Spark in Action

Spark in Action

PETAR ZEČEVIĆ
MARKO BONAČI

MANNING
Shelter Island

For online information and ordering of this and other Manning books, please visit
www.manning.com. The publisher offers discounts on this book when ordered in quantity.
For more information, please contact

    Special Sales Department
    Manning Publications Co.
    20 Baldwin Road
    PO Box 761
    Shelter Island, NY 11964
    Email: orders@manning.com

Manning Publications Co.
20 Baldwin Road
PO Box 761
Shelter Island, NY 11964

Development editor:	Marina Michaels
Technical development editor:	Andy Hicks
Project editor:	Karen Gulliver
Copyeditor:	Tiffany Taylor
Proofreader:	Elizabeth Martin
Technical proofreaders:	Michiel Trimpe
	Robert Ormandi
Typesetter:	Gordan Salinovic
Cover designer:	Marija Tudor

ISBN 9781617292606
Printed in the United States of America
1 2 3 4 5 6 7 8 9 10 – EBM – 21 20 19 18 17 16

To my mother in heaven.

—P.Z.

To my dear wife Suzana and our twins, Frane and Luka.

—M.B.

brief contents

                13   ■   Case study: real-time dashboard   363

                14   ■   Deep learning on Spark with H2O   383

contents

ix

preface

Looking back at the last year and a half, I can't help but wonder: how on Earth did I manage to survive this? These were the busiest 18 months of my life! Ever since Manning asked Marko and me to write a book about Spark, I have spent most of my free time on Apache Spark. And that made this period all the more interesting. I learned a lot, and I can honestly say it was worth it.

Spark is a super-hot topic these days. It was conceived in Berkeley, California, in 2009 by Matei Zaharia (initially as an attempt to prove the Mesos execution platform feasible) and was open sourced in 2010. In 2013, it was donated to the Apache Software Foundation, and it has been the target of lightning-fast development ever since. In 2015, Spark was one of the most active Apache projects and had more than 1,000 contributors. Today, it's a part of all major Hadoop distributions and is used by many organizations, large and small, throughout the world in all kinds of applications.

The trouble with writing a book about a project such as Spark is that it develops very quickly. Since we began writing *Spark in Action*, we've seen six minor releases of Spark, with many new, important features that needed to be covered. The first major release (version 2.0) came out after we'd finished writing most of the book, and we had to delay publication to cover the new features that came with it.

Another challenge when writing about Spark is the breadth of the topic: Spark is more of a platform than a framework. You can use it to write all kinds of applications (in four languages!): batch jobs, real-time processing systems and web applications executing Spark jobs, processing structured data using SQL and unstructured data using traditional programming techniques, various machine learning and data-munging tasks, interacting with distributed file systems, various relational and no-SQL databases, real-time systems, and so on. Then there are the runtime aspects—installing, configuring, and running Spark—which are equally relevant.

We tried to do justice to these important topics and make this book a thorough but gentle guide to using Spark. We hope you'll enjoy it.

acknowledgments

Our technical proofreader, Michiel Trimpe, made countless valuable suggestions. Thanks, too, to Robert Ormandi for reviewing chapter 7. We would also like to thank the reviewers of *Spark in Action*, including Andy Kirsch, Davide Fiorentino, lo Regio, Dimitris Kouzis-Loukas, Gaurav Bhardwaj, Ian Stirk, Jason Kolter, Jeremy Gailor, John Guthrie, Jonathan Miller, Jonathan Sharley, Junilu Lacar, Mukesh Kumar, Peter J. Krey Jr., Pranay Srivastava, Robert Ormandi, Rodrigo Abreu, Shobha Iyer, and Sumit Pal.

We want to thank the people at Manning who made this book possible: publisher Marjan Bace and the Manning reviewers and the editorial team, especially Marina Michaels, for guidance on writing a higher-quality book. We would also like to thank the production team for their work in ushering the project through to completion.

Petar Zečević

I'd like to thank my wife for her continuous support and patience in all my endeavors. I owe thanks to my parents, for raising me with love and giving me the best learning environment possible. And finally, I'd like to thank my company, SV Group, for providing the resources and time necessary for me to write this book.

Marko Bonaći

I'd like to thank my co-author, Petar. Without his perseverance, this book would not have been written.

about this book

Apache Spark is a general data processing framework. That means you can use it for all kinds of computing tasks. And *that* means any book on Apache Spark needs to cover a lot of different topics. We've tried to describe all aspects of using Spark: from configuring runtime options and running standalone and interactive jobs, to writing batch, streaming, or machine learning applications. And we've tried to pick examples and example data sets that can be run on your personal computer, that are easy to understand, and that illustrate the concepts well.

We hope you'll find this book and the examples useful for understanding how to use and run Spark and that it will help you write future, production-ready Spark applications.

Who should read this book

Although the book contains lots of material appropriate for business users and managers, it's mostly geared toward developers—or, rather, people who are able to understand and execute code. The Spark API can be used in four languages: Scala, Java, Python, and R. The primary examples in the book are written in Scala (Java and Python versions are available at the book's website, www.manning.com/books/spark-in-action, and in our online GitHub repository at https://github.com/spark-in-action/first-edition), but we don't assume any prior knowledge of Scala, and we explain Scala specifics throughout the book. Nevertheless, it will be beneficial if you have Java or Scala skills before starting the book. We list some resources to help with that in chapter 2.

Spark can interact with many systems, some of which are covered in the book. To fully appreciate the content, knowledge of the following topics is preferable (but not required):

- SQL and JDBC (chapter 5)
- Hadoop (HDFS and YARN, chapters 5 and 12)
- Kafka (chapter 6)
- Amazon EC2 (chapter 11)
- Basics of linear algebra, and the ability to understand mathematical formulas (chapters 7 and 8)
- Mesos (chapter 12)

We've prepared a virtual machine to make it easy for you to run the examples in the book. In order to use it, your computer should meet the software and hardware prerequisites listed in chapter 1.

How this book is organized

This book has 14 chapters, organized in 4 parts. Part 1 introduces Apache Spark and its rich API. An understanding of this information is important for writing high-quality Spark programs and is an excellent foundation for the rest of the book:

- Chapter 1 roughly describes Spark's main features and compares them with Hadoop's MapReduce and other tools from the Hadoop ecosystem. It also includes a description of the spark-in-action virtual machine, which you can use to run the examples in the book.
- Chapter 2 further explores the virtual machine, teaches you how to use Spark's command-line interface (the *spark-shell*), and uses several examples to explain resilient distributed datasets (RDDs): the central abstraction in Spark.
- In chapter 3, you'll learn how to set up Eclipse to write standalone Spark applications. Then you'll write an application for analyzing GitHub logs and execute the application by submitting it to a Spark cluster.
- Chapter 4 explores the Spark core API in more detail. Specifically, it shows how to work with key-value pairs and explains how data partitioning and shuffling work in Spark. It also teaches you how to group, sort, and join data, and how to use accumulators and broadcast variables.

In part 2, you'll get to know other components that make up Spark, including Spark SQL, Spark Streaming, Spark MLlib, and Spark GraphX:

- Chapter 5 introduces Spark SQL. You'll learn how to create and use Data-Frames, how to use SQL to query DataFrame data, and how to load data to and save it from external data sources. You'll also learn about optimizations done by Spark's SQL Catalyst optimization engine and about performance improvements introduced with the Tungsten project.
- Spark Streaming, one of the more popular Spark family members, is introduced in chapter 6. You'll learn about discretized streams, which periodically produce RDDs as a streaming application is running. You'll also learn how to save computation state over time and how to use window operations. We'll

examine ways of connecting to Kafka and how to obtain good performance
from your streaming jobs. We'll also talk about structured streaming, a new concept included in Spark 2.0.

- Chapters 7 and 8 are about machine learning, specifically about the Spark
  MLlib and Spark ML sections of the Spark API. You'll learn about machine
  learning in general and about linear regression, logistic regression, decision
  trees, random forests, and k-means clustering. Along the way, you'll scale and
  normalize features, use regularization, and train and evaluate machine learning
  models. We'll explain API standardizations brought by Spark ML.
- Chapter 9 explores how to build graphs with Spark's GraphX API. You'll transform and join graphs, use graph algorithms, and implement the A* search algorithm using the GraphX API.

Using Spark isn't just about writing and running Spark applications. It's also about
configuring Spark clusters and system resources to be used efficiently by applications.
Part 3 explains the necessary concepts and configuration options for running Spark
applications on Spark standalone, Hadoop YARN, and Mesos clusters:

- Chapter 10 explores Spark runtime components, Spark cluster types, job and
  resource scheduling, configuring Spark, and the Spark web UI. These are concepts common to all cluster managers Spark can run on: the Spark standalone
  cluster, YARN, and Mesos. The two local modes are also explained in chapter 10.
- You'll learn about the Spark standalone cluster in chapter 11: its components,
  how to start it and run applications on it, and how to use its web UI. The Spark
  History server, which keeps details about previously run jobs, is also discussed.
  Finally, you'll learn how to use Spark's scripts to start up a Spark standalone
  cluster on Amazon EC2.
- Chapter 12 goes through the specifics of setting up, configuring, and using
  YARN and Mesos clusters to run Spark applications.

Part 4 covers higher-level aspects of using Spark:

- Chapter 13 brings it all together and explores a Spark streaming application for
  analyzing log files and displaying the results on a real-time dashboard. The
  application implemented in chapter 13 can be used as a basis for your own
  future applications.
- Chapter 14 introduces H2O, a scalable and fast machine-learning framework
  with implementations of many machine-learning algorithms, most notably deep
  learning, which Spark lacks; and Sparkling Water, H2O's package that enables
  you to start and use an H2O cluster from Spark. Through Sparkling Water, you
  can use Spark's Core, SQL, Streaming, and GraphX components to ingest, prepare, and analyze data, and transfer it to H2O to be used in H2O's deep-learning
  algorithms. You can then transfer the results back to Spark and use them in subsequent computations.

Appendix A gives you instructions for installing Spark. Appendix B provides a short overview of MapReduce. And appendix C is a short primer on linear algebra.

About the code

All source code in the book is presented in a `mono-spaced typeface like this`, which sets it off from the surrounding text. In many listings, the code is annotated to point out key concepts, and numbered bullets are sometimes used in the text to provide additional information about the code.

Source code in Scala, Java, and Python, along with the data files used in the examples, are available for download from the publisher's website at www.manning.com/books/spark-in-action and from our online repository at https://github.com/spark-in-action/first-edition. The examples were written for and tested with Spark 2.0.

Author Online

Purchase of *Spark in Action* includes free access to a private web forum run by Manning Publications where you can make comments about the book, ask technical questions, and receive help from the lead author and from other users. To access the forum and subscribe to it, point your web browser to www.manning.com/books/spark-in-action. This page provides information on how to get on the forum once you're registered, what kind of help is available, and the rules of conduct on the forum.

Manning's commitment to our readers is to provide a venue where a meaningful dialog between individual readers and between readers and the authors can take place. It isn't a commitment to any specific amount of participation on the part of the authors, whose contribution to the Author Online forum remains voluntary (and unpaid). We suggest you try asking the authors some challenging questions lest their interest stray! The forum and the archives of previous discussions will be accessible from the publisher's website as long as the book is in print.

about the authors

Petar Zečević has been working in the software industry for more than 15 years. He started as a Java developer and has since worked on many projects as a full-stack developer, consultant, analyst, and team leader. He currently occupies the role of CTO for SV Group, a Croatian software company working for large Croatian banks, government institutions, and private companies. Petar organizes monthly Apache Spark Zagreb meetups, regularly speaks at conferences, and has several Apache Spark projects behind him.

Marko Bonaći has worked with Java for 13 years. He works for Sematext as a Spark developer and consultant. Before that, he was team lead for SV Group's IBM Enterprise Content Management team.

about the cover

The figure on the cover of *Spark in Action* is captioned "Hollandais" (a Dutchman). The illustration is taken from a collection of dress costumes from various countries by Jacques Grasset de Saint-Sauveur (1757–1810), titled *Costumes de Différents Pays*, published in France in 1797. Each illustration is finely drawn and colored by hand.

The rich variety of Grasset de Saint-Sauveur's collection reminds us vividly of how culturally apart the world's towns and regions were just 200 years ago. Isolated from each other, people spoke different dialects and languages. In the streets or in the countryside, it was easy to identify where they lived and what their trade or station in life was just by their dress.

The way we dress has changed since then, and the diversity by region, so rich at the time, has faded away. It's now hard to tell apart the inhabitants of different continents, let alone different towns, regions, or countries. Perhaps we have traded cultural diversity for a more varied personal life—certainly for a more varied and fast-paced technological life.

At a time when it's hard to tell one computer book from another, Manning celebrates the inventiveness and initiative of the computer business with book covers based on the rich diversity of regional life of two centuries ago, brought back to life by Grasset de Saint-Sauveur's pictures.

Part 1

First steps

We begin this book with an introduction to Apache Spark and its rich API. Understanding the information in part 1 is important for writing high-quality Spark programs and is an excellent foundation for the rest of the book.

Chapter 1 roughly describes Spark's main features and compares them with Hadoop's MapReduce and other tools from the Hadoop ecosystem. It also includes a description of the spark-in-action virtual machine we've prepared for you, which you can use to run the examples in the book.

Chapter 2 further explores the VM, teaches you how to use Spark's command-line interface (*spark-shell*), and uses several examples to explain *resilient distributed datasets* (RDDs)—the central abstraction in Spark.

In chapter 3, you'll learn how to set up Eclipse to write standalone Spark applications. Then you'll write such an application to analyze GitHub logs and execute the application by submitting it to a Spark cluster.

Chapter 4 explores the Spark core API in more detail. Specifically, it shows you how to work with key-value pairs and explains how data partitioning and *shuffling* work in Spark. It also teaches you how to group, sort, and join data, and how to use accumulators and broadcast variables.

Introduction to Apache Spark

Apache Spark is usually defined as a fast, general-purpose, distributed computing platform. Yes, it sounds a bit like marketing speak at first glance, but we could hardly come up with a more appropriate label to put on the Spark box.

Apache Spark really did bring a revolution to the big data space. Spark makes efficient use of memory and can execute equivalent jobs 10 to 100 times faster than Hadoop's MapReduce. On top of that, Spark's creators managed to abstract away the fact that you're dealing with a cluster of machines, and instead present you with a set of collections-based APIs. Working with Spark's collections feels like working with local Scala, Java, or Python collections, but Spark's collections reference data distributed on many nodes. Operations on these collections get translated to complicated parallel programs without the user being necessarily aware of the fact, which is a truly powerful concept.

In this chapter, we first shed light on the main Spark features and compare Spark to its natural predecessor: Hadoop's MapReduce. Then we briefly explore Hadoop's ecosystem—a collection of tools and languages used together with Hadoop for big data operations—to see how Spark fits in. We give you a brief overview of Spark's components and show you how a typical Spark program executes using a simple "Hello World" example. Finally, we help you download and set up the spark-in-action virtual machine we prepared for running the examples in the book.

We've done our best to write a comprehensive guide to Spark architecture, its components, its runtime environment, and its API, while providing concrete examples and real-life case studies. By reading this book and, more important, by sifting through the examples, you'll gain the knowledge and skills necessary for writing your own high-quality Spark programs and managing Spark applications.

1.1   *What is Spark?*

Apache Spark is an exciting new technology that is rapidly superseding Hadoop's MapReduce as the preferred big data processing platform. Hadoop is an open source, distributed, Java computation framework consisting of the Hadoop Distributed File System (HDFS) and MapReduce, its execution engine. Spark is similar to Hadoop in that it's a distributed, general-purpose computing platform. But Spark's unique design, which allows for keeping large amounts of data in memory, offers tremendous performance improvements. Spark programs can be 100 times faster than their MapReduce counterparts.

Spark was originally conceived at Berkeley's AMPLab by Matei Zaharia, who went on to cofound Databricks, together with his mentor Ion Stoica, as well as Reynold Xin, Patrick Wendell, Andy Konwinski, and Ali Ghodsi. Although Spark is open source, Databricks is the main force behind Apache Spark, contributing more than 75% of Spark's code. It also offers Databricks Cloud, a commercial product for big data analysis based on Apache Spark.

By using Spark's elegant API and runtime architecture, you can write distributed programs in a manner similar to writing local ones. Spark's collections abstract away the fact that they're potentially referencing data distributed on a large number of nodes. Spark also allows you to use functional programming methods, which are a great match for data-processing tasks.

By supporting Python, Java, Scala, and, most recently, R, Spark is open to a wide range of users: to the science community that traditionally favors Python and R, to the still-widespread Java community, and to people using the increasingly popular Scala, which offers functional programming on the Java virtual machine (JVM).

Finally, Spark combines MapReduce-like capabilities for batch programming, real-time data-processing functions, SQL-like handling of structured data, graph algorithms, and machine learning, all in a single framework. This makes it a one-stop shop for most of your big data-crunching needs. It's no wonder, then, that Spark is one of the busiest and fastest-growing Apache Software Foundation projects today.

But some applications aren't appropriate for Spark. Because of its distributed architecture, Spark necessarily brings some overhead to the processing time. This overhead is negligible when handling large amounts of data; but if you have a dataset that can be handled by a single machine (which is becoming ever more likely these days), it may be more efficient to use some other framework optimized for that kind of computation. Also, Spark wasn't made with online transaction processing (OLTP) applications in mind (fast, numerous, atomic transactions). It's better suited for online analytical processing (OLAP): batch jobs and data mining.

1.1.1 The Spark revolution

Although the last decade saw Hadoop's wide adoption, Hadoop is not without its shortcomings. It's powerful, but it can be slow. This has opened the way for newer technologies, such as Spark, to solve the same challenges Hadoop solves, but more efficiently. In the next few pages, we'll discuss Hadoop's shortcomings and how Spark answers those issues.

The Hadoop framework, with its HDFS and MapReduce data-processing engine, was the first that brought distributed computing to the masses. Hadoop solved the three main problems facing any distributed data-processing endeavor:

- *Parallelization*—How to perform subsets of the computation simultaneously
- *Distribution*—How to distribute the data
- *Fault tolerance*—How to handle component failure

NOTE Appendix A describes MapReduce in more detail.

On top of that, Hadoop clusters are often made of commodity hardware, which makes Hadoop easy to set up. That's why the last decade saw its wide adoption.

1.1.2 MapReduce's shortcomings

Although Hadoop is the foundation of today's big data revolution and is actively used and maintained, it still has its shortcomings, and they mostly pertain to its Map-Reduce component. MapReduce job results need to be stored in HDFS before they can be used by another job. For this reason, MapReduce is inherently bad with iterative algorithms.

Furthermore, many kinds of problems don't easily fit MapReduce's two-step paradigm, and decomposing every problem into a series of these two operations can be difficult. The API can be cumbersome at times.

Hadoop is a rather low-level framework, so myriad tools have sprung up around it: tools for importing and exporting data, higher-level languages and frameworks for manipulating data, tools for real-time processing, and so on. They all bring additional complexity and requirements with them, which complicates any environment. Spark solves many of these issues.

1.1.3   *What Spark brings to the table*

Spark's core concept is an in-memory execution model that enables caching job data in memory instead of fetching it from disk every time, as MapReduce does. This can speed the execution of jobs up to 100 times,[1] compared to the same jobs in Map-Reduce; it has the biggest effect on iterative algorithms such as machine learning, graph algorithms, and other types of workloads that need to reuse data.

Imagine you have city map data stored as a graph. The vertices of this graph represent points of interest on the map, and the edges represent possible routes between them, with associated distances. Now suppose you need to find a spot for a new ambulance station that will be situated as close as possible to all the points on the map. That spot would be the center of your graph. It can be found by first calculating the shortest path between all the vertices and then finding the *farthest point distance* (the maximum distance to any other vertex) for each vertex, and finally finding the vertex with the smallest farthest point distance. Completing the first phase of the algorithm, finding the shortest path between all vertices, in a parallel manner is the most challenging (and complicated) part, but it's not impossible.[2]

In the case of MapReduce, you'd need to store the results of each of these three phases on disk (HDFS). Each subsequent phase would read the results of the previous one from disk. But with Spark, you can find the shortest path between all vertices and cache that data in memory. The next phase can use that data from memory, find the farthest point distance for each vertex, and cache its results. The last phase can go through this final cached data and find the vertex with the minimum farthest point distance. You can imagine the performance gains compared to reading and writing to disk every time.

Spark performance is so good that in October 2014 it won the Daytona Gray Sort contest and set a world record (jointly with TritonSort, to be fair) by sorting 100 TB in 1,406 seconds (see http://sortbenchmark.org).

SPARK'S EASE OF USE

The Spark API is much easier to use than the classic MapReduce API. To implement the classic word-count example from appendix A as a MapReduce job, you'd need three classes: the main class that sets up the job, a `Mapper`, and a `Reducer`, each 10 lines long, give or take a few.

---

[1] See "Shark: SQL and Rich Analytics at Scale" by Reynold Xin et al., http://mng.bz/gFry.
[2] See "A Scalable Parallelization of All-Pairs Shortest Path Algorithm for a High Performance Cluster Environment" by T. Srinivasan et al., http://mng.bz/5TMT.

By contrast, the following is all it takes for the same Spark program written in Scala:

```
val spark = SparkSession.builder().appName("Spark wordcount")
val file = spark.sparkContext.textFile("hdfs://...")
val counts = file.flatMap(line => line.split(" "))
    .map(word => (word, 1)).countByKey()
counts.saveAsTextFile("hdfs://...")
```

Figure 1.1. shows this graphically.

Spark supports the Scala, Java, Python, and R programming languages, so it's accessible to a much wider audience. Although Java is supported, Spark can take advantage of Scala's versatility, flexibility, and functional programming concepts, which are a much better fit for data analysis. Python and R are widespread among data scientists and in the scientific community, which brings those users on par with Java and Scala developers.

Furthermore, the Spark shell (read-eval-print loop [REPL]) offers an interactive console that can be used for experimentation and idea testing. There's no need for compilation and deployment just to find out something isn't working (again). REPL can even be used for launching jobs on the full set of data.

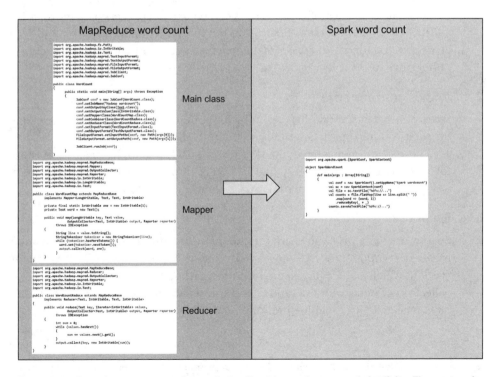

Figure 1.1 A word-count program demonstrates Spark's conciseness and simplicity. The program is shown implemented in Hadoop's MapReduce framework on the left and as a Spark Scala program on the right.

Finally, Spark can run on several types of clusters: Spark standalone cluster, Hadoop's YARN (yet another resource negotiator), and Mesos. This gives it additional flexibility and makes it accessible to a larger community of users.

SPARK AS A UNIFYING PLATFORM

An important aspect of Spark is its combination of the many functionalities of the tools in the Hadoop ecosystem into a single unifying platform. The execution model is general enough that the single framework can be used for stream data processing, machine learning, SQL-like operations, and graph and batch processing. Many roles can work together on the same platform, which helps bridge the gap between programmers, data engineers, and data scientists. And the list of functions that Spark provides is continuing to grow.

SPARK ANTI-PATTERNS

Spark isn't suitable, though, for asynchronous updates to shared data[3] (such as online transaction processing, for example), because it has been created with batch analytics in mind. (Spark streaming is simply batch analytics applied to data in a time window.) Tools specialized for those use cases will still be necessary.

Also, if you don't have a large amount of data, Spark may not be required, because it needs to spend some time setting up jobs, tasks, and so on. Sometimes a simple relational database or a set of clever scripts can be used to process data more quickly than a distributed system such as Spark. But data has a tendency to grow, and it may outgrow your relational database management system (RDBMS) or your clever scripts rather quickly.

1.2   *Spark components*

Spark consists of several purpose-built components. These are Spark Core, Spark SQL, Spark Streaming, Spark GraphX, and Spark MLlib, as shown in figure 1.2.

These components make Spark a feature-packed *unifying platform*: it can be used for many tasks that previously had to be accomplished with several different frameworks. A brief description of each Spark component follows.

1.2.1   *Spark Core*

Spark Core contains basic Spark functionalities required for running jobs and needed by other components. The most important of these is the *resilient distributed dataset* (RDD),[4] which is the main element of the Spark API. It's an abstraction of a *distributed* collection of items with operations and transformations applicable to the dataset. It's *resilient* because it's capable of rebuilding datasets in case of node failures.

---

[3]   See "Resilient Distributed Datasets: A Fault-Tolerant Abstraction for In-Memory Cluster Computing" by Matei Zaharia et al., http://mng.bz/57uJ.

[4]   RDDs are explained in chapter 2. Because they're the fundamental abstraction of Spark, they're also covered in detail in chapter 4.

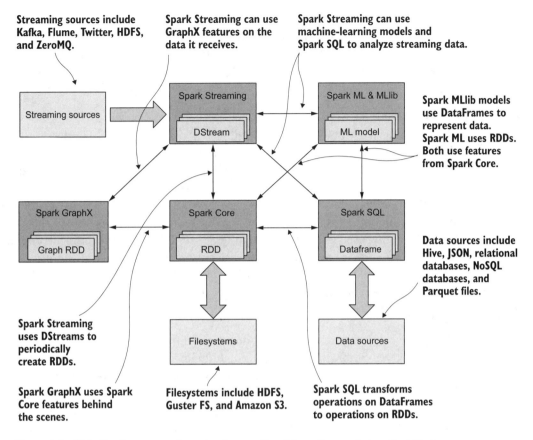

Figure 1.2   Main Spark components and various runtime interactions and storage options

Spark Core contains logic for accessing various filesystems, such as HDFS, GlusterFS, Amazon S3, and so on. It also provides a means of information sharing between computing nodes with broadcast variables and accumulators. Other fundamental functions, such as networking, security, scheduling, and data shuffling, are also part of Spark Core.

1.2.2   *Spark SQL*

Spark SQL provides functions for manipulating large sets of distributed, structured data using an SQL subset supported by Spark and Hive SQL (HiveQL). With Data-Frames introduced in Spark 1.3, and DataSets introduced in Spark 1.6, which simplified handling of structured data and enabled radical performance optimizations, Spark SQL became one of the most important Spark components. Spark SQL can also be used for reading and writing data to and from various structured formats and data sources, such as JavaScript Object Notation (JSON) files, Parquet files (an increasingly popular file format that allows for storing a schema along with the data), relational databases, Hive, and others.

Operations on `DataFrames` and `DataSets` at some point translate to operations on RDDs and execute as ordinary Spark jobs. Spark SQL provides a query optimization framework called Catalyst that can be extended by custom optimization rules. Spark SQL also includes a Thrift server, which can be used by external systems, such as business intelligence tools, to query data through Spark SQL using classic JDBC and ODBC protocols.

1.2.3 Spark Streaming

Spark Streaming is a framework for ingesting real-time streaming data from various sources. The supported streaming sources include HDFS, Kafka, Flume, Twitter, ZeroMQ, and custom ones. Spark Streaming operations recover from failure automatically, which is important for online data processing. Spark Streaming represents streaming data using *discretized streams* (DStreams), which periodically create RDDs containing the data that came in during the last time window.

Spark Streaming can be combined with other Spark components in a single program, unifying real-time processing with machine learning, SQL, and graph operations. This is something unique in the Hadoop ecosystem. And since Spark 2.0, the new Structured Streaming API makes Spark streaming programs more similar to Spark batch programs.

1.2.4 Spark MLlib

Spark MLlib is a library of machine-learning algorithms grown from the MLbase project at UC Berkeley. Supported algorithms include logistic regression, naïve Bayes classification, support vector machines (SVMs), decision trees, random forests, linear regression, and k-means clustering.

Apache Mahout is an existing open source project offering implementations of distributed machine-learning algorithms running on Hadoop. Although Apache Mahout is more mature, both Spark MLlib and Mahout include a similar set of machine-learning algorithms. But with Mahout migrating from MapReduce to Spark, they're bound to be merged in the future.

Spark MLlib handles machine-learning models used for transforming datasets, which are represented as RDDs or `DataFrames`.

1.2.5 Spark GraphX

Graphs are data structures comprising vertices and the edges connecting them. GraphX provides functions for building graphs, represented as *graph RDDs*: `EdgeRDD` and `VertexRDD`. GraphX contains implementations of the most important algorithms of graph theory, such as page rank, connected components, shortest paths, SVD++, and others. It also provides the Pregel message-passing API, the same API for large-scale graph processing implemented by Apache Giraph, a project with implementations of graph algorithms and running on Hadoop.

1.3   Spark program flow

Let's see what a typical Spark program looks like. Imagine that a 300 MB log file is stored in a three-node HDFS cluster. HDFS automatically splits the file into 128 MB

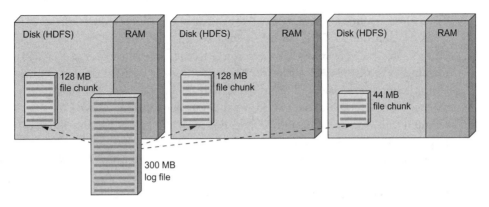

Figure 1.3 Storing a 300 MB log file in a three-node Hadoop cluster

parts (*blocks*, in Hadoop terminology) and places each part on a separate node of the cluster[5] (see figure 1.3). Let's assume Spark is running on YARN, inside the same Hadoop cluster.

A Spark data engineer is given the task of analyzing how many errors of type Out-OfMemoryError have happened during the last two weeks. Mary, the engineer, knows that the log file contains the last two weeks of logs of the company's application server cluster. She sits at her laptop and starts to work.

She first starts her *Spark shell* and establishes a connection to the Spark cluster. Next, she loads the log file from HDFS (see figure 1.4) by using this (Scala) line:

```
val lines = sc.textFile("hdfs://path/to/the/file")
```

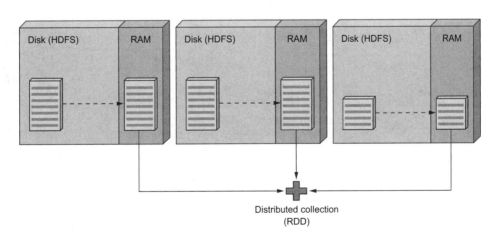

Figure 1.4 Loading a text file from HDFS

---

[5] Although it's not relevant to our example, we should probably mention that HDFS replicates each block to two additional nodes (if the default replication factor of 3 is in effect).

To achieve maximum *data locality*,[6] the loading operation asks Hadoop for the locations of each block of the log file and then transfers all the blocks into RAM of the cluster's nodes. Now Spark has a reference to each of those blocks (*partitions*, in Spark terminology) in RAM. The sum of those partitions is a distributed collection of lines from the log file referenced by an RDD. Simplifying, we can say that RDDs allow you to work with a distributed collection the same way you would work with any local, nondistributed one. You don't have to worry about the fact that the collection is distributed, nor do you have to handle node failures yourself.

In addition to automatic fault tolerance and distribution, the RDD provides an elaborate API, which allows you to work with a collection in a functional style. You can filter the collection; map over it with a function; reduce it to a cumulative value; subtract, intersect, or create a union with another RDD, and so on.

Mary now has a reference to the RDD, so in order to find the error count, she first wants to remove all the lines that don't have an OutOfMemoryError substring. This is a job for the filter function, which she calls like this:

```
val oomLines = lines.filter(l => l.contains("OutOfMemoryError")).cache()
```

After filtering the collection so it contains the subset of data that she needs to analyze (see figure 1.5), Mary calls cache on it, which tells Spark to leave that RDD in memory across jobs. Caching is the basic component of Spark's performance improvements we mentioned before. The benefits of caching the RDD will become apparent later.

Now she is left with only those lines that contain the error substring. For this simple example, we'll ignore the possibility that the OutOfMemoryError string might occur in multiple lines of a single error. Our data engineer counts the remaining lines

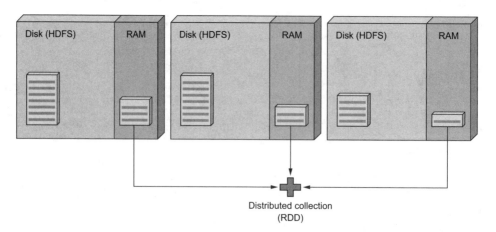

Distributed collection
(RDD)

Figure 1.5   Filtering the collection to contain only lines containing the OutOfMemoryError string

---

[6] Data locality is honored if each block gets loaded in the RAM of the same node where it resides in HDFS. The whole point is to try to avoid having to transfer large amounts of data over the wire.

and reports the result as the number of out-of-memory errors that occurred in the last two weeks:

```
val result = oomLines.count()
```

Spark enabled her to perform distributed filtering and counting of the data with only three lines of code. Her little program was executed on all three nodes in parallel.

If she now wants to further analyze lines with `OutOfMemoryErrors`, and perhaps call `filter` again (but with other criteria) on an `oomLines` object that was previously cached in memory, Spark won't load the file from HDFS again, as it would normally do. Spark will load it from the cache.

1.4   *Spark ecosystem*

We've already mentioned the Hadoop ecosystem, consisting of interface, analytic, cluster-management, and infrastructure tools. Some of the most important ones are shown in figure 1.6.

Figure 1.6 is by no means complete.[7] You could argue that we failed to add one tool or another, but a complete list of tools would be hard to fit in this section. We believe, though, that this list represents a good subset of the most prominent tools in the Hadoop ecosystem.

If you compare the functionalities of Spark components with the tools in the Hadoop ecosystem, you can see that some of the tools are suddenly superfluous. For example, Apache Giraph can be replaced by Spark GraphX, and Spark MLlib can be

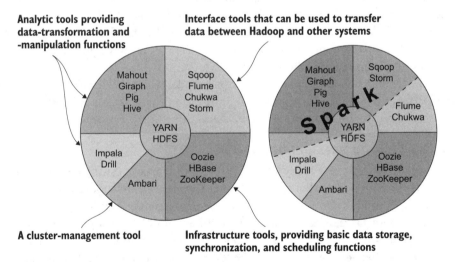

Figure 1.6   **Basic infrastructure, interface, analytic, and management tools in the Hadoop ecosystem, with some of the functionalities that Spark incorporates or makes obsolete**

---

[7] If you're interested, you can find a (hopefully) complete list of Hadoop-related tools and frameworks at http://hadoopecosystemtable.github.io.

used instead of Apache Mahout. Apache Storm's capabilities overlap greatly with those of Spark Streaming, so in many cases Spark Streaming can be used instead.

Apache Pig and Apache Sqoop aren't needed any longer, because the same functionalities are covered by Spark Core and Spark SQL. But even if you have legacy Pig workflows and need to run Pig, the Spork project enables you to run Pig on Spark.

Spark has no means of replacing the infrastructure and management of the Hadoop ecosystem tools (Oozie, HBase, and ZooKeeper), though. Oozie is used for scheduling different types of Hadoop jobs and now even has an extension for scheduling Spark jobs. HBase is a distributed and scalable database, which is something Spark doesn't provide. ZooKeeper provides fast and robust implementation of common functionalities many distributed applications need, like coordination, distributed synchronization, naming, and provisioning of group services. It is used for these purposes in many other distributed systems, too.

Impala and Drill can coexist alongside Spark, especially with Drill's coming support for Spark as an execution engine. But they're more like competing frameworks, mostly spanning the features of Spark Core and Spark SQL, which makes Spark feature-richer (pun not intended).

We said earlier that Spark doesn't need to use HDFS storage. In addition to HDFS, Spark can operate on data stored in Amazon S3 buckets and plain files. More exciting, it can also use Alluxio (formerly Tachyon), which is a memory-centric distributed filesystem, or other distributed filesystems, such as GlusterFS.

Another interesting fact is that Spark doesn't have to run on YARN. Apache Mesos and the Spark standalone cluster are alternative cluster managers for Spark. Apache Mesos is an advanced distributed systems kernel bringing distributed resource abstractions. It can scale to tens of thousands of nodes with full fault tolerance (we'll visit it in chapter 12). Spark Standalone is a Spark-specific cluster manager that is used in production today on multiple sites.

So if we switch from MapReduce to Spark and get rid of YARN and all the tools that Spark makes obsolete, what's left of the Hadoop ecosystem? To put it another way: Are we slowly moving toward a new big data standard: a *Spark ecosystem?*

1.5   *Setting up the spark-in-action VM*

In order to make it easy for you to set up a Spark learning environment, we prepared a virtual machine (VM) that you'll be using throughout this book. It will allow you to run all the examples from the book without surprises due to different versions of Java, Spark, or your OS. For example, you could have problems running the Spark examples on Windows; after all, Spark is developed on OS X and Linux, so, understandably, Windows isn't exactly in the focus. The VM will guarantee we're all on the same page, so to speak.

The VM consists of the following software stack:

- *64-bit Ubuntu OS, 14.04.4 (nicknamed Trusty)*—Currently the latest version with long-term support (LTS).

- *Java 8 (OpenJDK)*—Even if you plan on only using Spark from Python, you have to install Java, because Spark's Python API communicates with Spark running in a JVM.
- *Hadoop 2.7.2*—Hadoop isn't a hard requirement for using Spark. You can save and load files from your local filesystem, if you're running a local cluster, which is the case with our VM. But as soon as you set up a truly distributed Spark cluster, you'll need a distributed filesystem, such as Hadoop's HDFS. Hadoop installation will also come in handy in chapter 12 for trying out the methods of running Spark on YARN, Hadoop's execution environment.
- *Spark 2.0*—We included the latest Spark version at the time this book was finished. You can easily upgrade the Spark version in the VM, if you wish to do so, by following the instructions in chapter 2.
- *Kafka 0.8.2*—Kafka is a distributed messaging system, used in chapters 6 and 13.

We chose Ubuntu because it's a popular Linux distribution and Linux is the preferred Spark platform. If you've never worked with Ubuntu before, this could be your chance to start. We'll guide you, explaining commands and concepts as you progress through the chapters.

Here we'll explain only the basics: how to download, start, and stop the VM. We'll go into more details about using it in the next chapter.

1.5.1 *Downloading and starting the virtual machine*

To run the VM, you'll need a 64-bit OS with at least 3 GB of free memory and 15 GB of free disk space. You first need to install these two software packages for your platform:

- *Oracle VirtualBox*—Oracle's free, open source hardware virtualization software (www.virtualbox.org)
- *Vagrant*—HashiCorp's software for configuring portable development environments (www.vagrantup.com/downloads.html)

When you have these two installed, create a folder for hosting the VM (called, for example, spark-in-action), and enter it. Then download the Vagrant box metadata JSON file from our online repository. You can download it manually or use the wget command on Linux or Mac:

```
$ wget https://raw.githubusercontent.com/spark-in-action/first-edition/
➥ master/spark-in-action-box.json
```

Then issue the following command to download the VM itself:

```
$ vagrant box add spark-in-action-box.json
```

The Vagrant box metadata JSON file points to the Vagrant box file. The command will download the 5 GB VM box (this will probably take some time) and register it as the manning/spark-in-action Vagrant box. To use it, initialize the Vagrant VM in the current directory by issuing this command:

```
$ vagrant init manning/spark-in-action
```

Finally, start the VM with the vagrant up command (this will also allocate approximately 10 GB of disk space):

```
$ vagrant up
Bringing machine 'default' up with 'virtualbox' provider...
==> default: Checking if box 'manning/spark-in-action' is up to date...
==> default: Clearing any previously set forwarded ports...
==> default: Clearing any previously set network interfaces...
...
```

If you have several network interfaces on your machine, you'll be asked to choose one of them for connecting it to the VM. Choose the one with an access to the internet. For example:

```
==> default: Available bridged network interfaces:
1) 1x1 11b/g/n Wireless LAN PCI Express Half Mini Card Adapter
2) Cisco Systems VPN Adapter for 64-bit Windows
==> default: When choosing an interface, it is usually the one that is
==> default: being used to connect to the internet.
    default: Which interface should the network bridge to? 1
==> default: Preparing network interfaces based on configuration...
...
```

1.5.2 Stopping the virtual machine

You'll learn how to use the VM in the next chapter. For now, we'll only show you how to stop it. To power off the VM, issue the following command:

```
$ vagrant halt
```

This will stop the machine but preserve your work. If you wish to completely remove the VM and free up its space, you need to *destroy* it:

```
$ vagrant destroy
```

You can also remove the downloaded Vagrant box, which was used to create the VM, with this command:

```
$ vagrant box remove manning/spark-in-action
```

But we hope you won't feel the need for that for quite some time.

1.6 Summary

- Apache Spark is an exciting new technology that is rapidly superseding Hadoop's MapReduce as the preferred big data processing platform.
- Spark programs can be 100 times faster than their MapReduce counterparts.
- Spark supports the Java, Scala, Python, and R languages.
- Writing distributed programs with Spark is similar to writing local Java, Scala, or Python programs.

- Spark provides a unifying platform for batch programming, real-time data-processing functions, SQL-like handling of structured data, graph algorithms, and machine learning, all in a single framework.
- Spark isn't appropriate for small datasets, nor should you use it for OLTP applications.
- The main Spark components are Spark Core, Spark SQL, Spark Streaming, Spark MLlib, and Spark GraphX.
- RDDs are Spark's abstraction of distributed collections.
- Spark supersedes some of the tools in the Hadoop ecosystem.
- You'll use the spark-in-action VM to run the examples in this book.

Spark fundamentals

2

This chapter covers

- Exploring the spark-in-action VM
- Managing multiple Spark versions
- Getting to know Spark's command line interface (spark-shell)
- Playing with simple examples in spark-shell
- Exploring RDD actions and transformations and double functions

It's finally time to get down to business. In this chapter, you'll start using the VM we prepared for you and write your first Spark programs. All you need is a laptop or a desktop machine with a usable internet connection and the prerequisites described in chapter 1.

To avoid overwhelming you this early in the book with various options for running Spark, for now you'll be using the so-called *Spark standalone local* cluster. *Standalone* means Spark is using its own cluster manager (rather than Mesos or Hadoop's YARN). *Local* means the whole system is running locally—that is, on your laptop or a desktop machine. We'll talk extensively about Spark running modes and deployment options in the second part of the book. Strap in: things are about to get real!

Rest assured, we aren't assuming any prior Spark or Scala knowledge; in this chapter, you'll start slowly and progress step-by-step, tutorial style, through the process of setting up prerequisites, downloading and installing Spark, and playing with simple code examples in spark-shell (used for accessing Spark from the command prompt).

Although we intend to explain all the Scala specifics throughout the book, we don't have the illusion that you can learn Scala using a book about Spark. Therefore, it might be beneficial to get a dedicated Scala book, such as Nilanjan Raychaudhuri's *Scala in Action* (Manning, 2013). Or you can use the second edition of *Programming in Scala* (Artima Inc., 2010), an excellent book by Martin Odersky, father of the Scala programming language. Another awesome, readily available resource we can recommend is Twitter's online Scala School (http://twitter.github.io/scala_school). As you come across a new Scala topic, look it up in your book or online, because that will make it much easier to put things into perspective—especially Scala topics that you need more details on (than we have room to provide).

We hope you've followed our instructions from the last chapter and successfully set up the spark-in-action VM. If for some reason you can't use the VM, check out appendix B for instructions on installing Spark.

You'll now use the spark-in-action VM for writing and executing your first Spark program. We guess you're eager to start, so let's get to it!

2.1 *Using the spark-in-action VM*

To start using the VM, change to the folder where you put `Vagrantfile`, and, if it's not already running, start the machine with the following command:

```
$ vagrant up
```

When the command finishes, you can log in to the VM. Open an SSH connection to the machine, either by issuing Vagrant's `ssh` command

```
$ vagrant ssh
```

or by using your favorite SSH program (such as ssh on Linux and Mac, or Putty, Kitty, or MobaXTerm if you're running on Windows) to connect directly to 192.168.10.2, which is the IP address we configured for the spark-in-action VM. Both methods should present the same login prompt. Enter username `spark` and password `spark`, and you should be greeted with the following prompt:

```
Welcome to Ubuntu 14.04.4 LTS (GNU/Linux 3.13.0-85-generic x86_64)
... several omitted lines ...
spark@spark-in-action:~$
```

You're in. The first step is behind you!

2.1.1 *Cloning the Spark in Action GitHub repository*

Before doing anything else, clone our *Spark in Action* GitHub repository into your home directory by issuing the following command (Git is already installed in the VM):

```
$ git clone https://github.com/spark-in-action/first-edition
```

This creates the first-edition folder in your home directory.

2.1.2 *Finding Java*

We configured the spark user's PATH so that you can easily invoke Java, Hadoop, and Spark commands from wherever you're positioned in the VM. Let's first see where Java is installed. The which command shows the location of the executable file specified, if it can be found in the current PATH:

```
$ which java
/usr/bin/java
```

> ## Code formatting and notation
> We've established the following notation and formatting rules to distinguish commands entered into the terminal from those entered into the Spark shell, from terminal and the Spark-shell outputs. Terminal commands start with a dollar sign, while code entered into the Spark-shell starts with scala>:
>
> ```
> $ terminal command
> terminal output
> scala> a line of code
> spark shell output
> ```

That's the default location for system-wide user programs, so it's hardly surprising. But the file is a *symbolic link*, which you can trace to Java's real install location:

```
spark@spark-in-action:~$ ls -la /usr/bin/java
lrwxrwxrwx 1 root root 22 Apr 19 18:36 /usr/bin/java -> /etc/alternatives
➥ /java
spark@spark-in-action:~$ ls -la /etc/alternatives/java
lrwxrwxrwx 1 root root 46 Apr 19 18:36 /etc/alternatives/java -> /usr/lib/
➥ jvm/java-8-openjdk-amd64/jre/bin/java
```

So, the Java install location is /usr/lib/jvm/java-8-openjdk-amd64. The JAVA_HOME variable, which is important for running Hadoop and Spark, has also been set up for you:

```
$ echo $JAVA_HOME
/usr/lib/jvm/java-8-openjdk-amd64/jre
```

> **Symbolic links**
> A symbolic link (or *symlink*) is a reference to a file or a folder. It behaves as though you have access to the same file or folder from two different places in your filesystem. The symlink isn't a copy; it's a reference to the target folder (in the case of a *folder symlink*) with the ability to navigate inside, as if it were the target folder. Every change you make inside the symlink is applied directly to the target folder and reflected in the symlink. If you were to edit a file symlink using the vi editor, for example, you would be editing the target file, and the changes would be visible in both places.

2.1.3 Using the VM's Hadoop installation

With the spark-in-action VM, you also get a fully functioning Hadoop installation. You'll need it for reading and writing files to and from the HDFS and for running YARN later in the book.

Hadoop is installed in the folder /usr/local/hadoop. But that is a symlink again, pointing to /opt/hadoop-2.7.2, which is where the Hadoop binaries are located.

Many HDFS shell commands are available in Hadoop, mimicking the usual filesystem commands (for creating, copying, moving files and folders, and so on). They're issued as arguments to the `hadoop fs` command. For example, to list the files and folders in the /user HDFS folder, you use the following:

```
$ hadoop fs -ls /user
Found 1 items
drwxr-xr-x   - spark supergroup          0 2016-04-19 18:49 /user/spark
```

We don't have the time or space here to explain other Hadoop commands, but you can find the complete Hadoop filesystem command reference in the official documentation: http://mng.bz/Y9FP.

The last command (`hadoop fs -ls`) works because the spark-in-action VM is configured to automatically start HDFS daemon processes during its startup, so the command can connect to HDFS and query the filesystem. HDFS startup is done by invoking a single script (note that Hadoop's sbin directory isn't on the `spark` user's PATH):

```
$ /usr/local/hadoop/sbin/start-dfs.sh
```

If you wish to stop HDFS daemons, you can invoke the equivalent `stop-dfs.sh` script:

```
$ /usr/local/hadoop/sbin/stop-dfs.sh
```

You should note that the `spark` user has full access rights (read/write/execute [rwx]) to the /usr/local/hadoop directory, so you won't have to fiddle with `sudo` every time you need to make a change (for example, to a configuration file) or start or stop the daemons.

2.1.4 *Examining the VM's Spark installation*

When installing Spark, you download the appropriate Spark archive from the Spark downloads page (https://spark.apache.org/downloads.html) and unpack it to the folder of your choice. In the spark-in-action VM, similar to Hadoop, Spark is available from the /usr/local/spark folder, which is a symlink pointing to /opt/spark-2.0.0-bin-hadoop2.7, where the Spark binary archive was unpacked. As the folder name suggests, the installed version is 2.0, prebuilt for Hadoop 2.7 or higher, which is what we needed for this VM.

Instead of downloading a prebuilt version, you can build Spark yourself. Please see appendix B for details. The examples in this book were tested with Spark 2.0.0 (the latest version at the time of writing), so make sure you install that version.

MANAGING SPARK RELEASES

Because new versions of Spark are flying out every couple of months, you need a way to manage them so you can have multiple versions installed and easily choose which one to use. By using a symlink in the described way, regardless of the current version of Spark, you can always use /usr/local/spark to reference a Spark installation in all of your programs, scripts, and configuration files. You switch versions by deleting the symlink and creating a new one, pointing to the root installation folder of the Spark version you want to work with.

For example, after unpacking several Spark versions, your /opt folder might contain the following folders:

```
$ ls /opt | grep spark
spark-1.3.0-bin-hadoop2.4
spark-1.3.1-bin-hadoop2.4
spark-1.4.0-bin-hadoop2.4
spark-1.5.0-bin-hadoop2.4
spark-1.6.1-bin-hadoop2.6
spark-2.0.0-bin-hadoop2.7
```

To switch from the current version of 2.0 back to 1.6.1, for example, you would remove the current symlink (you would need to use sudo here because the spark user doesn't have the rights for changing the /usr/local folder)

```
$ sudo rm -f /usr/local/spark
```

and then create a new one pointing to version 1.6.1:

```
$ sudo ln -s /opt/spark-1.6.1-bin-hadoop2.4 /usr/local/spark
```

The idea is to always refer to the current Spark installation the same way, using the spark symlink.

OTHER SPARK INSTALLATION DETAILS

Many Spark scripts require the SPARK_HOME environment variable to be set. It's already set up for you in the VM, and it points to the spark symlink, as you can check yourself:

```
$ export | grep SPARK
declare -x SPARK_HOME="/usr/local/spark"
```

Spark's bin and sbin directories have been added to the `spark` user's PATH. The `spark` user is also the owner of the files and folders under /usr/local/spark, so you can change them as necessary without using `sudo`.

2.2 Using Spark shell and writing your first Spark program

In this section, you'll start the Spark shell and use it to write your first Spark example program. So what is this Spark shell all about?

There are two different ways you can interact with Spark. One way is to write a program in Scala, Java, or Python that uses Spark's library—that is, its API (more on programs in chapter 3). The other is to use the *Scala shell* or the *Python shell*.

The shell is primarily used for exploratory data analysis, usually for *one-off* jobs, because a program written in the shell is discarded after you exit the shell. The other common shell-usage scenario is testing and developing Spark applications. It's much easier to test a hypothesis in a shell (for example, probe a dataset and experiment) than to write an application, submit it to be executed, write results to an output file, and then analyze that output.

Spark shell is also known as *Spark REPL*, where the REPL acronym stands for *read-eval-print loop*. It reads your input, evaluates it, prints the result, and then does it all over again—that is, after a command returns a result, it doesn't exit the scala> prompt; it stays ready for your next command (thus *loop*).

2.2.1 Starting the Spark shell

You should be logged in to the VM as the `spark` user by now. As we said earlier, Spark's bin directory is in the `spark` user's PATH, so you should be able to start the Spark shell by entering the following:

```
$ spark-shell
Spark context Web UI available at http://10.0.2.15:4040
Spark context available as 'sc' (master = local[*], app id = local-1474054368520).
Spark session available as 'spark'.
Welcome to
      ____              __
     / __/__  ___ _____/ /__
    _\ \/ _ \/ _ `/ __/  '_/
   /___/ .__/\_,_/_/ /_/\_\   version 2.0.0
      /_/

Using Scala version 2.11.8 (OpenJDK 64-Bit Server VM, Java 1.8.0_72-internal)
Type in expressions to have them evaluated.
Type :help for more information.

scala>
```

And boom! You have a running spark-shell on your machine.

NOTE To write Python programs in the Spark Python shell, type `pyspark`.

In previous Spark versions, Spark logged all the detailed INFO messages to the console and cluttered the view. That was toned down in later versions, but now those messages, which may be valuable, are no longer available. Let's correct that.

You'll make spark-shell print only errors, but you'll maintain the complete log in the logs/info.log file (relative to the *Spark root*) for troubleshooting. Exit the shell by typing :quit (or pressing Ctrl-D) and create a log4j.properties file in the conf subfolder, like this:

```
$ nano /usr/local/spark/conf/log4j.properties
```

nano is a text editor for UNIX-like systems, available in Ubuntu by default. You are, of course, free to use any other text editor. Copy the contents of the following listing into the newly created log4j.properties file.

Listing 2.1   Contents of Spark's log4j.properties file

```
# set global logging severity to INFO (and upwards: WARN, ERROR, FATAL)
log4j.rootCategory=INFO, console, file

# console config (restrict only to ERROR and FATAL)
log4j.appender.console=org.apache.log4j.ConsoleAppender
log4j.appender.console.target=System.err
log4j.appender.console.threshold=ERROR
log4j.appender.console.layout=org.apache.log4j.PatternLayout
log4j.appender.console.layout.ConversionPattern=%d{yy/MM/dd HH:mm:ss}
➥ %p %c{1}: %m%n

# file config
log4j.appender.file=org.apache.log4j.RollingFileAppender
log4j.appender.file.File=logs/info.log
log4j.appender.file.MaxFileSize=5MB
log4j.appender.file.MaxBackupIndex=10
log4j.appender.file.layout=org.apache.log4j.PatternLayout
log4j.appender.file.layout.ConversionPattern=%d{yy/MM/dd HH:mm:ss}
➥ %p %c{1}: %m%n

# Settings to quiet third party logs that are too verbose
log4j.logger.org.eclipse.jetty=WARN
log4j.logger.org.eclipse.jetty.util.component.AbstractLifeCycle=ERROR
log4j.logger.org.apache.spark.repl.SparkIMain$exprTyper=INFO
log4j.logger.org.apache.spark.repl.SparkILoop$SparkILoopInterpreter=INFO
log4j.logger.org.apache.spark=WARN
log4j.logger.org.apache.hadoop=WARN
```

Exit nano by pressing Ctrl-X and then Y, confirming that you wish to save the file, and press Enter if you're asked for the file's name.

LOG4J   Although it has been superseded by the logback library and is almost two decades old, log4j is still one of the most widely used Java logging libraries, due to the simplicity of its design.

Then use the same command as before to start the Spark shell:

```
$ spark-shell
```

As you can see in the output, you're provided with the *Spark context* in the form of the `sc` variable and the *SQL context* as `sqlContext`. The Spark context is the entry point for interacting with Spark. You use it for things like connecting to Spark from an application, configuring a session, managing job execution, loading or saving a file, and so on.

2.2.2 *The first Spark code example*

It's time for your first Spark example. Suppose you want to find out how many third-party libraries that Spark uses are licensed under the BSD license (acronym for Berkeley Software Distribution). Luckily, Spark comes with a file named LICENSE, located in the Spark root directory. The LICENSE file contains the list of all libraries used by Spark and the licenses they're provided under. Lines in the file, which names packages licensed under the BSD license, contain the word BSD. You could easily use a Linux shell command to count those lines, but that's not the point. Let's see how you can ingest that file and count the lines using the Spark API:

Think of licLines variable as a collection of lines constructed by splitting LICENSE on the newline character.

```
scala> val licLines = sc.textFile("/usr/local/spark/LICENSE")
licLines: org.apache.spark.rdd.RDD[String] = LICENSE MapPartitionsRDD[1] at
    textFile at <console>:27
scala> val lineCnt = licLines.count          ◁——— Retrieves the number of lines
lineCnt: Long = 294                          ◁———    in the licLines collection
```

The number of lines in LICENSE may vary (and often does) between Spark versions.

You now know the total number of lines in the file. What good does that do? You need to find out the number of lines BSD appears in. The idea is to run the `licLines` collection through a filter that sifts out the lines that don't contain BSD:

**Forms a new collection, ❶
bsdLines, that contains only
lines with the "BSD" substring**

```
scala> val bsdLines = licLines.filter(line => line.contains("BSD"))   ◁——
bsdLines: org.apache.spark.rdd.RDD[String] = MapPartitionsRDD[2] at filter
➥ at <console>:23
scala> bsdLines.count        ◁——— count how many
res0: Long = 34                    elements (lines) the
                                   collection bsdLines has
```

Function literals

If you've never used Scala, you may be wondering what the snippet with the *fat arrow* (=>) means ❶. That is a Scala function literal; it defines an anonymous function that takes a string and returns `true` or `false`, depending on whether `line` contains the "BSD" substring.

The fat arrow basically designates the transformation that a function does on the left side of the expression, converting it to the right side, which is then returned. In this case, `String` (line) is transformed into a `Boolean` (the result of `contains`), which is then returned as the function's result.

The `filter` function evaluates the fat-arrow function on each element of the `licLines` collection (each line) and returns a new collection, `bsdLines`, that has only those elements for which the fat-arrow function returned `true`.

The fat-arrow function you use for filtering lines is anonymous, but you could also define the equivalent named function, like this

```
scala> def isBSD(line: String) = { line.contains("BSD") }
isBSD: (line: String)Boolean
```

or store (a reference to) the function definition in a variable

```
scala> val isBSD = (line: String) => line.contains("BSD")
isBSD: String => Boolean = <function1>
```

and then use it in place of the anonymous function:

```
scala> val bsdLines1 = licLines.filter(isBSD)
bsdLines1: org.apache.spark.rdd.RDD[String] = MapPartitionsRDD[5] at filter
➥ at <console>:25
scala> bsdLines1.count
res1: Long = 34
```

To print the lines containing BSD to the console, you call `println` for each line:

```
scala> bsdLines.foreach(bLine => println(bLine))
BSD-style licenses
The following components are provided under a BSD-style license. See
➥ project link for details.
    (BSD 3 Clause) netlib core (com.github.fommil.netlib:core:1.1.2 -
➥ https://github.com/fommil/netlib-java/core)
    (BSD 3 Clause) JPMML-Model (org.jpmml:pmml-model:1.1.15 -
➥ https://github.com/jpmml/jpmml-model)
    (BSD 3-clause style license) jblas (org.jblas:jblas:1.2.4 -
➥ http://jblas.org/)
    (BSD License) AntLR Parser Generator (antlr:antlr:2.7.7 -
➥ http://www.antlr.org/)
...
```

To accomplish the same thing with less typing, you can also use a shortcut version:

```
scala> bsdLines.foreach(println)
```

2.2.3 *The notion of a resilient distributed dataset*

Although `licLines` and `bsdLines` feel and look like ordinary Scala collections (`filter` and `foreach` methods are available in ordinary Scala collections, too), they aren't. They're distributed collections, specific to Spark, called resilient distributed datasets or RDDs.

The RDD is the fundamental abstraction in Spark. It represents a collection of elements that is

- *Immutable* (read-only)
- *Resilient* (fault-tolerant)
- *Distributed* (dataset spread out to more than one node)

RDDs support a number of transformations that do useful data manipulation, but they always yield a new RDD instance. Once created, RDDs never change; thus the adjective *immutable*. Mutable state is known to introduce complexity, but besides that, having immutable collections allows Spark to provide important fault-tolerance guarantees in a straightforward manner.

The fact that the collection is *distributed* on a number of machines (execution contexts, JVMs) is transparent[1] to its users, so working with RDDs isn't much different than working with ordinary local collections like plain old lists, maps, sets, and so on. To summarize, the purpose of RDDs is to facilitate parallel operations on large datasets in a straightforward manner, abstracting away their distributed nature and inherent fault tolerance.

RDDs are *resilient* because of Spark's built-in fault recovery mechanics. Spark is capable of healing RDDs in case of node failure. Whereas other distributed computation frameworks facilitate fault tolerance by replicating data to multiple machines (so it can be restored from healthy replicas once a node fails), RDDs are different: they provide fault tolerance by logging the transformations used to build a dataset (how it came to be) rather than the dataset itself. If a node fails, only a subset of the dataset that resided on the failed node needs to be recomputed.

For example, in the previous section, the process of loading the text file yielded the `licLines` RDD. Then you applied the `filter` function to `licLines`, which produced the new `bsdLines` RDD. Those transformations and their ordering are referred to as *RDD lineage*. It represents the exact recipe for creating the `bsdLines` RDD, from start to finish. We'll talk more about RDD lineage in later chapters. For now, let's see what else you can do with RDDs.

---

[1] Well, almost transparent. In order to optimize computation and thus gain performance benefits, there are ways to control dataset partitioning (how the RDD is distributed among nodes in a cluster) and persistence options. We'll talk about both features extensively later in the book.

2.3   *Basic RDD actions and transformations*

There are two types of RDD operations: transformations and actions. *Transformations* (for example, `filter` or `map`) are operations that produce a new RDD by performing some useful data manipulation on another RDD. *Actions* (for example, `count` or `foreach`) trigger a computation in order to return the result to the calling program or to perform some actions on an RDD's elements.

> **Laziness of Spark transformations**
>
> It's important to understand that transformations are evaluated *lazily*, meaning computation doesn't take place until you invoke an action. Once an action is triggered on an RDD, Spark examines the RDD's lineage and uses that information to build a "graph of operations" that needs to be executed in order to compute the action. Think of a transformation as a sort of diagram that tells Spark which operations need to happen and in which order once an action gets executed.

In this section, you'll be introduced to a number of other important RDD operations, such as `map`, `flatMap`, `take`, and `distinct`. We hope you still have your Spark shell open so that you can follow along. Feel free to experiment, turn things around, and make some mistakes. That way, you'll learn much more efficiently.

2.3.1   *Using the map transformation*

You saw that `filter` is used to conditionally remove[2] some elements from an RDD. Now let's look at how you can take one RDD's elements, transform them, and create a brand-new RDD with those transformed elements.

The `map` transformation allows you to apply an arbitrary function to all elements of an RDD. Here is how the `map` method is declared (we removed parts of the signature that aren't relevant for this discussion):

```
class RDD[T] {                          Defines the RDD as a class
  // ... other methods ...              with parameterized type T
  def map[U](f: (T) => U): RDD[U]       map takes another function as
  // ... other methods ...              a parameter and returns an
}                                       RDD of a different type.
```

You can read the function signature like this: "Declare a function called `map` that takes some other function as a parameter and returns an RDD. The RDD that is returned contains elements of a different type than the RDD on which `map` was called." So the resulting RDD, unlike with `filter`, may or may not be of the same type as the RDD that `map` was called on (`this`).

---

[2] RDDs are immutable, remember? So when we say "remove" we mean "create a new RDD where some elements are conditionally missing, compared to the RDD you started with (the one on which `filter` was called)."

Let's start with a basic example. If you wanted to calculate the squares of an RDD's elements, you could easily do that using `map`.

Listing 2.2   Calculating the squares of an RDD's elements using `map`

```
scala> val numbers = sc.parallelize(10 to 50 by 10)
numbers: org.apache.spark.rdd.RDD[Int] = ParallelCollectionRDD[2] at
➥ parallelize at <console>:12
scala> numbers.foreach(x => println(x))
30
40
50
10
20
scala> val numbersSquared = numbers.map(num => num * num)
numbersSquared: org.apache.spark.rdd.RDD[Int] = MapPartitionsRDD[7] at map
➥ at <console>:23
scala> numbersSquared.foreach(x => println(x))
100
400
1600
2500
900
```

The first command in the listing, Spark context's `parallelize` method, takes a `Seq` (`Array` and `List` classes both implement the `Seq` interface) and creates an RDD from its elements. The `Seq`'s elements get distributed to Spark executors in the process. `makeRDD` is an alias for `parallelize`, so you can use either of the two. The expression passed in as an argument (10 to 50 by 10) is Scala's way of creating a `Range`, which is also an implementation of `Seq`.

Using a slightly different example to illustrate how `map` can change RDD's type, imagine a situation where you want to convert an RDD of integers to an RDD of strings and then reverse each of those strings:

```
scala> val reversed = numbersSquared.map(x => x.toString.reverse)
reversed: org.apache.spark.rdd.RDD[String] = MappedRDD[4] at map at
➥ <console>:16
scala> reversed.foreach(x => println(x))
001
004
009
0061
0052
```

An underscore in Scala, in this ➊
context, is called a placeholder.

You can also write this last transformation so it's even shorter:

```
scala> val alsoReversed = numbersSquared.map(_.toString.reverse)          ◄──┐
alsoReversed: org.apache.spark.rdd.RDD[String] = MappedRDD[4] at map at
➥ <console>:16
scala> alsoReversed.first          ◄─── Returns the first elements from an RDD
```

```
res6: String = 001
scala> alsoReversed.top(4)
res7: Array[String] = Array(009, 0061, 0052, 004)
```

009 is bigger than 0061; because these are strings they're sorted alphabetically.[3]

top returns an ordered array of the k largest elements from an RDD Set.

Placeholder syntax

You can read the placeholder syntax in the previous example ❶ like this: "Whatever I'm invoked with, call `toString` and then `reverse` on it." We call it a *placeholder*[4] because it holds the place to be filled in with the argument to a function when the function is invoked.

In this case, as `map` starts going over elements, the placeholder is first replaced with the first element from the `numbersSquared` collection (100), then the second element (400), and so on.

2.3.2 *Using the distinct and flatMap transformations*

We continue our tour of RDD operations with the `distinct` and `flatMap` transformations. They're similar to the functions of the same name available in some Scala collections (such as `Array` objects), so they may be familiar to you. The difference is that, when used on RDDs, they operate on distributed data and are lazily evaluated, as we said earlier.

Let's use another example. Imagine that you have a large file containing clients' transaction logs from the last week. Every time a client makes a purchase, the server appends a unique client ID to the end of the log file. At the end of each day, the server adds a new line, so you have a nice file structure of one line of comma-separated user IDs per day. Suppose you're given the task of finding out how many clients bought at least one product during a week. To get that number, you need to remove all duplicate clients: that is, reduce all clients who made multiple purchases to a single entry. After that, all that is left to do is count the remaining entries.

To prepare for this example, you'll create a sample file with several client IDs. Open a new terminal (not spark-shell), and execute the following commands:[5]

~ is another way to refer to your Linux home directory (equivalent to $HOME).

```
$ echo "15,16,20,20
77,80,94
94,98,16,31
31,15,20" > ~/client-ids.log
```

echo prints its argument to the standard output, which here is redirected to the client-ids.log file. The numbers represent client IDs.

---

[3] Alphabetical order: http://en.wikipedia.org/wiki/Alphabetical_order.

[4] More on placeholder syntax: http://mng.bz/c52S.

[5] If you're reading the printed version of the book, use the book's GitHub repository to copy the snippets: http://mng.bz/RCb9.

Back in spark-shell, load the log file:

```
scala> val lines = sc.textFile("/home/spark/client-ids.log")
lines: org.apache.spark.rdd.RDD[String] = client-ids.log
➥ MapPartitionsRDD[1] at textFile at <console>:21
```

Then you split each line on the comma character, which yields an array of strings for each line:

```
scala> val idsStr = lines.map(line => line.split(","))
idsStr: org.apache.spark.rdd.RDD[Array[String]] = MapPartitionsRDD[2] at
➥ map at <console>:14
scala> idsStr.foreach(println(_))
[Ljava.lang.String;@65d795f9
[Ljava.lang.String;@2cb742ab
... 4 of these ...
```

Wait, what just happened? Isn't the expected output an array of IDs?

Actually, no: you created `idsStr` by splitting each of the four lines on the comma character, which created four arrays of IDs. Thus the printout contains four return values of `Array.toString`:[6]

```
scala> idsStr.first
res0: Array[String] = Array(15, 16, 20, 20)
```

How could you visualize these arrays that found themselves inside your `idsStr` RDD? Let's use the RDD's `collect` action (you do remember section 2.3, where we explained that RDD operations can either be transformations or actions, right?). `collect` is an action that creates an array and then, well, collects all elements of an RDD into that array, which it then returns as the result to your shell:

```
scala> idsStr.collect
res1: Array[Array[String]] = Array(Array(15, 16, 20, 20), Array(77, 80,
➥ 94), Array(94, 98, 16, 31), Array(31, 15, 20))
```

If only there was a function that knows how to flatten those seven arrays into a single, *union array*. There is, and it is called `flatMap`, and it's used exactly for situations like these, where the result of a transformation yields multiple arrays and you need to get all elements into one array. It basically works the same as `map`, in that it applies the provided function to all of the RDD's elements, but the difference is that it concatenates multiple arrays into a collection that has one level of nesting less than what it received. This is its signature:

```
def flatMap[U](f: (T) => TraversableOnce[U]): RDD[U]
```

To simplify things and avoid confusion, we'll say that `TraversableOnce`[7] is a weird name for a collection.

---

[6] What is this `[Ljava.lang.String;@...` thing? See http://stackoverflow.com/a/3442100/465710.

[7] If you like a good puzzle, you can look up `TraversableOnce` in the Scala API (called *scaladoc*): http://mng.bz/OTvD.

The game plan

It isn't yet time to go deeper into Scala; after all, we're sticking to the game plan of not assuming any prior Scala knowledge. Overwhelming you with Scala definitions wouldn't be productive at this point. Instead, we'll keep explaining relevant Scala concepts in context, as we come across them. We'll skip the topics that are hard for a Scala beginner to understand, unless we think that understanding the topic is crucial for working with Spark. TraversableOnce is definitely not (yet) in that category.

For more experienced Scala developers, for each such topic, we'll make sure to include a footnote that contains a link to an online resource.

Now that you know about `flatMap`, let's start over with this example. You'll once again split the lines you loaded into the `lines` RDD, but this time you'll use `flatMap` instead of the regular `map`:

```
scala> val ids = lines.flatMap(_.split(","))
ids: org.apache.spark.rdd.RDD[String] = MapPartitionsRDD[8] at flatMap at
➥ <console>:23
```

Let's use `collect` to see what `flatMap` returned:

```
scala> ids.collect
res11: Array[String] = Array(15, 16, 20, 20, 77, 80, 94, 94, 98, 16, 31,
➥ 31, 15, 20)
```

This `Array` that wraps the IDs, as we already mentioned, is just the way `collect` returns results. When you used `collect` the first time, after applying the regular `map` function, you got back an *array of arrays*. `flatMap` yielded one level of nesting less than `map`. Let's make sure you don't have any arrays in the `ids` RDD:

```
scala> ids.first
res12: String = 15
```

We told you so: you get back a single string. If you want to format the output of the `collect` method, you can use a method of the `Array` class called `mkString`:

```
scala> ids.collect.mkString("; ")
res13: String = 15; 16; 20; 20; 77; 80; 94; 94; 98; 16; 31; 31; 15; 20
```

`mkString` isn't specific to Spark; it's a method of the `Array` class from Scala's standard library, which is used to concatenate all the array elements into a `String`, dividing them with the provided parameter.

For no particular reason, apart from practicing the `map` transformation and the placeholder syntax, let's transform the RDD's elements from `String` to `Int` (this could perhaps be used to avoid sorting elements alphabetically as strings, where "10" is smaller than "2"):

```
scala> val intIds = ids.map(_.toInt)
intIds: org.apache.spark.rdd.RDD[Int] = MapPartitionsRDD[9] at map at
➥ <console>:25
scala> intIds.collect
res14: Array[Int] = Array(15, 16, 20, 20, 77, 80, 94, 94, 98, 16, 31, 31,
➥ 15, 20)
```

Your task was to find the number of unique clients who bought anything. To find that number, you need `distinct`. `distinct` is a method that returns a new RDD with duplicate elements removed:

```
def distinct(): RDD[T]
```

When called on an RDD, it creates a new RDD with unique elements (of the same type, of course). So, let's finally make the list of IDs unique:

```
scala> val uniqueIds = intIds.distinct
uniqueIds: org.apache.spark.rdd.RDD[Int] = MapPartitionsRDD[12] at distinct
➥ at <console>:27
scala> uniqueIds.collect
res15: Array[Int] = Array(16, 80, 98, 20, 94, 15, 77, 31)
scala> val finalCount = uniqueIds.count
finalCount: Long = 8
```

You now know that only eight distinct clients made purchases during that week. How many transactions were made in total?

```
scala> val transactionCount = ids.count
transactionCount: Long = 14
```

So, 8 clients made 14 transactions. You end up concluding that you have a small set of loyal clients.

Pasting blocks of code into the Spark Scala shell

Just so you know, you don't have to paste line by line into your shell. You can copy whole blocks of code, together with their outputs, which can make things a little easier.

Execute the following block of slightly modified commands from this section. If you're reading the print edition, you can copy the snippet from the book's GitHub repository; otherwise, copy and paste the entire block, together with the results, into spark-shell. It will detect that you pasted a shell transcript, and all the commands that start with the `scala>` prompt will be replayed, after you confirm your intention with a secret keyboard shortcut that will be revealed to you (watch out for `// Detected repl transcript` in the output):

```
(continued)
scala> val lines = sc.textFile("/home/spark/client-ids.log")
lines: org.apache.spark.rdd.RDD[String] = client-ids.log
 ➥ MapPartitionsRDD[12] at textFile at <console>:21
scala> val ids = lines.flatMap(_.split(","))
ids: org.apache.spark.rdd.RDD[String] = MapPartitionsRDD[13] at flatMap at
 ➥ <console>:23
scala> ids.count
res8: Long = 14
scala> val uniqueIds = ids.distinct
uniqueIds: org.apache.spark.rdd.RDD[String] = MapPartitionsRDD[16] at
 ➥ distinct at <console>:25
scala> uniqueIds.count
res17: Long = 8
scala> uniqueIds.collect
res18: Array[String] = Array(16, 80, 98, 20, 94, 15, 77, 31)
```

Now that you have witnessed a small miracle, let's continue on with our business.

Still with us? Great! But hold your horses—after all, these are still basics. Let's see whether you can grasp the next transformation, the dreaded `sample`.

2.3.3 *Obtaining RDD's elements with the sample, take, and takeSample operations*

Suppose you need to prepare a sample set that contains 30% of client IDs randomly picked from the same log. Good thing the authors of the RDD API anticipated this exact situation, because they implemented a `sample` method in the RDD class. It's a transformation that creates a new RDD with random elements from the calling RDD (`this`):

The signature looks like this:

```
def sample(withReplacement: Boolean, fraction: Double, seed: Long =
 ➥ Utils.random.nextLong): RDD[T]
```

The first parameter, `withReplacement`, determines whether the same element may be sampled multiple times. If it's set to `false`, an element, once sampled, won't be considered for the subsequent sampling (it's removed—that is, not replaced) during the life of that method call. To use an example from Wikipedia (http://mng.bz/kQ7W), if we catch fish, measure them, and immediately return them to the water before continuing with the sample, this is a *with replacement* design, because we might end up catching and measuring the same fish more than once. But if we don't return the fish to the water (for example, if we eat the fish), this becomes a *without replacement* design.

The second parameter, `fraction`, determines the expected number of times each element is going to be sampled (as a number greater than zero), when replacement is used. When used without replacement, it determines the expected probability that each element is going to be sampled, expressed as a floating-point number between 0 and 1. Keep in mind that sampling is a probabilistic method, so don't expect the results to be exact every time.

The third parameter represents the *seed* for random-number generation. The same seed always produces the same quasi-random numbers, which is useful for testing. Under the hood, this method uses `scala.util.Random`, which in turn uses `java.util.Random`.

The one new thing you should notice in the method signature is that the `seed` parameter has a default value, `Utils.random.nextLong`. In Scala, a parameter's default value is used if you don't provide that argument when calling a function.

You needed to prepare a set of 30% (0.3) of all client IDs. You'll do sampling without replacement:

```
scala> val s = uniqueIds.sample(false, 0.3)
s: org.apache.spark.rdd.RDD[String] = PartitionwiseSampledRDD[19] at sample
➡ at <console>:27
scala> s.count
res19: Long = 2
scala> s.collect
res20: Array[String] = Array(94, 21)
```

You sampled two elements, which is about 30% of the unique set of client IDs. Don't be surprised if you get 1 or 3 elements; as we mentioned, 0.3 is only the probability that each of the elements will end up in the sampled subset.

Let's now see what a with replacement does. A 50% with replacement will make results more apparent:

```
scala> val swr = uniqueIds.sample(true, 0.5)
swr: org.apache.spark.rdd.RDD[String] = PartitionwiseSampledRDD[20] at
➡ sample at <console>:27
scala> swr.count
res21: Long = 5
scala> swr.collect
res22: Array[String] = Array(16, 80, 80, 20, 94)
```

Notice that you get back the string "80" two times from the *unique* set of strings. That wouldn't be possible if you hadn't used replacement (the algorithm doesn't remove elements from the pool of potential sample candidates once they're picked).

If you want to sample an exact number of elements from an RDD, you can use the `takeSample` action:

```
def takeSample(withReplacement: Boolean, num: Int, seed: Long =
➡ Utils.random.nextLong): Array[T]
```

There are two differences between `sample` and `takeSample`. The first is that `takeSample` takes an `Int` as its second parameter, which determines the number of sampled elements it returns (notice that we didn't say "expected number of elements"—it always returns exactly `num` number of elements). The second difference is that, whereas `sample` is a transformation, `takeSample` is an action, which returns an array (like `collect`):

```
scala> val taken = uniqueIds.takeSample(false, 5)
taken: Array[String] = Array(80, 98, 77, 31, 15)
```

Another useful action for obtaining a subset of your data is take. It scans enough of an RDD's *partitions* (parts of data residing on different nodes in the cluster) to return the requested number of elements. Remember this one well, because you'll find your-self needing a simple action for peeking into the data in your RDDs:

```
scala> uniqueIds.take(3)
res23: Array[String] = Array(80, 20, 15)
```

Of course, you shouldn't request too many elements, because they all need to be transferred to a single machine.

2.4   Double RDD functions

If you create an RDD containing only Double elements, several extra functions automagically become available, through the concept known as *implicit conversion.*

Scala's implicit conversion

Implicit conversion is a useful concept, heavily used in Spark, but it can be a bit tricky to understand at first, so we'll explain it here. Let's say you have a Scala class defined like this:

```
class ClassOne[T](val input: T) { }
```

ClassOne is type parameterized, so the argument input can be a string, an integer, or any other object. And let's say you want objects of ClassOne to have a method duplicatedString(), but only if input is a string, and to have a method duplicated-Int(), only if input is an integer. You can accomplish this by creating two classes, each containing one of these new methods. Additionally, you have to define two implicit methods that will be used for conversion of ClassOne to these new classes, like this:

```
class ClassOneStr(val one: ClassOne[String]) {
    def duplicatedString() = one.input + one.input
}
class ClassOneInt(val one: ClassOne[Int]) {
    def duplicatedInt() = one.input.toString + one.input.toString
}
implicit def toStrMethods(one: ClassOne[String]) = new ClassOneStr(one)
implicit def toIntMethods(one: ClassOne[Int]) = new ClassOneInt(one)
```

The compiler can now perform automatic conversion from type ClassOne[String] to ClassOneStr and from ClassOne[Int] to ClassOneInt, and you can use their methods on ClassOne objects. You can now perform something like this:

```
scala> val oneStrTest = new ClassOne("test")
oneStrTest: ClassOne[String] = ClassOne@516a4aef

scala> val oneIntTest = new ClassOne(123)
oneIntTest: ClassOne[Int] = ClassOne@f8caa36

scala> oneStrTest.duplicatedString()
res0: String = testtest

scala> oneIntTest.duplicatedInt()
res1: 123123
```

(continued)

But the following snippet gives an error:

```scala
scala> oneIntTest.duplicatedString()
      error: value duplicatedString is not a member of ClassOne[Int]
            oneIntTest.duplicatedString()
```

Neat, eh?

This is exactly what happens with RDDs in Spark. RDDs have new methods added to them automatically, depending on the type of data they hold. RDDs containing only `Double` objects are automatically converted into instances of the `org.apache.spark` `.rdd.DoubleRDDFunctions` class, which contains all the double RDD functions described in this section.

For the curious, the only difference between RDDs in Spark and the preceding example is where the implicit methods are defined. You can find them in the RDD companion object, which is an *object* RDD defined in the same file as the *class* RDD (and having the same name). Companion objects in Scala hold what would be static members in Java.

We're glad that's out of the way. So, what functions are implicitly added to RDDs containing `Double` elements? Double RDD functions can give you the total sum of all elements along with their mean value, standard deviation, variance, and histogram. These functions can come in handy when you get new data and you need to obtain information about its distribution.

2.4.1 Basic statistics with double RDD functions

Let's use the `intIds` RDD you created previously to illustrate the concepts in this section. Although it contains `Int` objects, they can be automatically converted to `Doubles`, so double RDD functions can be implicitly applied.

Using `mean` and `sum` is trivial:

```scala
scala> intIds.mean
res0: Double = 44.785714285714285
scala> intIds.sum
res1: Double = 627.0
```

A bit more involved is the `stats` action. It calculates the count and sum of all elements; their mean, maximum, and minimum values; and their variance and standard deviation, all in one pass, and returns an `org.apache.spark.util.StatCounter` object that has methods for accessing all these metrics.

`variance` and `stdev` actions are just shortcuts for calling `stats().variance` and `stats().stdev`:

```scala
scala> intIds.variance
res2: Double = 1114.8826530612246
scala> intIds.stdev
res3: Double = 33.38985853610681
```

2.4.2   *Visualizing data distribution with histograms*

Histograms are used for graphical representation of data. The X axis has value intervals and the Y axis has the data density, or number of elements in the corresponding interval.

The `histogram` action on double RDDs has two versions. The first version takes an array of `Double` values that represent interval limits and returns an `Array` with counts of elements belonging to each interval. Interval limits have to be sorted, must contain at least two elements (that represent one interval), and must not contain any duplicates:

```
scala> intIds.histogram(Array(1.0, 50.0, 100.0))
res4: Array[Long] = Array(9, 5)
```

The second version takes a number of intervals, which is used to split the input data range into intervals of equal size, and returns a tuple whose second element contains the counts (just like the first version) and whose first element contains the calculated interval limits:

```
scala> intIds.histogram(3)
res5: (Array[Double], Array[Long]) = (Array(15.0, 42.66666666666667,
➥ 70.33333333333334, 98.0),Array(9, 0, 5))
```

Histograms can offer some insight into data distribution, which usually isn't obvious from standard deviation and mean values.

2.4.3   *Approximate sum and mean*

If you have a really large dataset of `Double` values, calculating their statistics can take longer than you care to spend. You can use two experimental actions, `sumApprox` and `meanApprox`, to calculate the approximate sum and mean, respectively, in a specified timeframe:

```
sumApprox(timeout: Long, confidence: Double = 0.95):
    PartialResult[BoundedDouble]
meanApprox(timeout: Long, confidence: Double = 0.95):
    PartialResult[BoundedDouble]
```

They both take a timeout value in milliseconds, which determines the maximum amount of time the action can run for. If it doesn't return by then, the result computed until that point is returned. The `confidence` parameter influences the values returned.

Approximate actions return a `PartialResult` object, which gives access to `finalValue` and `failure` fields (the `failure` field is available only if an exception occurred). `finalValue` is of type `BoundedDouble`, which expresses not a single value, but a probable range (low and high), its mean value, and the associated confidence.

2.5 Summary

- Symbolic links can help you manage multiple Spark releases.
- The Spark shell is used for interactive one-off jobs and exploratory data analysis.
- The resilient distributed dataset (RDD) is the fundamental abstraction in Spark. It represents a collection of elements that is immutable, resilient, and distributed.
- There are two types of RDD operations: transformations and actions. Transformations (for example, `filter` or `map`) are operations that produce a new RDD by performing useful data manipulation on another RDD. Actions (for example, `count` or `foreach`) trigger a computation in order to return the result to the calling program or to perform some actions on an RDD's elements.
- The `map` transformation is the main operation for transforming RDD data.
- `distinct` returns another RDD containing only unique elements.
- `flatMap` concatenates multiple arrays into a collection that has one level of nesting less than what it received.
- With `sample`, `take`, and `takeSample`, you can obtain a subset of an RDD's elements.
- Double RDD functions become available through Scala's implicit conversion and give you the total sum of all of an RDD's elements and their mean value, standard deviation, variance, and histogram.

Writing
Spark applications

3

This chapter covers

- Generating a new Spark project in Eclipse
- Loading a sample dataset from the GitHub archive
- Writing an application that analyzes GitHub logs
- Working with DataFrames in Spark
- Submitting your application to be executed

In this chapter, you'll learn to write Spark applications. Most Spark programmers use an integrated development environment (IDE), such as IntelliJ or Eclipse. There are readily available resources online that describe how to use IntelliJ IDEA with Spark, whereas Eclipse resources are still hard to come by. That is why, in this chapter, you'll learn how to use Eclipse for writing Spark programs. Nevertheless, if you choose to stick to IntelliJ, you'll still be able to follow along. After all, these two IDEs have similar sets of features.

You'll start by downloading and configuring Eclipse and then installing Eclipse plug-ins that are necessary for working with Scala. You'll use Apache Maven (a software project-management tool) to configure Spark application projects in this chapter. The Spark project itself is configured using Maven. We prepared a Maven Archetype (a template for quickly bootstrapping Maven projects) in the book's GitHub repository at https://github.com/spark-in-action, which will help you bootstrap your new Spark application project in just a few clicks.

Throughout this chapter, you'll be developing an application that counts GitHub push events (code commits to GitHub) made by your company's employees. You'll use an exciting new construct, the `DataFrame`, which saw the light of day in Spark 1.3.0.

Lots of content awaits you. Ready?

3.1 Generating a new Spark project in Eclipse

This section describes how to create a Spark project in Eclipse. We trust you know how to install Eclipse (you can follow the online instructions at http://wiki.eclipse.org/Eclipse/Installation), so we won't go into details. You can install it onto your development machine or in the spark-in-action VM. The decision is all yours, because it won't significantly affect how you build your Spark project. We installed it in the VM, in the /home/spark/eclipse folder, and used /home/spark/workspace as the workspace folder. To view the Eclipse GUI started from the VM, you'll need to set up an X Window system (on Windows, you can use Xming: https://sourceforge.net/projects/xming) and set the `DISPLAY` variable in your VM Linux shell to point to the IP address of your running X Window system.

If you wish to use some other IDE, such as IntelliJ, you can skip this section and start from section 3.2. If you wish to continue using Eclipse, you also need to install these two plug-ins:

- Scala IDE plug-in
- Scala Maven integration for Eclipse (`m2eclipse-scala`)

To install the Scala IDE plug-in, follow these steps:

1 Go to Help[1] > Install new Software, and click Add in the upper-right corner.
2 When the Add Repository window appears, enter `scala-ide` in the Name field.
3 Enter `http://download.scala-ide.org/sdk/lithium/e44/scala211/stable/site` in the Location field
4 Confirm by clicking OK.
5 Eclipse looks up the URL you entered and displays the available software it found there. Select only the Scala IDE for Eclipse entry and all its subentries.
6 Confirm the selection on the next screen, and accept the license on the one after that. Restart Eclipse when prompted.

---

[1] Readers new to Ubuntu may not know that the toolbar of the currently active window is always located at the top of the screen, and it's revealed when you hover the cursor near the top.

To install the Scala Maven integration for Eclipse plug-in, follow the same steps as for the Scala IDE plug-in, only enter `http://alchim31.free.fr/m2e-scala/update-site` in the Location field and `m2eclipse-scala` in the Name field.

Once you have all these set up, you're ready to start a new Eclipse project that will host your application. To simplify setting up new projects (either for examples in this book or for your future Spark projects), we have prepared an Archetype called `scala-archetype-sparkinaction` (available from our GitHub repository), which is used to create a starter Spark project in which versions and dependencies have already been taken care of.

To create a project in Eclipse, on your toolbar menu select File > New > Project > Maven > Maven Project. Don't make any changes on the first screen of the New Maven Project Wizard, but click Next.

On the second screen, click Configure (which opens the Maven > Archetypes section of the Eclipse Preferences). Click the Add Remote Catalog button, and fill in the following values in the dialog that pops up (see figure 3.1):

- *Catalog File:* `https://github.com/spark-in-action/scala-archetype-sparkinaction/raw/master/archetype-catalog.xml`
- *Description:* `Spark in Action`

Click OK, and then close the Preferences window. You should see a progress bar in the lower-right corner, which is how Eclipse notifies you that it went to look up the catalog you just added.

You're now back in the New Maven Project wizard. Select Spark in Action in the Catalog drop-down field and scala-archetype-sparkinaction artifact (see figure 3.2).

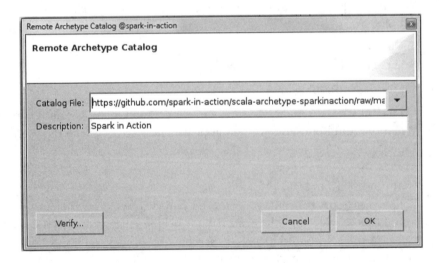

Figure 3.1 Adding the *Spark in Action* Maven Remote Archetype Catalog to your Eclipse Preferences

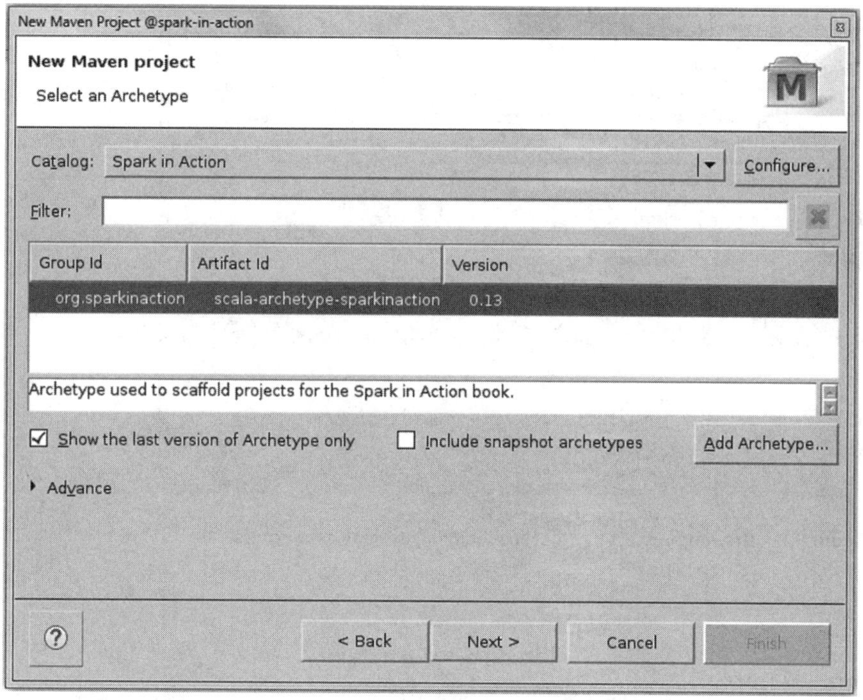

Figure 3.2 Choosing the Maven Archetype that you want to use as the new project's template. Select scala-archetype-sparkinaction.

The next screen prompts you to enter your project's parameters. Notice (in figure 3.3) that your root package consists of groupId and artifactId.

> ### groupId and artifactId
>
> If you're new to Maven, it may be easier for you to look at artifactId as your project name and groupId as its fully qualified organization name. For example, Spark has groupId org.apache and artifactId spark. The Play framework has com.typesafe as its groupId and play as its artifactId.

You can specify whichever values you like for groupId and artifactId, but it may be easier for you to follow along if you choose the same values as we did (see figure 3.3). Confirm by clicking Finish.

Let's examine the structure of the generated project. Looking from the top, the first (root) entry is the project's main folder, always named the same as the project. We call this folder the project's *root* (or *project root*, interchangeably).

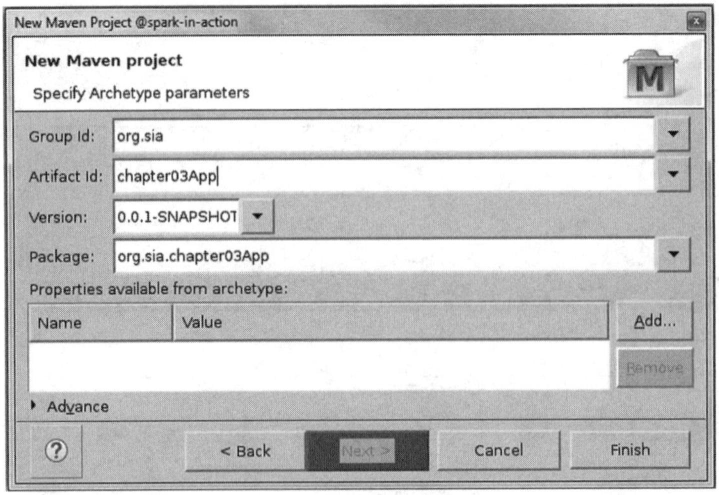

Figure 3.3   Creating a Maven project: specifying project parameters

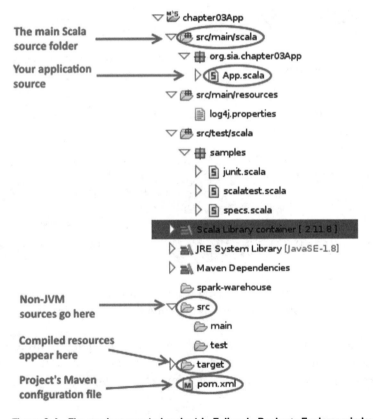

Figure 3.4   The newly generated project in Eclipse's Package Explorer window

src/main/scala is your main Scala source folder (if you were to add Java code to your project, you would create an src/main/java source folder). In the scala folder, you have the root package,[2] `org.sia.chapter03App`, with a single Scala source file in it: App.scala. This is the Scala file where you'll start writing your application.

Next comes the main test folder with prepared samples for various test types, followed by the container for your Scala library. You're using the Scala that came with the Scala IDE Eclipse plug-in. Next is Maven Dependencies, described a bit later. Below Maven Dependencies is JDK (Eclipse refers to JRE and JDK in the same way, as JRE System Library). Further down in the Package Explorer window is again the src folder, but this time in the role of an ordinary folder (non-source or, more precisely, non-jvm-source folder), in case you want to add other types of resources to your project, such as images, JavaScript, HTML, CSS, anything you don't want to be processed by the Eclipse JVM tooling. Then there is the target folder, which is where compiled resources go (like .class or .jar files).

Finally, there is the all-encompassing pom.xml, which is the project's Maven specification. If you open pom.xml from the project root and switch to the Dependency Hierarchy tab, you'll have a much better view of the project's dependencies and their causality (see figure 3.5).

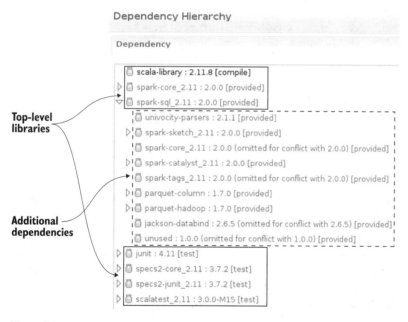

Figure 3.5   Project's libraries dependency hierarchy (in pom.xml)

---

[2] On the filesystem level, `org.sia.chapter03App` consists of three folders. In other words, this is the path to the App.scala file: chapter03App/src/main/scala/org/sia/chapter03App/App.scala.

There are only six libraries at the top level (all explicitly listed in pom.xml). Each of those libraries brought with it its own dependencies; and many of those dependencies, in turn, have their own dependencies, and so on

In the next section, you'll see a plausible real-world example of developing a Spark application. You'll need Eclipse, so don't close it just yet.

3.2   *Developing the application*

Say you need to create a daily report that lists all employees of your company and the number of *pushes*[3] they've made to GitHub. You can implement this using the GitHub archive site (www.githubarchive.org/), put together by Ilya Grigorik from Google (with the help of the GitHub folks), where you can download GitHub archives for arbitrary time periods. You can download a single day from the archive and use it as a sample for building the daily report.

3.2.1   *Preparing the GitHub archive dataset*

Open your VM's terminal, and type in the following commands:

```
$ mkdir -p $HOME/sia/github-archive
$ cd $HOME/sia/github-archive
$ wget http://data.githubarchive.org/2015-03-01-{0..23}.json.gz
```

This downloads all public GitHub activity from March 1, 2015, in the form of 24 JSON files, one for each hour of the day:

```
2015-03-01-0.json.gz
2015-03-01-1.json.gz
...
2015-03-01-23.json.gz
```

To decompress the files, you can run

```
$ gunzip *
```

After a few seconds, you're left with 24 JSON files. You'll notice that the files are rather large (around 1 GB in total, decompressed), so you can use just the first hour of the day (44 MB) as a sample during development, instead of the entire day.

But the extracted files aren't valid JSON. Each file is a set of valid JSON strings separated with newlines, where each line is a single JSON object—that is, a GitHub event (push, branch, create repo, and so on).[4] You can preview the first JSON object with head (which is used to list n lines from the top of a file), like this:

---

[3] To *push changes*, in distributed source control management systems (such as Git), means to transfer content from your local repository to a remote repository. In earlier SCM systems, that was known as *commit*.

[4] GitHub API documentation on types of events: https://developer.github.com/v3/activity/events/types/.

```
$ head -n 1 2015-03-01-0.json
{"id":"2614896652","type":"CreateEvent","actor":{"id":739622,"login":
➥ "treydock","gravatar_id":"","url":"https://api.github.com/users/
➥ treydock","avatar_url":"https://avatars.githubusercontent.com/u/
➥ 739622?"},"repo":{"id":23934080,"name":"Early-Modern-OCR/emop-
➥ dashboard","url":"https://api.github.com/repos/Early-Modern-OCR/emop-
➥ dashboard"},"payload":{"ref":"development","ref_type":"branch","master_
➥ branch":"master","description":"","pusher_type":"user"},"public":true,
➥ "created_at":"2015-03-01T00:00:00Z","org":{"id":10965476,"login":
➥ "Early-Modern-OCR","gravatar_id":"","url":"https://api.github.com/
➥ orgs/Early-Modern-OCR","avatar_url":
➥ "https://avatars.githubusercontent.com/u/10965476?"}}
```

Uh, that's tough to read. Fortunately, an excellent program called jq (http://stedolan
.github.io/jq) makes working with JSON from the command line much easier. Among
other things, it's great for pretty-printing and color highlighting JSON. You can
download it from http://stedolan.github.io/jq/download. If you're working in the
spark-in-action VM, it's already installed for you.

To try it out, you can pipe a JSON line to jq:

```
$ head -n 1 2015-03-01-0.json | jq '.'
{
  "id": "2614896652",
  "type": "CreateEvent",
  "actor": {
    "id": 739622,
    "login": "treydock",
    "gravatar_id": "",
    "url": "https://api.githb.com/users/treydock",
    "avatar_url": "https://avatars.githubusercontent.com/u/739622?"
  },
  "repo": {
    "id": 23934080,
    "name": "Early-Modern-OCR/emop-dashboard",
    "url": "https://api.github.com/repos/Early-Modern-OCR/emop-dashboard"
  },
  "payload": {
    "ref": "development",
    "ref_type": "branch",
    "master-branch": "master",
    "description": "",
    "pusher_type": "user",
  },
  "public": true,
  "created_at": "2015-03-01T00:00:00Z",
  "org": {
    "id": 10965476,
    "login": "Early-Modern-OCR",
    "gravatar_id": "",
    "url": "https://api.github.com/orgs/Early-Modern-OCR",
    "avatar_url": "https://avatars.githubusercontent.com/u/10965476?"
  }
}
```

Wow! That certainly is pretty. Now you can easily see that this first log entry from the file has `"CreateEvent"` type and that its `payload.ref_type` is `"branch"`. So someone named `"treydock"` (`actor.login`) created a repository branch called `"development"` (`payload.ref`) in the first second of March 1, 2015 (`created_at`). This is how you'll distinguish types of events, because all you need to count are push events. Looking at the GitHub API (https://developer.github.com/v3/activity/events/types/#pushevent), you find out that the push event's `type` is, unsurprisingly, `"PushEvent"`.

OK, you obtained the files needed to develop a prototype, and you know how to prettify its contents so you can understand the structure of GitHub log files. Next, you can start looking into the problem of ingesting a JSON-like structured file into Spark.

3.2.2 Loading JSON

Spark SQL and its `DataFrame` facility, which was introduced in Spark v.1.3.0, provide a means for ingesting JSON data into Spark. At the time of this announcement, everyone was talking about `DataFrames` and the benefits they were going to bring to computation speed and data interchange between Spark components (Spark Streaming, MLlib, and so on). In Spark 1.6.0 `DataSets` were introduced as generalized and improved `DataFrames`.

> **DataFrame API**
>
> A `DataFrame` is an RDD that has a schema. You can think of it as a relational database table, in that each column has a name and a known type. The power of `DataFrames` comes from the fact that, when you create a `DataFrame` from a structured dataset (in this case, JSON), Spark is able to infer a schema by making a pass over the entire JSON dataset that's being loaded. Then, when calculating the execution plan, Spark can use the schema and do substantially better computation optimizations. Note that `DataFrame` was called `SchemaRDD` before Spark v1.3.0.

SQL is so ubiquitous that the new `DataFrame` API was quickly met with acclamation by the wider Spark community. It allows you to attack a problem from a higher vantage point when compared to Spark Core transformations. The SQL-like syntax lets you express your intent in a more declarative fashion: you describe what you want to achieve with a dataset, whereas with the Spark Core API you basically specify how to transform the data (to reshape it so you can come to a useful conclusion).

You may therefore think of Spark Core as a set of fundamental building blocks on which all other facilities are built. The code you write using the `DataFrame` API gets translated to a series of Spark Core transformations under the hood.

We'll talk about `DataFrames` extensively in chapter 5. For now, let's focus on features relevant to the task at hand.

SQLContext is the main interface to Spark SQL (analogous to what SparkContext is to Spark Core). Since Spark 2.0, both contexts are merged into a single class: SparkSession. Its read method gives access to the DataFrameReader object, which you use for getting various data. DataFrameReader's json method is for reading the JSON data. Here's what the scaladocs (http://mng.bz/amo7) say:

```
def json(paths: String*): DataFrame
Loads a JSON file (one object per line) and returns the result as a
➥ [[DataFrame]].
```

One object per line: that's exactly how the GitHub archive files are structured.

Bring your Eclipse forward, and switch to the Scala perspective (Window > Open Perspective > Other > Scala). Then open the App.scala file (to quickly locate the file, you can use Ctrl-Shift-R and then type the first few letters of the filename in the dialog that pops up), clean it up, and leave only the SparkContext initialization, like this:

```
import org.apache.spark.sql.SparkSession

object App {
  def main(args : Array[String]) {
    val spark = SparkSession.builder()
      .appName("GitHub push counter")
      .master("local[*]")
      .getOrCreate()

    val sc = spark.sparkContext
  }
}
```

To load the first JSON file, add the following snippet. Because neither a tilde (~)[5] nor $HOME can be used directly in the path, you end up first retrieving the HOME environment variable so you can use it to compose the JSON file path:

```
val homeDir = System.getenv("HOME")
val inputPath = homeDir + "/sia/github-archive/2015-03-01-0.json"
val ghLog = spark.read.json(inputPath)
```

The json method returns a DataFrame, which has many of the standard RDD methods you used before, like filter, map, flatMap, collect, count, and so on.

The next task to tackle is filtering the log entries so you're left only with push events. By taking a peek at DataFrame (since Spark 2.0, DataFrame is a special case of DataSet; it's a DataSet containing Row objects) in the scaladocs (http://mng.bz/3EQc), you can quickly find out that the filter function is overloaded and that one version takes a condition expression in the form of a String and another one takes a Column.

---

[5] The tilde is equivalent to $HOME. You can use them interchangeably.

The `String` argument will be parsed as SQL, so you can write the following line below the line that loads JSON into ghLog:

```
val pushes = ghLog.filter("type = 'PushEvent'")
```

It's time to see whether the code you have so far works. Will the application compile and start successfully? How will the loading go? Will the schema be inferred successfully? Have you specified the filter expression correctly?

3.2.3 *Running the application from Eclipse*

For the purpose of finding out answers to these questions, add the following code below `filter`:

```
pushes.printSchema          ◁─┐  Pretty-prints the schema
println("all events: " + ghLog.count)      of the pushes DataFrame
println("only pushes: " + pushes.count)
pushes.show(5)      ◁─┐  Prints the first 5 rows (defaults to 20
                         if you call it with no arguments) from
                         a DataFrame in a tabular format
```

Then, build the project by right-clicking the main project folder and choosing Run As > Maven Install. Once the process finishes, right-click App.scala in the Package Explorer, and choose Run As > Scala Application.

If there is no such option, you will need to create a new Run Configuration. To do this, click Run As > Run Configurations …, then choose `Scala Application` and press the `New` button. Enter *Chapter03App* in the `Name` field and *org.sia.chapter03App.App* in the `Main class` field and hit `Run`.

> ### Keyboard shortcut for running a Scala application
> You may have noticed the keyboard shortcut located next to Scala Application (in Package Explorer > Run As). It says Alt-Shift-X S. This means you first need to press together on Alt, Shift, and X, then release all the keys, and then press S by itself.

From now on, we won't always explicitly tell you when to run the application. Follow the code (always inserting it at the bottom of the existing code), and every time you see the output, run the application using either of the two methods described here.

Hopefully, you can now see the output in Eclipse's console window, where the `printSchema` method outputs the inferred schema (if the output is buried in many `INFO` and `WARN` messages, you probably skipped the logging-configuration step in section 2.2.1). The inferred schema consists of the union of all JSON keys, where each key has been assigned a type and the `nullable` attribute (which is always `true` in inferred schemas because, understandably, Spark leaves that decision to you):

```
root
 |-- actor: struct (nullable = true)
 |    |-- avatar_url: string (nullable = true)
 |    |-- gravatar_id: string (nullable = true)
 |    |-- id: long (nullable = true)
 |    |-- login: string (nullable = true)
 |    |-- url: string (nullable = true)
 |-- created_at: string (nullable = true)
 |-- id: string (nullable = true)
 |-- org: struct (nullable = true)
 |    |-- avatar_url: string (nullable = true)
 |    |-- gravatar_id: string (nullable = true)
 |    |-- id: long (nullable = true)
 |    |-- login: string (nullable = true)
 |    |-- url: string (nullable = true)
 |-- payload: struct (nullable = true)
 |    |-- action: string (nullable = true)
 |    |-- before: string (nullable = true)
 |    |-- comment: struct (nullable = true)
 |    |    |-- _links: struct (nullable = true)
 |    |    |    |-- html: struct (nullable = true)
 |    |    |    |    |-- href: string (nullable = true)
 ...
```

You can see that the inferred schema fits your previous findings regarding the GitHub username. You'll have to use the `actor` object and its property `login`, thus `actor.login`. You'll need that information soon, to count the number of pushes per employee. Scroll down to find the first count (`all events`) and then a bit more to find the second one (`only pushes`):

```
...
all events: 17786
...
only pushes: 8793
...
```

At the bottom of the output, you can see the first five rows (we removed four columns—id, org, payload, and `public`—from the middle so the output can fit on a single line):

```
+------------------+------------------+<->+------------------+--------+
|             actor|        created_at|<->|              repo|    type|
+------------------+------------------+<->+------------------+--------+
|[https://avatars...|2015-03-01T00:00:00Z|<->|[31481156,bezerra...|PushEvent|
|[https://avatars...|2015-03-01T00:00:00Z|<->|[31475673,demianb...|PushEvent|
|[https://avatars...|2015-03-01T00:00:00Z|<->|[31481269,ricardo...|PushEvent|
|[https://avatars...|2015-03-01T00:00:00Z|<->|[24902852,actorap...|PushEvent|
|[https://avatars...|2015-03-01T00:00:00Z|<->|[24292601,komasui...|PushEvent|
+------------------+------------------+<->+------------------+--------+
```

To summarize, there were 17,786 events, out of which 8,793 were push events, in the first hour of March 1, 2015. So, it's all working as expected.

3.2.4   Aggregating the data

You managed to filter out every type of event but PushEvent, and that's a good start. Next, you need to group the push events by username and, in the process, count the number of pushes in each group (rows for each username):

```
val grouped = pushes.groupBy("actor.login").count
grouped.show(5)
```

This groups all rows by actor.login column and, similar to regular SQL, performs count as the aggregate operation during grouping. Think about it: as multiple rows (with the same value in the actor.login column) get collapsed down to a single row (that's what *grouping* means), what happens with values in other columns? count[6] tells Spark to ignore the values in those columns and count the number of rows that get collapsed for each unique login. The result answers the question of how many push events each unique login has. In addition to count, the API lists other aggregation functions including min, max, avg, and sum.

The first five rows of the resulting DataFrame, grouped, are displayed in Eclipse Console View:

```
+----------+-----+
|     login|count|
+----------+-----+
|    gfgtdf|    1|
|   mdorman|    1|
|quinngrier|    1|
|  aelveborn|    1|
|  jwallesh|    3|
+----------+-----+
```

That looks good, but it's impossible to see who had the highest number of pushes. The only thing left to do is to sort the dataset by the count column:

```
val ordered = grouped.orderBy(grouped("count").desc)
ordered.show(5)
```

This orders the grouped DataFrame by the value in the count column and names the new, sorted DataFrame ordered. The expression grouped("count") returns the count column from the grouped DataFrame (it implicitly calls DataFrame.apply[7]), on which you call desc to order the output by count in descending order (the default ordering is asc):

---

[6]   For other operations (such as sum, avg, max, and so on), consult the GroupedData scaladoc: http://mng.bz/X8lA.
[7]   See the apply method and the examples at the top of the DataFrame API for more info: http://mng.bz/X8lA.

```
+------------------+-----+
|            login|count|
+------------------+-----+
|      greatfirebot|  192|
|diversify-exp-user|  146|
|     KenanSulayman|   72|
|        manuelrp07|   45|
|    mirror-updates|   42|
+------------------+-----+
```

It works! That's great—but this is the list of all users pushing to GitHub, not only employees of your company. So, you need to exclude non-employees from the list.

3.2.5   *Excluding non-employees*

We prepared a file on our GitHub repository containing GitHub usernames for employees of your imaginary company. It should already be downloaded in your home directory at first-edition/ch03/ghEmployees.txt.

To use the employee list, load it into some type of Scala collection. Because Set has faster random lookup than Seq (sequential collection types, such as Array and List), let's use Set. To load the entire file[8] into a new Set, you can do the following (this is only a piece of the complete application, which will be given in the next section):

The for expression[9] reads each line from the file and stores it into the line variable.

```
import scala.io.Source.fromFile

val empPath = homeDir + "/first-edition/ch03/ghEmployees.txt"
val employees = Set() ++ (
  for {
    line <- fromFile(empPath).getLines
  } yield line.trim
)
```

Set() creates an empty, immutable set. The method named ++ adds multiple elements to the set.

yield also operates on every cycle of the for loop, adding a value to a hidden collection that will be returned (and destroyed) as the result of the entire for expression, once the loop ends.

This code snippet works like the following pseudocode:

```
In each iteration of the for loop:
    Read the next line from the file
    Initialize a new line variable so that it contains the current line
        as its value
    Take the value from the line variable, trim it, and add it to the
        temporary collection
Once the last iteration finishes:
    Return the temporary, hidden collection as the result of for
    Add the result of for to an empty set
    Assign the set to the employees variable
```

---

[8] Loading an entire file isn't considered good practice, but because you know ghEmployees.txt should never go over 1 MB, in this case it's fine (with 208 employees, it weighs only 2 KB).

[9] More about for expressions in Scala: http://mng.bz/k8q2.

This `for` expression probably looks complicated if you're new to Scala, but give it a couple of tries; Scala's `for` comprehensions are a powerful and succinct way of dealing with iteration. There are no index variables unless you need them. We encourage you to try a few `for`-related examples from that Scala book of yours (or other Scala resource you choose to use).

You now have the set of employee usernames, but how do you compare it with your ordered `DataFrame` that contains usernames and the corresponding counts? Well, you already used `DataFrame`'s `filter` method. Its scaladocs (http://mng.bz/3EQc) say

```
def filter(conditionExpr: String): DataSet
```

filters rows using the given SQL expression:

```
val oldPeopleDf = peopleDf.filter("age > 15")
```

But this is only a simple example that compares values of the `peopleDf` DataFrame's age with the literal number 15. If a row's age is greater than 15, the row is included in `oldPeopleDf`.

You, on the other hand, need to compare the `login` column *against the set* of employees and filter out each row whose `login` value isn't in that set. You could use `DataSet`'s `filter` function to specify filtering criteria based on the contents of individual `Row` objects (`DataFrames` are just `DataSets` containing `Row` objects), but you couldn't use that method in `DataFrame` SQL expressions. That's where user-defined functions (UDFs) come into play.

The `SparkSession` (http://mng.bz/j9As) class contains the `udf` method, which is used for registering UDFs. Because you need to check whether each login is in the set of your company's employees, the first thing you need to do is write a general filtering function that checks whether a string is in a set:

```
val isEmp: (String => Boolean) = (arg: String) => employees.contains(arg)
```

You explicitly define `isEmp` as a function that takes a `String` and returns a `Boolean` (often said as "function from String to Boolean"), but thanks to Scala's type inference, you could have made it more terse:

```
val isEmp = user => employees.contains(user)
```

Because `employees` is a `Set` of `Strings`, Scala knows that the `isEmp` function should take a `String`.

In Scala, the return value of a function is the value of its last statement, so it isn't difficult to infer that the function should return whatever the method `contains` returns, which is a `Boolean`.

Next you register `isEmp` as a UDF:

```
val isEmployee = spark.udf.register("isEmpUdf", isEmp)
```

Now, when Spark goes to execute the UDF, it will take all of its dependencies (only the employees set, in this case) and send them along with *each and every task*, to be executed on a cluster.

3.2.6 *Broadcast variables*

We'll talk more about tasks and Spark execution in general in the coming chapters; for now, to explain broadcast variables, we'll tell you that if you were to leave the program like this, you'd be sending the employees set some 200 times over the network (the approximate number of tasks your application will generate for the purpose of excluding non-employees). You don't need to imagine this, because you'll soon see it in your program's output.

Broadcast variables are used for this purpose, because they allow you to send a variable *exactly once* to each node in a cluster. Moreover, the variable is automatically cached in memory on the cluster nodes, ready to be used during the execution of the program.

Spark uses a peer-to-peer protocol, similar to BitTorrent, to distribute broadcast variables, so that, in the case of large clusters, the master doesn't get clogged while broadcasting a potentially large variable to all nodes. This way, worker nodes know how to exchange the variable among themselves, so it spreads out through the cluster organically, like a virus or gossip. In fact, you'll often hear this type of communication between nodes referred to as a *gossip protocol*, further explained at http://en.wikipedia.org/wiki/Gossip_protocol.

The good thing about broadcast variables is that they're simple to use. All you have to do to "fix" your program is to turn your regular employees variable into a broadcast variable, which you then use in place of employees.

You need to add an additional line, just above the isEmp function's definition:

```
val bcEmployees = sc.broadcast(employees)
```

Then change how you refer to this variable, because broadcast variables are accessed using their value method (you need to change this line and not add it; the complete source code of the program is given in listing 3.1):

```
val isEmp = user => bcEmployees.value.contains(user)
```

That's all—everything else stays unchanged. The last thing to do here is to finally filter the ordered DataFrame using your newly created isEmployee UDF function:

```
import sqlContext.implicits._
val filtered = ordered.filter(isEmployee($"login"))
filtered.show()
```

By writing the previous line, you basically tell filter to apply the isEmployee UDF on the login column. If isEmployee returns true, the row gets included in the filtered DataFrame.

Listing 3.1   Complete source code of the program

```scala
package org.sia.chapter03App
import org.apache.spark.sql.SparkSession
import scala.io.Source.fromFile

object App {

  def main(args : Array[String]) {
    // TODO expose appName and master as app. params
    val spark = SparkSession.builder()
        .appName("GitHub push counter")
        .master("local[*]")
        .getOrCreate()

        val sc = spark.sparkContext

    // TODO expose inputPath as app. param
    val homeDir = System.getenv("HOME")
    val inputPath = homeDir + "/sia/github-archive/2015-03-01-0.json"
    val ghLog = spark.read.json(inputPath)

    val pushes = ghLog.filter("type = 'PushEvent'")
    val grouped = pushes.groupBy("actor.login").count
    val ordered = grouped.orderBy(grouped("count").desc)

    // TODO expose empPath as app. param
    val empPath = homeDir + "/first-edition/ch03/ghEmployees.txt"
    val employees = Set() ++ (
      for {
        line <- fromFile(empPath).getLines
      } yield line.trim
    )
    val bcEmployees = sc.broadcast(employees)        // Broadcasts the
                                                     // employees set

    import spark.implicits._
    val isEmp = user => bcEmployees.value.contains(user)
    val isEmployee = spark.udf.register("SetContainsUdf", isEmp)
    val filtered = ordered.filter(isEmployee($"login"))
    filtered.show()
  }
}
```

If you were writing this application for real, you would parameterize appName, appMaster, inputPath, and empPath before sending the application to be tested in a production-simulation environment. Who knows which Spark cluster the application is ultimately going to run on? Even if you knew all the parameters in advance, it would still be prudent to specify those parameters from the outside. It makes the application more flexible. One obvious consequence of hard-coding the parameters in the application code is that every time a parameter changes, the application has to be recompiled.

To run the application, follow these steps:

1 In the top menu, go to Run > Run Configurations.
2 At left in the dialog, select Scala Application > App$.
3 Click Run.

The top 20 commit counts are displayed at the bottom of your Eclipse output:

```
+----------------+-----+
|           login|count|
+----------------+-----+
|   KenanSulayman|   72|
|      manuelrp07|   45|
|         Somasis|   26|
| direwolf-github|   24|
|  EmanueleMinotto|  22|
|         hansliu|   21|
|          digipl|   20|
|       liangyali|   19|
|        fbennett|   18|
|          shryme|   18|
|       jmarkkula|   18|
|         chapuni|   18|
|          qeremy|   16|
|      martagalaz|   16|
|      MichaelCTH|   15|
|         mfonken|   15|
|          tywins|   14|
|          lukeis|   12|
|      jschnurrer|   12|
|     eventuserum|   12|
+----------------+-----+
```

That's it! You have an application that's working on a one-hour subset of data.

It's obvious what you need to tackle next. The task was to run the report daily, which means you need to include all 24 JSON files in the calculation.

3.2.7 *Using the entire dataset*

First, let's create a new Scala source file, to avoid messing with the working one-hour example. In the Package Explorer, right-click the App.scala file, select Copy, right-click App.scala again, and choose Paste. In the dialog that appears, enter GitHub-Day.scala as the object's name, and click OK. When you double-click the new file to open it, notice the red around the filename.

In the GitHubDay.scala file, you can see the reason for the error: the object's name[10] is still App. Piece of cake: rename the object App to GitHubDay, and—nothing happens. Still red. Press Ctrl-S to save the file. Now the red is gone.

Next, open the SparkSession scaladoc (http://mng.bz/j9As) to see whether there is a way to create a DataFrame by ingesting multiple files with a single command.

---

[10] Objects are Scala's singletons. For more details, see http://mng.bz/y2ja.

Although the read method in the scaladoc says nothing about ingesting multiple files, let's try it.

Change the line starting with val inputPath to include all JSON files in the github-archive folder, like this:

```
val inputPath = homeDir + "/sia/github-archive/*.json"
```

Run the application. In about 90 seconds, depending on your machine, you get the result for March 1, 2015:

```
+---------------+-----+
|          login|count|
+---------------+-----+
|  KenanSulayman| 1727|
|direwolf-github|  561|
|         lukeis|  288|
|           keum|  192|
|        chapuni|  184|
|      manuelrp07|  104|
|         shryme|  101|
|            uqs|   90|
|    jefflevesque|   79|
|         BitKiwi|   68|
|         qeremy|   66|
|        Somasis|   59|
|         jvodan|   57|
|      BhawanVirk|   55|
|        Valicek1|   53|
|       evelynluu|   49|
|  TheRingMaster|   47|
|    larperdoodle|   42|
|          digip1|   42|
|       jmarkkula|   39|
+---------------+-----+
```

Yup, this really works. There is just one more thing to do: you need to assure yourself that all the dependencies are available when the application is run, so it can be used from anywhere and run on any Spark cluster.

3.3 *Submitting the application*

The application will be run on your in-house Spark cluster. When an application is run, it must have access to all the libraries it depends on; and because your application will be shipped off to be executed on a Spark cluster, you know it'll have access to all Spark libraries and their dependencies (Spark is always installed on all nodes of a cluster).

To visualize the application's dependencies, open pom.xml from the root of your project and switch to the Dependency Hierarchy tab. You can see that your application depends only on libraries that are available in your cluster (scala, spark-core, and spark-sql).

After you finish packaging the application, you'll probably first send it to the testing team, so it can be tested before the word *production* is even spoken out loud. But there is a potential problem: you can't be 100% sure that the Spark operations team (with their custom Spark builds) include `spark-sql` when they prepare the testing environment. It may well happen that you send your app to be tested, only to get an angry email.

3.3.1 Building the uberjar

You have two options for including additional JAR files in Spark programs that are going to be run in production (there are others ways, but only these two are production-grade).

- Use the `--jars` parameter of the `spark-submit` script, which will transfer all the listed JARs to the executors.
- Build a so-called *uberjar*: a JAR that contains all needed dependencies.

To avoid fiddling with libraries manually[11] on multiple clusters, let's build an uberjar.

To illustrate this concept, you'll introduce another dependency into the application: another library you need to include and distribute along with it. Let's say you would like to include the `commons-email` library for simplified email sending, provided by Apache Commons (although you won't be using it in the code of the current example). The uberjar will need to contain only the code you wrote, the `commons-email` library, and all the libraries that `commons-email` depends on.

Add the following dependency to pom.xml (right below the Spark SQL dependency):

```
<dependency>
  <groupId>org.apache.commons</groupId>
  <artifactId>commons-email</artifactId>
  <version>1.3.1</version>
  <scope>compile</scope>
</dependency>
```

Looking again at the dependency hierarchy in pom.xml, you can see that `commons-email` depends on the `mail` and `activation` libraries. Some of those libraries may, in turn, have their own dependencies. For instance, `mail` also depends on `activation`. This dependency tree can grow arbitrarily long and branchy.

You would probably start worrying, if you didn't know about `maven-shade-plugin`. Yes, Maven comes to the rescue yet again: `maven-shade-plugin` is used to build uberjars. We've also included a `maven-shade-plugin` configuration in pom.xml.

Because you wish to include the `commons-email` library in the uberjar, its *scope* needs to be set to `compile`. Maven uses the `scope` property of each dependency to determine the phase during which a dependency is required. `compile`, `test`, `package`, and `provided` are some of the possible values for `scope`.

If `scope` is set to `provided`, the library and all its dependencies won't be included in uberjar. If you omit the scope, Maven defaults to `compile`, which means the library is needed during application compilation and at runtime.

---

[11] For example, in the test environment, you can provide libraries locally and let the driver (a machine from which you connect to a cluster) expose the libraries over a provisional HTTP server to all other nodes (see "Advanced Dependency Management" at http://spark.apache.org/docs/latest/submitting-applications.html).

As always, after you change pom.xml, update the project by right-clicking its root and selecting Maven > Update Project; then click OK without changing the defaults. Depending on the type of changes made in pom.xml, updating the project may or may not be necessary. If a project update is needed and you haven't yet done so, Eclipse draws your attention to the fact by displaying an error in the Problems view and putting a red marker on the project root.

3.3.2   *Adapting the application*

To adapt your application to be run using the `spark-submit` script, you need to make some modifications. First remove the assignment of the application name and Spark master parameters from `SparkConf` (because those will be provided as arguments to `spark-submit`) and instead provide an empty `SparkConf` object when creating `Spark-Context`. The final result is shown in the following listing.

Listing 3.2   Final version of the adapted, parameterized application

```
package org.sia.chapter03App

import scala.io.Source.fromFile
import org.apache.spark.sql.SparkSession

object GitHubDay {
  def main(args : Array[String]) {
    val spark = SparkSession.builder().getOrCreate()

    val sc = spark.sparkContext

    val ghLog = spark.read.json(args(0))

    val pushes = ghLog.filter("type = 'PushEvent'")
    val grouped = pushes.groupBy("actor.login").count
    val ordered = grouped.orderBy(grouped("count").desc)

    val employees = Set() ++ (
      for {
        line <- fromFile(args(1)).getLines
      } yield line.trim
    )
    val bcEmployees = sc.broadcast(employees)

    import spark.implicits._
    val isEmp = user => bcEmployees.value.contains(user)
    val sqlFunc = spark.udf.register("SetContainsUdf", isEmp)
    val filtered = ordered.filter(sqlFunc($"login"))

    filtered.write.format(args(3)).save(args(2))
  }
}
```

The last line saves the result to an output file, but you do it in such a way that the person who's invoking `spark-submit` decides on the path and format of the written output (currently available built-in formats: JSON, Parquet,[12] and JDBC).

---

[12] Parquet is a fast columnar file format that contains a schema: http://parquet.apache.org/.

So, the application will take four arguments:

- Path to the input JSON files
- Path to the employees file
- Path to the output file
- Output format

To build the uberjar, select the project root in the Package Explorer, and then choose Run > Run Configurations. Choose Maven Build, and click New Launch Configuration. In the dialog that appears (see figure 3.6), enter `Build uberjar` in the Name field, click the Variables button, and choose project_loc in the dialog (which fills the Base Directory field with the `${project_loc}` value).[13]

In the Goals field, enter `clean package`. Select the Skip Tests check box, save the configuration by clicking Apply, and trigger the build by clicking Run.

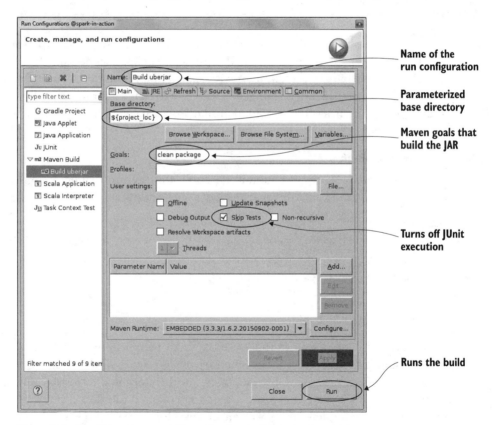

Figure 3.6   Specifying the run configuration for uberjar packaging

---

[13] You should use a variable so that any future project can also use this run configuration (which wouldn't be possible if you hard-coded the project's path with, for example, a Browse Workspace button). This way, the build will be triggered against the project that is currently selected in the Package Explorer.

After running the build, you should see a result similar to the following (truncated for a cleaner view):

```
[INFO] --- maven-shade-plugin:2.4.2:shade (default) @ chapter03App ---
[INFO] Including org.scala-lang:scala-library:jar:2.10.6 in the shaded jar.
[INFO] Replacing original artifact with shaded artifact.
[INFO] Replacing /home/spark/workspace/chapter03App/target/chapter03App...
[INFO] Dependency-reduced POM written at: /home/spark/workspace/chapter0...
[INFO] Dependency-reduced POM written at: /home/spark/workspace/chapter0...
    [INFO] Dependency-reduced POM written at: /home/spark/workspace/
    chapter0...
[INFO] ------------------------------------------------------------------------
[INFO] BUILD SUCCESS
[INFO] ------------------------------------------------------------------------
[INFO] Total time: 23.670 s
[INFO] Finished at: 2016-04-23T10:55:06+00:00
[INFO] Final Memory: 20M/60M
[INFO] ------------------------------------------------------------------------
```

You should now have a file named chapter03App-0.0.1-SNAPSHOT.jar in your project's target folder. Because the file isn't visible in Eclipse, check the filesystem by right-clicking the target folder in the Package Explorer and selecting Show In > System Explorer (or open a terminal and navigate to that folder manually).

Let's do a quick test on a local Spark installation. That should flush out most of the potential errors.

3.3.3 *Using spark-submit*

The Spark documentation on submitting applications (http://mng.bz/WY2Y) gives docs and examples of using the spark-submit shell script:

```
spark-submit \
    --class <main-class> \
    --master <master-url> \
    --deploy-mode <deploy-mode> \
    --conf <key>=<value> \
    ... # other options
    <application-jar> \
    [application-arguments]
```

spark-submit is a helper script that's used to submit applications to be executed on a Spark cluster. It's located in the bin subfolder of your Spark installation.

Before submitting the application, open another terminal to display the application log as it runs. Recall in chapter 2 that you changed the default log4j configuration so that the complete log is written in /usr/local/spark/logs/info.log. You can still see the log in real time by using the tail command, which displays content from the end of a file. It's similar to head, which you used to get the first line of that JSON file in section 3.3.2.

If you supply the `-f` parameter, `tail` waits until the content is appended to the file; as soon as that happens, `tail` outputs it in the terminal. Issue the following command in your second terminal:

```
$ tail -f /usr/local/spark/logs/info.log
```

Bring the first terminal back to the front, and enter the following:

```
$ spark-submit --class org.sia.chapter03App.GitHubDay --master local[*]
➡ --name "Daily GitHub Push Counter" chapter03App-0.0.1-SNAPSHOT.jar
➡ "$HOME/sia/github-archive/*.json"
➡ "$HOME/first-edition/ch03/ghEmployees.txt"
➡ "$HOME/sia/emp-gh-push-output" "json"
```

> ## Pasting blocks of code into the Spark Scala shell
> When submitting a Python application, you specify a Python file name instead of the application JAR file. You also skip the `--class` argument. For the GitHubDay example:
>
> ```
> $ spark-submit --master local[*] --name "Daily GitHub Push Counter"
> ➡ GitHubDay.py "$HOME/sia/github-archive/*.json"
> ➡ "$HOME/sia/ghEmployees. txt" "$HOME/sia/emp-gh-push-output" "json"
> ```
>
> For more information, see the Python version of the GitHubDay application in our online repository.

One or two minutes later, depending on your machine, the command will end without any errors. List the contents of the output folder:

```
$ cd $HOME/sia/emp-gh-push-output
$ ls -la
```

You see as many as 42 files (filenames are shortened here for nicer output):

```
-rw-r--r-- 1 spark spark   720 Apr 23 09:40 part-r-00000-b24f792c-...
-rw-rw-r-- 1 spark spark    16 Apr 23 09:40 .part-r-00000-b24f792c-....crc
-rw-r--r-- 1 spark spark   529 Apr 23 09:40 part-r-00001-b24f792c-...
-rw-rw-r-- 1 spark spark    16 Apr 23 09:40 .part-r-00001-b24f792c-....crc
-rw-r--r-- 1 spark spark   328 Apr 23 09:40 part-r-00002-b24f792c-...
-rw-rw-r-- 1 spark spark    12 Apr 23 09:40 .part-r-00002-b24f792c-....crc
-rw-r--r-- 1 spark spark   170 Apr 23 09:40 part-r-00003-b24f792c-...
-rw-rw-r-- 1 spark spark    12 Apr 23 09:40 .part-r-00003-b24f792c-....crc
-rw-r--r-- 1 spark spark     0 Apr 23 09:40 part-r-00004-b24f792c-...
-rw-rw-r-- 1 spark spark     8 Apr 23 09:40 .part-r-00004-b24f792c-....crc
...
-rw-r--r-- 1 spark spark     0 Apr 22 19:20 _SUCCESS
-rw-rw-r-- 1 spark spark     8 Apr 22 19:20 ._SUCCESS.crc
```

The presence of the _SUCCESS file signifies that the job finished successfully. The crc files are used to verify file validity by calculating the cyclic redundancy check (CRC)[14] code for each data file. The file named ._SUCCESS.crc signifies that the CRC calculation for all the files was successful.

To see the contents of the first data file, you can use the `cat` command, which sends the contents of the file to the standard output (terminal):

```
$ cat $HOME/sia/emp-gh-push-output/part-r-00000-b24f792c-c0d0-425b-85db-
  3322aab8f3e0
{"login":"KenanSulayman","count":1727}
{"login":"direwolf-github","count":561}
{"login":"lukeis","count":288}
{"login":"keum","count":192}
{"login":"chapuni","count":184}
{"login":"manuelrp07","count":104}
{"login":"shryme","count":101}
{"login":"uqs","count":90}
{"login":"jefflevesque","count":79}
{"login":"BitKiwi","count":68}
{"login":"qeremy","count":66}
{"login":"Somasis","count":59}
{"login":"jvodan","count":57}
{"login":"BhawanVirk","count":55}
{"login":"Valicek1","count":53}
{"login":"evelynluu","count":49}
{"login":"TheRingMaster","count":47}
{"login":"larperdoodle","count":42}
{"login":"digipl","count":42}
{"login":"jmarkkula","count":39}
```

3.4   Summary

- Online resources describe how to use IntelliJ IDEA with Spark, but Eclipse resources are still hard to come by. That's why we chose Eclipse for writing the Spark programs in this chapter.

- We've prepared an Archetype called `scala-archetype-sparkinaction` (available from our GitHub repository), which is used to create a starter Spark project in which the versions and dependencies are taken care of.

- The GitHub archive site (https://www.githubarchive.org/) provides GitHub archives for arbitrary time periods.

- Spark SQL and `DataFrame` (which is a `DataSet` containing `Row` objects) provide a means for ingesting JSON data into Spark.

- `SparkSession`'s `jsonFile` method provides a means for ingesting JSON data. Each line in an input file needs to be a complete JSON object.

---

[14] A cyclic redundancy check (CRC) is an error-detecting code commonly used in digital networks and storage devices to detect accidental changes to raw data. http://en.wikipedia.org/wiki/Cyclic_redundancy_check.

- `DataSet`'s `filter` method can parse SQL expressions and return a subset of the data.
- You can run a Spark application directly from Eclipse.
- The `SparkSession` class contains the `udf` method, which is used to register user-defined functions.
- Broadcast variables are used to send a variable exactly once to each node in a cluster.
- `maven-shade-plugin` is used to build an uberjar containing all of your application's dependencies.
- You can run a Spark application on a cluster using the `spark-submit` script.

The Spark API in depth

4

This chapter covers

- Working with key-value pairs
- Data partitioning and shuffling
- Grouping, sorting, and joining data
- Using accumulators and broadcast variables

The previous two chapters explained RDDs and how to manipulate them with basic actions and transformations. You've seen how to run Spark programs from Spark REPL and how to submit standalone applications to Spark.

In this chapter, you'll delve further into the Spark Core API and become acquainted with a large number of Spark API functions. But don't faint just yet! We'll be gentle, go slowly, and take you safely through these complicated and comprehensive, but necessary, topics.

You'll also learn how to use RDDs of key-value pairs called *pair RDDs*. You'll see how Spark partitions data and how you can change and take advantage of RDD partitioning. Related to partitioning is shuffling, which is an expensive operation, so you'll focus on avoiding unnecessary shuffling of data. You'll also learn how to group, sort, and join data. You'll learn about accumulators and broadcast variables and how to use them to share data among Spark executors while a job is running.

Finally, you'll get into more advanced aspects of the inner workings of Spark, including RDD dependencies. Roll up your sleeves!

4.1 Working with pair RDDs

Storing data as key-value pairs offers a simple, general, and extensible data model because each key-value pair can be stored independently and it's easy to add new types of keys and new types of values. This extensibility and simplicity have made this practice fundamental to several frameworks and applications. For example, many popular caching systems and NoSQL databases, such as memcached and Redis, are key-value stores. Hadoop's MapReduce also operates on key-value pairs (as you can see in appendix A).

Keys and values can be simple types such as integers and strings, as well as more-complex data structures. Data structures traditionally used to represent key-value pairs are *associative arrays*, also called *dictionaries* in Python and *maps* in Scala and Java.

In Spark, RDDs containing key-value tuples are called *pair RDDs*. Although you don't have to use data in Spark in the form of key-value pairs (as you've seen in the previous chapters), pair RDDs are well suited (and indispensable) for many use cases. Having keys along with the data enables you to aggregate, sort, and join the data, as you'll soon see. But before doing any of that, the first step is to create a pair RDD, of course.

4.1.1 Creating pair RDDs

You can create a pair RDD in a couple of ways. Some `SparkContext` methods produce pair RDDs by default (for example, methods for reading files in Hadoop formats, which are covered later). You can also use a `keyBy` transformation, which accepts a function (let's call it `f`) for generating keys from an ordinary RDD's elements and maps each element into a tuple `(f(element), element)`. You can also transform the data into two-element tuples manually.

> ### Creating pair RDDs in Java
> To create a pair RDD in Java, you need to use the `JavaPairRDD` class. You can create a `JavaPairRDD` object with the `JavaSparkContext.parallelizePairs` method by providing a list of `Tuple2[K, V]` objects. Or you can use the `mapToPair` transformation on a `JavaRDDLike` object and pass it a function that will be used to map each RDD's element into `Tuple2[K, V]` objects. A number of other Java RDD transformations return RDDs of type `JavaPairRDD`.

No matter which method you use, if you create an RDD of two-element tuples, the pair RDD functions automagically become available, through the concept known as implicit conversion. This concept was described in chapter 2, so feel free to glance back if you don't remember how it functions. The class hosting these special pair RDD functions is `PairRDDFunctions`, and RDDs of two-element tuples get implicitly converted to an instance of this class.

Let's see what functionalities are implicitly added to pair RDDs.

4.1.2 Basic pair RDD functions

Let's say your marketing department wants to give complimentary products to customers according to some rules. They want you to write a program that will go through yesterday's transactions and add the complimentary ones. The rules for adding complimentary products are these:

- Send a bear doll to the customer who made the most transactions
- Give a 5% discount for two or more Barbie Shopping Mall Playsets bought
- Add a toothbrush for more than five dictionaries bought
- Send a pair of pajamas to the customer who spent the most money overall

The complimentary products should be represented as additional transactions with price 0.00. Marketing would also like to know which transactions were made by the customers who are getting the complimentary products.

To begin this task, start up your Spark shell. Assuming you're running in the spark-in-action VM, logged in as spark (in which case spark-shell is on your PATH), you can issue the spark-shell command. Make sure you're starting it from the /home/spark directory. The Spark in the VM is already configured to start a cluster with the local[*] master by default, so you don't have to provide the --master argument:

```
$ spark-shell
```

We assume you cloned our GitHub repository and that the ch04_data_transactions.txt file[1] is available from the first-edition/ch04 directory (otherwise, you can get the file from https://github.com/spark-in-action/first-edition/tree/master/ch04).

Each line in the file contains a transaction date, time, customer ID, product ID, quantity, and product price, delimited with hash signs. The following snippet creates a pair RDD with customer IDs as keys and the complete transaction data as values:

```scala
scala> val tranFile = sc.textFile("first-edition/ch04/"+      ❶ Loads data   ❷ Parses
    "ch04_data_transactions.txt")                                                   data
scala> val tranData = tranFile.map(_.split("#"))
scala> var transByCust = tranData.map(tran => (tran(2).toInt, tran))
```

Creates the pair RDD ❸

After you execute the code, tranFile ❶ contains lines from the file and tranData ❷ contains an array of strings containing the parsed data. The customer ID is in the third column, so in order to create the pair RDD transByCust ❸, you map the parsed data into a tuple whose first element is the element with index 2 (converted to an integer)

---

[1] The file was generated using the Mockaroo website: www.mockaroo.com.

and whose second element is the complete parsed transaction. You declare `transBy-Cust` to be a variable so that you can keep RDDs containing new and changed transactions (which you'll calculate later) in a single variable and just update it.

GETTING KEYS AND VALUES

Now that you have your pair RDD, you decide to first see how many customers bought anything yesterday. You can get a new RDD containing only the keys or only the values with pair RDD transformations prosaically named `keys` and `values`.

You use this line to get a list of customer IDs, remove any duplicates, and count the number of unique customer IDs:

```
scala> transByCust.keys.distinct().count()
res0: Long = 100
```

The RDD returned by the `keys` transformation should contain 1,000 elements and include duplicate IDs. To get the number of different customers who bought a product, you first need to eliminate the duplicates with the `distinct()` transformation, which gives you 100 as a result.

The `values` transformation behaves analogously, but you don't need it right now. These two transformations are shortcuts for `map(_._1)` and `map(_._2)`, only easier to type.

COUNTING VALUES PER KEY

What was the task, again? Oh, yes. Give a complimentary bear doll to the customer who made the most transactions.

Each line in the transactions file is one transaction. So, to find out how many transactions each customer made, it's enough to count the lines per customer.

The corresponding RDD function is the `countByKey` action. As a reminder: unlike RDD transformations, RDD actions immediately return the result as a Java (Scala or Python) object. `countByKey` gives you a Scala `Map` containing the number of occurrences of each key:

```
scala> transByCust.countByKey()
res1: scala.collection.Map[Int,Long] = Map(69 -> 7, 88 -> 5, 5 -> 11,
10 -> 7, 56 -> 17, 42 -> 7, 24 -> 9, 37 -> 7, 25 -> 12, 52 -> 9, 14 -> 8,
20 -> 8, 46 -> 9, 93 -> 12, 57 -> 8, 78 -> 11, 29 -> 9, 84 -> 9, 61 -> 8,
89 -> 9, 1 -> 9, 74 -> 11, 6 -> 7, 60 -> 4,...
```

The sum of all values of this `Map` is 1,000, of course, which is the total number of transactions in the file. To calculate this you can use the following snippet:

```
scala> transByCust.countByKey().values.sum
res3: Long = 1000
```

`map` and `sum` are Scala's standard methods and aren't part of Spark's API.

You can also use standard Scala methods to find the customer who made the most purchases:

```
scala> val (cid, purch) = transByCust.countByKey().toSeq.sortBy(_._2).last
cid: Int = 53
purch: Long = 19
```

The customer with ID 53 made 19 transactions, and you need to give them a complimentary bear doll (product ID 4). Let's create a variable, complTrans, which will hold the complimentary products (transactions) as Arrays of Strings:

```
scala> var complTrans = Array(Array("2015-03-30", "11:59 PM", "53", "4",
"1", "0.00"))
```

You'll later add the transactions from this Array to the final transactions RDD.

LOOKING UP VALUES FOR A SINGLE KEY

Marketing would also like to know exactly which transactions were made by the customers who are getting the complimentary products. You can get that information for the customer with ID 53 using the lookup() action:

```
scala> transByCust.lookup(53)
res1: Seq[Array[String]] = WrappedArray(Array(2015-03-30, 6:18 AM, 53, 42,
5, 2197.85), Array(2015-03-30, 4:42 AM, 53, 3, 6, 9182.08), ...
```

The WrappedArray class that you see in the result is Scala's way to present an Array as a Seq (mutable sequence) object through implicit conversion. A warning, though. A lookup transaction will transfer the values to the driver, so you have to make sure the values will fit in its memory.

You can use some plain Scala functions to pretty-print the result so that you can copy it into an e-mail and send it to the marketing folks:

```
scala> transByCust.lookup(53).foreach(tran => println(tran.mkString(", ")))
2015-03-30, 6:18 AM, 53, 42, 5, 2197.85
2015-03-30, 4:42 AM, 53, 3, 6, 9182.08
...
```

USING THE MAPVALUES TRANSFORMATION TO CHANGE VALUES IN A PAIR RDD

The second task is to give a 5% discount for two or more Barbie Shopping Mall Playsets bought. The mapValues transformation helps you do this: it changes the values contained in a pair RDD without changing the associated keys. And that's exactly what you need. Barbie Shopping Mall Playset has ID 25, so you apply the discount like this:

```
scala> transByCust = transByCust.mapValues(tran => {
    if(tran(3).toInt == 25 && tran(4).toDouble > 1)
        tran(5) = (tran(5).toDouble * 0.95).toString
    tran })
```

The function you give to the `mapValues` transformation checks whether the product ID (third element of the transaction array) is 25 and the quantity (fourth element) is greater than 1; in that case, it decreases the total price (fifth element) by 5%. Otherwise, it leaves the transaction array untouched. You assign the new RDD to the same variable, `transByCust`, just to make things simpler.

USING THE FLATMAPVALUES TRANSFORMATION TO ADD VALUES TO KEYS

You still have two more tasks to do. Let's tackle the dictionary one first: you need to add a complimentary toothbrush (ID 70) to customers who bought five or more dictionaries (ID 81). That means you need to add transactions (represented as arrays) to the `transByCust` RDD.

The `flatMapValues` transformation fits the bill because it enables you to change the number of elements corresponding to a key by mapping each value to *zero or more* values. That means you can add new values for a key or remove a key altogether. The signature of the transformation function it expects is `V => TraversableOnce[U]` (we said in chapter 2 that `TraversableOnce` is just a special name for a collection). From each of the values in the return collection, a new key-value pair is created for the corresponding key. If the transformation function returns an empty list for one of the values, the resulting pair RDD will have one fewer element. If the transformation function returns a list with two elements for one of the values, the resulting pair RDD will have one more element. Note that the mapped values can be of a different type than before.

So this is what you do:

```scala
scala> transByCust = transByCust.flatMapValues(tran => {
    if(tran(3).toInt == 81 && tran(4).toDouble >= 5) {
        val cloned = tran.clone()
        cloned(5) = "0.00"; cloned(3) = "70"; cloned(4) = "1";
        List(tran, cloned)
    }
    else
        List(tran)
})
```

Clones the transaction array

Returns two elements

Filters by product and quantity

Sets the clone's price to 0.00, product ID to 70, and quantity to 1

Returns one element

The anonymous function given to the transformation maps each transaction into a list. The list contains only the original transaction if the condition isn't met, or an additional transaction with a complimentary toothbrush if the condition holds true. The final `transByCust` RDD now contains 1,006 elements (because there are 6 transactions with 5 or more dictionaries in the file).

USING THE REDUCEBYKEY TRANSFORMATION TO MERGE ALL VALUES OF A KEY

`reduceByKey` lets you merge all the values of a key into a single value of the same type. The `merge` function you pass to it merges two values at a time until there is only one value left. The function should be associative; otherwise you won't get the same result every time you perform the `reduceByKey` transformation on the same RDD.

You could use reduceByKey for your final task—finding the customer who spent the most overall—but you can also use the similar foldByKey transformation.

USING THE FOLDBYKEY TRANSFORMATION AS AN ALTERNATIVE TO REDUCEBYKEY

foldByKey does the same thing as reduceByKey, except that it requires an additional parameter, zeroValue, in an extra parameter list that comes before the one with the reduce function. The complete method signature is as follows:

```
foldByKey(zeroValue: V)(func: (V, V) => V): RDD[(K, V)]
```

zeroValue should be a neutral value (0 for addition, 1 for multiplication, Nil for lists, and so forth). It's applied on the first value of a key (using the input function), and the result is applied on the second value. You should be careful here, because, unlike in the foldLeft and foldRight methods in Scala, zeroValue may be applied multiple times. This happens because of RDD's parallel nature.

You finally get to the last task: finding the customer who spent the most. But your original dataset isn't appropriate for that, because you need to sum up the prices, and the dataset contains arrays of strings. So you first map values to contain only the prices and then use foldByKey. Finally, you sort the resulting Array by price and take the largest element:

```
scala> val amounts = transByCust.mapValues(t => t(5).toDouble)
scala> val totals = amounts.foldByKey(0)((p1, p2) => p1 + p2).collect()
res0: Array[(String, Double)] = Array((84,53020.619999999995),
(96,36928.57), (66,52130.01), (54,36307.04), ...
scala> totals.toSeq.sortBy(_._2).last
res1: (Int, Double) = (76,100049.0)
```

Whoa! Not bad! This person spent $100,049 on your company's website! They definitely deserve a pair of pajamas. But before giving it to them, let's illustrate the point about zeroValue being applied multiple times and try the same foldByKey operation with a zeroValue of 100,000:

```
scala> amounts.foldByKey(100000)((p1, p2) => p1 + p2).collect()
res2: Array[(String, Double)] = Array((84,453020.62), (96,436928.57),
(66,452130.0099999999), (54,436307.04), ...
```

You can see that a "zero value" of 100,000 was added to the values more than once (as many times as there are partitions in the RDD), which isn't something you typically want to do (unless you like random results).

Now you give a pair of pajamas (ID 63) to the customer with ID 76 by adding a transaction to the temporary array complTrans that you created before:

```
scala> complTrans = complTrans :+ Array("2015-03-30", "11:59 PM", "76",
"63", "1", "0.00")
```

The `complTrans` array should have two transactions now. All that is left for you to do is add these two transactions to the `transByCust` RDD (adding client IDs as keys and complete transactions arrays as values), which holds the other changes you made, and save everything to a new file:

```
scala> transByCust = transByCust.union(sc.parallelize(complTrans).map(t =>
(t(2).toInt, t)))
scala> transByCust.map(t => t._2.mkString("#")).saveAsTextFile("ch04output-
transByCust")
```

Someone else will now use a batch job to transform this file into shipping orders. You can relax now; you've finished all the tasks marketing gave you.

USING AGGREGATEBYKEY TO GROUP ALL VALUES OF A KEY

While you're relaxing, we'll go on to explain a few things about the `aggregateByKey` transformation. But don't relax too much: leave your Spark shell open, because you're still going to need it.

`aggregateByKey` is similar to `foldByKey` and `reduceByKey` in that it merges values and takes a zero value, but it also transforms values to another type. In addition to the `zeroValue` argument, it takes two functions as arguments: a *transform* function for transforming values from type V to type U (with the signature `(U, V) => U`) and a *merge* function for merging the transformed values (with the signature `(U, U) => U`). The double parameter list is a Scala feature known as *currying* (www.scala-lang.org/old/node/135). If given only the `zeroValue` argument (the only argument in the first parentheses), `aggregateByKey` returns a parameterized function that takes the other two arguments. But you wouldn't normally use `aggregateByKey` like that; you would provide both sets of parameters at the same time.

Let's say you need a list of all products your customers purchased. You can use `aggregateByKey` to accomplish that:

❶ **Empty list as a zero value**

❷ **Adds products to lists**

```
scala> val prods = transByCust.aggregateByKey(List[String]())(      ⟵
    (prods, tran) => prods ::: List(tran(3)),
    (prods1, prods2) => prods1 ::: prods2)                          ⟵
scala> prods.collect()
res0: Array[(String, List[String])] = Array((88,List(47.149.147.123,
74.211.5.196,...), (82,List(8.140.151.84, 23.130.185.187,...), ...)
```

❸ **Concatenates two lists of the same key**

NOTE The `:::` operator is a Scala list operator for concatenating two lists.

The `zeroValue` ❶ is an empty `List`. The first combine function ❷ in `aggregate-ByKey` is applied to elements of each of the RDD's partitions, and the second one ❸ is used for merging the results. But to understand fully what is going on here, you should first understand data partitioning.

4.2   *Understanding data partitioning and reducing data shuffling*

D*ata partitioning* is Spark's mechanism for dividing data between multiple nodes in a cluster. It's a fundamental aspect of RDDs that can have a big effect on performance and resource consumption. Shuffling is another important aspect of Spark, closely related to data partitioning, that you'll learn about in this section. Many RDD operations offer ways of manipulating data partitioning and shuffling, so our in-depth exploration of the Spark API wouldn't be complete without explaining them.

In part 3 of the book, we'll talk about Spark deployment types, where we discuss *Spark cluster* options in depth. For the purpose of explaining partitions, think of a cluster as a set of interconnected machines (nodes) that are being used in parallel.

Each part (piece or slice) of an RDD is called a *partition*.[2] When you load a text file from your local filesystem into Spark, for example, the file's contents are split into partitions, which are evenly distributed to nodes in a cluster. More than one partition may end up on the same node. The sum of all those partitions forms your RDD. This is where the word *distributed* in *resilient distributed dataset* comes from. Figure 4.1 shows the distribution of lines of a text file loaded into an RDD in a five-node cluster. The original file had 15 lines of text, so each RDD partition was formed with 3 lines of text. Each RDD maintains a list of its partitions and an optional list of preferred locations for computing the partitions.

> **NOTE** The list of an RDD's partitions can be obtained from that RDD's `partitions` field. It's an `Array`, so you can get the number of RDD partitions by reading its `partitions.size` field (`aggrdd.partitions.size` for the previous example).

The number of RDD partitions is important because, in addition to influencing data distribution throughout the cluster, it also directly determines the number of tasks that will be running RDD transformations. If this number is too small, the cluster will be underutilized. Furthermore, memory problems could result, because working sets might get too big to fit into the memory of executors. We recommend using three to four times more partitions than there are cores in your cluster. Moderately larger values shouldn't pose a problem, so feel free to experiment. But don't get too crazy, because management of a large number of tasks could create a bottleneck.

Let's now see how data partitioning is achieved in Spark.

4.2.1   *Using Spark's data partitioners*

Partitioning of RDDs is performed by `Partitioner` objects that assign a partition index to each RDD element. Two implementations are provided by Spark: `HashPartitioner` and `RangePartitioner`. Pair RDDs also accept custom partitioners.

---

[2] Partitions were previously called *splits*. The term *split* can still be found in Spark's source code (it's eventually going to be refactored).

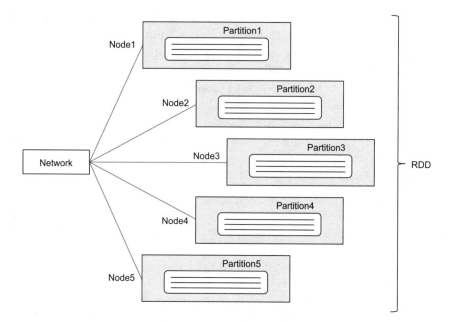

Figure 4.1 Simplified look at partitions of an RDD in a five-node cluster. The RDD was created by loading a text file using the `textFile` method of `SparkContext`. The loaded text file had 15 lines of text, so each partition was formed with 3 lines of text.

UNDERSTANDING HASHPARTITIONER

`HashPartitioner` is the default partitioner in Spark. It calculates a partition index based on an element's Java hash code (or a key's hash code in pair RDDs), according to this simple formula: `partitionIndex = hashCode % numberOfPartitions`. The partition index is determined quasi-randomly; consequently, the partitions most likely won't be exactly the same size. In large datasets with a relatively small number of partitions, though, the algorithm is likely to distribute data evenly among them.

The default number of data partitions when using `HashPartitioner` is determined by the Spark configuration parameter `spark.default.parallelism`. If that parameter isn't specified by the user, it will be set to the number of cores in the cluster. (Chapter 12 covers setting Spark configuration parameters.)

UNDERSTANDING RANGEPARTITIONER

`RangePartitioner` partitions data of *sorted RDDs* into roughly equal ranges. It samples the contents of the RDD passed to it and determines the range boundaries according to the sampled data. You aren't likely to use `RangePartitioner` directly.

UNDERSTANDING PAIR RDD CUSTOM PARTITIONERS

Pair RDDs can be partitioned with *custom partitioners* when it's important to be precise about the placement of data among partitions (and among tasks working on them). You may want to use a custom partitioner, for example, if it's important that each task processes only a specific subset of key-value pairs, where all of them belong to a single database, single database table, single user, or something similar.

Custom partitioners can be used only on pair RDDs, by passing them to pair RDD transformations. Most pair RDD transformations have two additional overloaded methods: one that takes an additional `Int` argument (the desired number of partitions) and another that takes an additional argument of the (custom) `Partitioner` type. The method that takes the number of partitions uses the default `Hash-Partitioner`. For example, these two lines of code are equal, because they both apply `HashPartitioner` with 100 partitions:

```
rdd.foldByKey(afunction, 100)
rdd.foldByKey(afunction, new HashPartitioner(100))
```

All other pair RDD transformations offer these two additional versions, except `mapValues` and `flatMapValues` (these two always preserve partitioning). You can specify a custom partitioner by using the second version.

If pair RDD transformations don't specify a partitioner, the number of partitions used will be the maximum number of partitions of parent RDDs (RDDs that were transformed into this one). If none of the parent RDDs have a partitioner defined, `HashPartitioner` will be used with the number of partitions specified by the `spark.default.parallelism` parameter.

Another method for changing the default placement of data among partitions in pair RDDs is using the default `HashPartitioner`, but changing the keys' hash code according to some algorithm. This might be simpler to do, depending on your use case, and it could perform better by avoiding inadvertent shuffling, which is covered next.

4.2.2 *Understanding and avoiding unnecessary shuffling*

Physical movement of data between partitions is called *shuffling*. It occurs when data from multiple partitions needs to be combined in order to build partitions for a new RDD. When grouping elements by key, for example, Spark needs to examine all of the RDD's partitions, find elements with the same key, and then physically group them, thus forming new partitions.

To visualize what happens with partitions during a shuffle, we'll use the previous example with the `aggregateByKey` transformation (from section 4.1.2). The shuffle that occurs during that transformation is illustrated in figure 4.2.

For this example, assume that you have only three partitions on three worker nodes and you'll simplify the data. As you may recall, `aggregateByKey` takes two functions: a transform function for transforming and merging two values to a value of the target type, and a merge function for merging the transformed values themselves. But what we didn't say before is that the first one merges values in partitions, and the second one merges them between partitions.

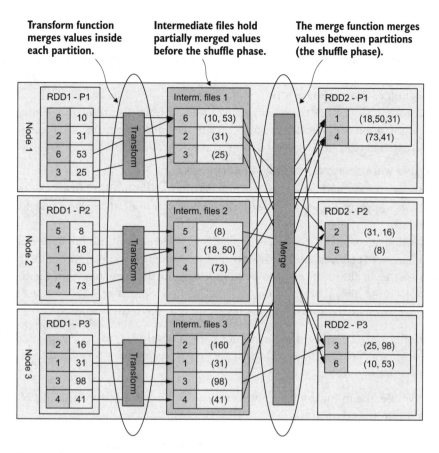

Figure 4.2 A shuffle during the example `aggregateByKey` transformation on an RDD with three partitions. The transform function, passed to `aggregateByKey`, merges values in partitions. The merge function merges values between partitions during the shuffle phase. Intermediate files hold values merged per partition and are used during the shuffle phase.

This was the example:

```scala
scala> val prods = transByCust.aggregateByKey(List[String]())(
    (prods, tran) => prods ::: List(tran(3)),
    (prods1, prods2) => prods1 ::: prods2)
```

This gathers all values of a single key into a list, so that `prods` has one list per key. The lists are presented in figure 4.2 in parentheses.

The transform function puts all values of each key in a single partition (partitions P1 to P3) into a list. Spark then writes this data to intermediate files on each node. In the next phase, the merge function is called to merge lists from different partitions, but of the same key, into a single list for each key. The default partitioner (`HashPartitioner`) then kicks in and puts each key in its proper partition.

Tasks that immediately precede and follow the shuffle are called *map* and *reduce* tasks, respectively. The results of map tasks are written to intermediate files (often to the OS's filesystem cache only) and read by reduce tasks. In addition to being written to disk, the data is sent over the network, so it's important to try to minimize the number of shuffles during Spark jobs.

Although most RDD transformations don't require shuffling, for some of them shuffling happens only under certain conditions. So to minimize the number of shuffle occurrences, you need to understand these conditions.

SHUFFLING WHEN EXPLICITLY CHANGING PARTITIONERS

We already mentioned pair RDD custom partitioners. Shuffling always occurs when using a custom partitioner in methods that allow you to do that (most pair RDD transformations).

Shuffling also occurs if a different `HashPartitioner` than the previous one is used. Two `HashPartitioners` are the same if they have the same number of partitions (because they'll always choose the same partition for the same object, if the number of partitions is the same). So shuffling will also occur if a `HashPartitioner` *with a different number of partitions* than the previous one is used in the transformation.

> **TIP** Because changing the partitioner provokes shuffles, the safest approach, performance-wise, is to use a default partitioner as much as possible and avoid inadvertently causing a shuffle.

For example, the following lines always cause shuffling to occur (assuming rdd's parallelism is different than 100):

```
rdd.aggregateByKey(zeroValue, 100)(seqFunc, comboFunc).collect()
rdd.aggregateByKey(zeroValue, new CustomPartitioner())(seqFunc,
⇒ comboFunc).collect()
```

In the first example, the number of partitions is changed; and in the second one, a custom partitioner is used. A shuffle is invoked in both cases.

SHUFFLE CAUSED BY PARTITIONER REMOVAL

Sometimes a transformation causes a shuffle, although you were using the default partitioner. `map` and `flatMap` transformations *remove* the RDD's partitioner, which doesn't cause a shuffle per se. But if you transform the resulting RDD (with one of the transformations previously mentioned, for example), *even using the default partitioner*, a shuffle will occur. In the following snippet, the second line doesn't induce a shuffle, but the third one does:

```
scala> val rdd:RDD[Int] = sc.parallelize(1 to 10000)
scala> rdd.map(x => (x, x*x)).map(_.swap).count()
scala> rdd.map(x => (x, x*x)).reduceByKey((v1, v2)=>v1+v2).count()
```

1 No shuffle

2 Shuffle occurs

The second line ❶ creates a pair RDD by using the `map` transformation, which removes the partitioner, and then switches its keys and values by using another `map` transformation. That alone won't cause a shuffle. The third line ❷ uses the same pair RDD as before, but this time the `reduceByKey` transformation instigates a shuffle.

Here's a complete list of transformations that cause a shuffle after `map` or `flatMap` transformations:

- Pair RDD transformations that can change the RDD's partitioner: `aggregate-ByKey`, `foldByKey`, `reduceByKey`, `groupByKey`, `join`, `leftOuterJoin`, `right-OuterJoin`, `fullOuterJoin`, and `subtractByKey`
- RDD transformations: `subtract`, `intersection`, and `groupWith`
- `sortByKey` transformation (which always causes a shuffle)
- `partitionBy` or `coalesce` with `shuffle=true` (covered in the next section)

OPTIMIZING SHUFFLING WITH AN EXTERNAL SHUFFLE SERVICE

During shuffling, executors need to read files from one another (a shuffle is pull-based). If some executors get killed, other executors can no longer get shuffle data from them, and the data flow is interrupted.

An external shuffle service is meant to optimize the exchange of shuffle data by providing a single point from which executors can read intermediate shuffle files. If an external shuffle service is enabled (by setting `spark.shuffle.service.enabled` to `true`), one external shuffle server is started per worker node.

PARAMETERS THAT AFFECT SHUFFLING

Spark has two shuffle implementations: sort-based and hash-based. *Sort-based shuffling* has been the default since version 1.2 because it's more memory efficient and creates fewer files.[3] You can define which shuffle implementation to use by setting the value of the `spark.shuffle.manager` parameter to either `hash` or `sort`.

The `spark.shuffle.consolidateFiles` parameter specifies whether to consolidate intermediate files created during a shuffle. For performance reasons, we recommend that you change this to `true` (the default value is `false`) if you're using an ext4 or XFS filesystem.[4]

Shuffling can require a lot of memory for aggregation and co-grouping. The `spark.shuffle.spill` parameter specifies whether the amount of memory used for these tasks should be limited (the default is `true`). In that case, any excess data will spill over to disk. The memory limit is specified by the `spark.shuffle.memoryFraction` parameter (the default is 0.2). Furthermore, the `spark.shuffle.spill.compress` parameter tells Spark whether to use compression for the spilled data (the default is again `true`).

---

[3] For more information, see http://mng.bz/s6EA.
[4] For more information, see http://mng.bz/O304.

The spill threshold shouldn't be too high, because it can cause out-of-memory exceptions. If it's too low, spilling can occur too frequently, so it's important to find a good balance. Keeping the default value should work well in most situations.

Some useful additional parameters are as follows:

- `spark.shuffle.compress` specifies whether to compress intermediate files (the default is `true`).
- `spark.shuffle.spill.batchSize` specifies the number of objects that will be serialized or deserialized together when spilling to disk. The default is 10,000.
- `spark.shuffle.service.port` specifies the port the server will listen on if an external shuffle service is enabled.

4.2.3 *Repartitioning RDDs*

Now you can return to your exploration of the Spark API with operations that let you change data partitioning at runtime. Why would you want to do that?

As we discussed previously, in some situations you need to explicitly repartition an RDD in order to distribute the workload more efficiently or avoid memory problems. Some Spark operations, for example, default to a small number of partitions, which results in partitions that have too many elements (take too much memory) and don't offer adequate parallelism. Repartitioning of RDDs can be accomplished with the `partitionBy`, `coalesce`, `repartition`, and `repartitionAndSortWithinPartition` transformations.

REPARTITIONING WITH PARTITIONBY

`partitionBy` is available only on pair RDDs. It accepts only one parameter: the desired `Partitioner` object. If the partitioner is the same as the one used before, partitioning is preserved and the RDD remains the same. Otherwise, a shuffle is scheduled and a new RDD is created.

REPARTITIONING WITH COALESCE AND REPARTITION

`coalesce` is used for either reducing or increasing the number of partitions. The full method signature is `coalesce (numPartitions: Int, shuffle: Boolean = false)`.

The second (optional) parameter specifies whether a shuffle should be performed (`false` by default). If you want to increase the number of partitions, it's *necessary* to set the `shuffle` parameter to `true`. The repartitioning algorithm balances new partitions so they're based on the same number of parent partitions, matching the preferred locality (machines) as much as possible, but also trying to balance partitions across the machines. The `repartition` transformation is just a `coalesce` with `shuffle` set to `true`.

It's important to understand that if a shuffle isn't specified, all transformations leading up to `coalesce`, if they themselves didn't include a shuffle, will be run using the newly specified number of executors (the number of partitions). If the shuffle is specified, the previous transformations are run using the original number of executors, and only the future ones (the ones after the `coalesce`) will be run with the new number of partitions.

REPARTITIONING WITH REPARTITIONANDSORTWITHINPARTITION

The final transformation for repartitioning RDDs is `repartitionAndSortWithin-Partition`. It's available only on sortable RDDs (pair RDDs with sortable keys), which are covered later, but we mention it here for the sake of completeness.

It also accepts a `Partitioner` object and, as its name suggests, sorts the elements within each partition. This offers better performance than calling `repartition` and manually sorting, because part of the sorting can be done during the shuffle. A shuffle is always performed when using `repartitionAndSortWithinPartition`.

4.2.4   *Mapping data in partitions*

The last aspect of data partitioning we want to tell you about is mapping data in partitions. Spark offers a way to apply a function not to an RDD as a whole, but to each of its partitions separately. This can be a precious tool in optimizing your transformations. Many can be rewritten to map data in partitions only, thus avoiding shuffles. RDD operations for working on partitions are `mapPartitions`, `mapPartitionsWithIndex`, and `glom`, a specialized partition-mapping transformation.

UNDERSTANDING MAPPARTITIONS AND MAPPARTITIONSWITHINDEX

Similar to `map`, `mapPartitions` accepts a mapping function, but the function has to have the signature `Iterator[T] => Iterator[U]`. This way, it can be used for iterating over elements within each partition and creating partitions for the new RDD.

`mapPartitionsWithIndex` is different in that its mapping function also accepts the partition's index: `(Int, Iterator[T]) => Iterator[U]`. The partition's index can then be used in the mapping function.

The mapping function can transform the input `Iterator` into a new one with some of Scala's `Iterator` functions.[5] For example:

- You can `map`, `flatMap`, `zip`, and `zipWithIndex` values in an `Iterator`.
- You can take only some elements with `take(n)` or `takeWhile(condition)`.
- You can skip elements with `drop(n)` or `dropWhile(condition)`.
- You can `filter` the elements.
- You can get an `Iterator` with a subset of elements with `slice(m,n)`.

All of these create a new `Iterator` that can be used as the result of the mapping function.

Both transformations accept an additional optional parameter `preservePartitioning`, which is `false` by default. If it's set to `true`, the new RDD will preserve partitioning of the parent RDD. If it's set to `false`, the partitioner will be removed, with all the consequences we discussed previously.

Mapping partitions can help you solve some problems more efficiently than using other transformations that don't operate on partitions explicitly. For example, if the mapping function involves expensive setup (such as opening a database connection), it's much better to do it once per partition than once per element.

---

[5]   For a complete reference, see http://mng.bz/CWA6.

COLLECTING PARTITION DATA WITH A GLOM TRANSFORMATION

glom (the word means *to grab*) gathers elements of each partition into an array and returns a new RDD with those arrays as elements. The number of elements in the new RDD is equal to the number of its partitions. The partitioner is removed in the process.

For a quick example of a glom transformation, we'll use parallelized random data:

```
scala> val list = List.fill(500)(scala.util.Random.nextInt(100))
list: List[Int] = List(88, 59, 78, 94, 34, 47, 49, 31, 84, 47, ...)
scala> val rdd = sc.parallelize(list, 30).glom()
rdd: org.apache.spark.rdd.RDD[Array[Int]] = MapPartitionsRDD[0]
scala> rdd.collect()
res0: Array[Array[Int]] = Array(Array(88, 59, 78, 94,...), ...)
scala> rdd.count()
res1: Long = 30
```

This creates an RDD of 30 partitions and gloms it. The count of array objects in the new RDD, containing data from each partition, is also 30.

glom could be used as a quick way to put all of an RDD's elements into a single array. You could first repartition the RDD into one partition and then call glom. The result is an RDD with a single array element containing all of the RDD's previous elements. Of course, this applies only to RDDs small enough so that all of their elements fit into a single partition.

4.3 Joining, sorting, and grouping data

Imagine now that marketing comes to you with another request. They want additional data for a report: names of products with totals sold, sorted alphabetically; a list of products the company didn't sell yesterday; and some statistics about yesterday's transactions per customer: average, maximum, minimum, and the total price of products bought. Being thorough and eager for knowledge as you are, you'll try out all the ways this can be done with the core Spark API.[6]

4.3.1 Joining data

Okay, you need names of products with totals sold (you'll do the sorting part later). You already have transaction data loaded in the RDD tranData (used in section 4.1), but you first need to key the transactions by product ID:

```
val transByProd = tranData.map(tran => (tran(3).toInt, tran))
```

Then you calculate the totals per product using the reduceByKey transformation:

```
val totalsByProd = transByProd.mapValues(t => t(5).toDouble).
    reduceByKey{case(tot1, tot2) => tot1 + tot2}
```

---

[6]   The list of transformations in these sections is rather long, but in order to write good Spark programs, it's necessary to become thoroughly acquainted with RDD transformations and know when to apply each of them. As your mother would probably say: it's for your own good!

Names of products are kept in a different file (ch04_data_products.txt from the online repository), and you'll obviously need to join the product names with yesterday's transaction data. You load the products file and convert it into a pair RDD:

```scala
scala> val products = sc.textFile("first-edition/ch04/"+
   "ch04_data_products.txt").
   map(line => line.split("#")).
   map(p => (p(0).toInt, p))
```

How can you join one with the other? To join contents of several RDDs, Spark offers classic joins, similar to joins in relational databases, but also transformations such as `zip`, `cartesian`, and `intersection`. Let's see how they work.

THE FOUR CLASSIC JOIN TRANSFORMATIONS

The four classic joins in Spark functions are just like RDBMS joins of the same names, but are performed on pair RDDs. When called on an RDD of `(K, V)` elements, and passing in an RDD of `(K, W)` elements, the four join transformations give different results:

- `join`—Equivalent to an inner join in RDBMS, this returns a new pair RDD with the elements `(K, (V, W))` containing all possible pairs of values from the first and second RDDs that have the same keys. For the keys that exist in only one of the two RDDs, the resulting RDD will have no elements.
- `leftOuterJoin`—Instead of `(K, (V, W))`, this returns elements of type `(K, (V, Option(W)))`. The resulting RDD will also contain the elements `(key, (v, None))` for those keys that don't exist in the second RDD. Keys that exist only in the second RDD will have no matching elements in the new RDD.
- `rightOuterJoin`—This returns elements of type `(K, (Option(V), W))`; the resulting RDD will also contain the elements `(key, (None, w))` for those keys that don't exist in the first RDD. Keys that exist only in the first RDD will have no matching elements in the new RDD.
- `fullOuterJoin`—This returns elements of type `(K, (Option(V), Option(W)))`; the resulting RDD will contain both `(key, (v, None))` and `(key, (None, w))` elements for those keys that exist in only one of the two RDDs.

If the RDDs you're trying to join have duplicate keys, these elements will be joined multiple times.

Similar to some of the other pair-RDD transformations, all four join transformations have two additional versions that expect a `Partitioner` object or a number of partitions. If a number of partitions is specified, `HashPartitioner` with that number of partitions will be used. If no partitioner is specified (nor the number of partitions), Spark takes the first partitioner from the two RDDs being joined. If even the two RDDs don't have the partitioner defined, a new `HashPartitioner` is created, using the number of partitions equal to either `spark.default.partitions` (if it's defined), or the largest number of partitions in the two RDDs. In a word, it's complicated.

Now that you know all this, you call `join` to attach product data to the totals:

```
scala> val totalsAndProds = totalsByProd.join(products)
scala> totalsAndProds.first()
res0: (Int, (Double, Array[String])) = (84,(75192.53,Array(84,
Cyanocobalamin, 2044.61, 8)))
```

And now you have, for each product ID, a tuple containing two elements: the total and the complete product data as an `Array` of `String`s.

Okay, that was easy. But what about the list of products the company didn't sell yesterday? That's obviously the `leftOuterJoin` or `rightOuterJoin` transformation, depending on the RDD you call it on. The RDD with more data (`products`, in this case) should be on the side mentioned in the transformation name. So these two lines have (almost) the same result:

```
val totalsWithMissingProds = products.leftOuterJoin(totalsByProd)
val totalsWithMissingProds = totalsByProd.rightOuterJoin(products)
```

The difference in the results is the position of the `Option` object. In the case of `rightOuterJoin`, `totalsWithMissingProds` will contain elements of type `(Int, (Option[Double], Array[String]))`. For missing products, the `Option` object will be equal to `None`. To retrieve the missing products, you filter the RDD and then map it so that you only get the product data, without the key and the `None` objects. Assuming you used `rightOuterJoin`:

```
val missingProds = totalsWithMissingProds.
  filter(x => x._2._1 == None).
  map(x => x._2._2)
```

Finally, you print out the contents of the `missingProds` RDD:

```
scala> missingProds.foreach(p => println(p.mkString(", ")))
43, Tomb Raider PC, 2718.14, 1
63, Pajamas, 8131.85, 3
3, Cute baby doll, battery, 1808.79, 2
20, LEGO Elves, 4589.79, 4
```

> **NOTE** The `Option` object in the result from `*OuterJoin` transformations is Scala's way to avoid `NullPointerExceptions`. The result from the `join` transformation doesn't contain `Option` objects because `null` elements aren't possible in that case. An `Option` object can be either a `None` or a `Some` object. To check whether an `Option` has a value, you can call `isEmpty`; and to get the value itself, you can call `get`. A convenient shortcut is to call `getOrElse(default)`. It will return the `default` expression if the `Option` is `None`, or `get` otherwise.

Well done! But you may be wondering if you can do this another way.

USING SUBTRACT AND SUBTRACTBYKEY TRANSFORMATIONS TO REMOVE COMMON VALUES

The answer is: *yes, you can.* subtract returns elements from the first RDD that aren't present in the second one. It works on ordinary RDDs and compares complete elements (not just their keys or values).

subtractByKey works on pair RDDs and returns an RDD with pairs from the first RDD whose keys aren't in the second RDD. The second RDD doesn't need to have values of the same type as the first one. This is perfect for your task. It gives you elements from products whose keys don't exist in totalsByProd:

```
val missingProds = products.subtractByKey(totalsByProd).values
```

The result is the same:

```
scala> missingProds.foreach(p => println(p.mkString(", ")))
20, LEGO Elves, 4589.79, 4
3, Cute baby doll, battery, 1808.79, 2
43, Tomb Raider PC, 2718.14, 1
63, Pajamas, 8131.85, 3
```

Both subtract and subtractByKey have two additional versions that accept the number of partitions and a Partitioner object.

JOINING RDDs WITH THE COGROUP TRANSFORMATION

Yet another way of finding both the names of purchased products and the products that no one bought is the cogroup transformation. cogroup performs a grouping of values from several RDDs by key and returns an RDD whose values are arrays of Iterable objects (a fancy name for a Scala collection) containing values from each RDD. So, cogroup groups values of several RDDs by key and then joins these grouped RDDs. You can pass up to three RDDs to it, all of which need to have the same key type as the enclosing RDD. For example, the signature of the cogroup function for cogrouping three RDDs (including the enclosing one) is as follows:

```
cogroup[W1, W2](other1: RDD[(K, W1)], other2: RDD[(K, W2)]):
  RDD[(K, (Iterable[V], Iterable[W1], Iterable[W2]))]
```

If you cogroup totalsByProd and products, you'll get an RDD containing keys present in one or the other and the matching values accessible through two Iterators:

```
scala> val prodTotCogroup = totalsByProd.cogroup(products)
prodTotCogroup: org.apache.spark.rdd.RDD[(Int, (Iterable[Double],
Iterable[Array[String]]))]...
```

If one of the two RDDs doesn't contain one of the keys, the corresponding iterator will be empty. So this is how you can filter out the missing products:

```
scala> prodTotCogroup.filter(x => x._2._1.isEmpty).
  foreach(x => println(x._2._2.head.mkString(", ")))
43, Tomb Raider PC, 2718.14, 1
```

```
63, Pajamas, 8131.85, 3
3, Cute baby doll, battery, 1808.79, 2
20, LEGO Elves, 4589.79, 4
```

The expression x._2._1 selects the iterator with matching values from totalsByProd (totals as Doubles), and x._2._2 selects the iterator with products as Arrays of Strings. The x._2._2.head expression takes the first element of the iterator (the two RDDs don't contain duplicates, so the Iterator objects contain at most one element).

You can obtain the totals and the products (the totalsAndProds RDD, which you created using the join transformation) in a similar way:

```
val totalsAndProds = prodTotCogroup.filter(x => !x._2._1.isEmpty).
  map(x => (x._2._2.head(0).toInt,(x._2._1.head, x._2._2.head)))
```

This totalsAndProds RDD now has the same elements as the one obtained with the join transformation.

USING THE INTERSECTION TRANSFORMATION

intersection and the cartesian, zip, and zipPartitions transformations aren't particularly useful for your current task, but we'll mention them here for the sake of completeness. intersection accepts an RDD of the same type as the enclosing one and returns a new RDD that contains elements present in both RDDs. It isn't useful for this use case because your transactions already contain only a subset of the products, and there is no point in intersecting them. But imagine that totalsByProd contains products from different departments, and you only want to see which products from a certain department (contained in products RDD) are among them. Then you need to map both RDDs to product IDs and then intersect them:

```
totalsByProd.map(_._1).intersection(products.map(_._1))
```

intersection has two additional versions: one accepting a number of partitions and the other accepting a Partitioner object.

COMBINING TWO RDDS WITH THE CARTESIAN TRANSFORMATION

A cartesian transformation makes a cartesian product (a mathematical operation) of two RDDs in the form of an RDD of tuples (T, U) containing all possible pairs of elements from the first RDD (containing elements of type T) and second RDD (containing elements of type U). For example, say you have rdd1 and rdd2 defined as follows:

```
scala> val rdd1 = sc.parallelize(List(7,8,9))
scala> val rdd2 = sc.parallelize(List(1,2,3))
```

cartesian gives you this:

```
scala> rdd1.cartesian(rdd2).collect()
res0: Array[(Int, Int)] = Array((7,1), (7,2), (7,3), (8,1), (9,1), (8,2),
(8,3), (9,2), (9,3))
```

Naturally, in large datasets, cartesian can incur a lot of data transfer because data from all partitions needs to be combined. And the resulting RDD will contain exponential number of elements, so the memory requirements also aren't negligible.

You can use cartesian to compare elements of two RDDs. For example, you could use it to get all pairs from the previous two RDDs that are divisible:

```scala
scala> rdd1.cartesian(rdd2).filter(el => el._1 % el._2 == 0).collect()
```

The result is as follows:

```scala
res1: Array[(Int, Int)] = Array((7,1), (8,1), (9,1), (8,2), (9,3))
```

You could also use it on your transactions data set to compare all transactions with each other (tranData.cartesian(tranData)) and detect fishy behavior (for example, too many transactions from the same customer in a short period of time).

JOINING RDDS WITH THE ZIP TRANSFORMATION

The zip and zipPartitions transformations are available on all RDDs (not only pair RDDs). zip functions just like the zip function in Scala: if you call it on an RDD with elements of type T and give it an RDD with elements of type U, it will create an RDD of pairs (T, U) with the first pair having the first elements from each RDD, the second pair having the second elements, and so forth.

Unlike Scala's zip function, though, it will throw an error if the two RDDs don't have the same number of partitions *and* the same number of elements in them. Two RDDs will satisfy these requirements if one of them is a result of a map transformation on the other one. But this makes zip a bit hard to use in Spark.

This is an operation that is otherwise not easy to do, if you think about it. That's because processing data sequentially isn't inherent to Spark, so it can come in handy, under the strict circumstances just outlined.

Here's an example:

```scala
scala> val rdd1 = sc.parallelize(List(1,2,3))
scala> val rdd2 = sc.parallelize(List("n4","n5","n6"))
scala> rdd1.zip(rdd2).collect()
res1: Array[(Int, Int)] = Array((1,"n4"), (2,"n5"), (3,"n6"))
```

You can get around the requirement for all partitions to have the same number of elements with the zipPartitions transformation.

JOINING RDDS WITH THE ZIPPARTITIONS TRANSFORMATION

zipPartitions is similar to mapPartitions, in that it enables you to iterate over elements in partitions, but you use it to combine several RDDs' partitions (four RDDs at most, including this). All RDDs need to have the same number of partitions (but not the same number of elements in them).

zipPartitions accepts two sets of arguments. In the first set, you give it RDDs; and in the second, a function that takes a matching number of Iterator objects used for accessing elements in each partition. The function must return a new Iterator, which can be a different type (matching the resulting RDD). This function has to take into account that RDDs may have different numbers of elements in partitions and guard against iterating beyond `Iterator` lengths.

NOTE `zipPartitions` still (v.1.4) isn't available in Python.

The `zipPartitions` transformation takes one more optional argument (in the first set of arguments): `preservesPartitioning`, which is `false` by default. If you're certain that your function will leave the data properly partitioned, you can set it to `true`. Otherwise, the partitioner is removed so a shuffle will be performed during one of the future transformations.

Again, a quick example. You'll take two RDDs—one containing 10 integers in 10 partitions, and the other one containing 8 strings in 10 partitions—and zip their partitions to create a string-formatted representation of their elements:

```scala
scala> val rdd1 = sc.parallelize(1 to 10, 10)
scala> val rdd2 = sc.parallelize((1 to 8).map(x=>"n"+x), 10)
scala> rdd1.zipPartitions(rdd2, true)((iter1, iter2) => {
        iter1.zipAll(iter2, -1, "empty")
        .map({case(x1, x2)=>x1+"-"+x2})
    }).collect()
res1: Array[String] = Array(1-empty, 2-n1, 3-n2, 4-n3, 5-n4, 6-empty, 7-n5,
    8-n6, 9-n7, 10-n8)
```

Scala's `zipAll` function is used here to combine two iterators because it can zip two collections of different sizes. If the first iterator has more elements than the second one, the remaining elements will be zipped along with the *dummy* value of `empty` (and with the value of `-1` in the opposite case). In the resulting RDD, you can see that rdd2 had zero elements in partitions 1 and 6. How you handle these `empty` values depends on your use case. Note that you can also change the number of elements in the partitions by using an iterator function such as `drop` or `flatMap`. For a refresher, consult section 4.2.4.

4.3.2 Sorting data

Okay, you have your products together with corresponding transaction totals in the RDD `totalsAndProds`. You also have to sort the results alphabetically. But how do you do that?

The main transformations for sorting RDD data are `sortByKey`, `sortBy`, and `repartitionAndSortWithinPartition`. The last one was covered in section 4.2.3. As we said, it can repartition and sort more efficiently than calling those two operations separately.

Using `sortBy` is easy:

```scala
scala> val sortedProds = totalsAndProds.sortBy(_._2._2(1))
scala> sortedProds.collect()
res0: Array[(Double, Array[String])] = Array((90,(48601.89,Array(90,
AMBROSIA TRIFIDA POLLEN, 5887.49, 1))), (94,(31049.07,Array(94, ATOPALM
MUSCLE AND JOINT, 1544.25, 7))), (87,(26047.72,Array(87, Acyclovir,
6252.58, 4))), ...
```

The expression `_._2` references the value, which is a tuple (total, transaction array). `_._2._2(1)` references the second element of the transaction Array. This is the same as keying the RDD by product name (`keyBy(_._2._2(1))`) and calling `sortByKey`. If you further map this RDD, the ordering will be preserved.

It's trickier if you have keys that are complex objects. Similar to pair RDD transformations, which are available only on RDDs with key-value tuples through implicit conversion, `sortByKey` and `repartitionAndSortWithinPartition` are available only on pair RDDs with orderable keys.

> **JAVA** In Java, the `sortByKey` method takes an object that implements the `Comparator` interface (http://mng.bz/5Suh). That's the standard way of sorting in Java. There is no `sortBy` method in the `JavaRDD` class.

You have two ways to make a class *orderable* in Scala and use it for sorting RDDs: via the `Ordered` trait and via the `Ordering` trait.

MAKING A CLASS ORDERABLE USING THE ORDERED TRAIT

The first way to make a class orderable is to create a class that extends Scala's `Ordered` trait, which is similar to Java's `Comparable` interface. The class extending `Ordered` has to implement the `compare` function, which takes as an argument an object of the same class against which to perform the comparison. The function returns a positive integer if the enclosing object (this) is greater than the one taken as an argument (other), a negative integer if the enclosing object is smaller, and zero if the two should be considered equal.

The `sortByKey` transformation requires an argument of type `Ordering` (discussed next), but there's an implicit conversion in Scala from `Ordered` to `Ordering` so you can safely use this method.

For example, the following case class can be used for keys in sortable RDDs for sorting employees according to their last names:

```
case class Employee(lastName: String) extends Ordered[Employee] {
    override def compare(that: Employee) =
        ➥ this.lastName.compare(that.lastName)
}
```

MAKING A CLASS ORDERABLE USING THE ORDERING TRAIT

The second way to make a class orderable uses the `Ordering` trait, which is similar to Java's `Comparator` interface. Let's presume you can't change the preceding `Employee` class and make it extend `Ordered`, but you'd still like to sort employees by their last names. In that case, you can define an object of type `Ordering[Employee]` somewhere in the scope of the function calling `sortByKey`. For example

```
implicit val emplOrdering = new Ordering[Employee] {
    override def compare(a: Employee, b: Employee) =
        ➥ a.lastName.compare(b.lastName)
}
```

or

```
implicit val emplOrdering: Ordering[Employee] = Ordering.by(_.lastName)
```

If defined within its scope, this implicit object will be picked up by the `sortByKey` transformation (called on an RDD with keys of type `Employee`), and the RDD will become *sortable*.

The previous sort by product name worked because the Scala standard library contains `Orderings` for simple types. But if you had a complex key, you would need to implement an approach similar to the one sketched previously.

PERFORMING A SECONDARY SORT

A few more things about sorting are worth mentioning. Sometimes you may also want to sort values within keys. For example, you may group transactions by customer ID and wonder how to further sort them by transaction time.

There's a relatively new `groupByKeyAndSortValues` transformation, which enables you to do exactly this. For an RDD of `(K, V)` pairs, it expects an implicit `Ordering[V]` object to be present in the scope and a single argument: either a `Partitioner` object or a number of partitions.

It will give you an RDD of `(K, Iter-able(V))` elements with values sorted according to the implicit `Ordering` object. But it will first group values by key, which can be expensive in terms of memory and network.

A cheaper method for performing a secondary sort, without grouping, is this:[7]

1 Map an `RDD[(K, V)]` to `RDD[((K, V),null)]`. For example: `rdd.map (kv => (kv, null))`.

2 Use a custom partitioner that partitions only on the `K` part of the new composite key, so that all elements with the same `K` part end up in the same partition.

3 Call `repartitionAndSortWithin-Partition`, which has to sort by the complete composite key `(K, V)`: first by keys, then by values.

4 Map the RDD back to `RDD[(K, V)]`.

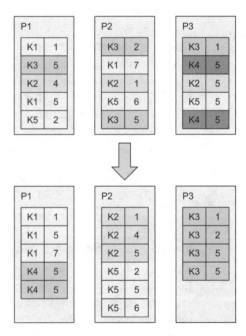

Figure 4.3   Example of a secondary sort using `repartitionAndSortWithinPartition`

---

[7] Thanks to Patrick Wendell for this idea. See https://issues.apache.org/jira/browse/SPARK-3655.

An example of the result of this operation is shown in figure 4.3.

As the figure shows, this procedure gives you partitions sorted first by key and then by value, and you can iterate over them by calling `mapPartitions`. No grouping of values occurs, which makes this method better from a performance point of view.

USING TOP AND TAKEORDERED TO FETCH SORTED ELEMENTS

To fetch the first or last n objects from an RDD, you can use the `takeOrdered(n)` and `top(n)` actions, respectively. What *first* or *last* means, on an RDD with elements of type T, is determined by an implicit `Ordering[T]` object defined in the scope.

Consequently, for pair RDDs, `top` and `takeOrdered` won't return elements sorted by keys (as `sortByKey` does), but by (K, V) tuples. So for pair RDDs, you need to have an implicitly defined `Ordering[(K, V)]` object in scope (which is true for simple keys and values).

`top` and `takeOrdered` don't perform full sorting of data among partitions. Instead, they first take the first (or last) n elements from each partition, merge the results, and then take the first (or last) n elements from the merged list. This is much faster than doing `sortBy` and then calling `take`, because much less data needs to be transferred over the network. But just like `collect`, `top` and `takeOrdered` bring all n results into the driver's memory, so you should make sure n isn't too big.

Wait a minute—we got carried away and drifted away from your task! You retrieved the products that no one bought yesterday, and you joined the products with their totals from yesterday's transactions (using several methods). And you managed to sort the results by product names.

There is one more task for you to do, and that is to calculate statistics about yesterday's transactions per customer: average, maximum, minimum, and total price of products bought. Transactions in your transaction file are organized per customer and product so you first need to group them by customer. The statistics can then be calculated in several ways. You'll use the `combineByKey` transformation. It's used for grouping data, so let's first say a few words about that.

4.3.3 Grouping data

To *group* data means to aggregate data into a single collection based on certain criteria. Several pair RDD transformations can be used for grouping data in Spark: `aggregateByKey` (used in section 4.1.2), `groupByKey` (and the related `groupBy`), and `combineByKey`.

GROUPING DATA WITH THE GROUPBYKEY AND GROUPBY TRANSFORMATIONS

The `groupByKey` transformation creates a pair RDD containing a single key-value pair for all elements with the same key. For example:

```
(A, 1)
(A, 2)                   (A, (1, 2))
(B, 1)      ->           (B, (1, 3))
(B, 3)                   (C, (1))
(C, 1)
```

Each pair's value becomes an `Iterable` for iterating over all the key's values. The resulting RDD, therefore, is of type `RDD[(K, Iterable[V])]`.

groupBy is available on non-pair RDDs and offers a shortcut for transforming an RDD to a pair RDD and then calling groupByKey. So, having an `rdd` of type `RDD[T]` (containing elements of type `T`) and the function `f: T => K` for creating keys of type `K`, the following two lines are equivalent:

```
rdd.map(x => (f(x), x)).groupByKey()
rdd.groupBy(f)
```

The groupByKey transformation can be memory expensive because it has to get all the values of each key in memory, so you have to be careful when using it. We recommend using aggregateByKey, reduceByKey, or foldByKey for simpler scenarios that don't require full grouping to occur, such as calculating the average per key. As is the case with other pair RDD transformations, groupByKey and groupBy can also accept the desired number of partitions or a custom partitioner (two additional implementations are available).

GROUPING DATA WITH THE COMBINEBYKEY TRANSFORMATION

combineByKey is the transformation you'll use to calculate the statistics per customer. It's a generic transformation that lets you specify custom functions for merging values into *combined values* and for merging the combined values themselves. It expects a partitioner to be specified. You can also specify two optional arguments: the mapSideCombine flag and a custom serializer.

The full function signature is as follows:

```
def combineByKey[C](createCombiner: V => C,
    mergeValue: (C, V) => C,
    mergeCombiners: (C, C) => C,
    partitioner: Partitioner,
    mapSideCombine: Boolean = true,
    serializer: Serializer = null): RDD[(K, C)]
```

The createCombiner function is used to create the first combined value (of type C) from the first key's value (of type V) in each partition. The mergeValue function is used to merge additional key values with the combined value, in a single partition, and the mergeCombiners function is used to merge combined values themselves among partitions.

As we said previously, if the partitioner (a required argument) is the same as the existing partitioner (which also means the existing one isn't missing), there's no need for a shuffle, because all the elements with the same key are already in the same (and correct) partition. That's why the mergeCombiners function won't be used if there's no shuffle (and if spilling to disk isn't enabled, which is another story), but you still have to provide it.

The last two optional parameters are relevant only if the shuffle will be performed. With the `mapSideCombine` parameter, you can specify whether to merge combined values in partitions before the shuffle. The default is `true`. This parameter isn't relevant if there's no shuffle, because in that case, combined values are always merged in partitions. Finally, with the `serializer` parameter, you can go into expert mode and specify a custom serializer to use if you don't want to use the default (as specified by the Spark configuration parameter `spark.serializer`).

The numerous options make `combineByKey` versatile and flexible. No wonder it was used to implement `aggregateByKey`, `groupByKey`, `foldByKey`, and `reduceByKey`. Feel free to check the Spark source code (http://mng.bz/Z6fp) to see how it was done.

Let's now look at how it can help you in your task. You have the `transByCust` pair RDD that you created in section 4.1.2. It holds transactions keyed by customer IDs (but not grouped by customers).

To calculate the average, maximum, minimum, and total price of products bought per customer, the combined values need to keep track of minimum, maximum, count, and total, while merging values. The average is then calculated by dividing the total by the count. Each transaction in `transByCust` contains a quantity (index 4 in the transaction array), so that value needs to be taken into account. And you also need to parse the numeric values because you have them as `Strings`:

```
def createComb = (t:Array[String]) => {          ←┐   Create combiners
  val total = t(5).toDouble                        ❶  function
  val q = t(4).toInt
  (total/q, total/q, q, total) }
def mergeVal:((Double,Double,Int,Double),Array[String])=>
  (Double,Double,Int,Double) =                     ←┐   Merge values
    { case((mn,mx,c,tot),t) => {                     ❷  function
      val total = t(5).toDouble
      val q = t(4).toInt
      (scala.math.min(mn,total/q),scala.math.max(mx,total/q),c+q,tot+total) } }
def mergeComb:((Double,Double,Int,Double),(Double,Double,Int,Double))=>
  (Double,Double,Int,Double) =
    { case((mn1,mx1,c1,tot1),(mn2,mx2,c2,tot2)) =>
      (scala.math.min(mn1,mn1),scala.math.max(mx1,mx2),c1+c2,tot1+tot2) }
val avgByCust = transByCust.combineByKey(createComb, mergeVal, mergeComb,
  new org.apache.spark.HashPartitioner(transByCust.partitions.size)).  ←┐
    mapValues({case(mn,mx,cnt,tot) => (mn,mx,cnt,tot,tot/cnt)})
```

❸ Merge combiners function

❹ Performs the combineByKey transformation

❺ Adds the average to the tuple

The create combiners function ❶ needs to set the count to the parsed quantity (variable q), the total to the parsed variable `total`, and the minimum and maximum to the price of a single product (`total/q`). The merge values function ❷ increases the count by the parsed quantity and the total by the parsed total and updates the minimum and maximum with the price of a single product (total/quantity).

The merge combiners function ❸ sums the counts and totals and compares the minimums and maximums of the two combined values. Then the combineByKey transformation is finally performed ❹ (the partitioning is preserved by using the previous number of partitions). This gives you an RDD containing tuples of minimum price, maximum price, count, and total price for each customer. Finally, you add the average value to the tuple ❺ by using the mapValues transformation.

You check the contents of avgByCust:

```
scala> avgByCust.first()
res0: (Int, (Double, Double, Int, Double, Double)) =
(96,(856.2885714285715,4975.08,57,36928.57,647.869649122807))
```

And that looks good. Finally, you're done!

You can save the results from avgByCust and totalsAndProds in a CSV format (with the # separator):

```
scala> totalsAndProds.map(_._2).map(x=>x._2.mkString("#")+", "+x._1).
    saveAsTextFile("ch04output-totalsPerProd")
scala> avgByCust.map{ case (id, (min, max, cnt, tot, avg)) =>
    "%d#%.2f#%.2f#%d#%.2f#%.2f".format(id, min, max, cnt, tot, avg)}.
    saveAsTextFile("ch04output-avgByCust")
```

But before calling it a day, let's learn a few more things about RDD dependencies, accumulators, and broadcast variables. You never know when those might come in handy.

4.4   *Understanding RDD dependencies*

In this section, we'll take a closer look at two aspects of Spark's inner workings: RDD dependencies and RDD checkpointing, both important mechanisms in Spark. We need these two to complete the picture of the Spark Core API. RDD dependencies make RDDs resilient. They also affect the creation of Spark jobs and tasks.

4.4.1   *RDD dependencies and Spark execution*

We said in the previous chapters that Spark's execution model is based on *directed acyclic graphs* (DAGs). You've surely seen graphs before: they consist of vertices (nodes) and edges (lines) connecting them. In directed graphs, edges have a direction from one vertex to another (but they can also be bidirectional). In acyclic directed graphs, edges connect vertices in such a way that you can never reach the same vertex twice if you follow the direction of the edges (there are no cycles in the graph; hence the name).

In Spark DAGs, RDDs are vertices and *dependencies* are edges. Every time a transformation is performed on an RDD, a new vertex (a new RDD) and a new edge (a dependency) are created. The new RDD depends on the old one, so the direction of the edge is from the *child* RDD to the *parent RDD*. This graph of dependencies is also called an *RDD lineage*.

Two basic types of dependencies exist: *narrow* and *wide* (or *shuffle*). They determine whether a shuffle will be performed, according to the rules explained in section 4.2.2. If no data transfer between partitions is required, a narrow dependency is created. A wide dependency is created in the opposite case, which means a shuffle is performed. By the way, a shuffle is always performed when joining RDDs.

Narrow dependencies can be divided further into *one-to-one dependencies* and *range dependencies*. Range dependencies are used only for the union transformation; they combine multiple parent RDDs in a single dependency. One-to-one dependencies are used in all other cases when no shuffling is required.

Let's illustrate all this with an example. This example is similar to the one used to examine shuffling after partitioner removal. The code looks like this:

Maps the RDD to create a pair RDD

Parallelizes a random list of integers and creates an RDD with five partitions

Sums up the RDD's values by keys

```
val list = List.fill(500)(scala.util.Random.nextInt(10))
val listrdd = sc.parallelize(list, 5)
val pairs = listrdd.map(x => (x, x*x))
val reduced = pairs.reduceByKey((v1, v2)=>v1+v2)
val finalrdd = reduced.mapPartitions(
            iter => iter.map({case(k,v)=>"K="+k+",V="+v}))
finalrdd.collect()
```

Maps the RDD's partitions to create a string representation of its key-value pairs

The transformations aren't meaningful or useful in real life, but they help illustrate the concept of RDD dependencies. The resulting lineage (DAG) is presented in figure 4.4; each rounded box containing lines represents a partition. Fat arrows in the figure represent transformations used to create an RDD. Each transformation produces a new RDD of a specific RDD subclass, and each new RDD becomes a child of the preceding one.

The arc arrows represent dependencies in the lineage chain. You can say that `finalrdd` (a `MapPartitionsRDD`) depends on `reduced`; `reduced` (a `ShuffleRDD`)

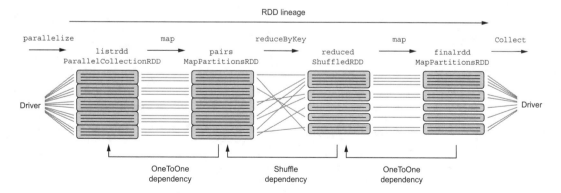

Figure 4.4   RDD example dependencies

depends on `pairs`; and `pairs` (a `MapPartitionsRDD`) depends on `listrdd`, itself of type `ParallelCollectionRDD`.

Light lines in the figure represent dataflow during the execution of the RDD program. As you can see, the two `map` transformations don't require data to be exchanged between partitions, and their dataflow is confined in partition boundaries. That's why they produce narrow (OneToOne) dependencies. `reduceByKey`, on the other hand, requires a shuffle, as discussed in section 4.2.2 (because the previous `map` transformation has removed the partitioner), so a wide (or shuffle) dependency is created. During execution, data is exchanged between the partitions of the `pairs` RDD and `reduced` RDD because each key-value pair needs to get into its proper partition.

You can get a textual representation of the RDD's DAG, with information similar to figure 4.4, by calling `toDebugString`. For the example `finalrdd`, the result is as follows:

```
scala> println(finalrdd.toDebugString)
(6) MapPartitionsRDD[4] at mapPartitions at <console>:20 []
 |  ShuffledRDD[3] at reduceByKey at <console>:18 []
 +-(5) MapPartitionsRDD[2] at map at <console>:16 []
    |  ParallelCollectionRDD[1] at parallelize at <console>:14 []
```

The RDDs in this output appear in reverse order from that in figure 4.4. Here the first RDD in the DAG appears last, so the direction of dependencies is upward. Examining this output can be useful in trying to minimize the number of shuffles your program performs. Every time you see a `ShuffledRDD` in the lineage chain, you can be sure that a shuffle will be performed at that point (if the RDD is executed). The numbers in parentheses (5 and 6) show the number of partitions of the corresponding RDD.

4.4.2 *Spark stages and tasks*

All of this is important when considering how Spark packages work to be sent to executors. Every job is divided into stages based on the points where shuffles occur. Figure 4.5 shows the two stages created in the example.

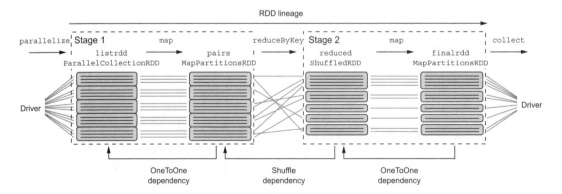

Figure 4.5 Example DAG divided into stages

Stage 1 encompasses transformations that result in a shuffle: `parallelize`, `map`, and `reduceByKey`. The results of Stage 1 are saved on disk as intermediate files on executor machines. During Stage 2, each partition receives data from these intermediate files belonging to it, and the execution is continued with the second `map` transformation and the final `collect`.

For each stage and each partition, tasks are created and sent to the executors. If the stage ends with a shuffle, the tasks created will be *shuffle-map tasks*. After all tasks of a particular stage complete, the driver creates tasks for the next stage and sends them to the executors, and so on. This repeats until the last stage (in this case, Stage 2), which will need to return the results to the driver. The tasks created for the last stage are called *result tasks*.

4.4.3 Saving the RDD lineage with checkpointing

Because the RDD lineage can grow arbitrarily long, by chaining any number of transformations, Spark provides a way to persist the entire RDD to stable storage. Then, in case of node failure, Spark doesn't need to recompute the missing RDD pieces from the start. It uses a snapshot and computes the rest of the lineage from there. This feature is called *checkpointing*.

During checkpointing, the entire RDD is persisted to disk—not just its data, as is the case with caching, but its lineage, too. After checkpointing, the RDD's dependencies are erased, as well as the information about its parent(s), because they won't be needed for its recomputation any more.

You can checkpoint an RDD by calling the `checkpoint` operation, but first you have to set the directory where the data will be saved by calling `SparkContext.setCheckpointDir()`. This directory is usually an HDFS directory, but it can also be a local one. `checkpoint` must be called before any jobs are executed on the RDD, *and* the RDD has to be materialized afterward (some action has to be called on it) for the checkpointing to be done.

So, when should you checkpoint an RDD? If you have an RDD with a long DAG (the RDD has lots of dependencies), rebuilding it could take a long time in case of a failure. If the RDD is checkpointed, reading it from a file could be much quicker than rebuilding it by using all the (possibly complicated) transformations. Checkpointing is also important in Spark Streaming, as you'll soon see.

4.5 Using accumulators and broadcast variables to communicate with Spark executors

The final topics for this chapter are accumulators and broadcast variables. They enable you to maintain a global state or share data across tasks and partitions in your Spark programs.

4.5.1 Obtaining data from executors with accumulators

Accumulators are variables shared across executors that you can only *add* to. You can use them to implement global sums and counters in your Spark jobs.

Accumulators are created with `SparkContext.accumulator(initialValue)`. You can also create one while specifying its name `sc.accumulator(initialValue, "accumulatorName")`. In that case, the accumulator will be displayed in the Spark web UI (on the stage details page), and you can use it to track the progress of your tasks. (For details about the Spark web UI, see chapter 11.)

NOTE   You can't name an accumulator in Python.

To add to an accumulator, you use the `add` method or `+=` operator. To get its value, you use the `value` method. You can access an accumulator's value only from within the driver. If you try to access it from an executor, an exception will be thrown.

Here's an accumulator example:

```
scala> val acc = sc.accumulator(0, "acc name")
scala> val list = sc.parallelize(1 to 1000000)
scala> list.foreach(x => acc.add(1))        Executes on executors
scala> acc.value            Executes on the driver
res0: Int = 1000000
scala> list.foreach(x => acc.value)
            Exception occurs
```

The last line gives you the exception `java.lang.UnsupportedOperationException: Can't read accumulator value in task`.

If you need to have an accumulated value of one type and add to it values of another type, you can create an `Accumulable` object. It's created with `SparkContext.accumulable(initialValue)`; and, similar to `Accumulator`, you can also assign it a name.

`Accumulator` is a special case of the `Accumulable` class, but is used more often. `Accumulable` objects are mostly used as custom accumulators (you'll see an example next).

WRITING CUSTOM ACCUMULATORS

The object in charge of adding values to an `Accumulator` is `AccumulatorParam` (or `AccumulableParam` for Accumulables). It has to be implicitly defined in the scope of the calling function. Spark already provides implicit `AccumulatorParam` objects for numeric types so they can be used as accumulator values without any special actions. But if you want to use a custom class as an accumulator value, you have to create a custom implicit `AccumulatorParam` object.

`AccumulatorParam` has to implement two methods:

- `zero(initialValue: T)`—Creates an initial value that's passed to executors. The global initial value stays the same.
- `addInPlace(v1: T, v2: T):T`—Merges two accumulated values.

`AccumulableParam` needs to implement one additional method:

- `addAccumulator(v1: T, v2: V): T`—Adds a new accumulator value to the accumulated value

For example, you could use a single `Accumulable` object to track both the sum and count of values (to get an average value) like this:

Creates an RDD of
integers from 1 to 100

Creates the implicit
AccumulableParam.

```
val rdd = sc.parallelize(1 to 100)
import org.apache.spark.AccumulableParam
implicit object AvgAccParam extends AccumulableParam[(Int, Int), Int] {
  def zero(v:(Int, Int)) = (0, 0)
  def addInPlace(v1:(Int, Int), v2:(Int, Int)) = (v1._1+v2._1, v1._2+v2._2)
  def addAccumulator(v1:(Int, Int), v2:Int) = (v1._1+1, v1._2+v2)
}
val acc = sc.accumulable((0,0))
rdd.foreach(x => acc += x)
val mean = acc.value._2.toDouble / acc.value._1
mean: Double = 50.5
```

Creates an Accumulable object;
compiler finds the AvgAccParam
object automatically

Accesses the accumulator
value to calculate the mean

Adds all values of the
RDD to the accumulator

The implicit `AccumulableParam` object in the previous snippet contains all the necessary methods for tracking counts and sums across the executors. `AvgAccParam` accepts integers and keeps the accumulated value in a tuple: the first element tracks the count, the second tracks the sum.

ACCUMULATING VALUES IN ACCUMULABLE COLLECTIONS

You can also accumulate values in mutable collections, without creating any implicit objects, by using `SparkContext.accumulableCollection()`. Custom accumulators are flexible, but if you only need to implement a collection accumulator, accumulable collections are much easier to use. For example, using the same `rdd` object generated in the previous example, you can accumulate its objects into a shared collection like this:

```
scala> import scala.collection.mutable.MutableList
scala> val colacc = sc.accumulableCollection(MutableList[Int]())
scala> rdd.foreach(x => colacc += x)
scala> colacc.value
res0: scala.collection.mutable.MutableList[Int] = MutableList(1, 2, 3, 4,
5, 6, 7, 8, 9, 10, 31, 32, 33, ...)
```

As you can see, the results aren't sorted, because there's no guarantee that the accumulator results from various partitions will return to the driver in any specific order.

4.5.2 Sending data to executors using broadcast variables

As we said in chapter 3, broadcast variables can be shared and accessed from across the cluster, similar to accumulators. But they're opposite from accumulators in that they can't be modified by executors. The driver creates a broadcast variable, and executors read it.

You should use broadcast variables if you have a large set of data that the majority of your executors need. Typically, variables created in the driver, needed by tasks for their execution, are serialized and shipped along with those tasks. But a single driver program can reuse the same variable in several jobs, and several tasks may get shipped to the same executor as part of the same job. So, a potentially large variable may get serialized and transferred over the network more times than necessary. In these cases, it's better to use broadcast variables, because they can transfer the data in a more optimized way and only once.

Broadcast variables are created with the `SparkContext.broadcast(value)` method, which returns an object of type `Broadcast`. The value can be any serializable object. It can then be read by executors using the `Broadcast.value` method. When an executor tries to read a broadcast variable, the executor will first check to see whether it's already loaded. If not, it requests the broadcast variable from the driver, one chunk at a time. This pull-based approach avoids network congestion at job startup.

You should always access its contents through the `value` method and never directly. Otherwise, Spark will automatically serialize and ship your variable along with tasks, and you'll lose all the performance benefits of broadcast variables.

DESTROYING AND UNPERSISTING BROADCAST VARIABLES

When a broadcast variable is no longer needed, you can `destroy` it. All information about it will be removed (from the executors and driver), and the variable will become unusable. If you try to access it after calling `destroy`, an exception will be thrown.

The other option is to call `unpersist`, which only removes the variable value from the cache in the executors. If you try to use it after unpersisting, it will be sent to the executors again.

Finally, broadcast variables are automatically unpersisted by Spark after they go out of scope (if all references to them cease to exist), so it's unnecessary to explicitly unpersist them. Instead, you can remove the reference to the broadcast variable in the driver program.

CONFIGURATION PARAMETERS THAT AFFECT BROADCAST VARIABLES

Several configuration parameters are available that can affect broadcast performance (for details about setting Spark configuration parameters, see chapter 11):

- `spark.broadcast.compress`—Specifies whether the variables will be compressed before transfer (you should leave this at `true`). Variables will be compressed with a codec specified by `spark.io.compression.codec`.
- `spark.broadcast.blockSize`—Indicates the size of the chunks of data used for transferring broadcast data. You should probably leave this at the battle-tested default of 4096.
- `spark.python.worker.reuse`—Can greatly affect broadcast performance in Python because, if workers aren't reused, broadcast variables will need to be transferred for each task. You should keep this at `true`, which is the default value.

The main points to remember are that you should use broadcast variables if you have a large set of data that the majority of your workers needs and to always use the `value` method to access the broadcast variables.

4.6   *Summary*

- Pair RDDs contain two-element tuples: keys and values.
- Pair RDDs in Scala are implicitly converted to instances of class `PairRDDFunctions`, which hosts special pair RDD operations.
- `countByKey` returns a map containing the number of occurrences of each key.
- `mapValues` changes the values contained in a pair RDD without changing the associated keys.
- `flatMapValues` enables you to change the number of elements corresponding to a key by mapping each value to zero or more values.
- `reduceByKey` and `foldByKey` let you merge all the values of a key into a single value of the same type.
- `aggregateByKey` merges values, but it also transforms values to another type.
- Data partitioning is Spark's mechanism for dividing data between multiple nodes in a cluster.
- The number of RDD partitions is important because, in addition to influencing data distribution throughout the cluster, it also directly determines the number of tasks that will be running RDD transformations.
- Partitioning of RDDs is performed by `Partitioner` objects that assign a partition index to each RDD element. Spark provides two implementations: `HashPartitioner` and `RangePartitioner`.
- Physical movement of data between partitions is called shuffling. It occurs when data from multiple partitions needs to be combined in order to build partitions for a new RDD.
- During shuffling, in addition to being written to disk, the data is also sent over the network, so it's important to try to minimize the number of shuffles during Spark jobs.
- RDD operations for working on partitions are `mapPartitions` and `mapPartitionsWithIndex`.
- The four classic joins in Spark function just like the RDBMS joins of the same names: `join` (inner join), `leftOuterJoin`, `rightOuterJoin`, and `fullOuterJoin`.
- `cogroup` performs grouping of values from several RDDs by key and returns an RDD whose values are arrays of `Iterable` objects containing values from each RDD.
- The main transformations for sorting RDD data are `sortByKey`, `sortBy`, and `repartitionAndSortWithinPartition`.

- Several pair RDD transformations can be used for grouping data in Spark: `aggregateByKey`, `groupByKey` (and the related `groupBy`), and `combineByKey`.
- RDD lineage is expressed as a directed acyclic graph (DAG) connecting an RDD with its parent RDDs, from which it was transformed.
- Every Spark job is divided into stages based on the points where shuffles occur.
- The RDD lineage can be saved with checkpointing.
- Accumulators and broadcast variables enable you to maintain a global state or share data across tasks and partitions in your Spark programs.

Part 2

Meet the Spark family

I't's time to get to know the other components that make up Spark: Spark SQL, Spark Streaming, Spark MLlib, and Spark GraphX. You've already made a brief acquaintance of Spark SQL in chapter 3. In chapter 5, you'll be formally introduced. You'll learn how to create and use `DataFrames`, how to use SQL to query `DataFrame` data, and how to load data to and save it from external data sources. You'll also learn about optimizations done by Spark's SQL Catalyst optimization engine and about performance improvements introduced with the Tungsten project.

Spark Streaming, one of the more popular family members, is introduced in chapter 6. There you'll learn about *discretized streams*, which periodically produce RDDs as the streaming application is running. You'll also learn how to save computation state over time and how to use window operations. We'll examine ways of connecting to Kafka and how to obtain good performance from your streaming jobs.

Chapters 7 and 8 are about machine learning, specifically about the Spark MLlib and Spark ML sections of Spark API. You'll learn about machine learning in general and about linear regression, logistic regression, decision trees, random forests, and k-means clustering. Along the way, you'll scale and normalize features, use regularization, and train and evaluate machine-learning models. We'll explain the API standardizations brought by Spark ML.

Finally, chapter 9 explores how to build graphs with Spark's GraphX API. You'll transform and join graphs, use graph algorithms, and implement the A* search algorithm using the GraphX API.

5

Sparkling queries with Spark SQL

This chapter covers

- Creating DataFrames
- Using the DataFrame API
- Using SQL queries
- Loading and saving data from/to external data sources
- Understanding the Catalyst optimizer
- Understanding Tungsten performance improvements
- Introducing DataSets

You had a taste of working with DataFrames in chapter 3. As you saw there, Data-Frames let you work with *structured data* (data organized in rows and columns, where each column contains only values of a certain type). SQL, frequently used in relational databases, is the most common way to organize and query this data. SQL also figures as part of the name of the first Spark component we're covering in part 2: Spark SQL.

In this chapter, we plunge deeper into the `DataFrame` API and examine it more closely. In section 5.1, you'll first learn how to convert RDDs to `DataFrames`. You'll then use the `DataFrame` API on a sample dataset from the Stack Exchange website to select, filter, sort, group, and join data. We'll show you all that you need to know about using SQL functions with `DataFrames` and how to convert `DataFrames` back to RDDs.

In section 5.2, we show you how to create `DataFrames` by running SQL queries and how to execute SQL queries on `DataFrame` data in three ways: from your programs, through Spark's SQL shell, and through Spark's Thrift server. In section 5.3, we show you how to save and load data to and from various external data sources. In the last two sections of this chapter, you learn about optimizations done by Spark's SQL Catalyst optimization engine and about performance improvements introduced with the Tungsten project.

In the last section of this chapter we give a brief overview of `DataSets`, which emerged in Spark 1.6. `DataFrames` have, since Spark 2.0, become a special case of `DataSets`; they are now implemented as `DataSets` containing `Row` objects.

You should have a basic knowledge of SQL to properly understand parts of this chapter. A good reference is w3schools.com's SQL tutorial (www.w3schools.com/SQL). Some familiarity with Hive, a distributed warehouse based on Hadoop, is also beneficial.

An HDFS cluster at your disposal would be helpful in this chapter. We hope you'll be using the spark-in-action VM, because HDFS is already installed there, in the standalone mode (http://mng.bz/Bu4d). There's a lot to cover, so let's get started.

5.1   *Working with DataFrames*

In the previous chapter, you learned how to manipulate RDDs. which is important because RDDs represent a low-level, direct way of manipulating data in Spark and the core of Spark runtime. Spark 1.3 introduced the `DataFrame` API for handling structured, distributed data in a table-like representation with named columns and declared column types.

Inspiration for `DataFrames` came from several languages that used a similar concept with the same name: `DataFrames` in Python's Pandas package, `DataFrames` in R, and `DataFrames` in the Julia language. What makes them different in Spark is their distributed nature and Spark's Catalyst, which optimizes resource use in real time, based on pluggable data sources, rules, and data types. We talk about Catalyst later in this chapter.

`DataFrames` translate SQL code and domain-specific language (DSL) expressions into optimized low-level RDD operations, so that the same API can be used from any supported language (Scala, Java, Python, and R) for accessing any supported data source (files, databases, and so forth) in the same way and with comparable performance characteristics. Since their introduction, `DataFrames` have become one of the most important features in Spark and made Spark SQL the most actively developed Spark component. Since Spark 2.0, `DataFrame` is implemented as a special case of `DataSet`.

Because you almost always know the structure of the data you're handling, `Data-Frames` are applicable in any instance that requires manipulation of structured data, which is the majority of cases in the big data world. `DataFrames` let you reference the data by column names and access it with "good ole" SQL queries, which is the most natural way for most users to handle data, and it provides many integration possibilities.

Let's say you have a table with user data in a relational database and user activity data in a Parquet file on HDFS, and you want to join the two data sources. (Parquet is a columnar file format that stores schema information along with the data.) Spark SQL lets you do that by loading both of these sources in `DataFrames`. Once available as `Data-Frames`, these two data sources can be joined, queried, and saved at a third location.

Spark SQL also lets you register `DataFrames` as tables in the table catalog, which doesn't hold the data itself; it merely saves information about how to access the structured data. Once registered, Spark applications can query the data when you provide the `DataFrames` name. What's also interesting is that third-party applications can use standard JDBC and ODBC protocols to connect to Spark and then use SQL to query the data from registered `DataFrames` tables. Spark's Thrift server is the component that enables this functionality. It accepts incoming JDBC client connections and executes them as Spark jobs using the `DataFrame` API.

Figure 5.1 illustrates all of this. It shows two types of clients: a Spark application executing a join on two tables using `DataFrame` DSL, and a non-Spark application executing

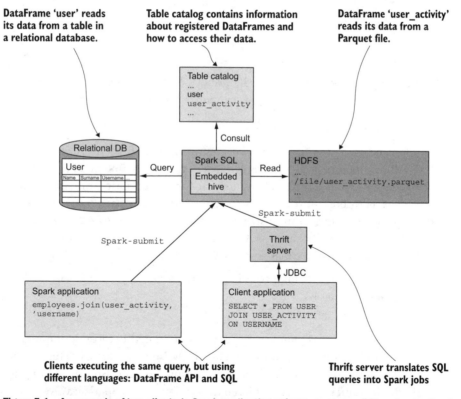

Figure 5.1 An example of two clients (a Spark application using `DataFrame` DSL and a non-Spark client application connecting through JDBC) executing the same query that joins two tables: one residing in a relational database and another residing in a Parquet file in HDFS

the same join, but as an SQL query through JDBC connected to Spark's Thrift server. We'll talk about Spark applications in this section and about JDBC tables in section 5.2. A permanent table catalog (surviving Spark context restarts) is available only when Spark is built with Hive support. In case you're wondering, Hive is a distributed warehouse built as a layer of abstraction on top of Hadoop's MapReduce. Initially built by Facebook, it's widely used today for data querying and analysis. It has its own dialect of SQL known as HiveQL. HiveQL is capable of running its jobs not only as MapReduce jobs, but also as Spark jobs.

When built with Hive support, Spark includes all of Hive's dependencies. Hive is included by default when you download archives from the Spark downloads page. In addition to bringing a more powerful SQL parser, Hive support enables you to access existing Hive tables and use existing, community-built Hive UDFs. For these reasons, we recommend using Spark built with Hive support.

DataFrames are comparable to, and are based on, RDDs, so the principles described in the previous chapter are valid for DataFrames too. Type information available for every column makes DataFrames much easier to use than RDDs because your query has fewer lines of code, and DataFrame-optimized queries offer better performance.

You can create DataFrames in three ways:

- Converting existing RDDs
- Running SQL queries
- Loading external data

The easiest method is to run an SQL query, but we'll leave that for later. First, we'll show you how to create DataFrames from existing RDDs.

5.1.1 *Creating DataFrames from RDDs*

It's often necessary to first load data into an RDD and then use it to create a DataFrame. If you want to load log files into DataFrames, you first need to load them as text, parse the lines, and identify elements that form each entry; only then does the data become structured and thus ready for consumption by DataFrames. In short, you use RDDs to load and transform unstructured data and then create DataFrames from RDDs if you want to use the DataFrame API.

You can create DataFrames from RDDs in three ways:

- Using RDDs containing row data as tuples
- Using case classes
- Specifying a schema

The first method is rudimentary. It's simple but limited because it doesn't allow you to specify all the schema attributes, which usually isn't satisfactory. The second method includes writing a case class, which is more involved but isn't as limiting as the first method. The third method, considered to be a standard in Spark, involves explicitly specifying a schema. In the first two methods, a schema is specified indirectly (it's inferred).

We cover each of these methods in this section. But first we need to discuss a few prerequisites: the `SparkSession` object, the necessary implicit methods, and the dataset used in this chapter.

CREATING SPARKSESSION AND IMPORTING IMPLICIT METHODS

To use Spark `DataFrames` and SQL expressions, begin with the `SparkSession` object. It's preconfigured in a Spark shell and available as the variable `spark`. In your own programs, you should construct it yourself, just as you did in previous chapters.

```
import org.apache.spark.sql.SparkSession
val spark = SparkSession.builder().getOrElse()
```

`SparkSession` is a wrapper around `SparkContext` and `SQLContext`, which was directly used for constructing `DataFrames` in the versions prior to Spark 2.0. The `Builder` object lets you specify master, `appName`, and other configuration options, but the defaults will do.

Spark provides a set of Scala implicit methods for automatically converting RDDs to `DataFrames`. You must import these methods before using this feature. Once you have your `SparkSession` in spark, the import can be accomplished with the following statement:

```
import spark.implicits._
```

Note that in Spark shell this is already done for you, but in your own programs you'll have to do it yourself.

These `implicits` add one method, called `toDF`, to your RDD if the RDD contains objects for which a `DataSet Encoder` is defined. `Encoders` are used for converting JVM objects to internal Spark SQL representation. For the list of `Encoders` that can be used for constructing `DataFrames`, and that come with Spark out of the box, see this list: http://mng.bz/Wa45. We'll illustrate how this works with an example.

UNDERSTANDING AND LOADING THE EXAMPLE DATASET

The examples in this chapter are based on the data obtained from Stack Exchange. You probably already know about or use the Stack Exchange website (www.stackexchange.com), especially its subcommunity Stack Overflow, a place for asking and answering programming-related questions.

Anybody can ask questions in Stack Exchange communities, and anybody can answer them. A system of upvotes and downvotes exists as a means for marking certain questions and answers useful (or less so). Users earn points for asking and answering questions and can also earn different types of *badges* for various activities on the site.

In 2009, Stack Exchange released[1] an anonymized *data dump* of all questions and answers in the Stack Exchange communities, and it continues to release data as new questions became available. One of the communities whose data was released is the Italian Language Stack Exchange, and we'll use its data to illustrate Spark SQL concepts in

---

[1] See the official announcement at http://mng.bz/Ct8l.

this chapter. We chose this community because of its small size (you can easily download and use it on your laptop) and because we like the language.

The original data is available in XML format. We preprocessed it and created a comma-separated values (CSV) file that you can find in our GitHub repository (which you have, hopefully, cloned) under the folder ch05. The first file you'll use is italian-Posts.csv. It contains Italian language–related questions (and answers) with the following fields (delimited with tilde signs):

- commentCount—Number of comments related to the question/answer
- lastActivityDate—Date and time of the last modification
- ownerUserId—User ID of the owner
- body—Textual contents of the question/answer
- score—Total score based on upvotes and downvotes
- creationDate—Date and time of creation
- viewCount—View count
- title—Title of the question
- tags—Set of tags the question has been marked with
- answerCount—Number of related answers
- acceptedAnswerId—If a question contains the ID of its accepted answer
- postTypeId—Type of the post; 1 is for questions, 2 for answers
- id—Post's unique ID

After downloading the file and starting your Spark shell, you can parse the data and load it into an RDD with the following snippet:

```
scala> val itPostsRows = sc.textFile("first-edition/ch05/italianPosts.csv")
scala> val itPostsSplit = itPostsRows.map(x => x.split("~"))
itPostsSplit: org.apache.spark.rdd.RDD[Array[String]] = ...
```

This gives you an RDD containing arrays of strings. You could convert this RDD to a DataFrame with only one column containing arrays of Strings, but that's not what we want to do here. We need to map each of those Strings to a different column.

CREATING A DATAFRAME FROM AN RDD OF TUPLES

So let's create a DataFrame by converting the RDD's element arrays to tuples and then calling toDF on the resulting RDD. There's no elegant way to convert an array to a tuple, so you have to resort to this ugly expression:

```
scala> val itPostsRDD = itPostsSplit.map(x => (x(0),x(1),x(2),x(3),x(4),
  x(5),x(6),x(7),x(8),x(9),x(10),x(11),x(12)))
itPostsRDD: org.apache.spark.rdd.RDD[(String, String, ...
```

Then use the `toDF` function:

```
scala> val itPostsDFrame = itPostsRDD.toDF()
itPostsDF: org.apache.spark.sql.DataFrame = [_1: string, ...
```

Now you have your `DataFrame`, and you can use all the goodies that come with it. First, you can get the contents of the first 10 rows in a nice, formatted textual output with the `show` method (the output is cropped to the right to fit on the page):

```
scala> itPostsDFrame.show(10)
+---+--------------------+---+--------------------+---+--------------------
| _1|                  _2| _3|                  _4| _5|                  _6
+---+--------------------+---+--------------------+---+--------------------
|  4|2013-11-11 18:21:...| 17|&lt;p&gt;The infi...| 23|2013-11-10 19:37:...
|  5|2013-11-10 20:31:...| 12|&lt;p&gt;Come cre...|  1|2013-11-10 19:44:...
|  2|2013-11-10 20:31:...| 17|&lt;p&gt;Il verbo...|  5|2013-11-10 19:58:...
|  1|2014-07-25 13:15:...|154|&lt;p&gt;As part ...| 11|2013-11-10 22:03:...
|  0|2013-11-10 22:15:...| 70|&lt;p&gt;&lt;em&g...|  3|2013-11-10 22:15:...
|  2|2013-11-10 22:17:...| 17|&lt;p&gt;There's ...|  8|2013-11-10 22:17:...
|  1|2013-11-11 09:51:...| 63|&lt;p&gt;As other...|  3|2013-11-11 09:51:...
|  1|2013-11-12 23:57:...| 63|&lt;p&gt;The expr...|  1|2013-11-11 10:09:...
|  9|2014-01-05 11:13:...| 63|&lt;p&gt;When I w...|  5|2013-11-11 10:28:...
|  0|2013-11-11 10:58:...| 18|&lt;p&gt;Wow, wha...|  5|2013-11-11 10:58:...
+---+--------------------+---+--------------------+---+--------------------
```

If you call the `show` method without arguments, it shows the first 20 rows. This is nice, but the column names are generic and aren't particularly helpful. You can rectify that by specifying column names when calling the `toDF` method:

```
scala> val itPostsDF = itPostsRDD.toDF("commentCount", "lastActivityDate",
  "ownerUserId", "body", "score", "creationDate", "viewCount", "title",
  "tags", "answerCount", "acceptedAnswerId", "postTypeId", "id")
```

If you call `show` now, you'll see that column names appear in the output. You can also examine the schema of the `DataFrame` with the `printSchema` method:

```
scala> itPostsDF.printSchema
root
 |-- commentCount: string (nullable = true)
 |-- lastActivityDate: string (nullable = true)
 |-- ownerUserId: string (nullable = true)
 |-- body: string (nullable = true)
 |-- score: string (nullable = true)
 |-- creationDate: string (nullable = true)
 |-- viewCount: string (nullable = true)
 |-- title: string (nullable = true)
 |-- tags: string (nullable = true)
 |-- answerCount: string (nullable = true)
 |-- acceptedAnswerId: string (nullable = true)
 |-- postTypeId: string (nullable = true)
 |-- id: string (nullable = true)
```

This method shows the information that the DataFrame has about its columns. You can see that column names are now available, but all the columns are of type String and they're all nullable. This could be desirable in some cases, but in this case it's obviously wrong. Here, the column ID should be of type long, counts should be integers, and the date columns should be timestamps. The following two RDD-to-DataFrame conversion methods let you specify the desirable column types and their names.

CONVERTING RDDs TO DATAFRAMES USING CASE CLASSES

The second option of converting RDDs to DataFrames is to map each row in an RDD to a case class and then use the toDF method. First you need to define the case class that will hold the data. Here's the Post class that can hold each row of the dataset:

```
import java.sql.Timestamp
case class Post(
  commentCount:Option[Int],
  lastActivityDate:Option[java.sql.Timestamp],
  ownerUserId:Option[Long],
  body:String,
  score:Option[Int],
  creationDate:Option[java.sql.Timestamp],
  viewCount:Option[Int],
  title:String,
  tags:String,
  answerCount:Option[Int],
  acceptedAnswerId:Option[Long],
  postTypeId:Option[Long],
  id:Long)
```

Nullable fields are declared to be of type Option[T], which means they can contain either a Some object with the value of type T, or a None (null in Java). For timestamp columns, Spark supports the java.sql.Timestamp class.

Before mapping itPostsRDD's rows to Post objects, first declare an implicit class that helps to write that in a more elegant way:[2]

```
object StringImplicits {
  implicit class StringImprovements(val s: String) {
    import scala.util.control.Exception.catching
    def toIntSafe = catching(classOf[NumberFormatException]) opt s.toInt
    def toLongSafe = catching(classOf[NumberFormatException]) opt s.toLong
    def toTimestampSafe = catching(classOf[IllegalArgumentException]) opt
      Timestamp.valueOf(s)
  }
}
```

The implicit StringImprovements class in the StringImplicits object defines three methods that can be implicitly added to Scala's String class and used to safely convert strings to integers, longs, and timestamps. Safely means that, if a string can't be

---

[2] Thanks to Pierre Andres for this idea: http://mng.bz/ih7n.

converted to the type, instead of throwing an exception, the methods return None. The catching function returns an object of type scala.util.control.Exception .Catch, whose opt method can be used to map the results of the specified function (s.toInt, for example) to an Option object, returning None if the specified exception occurs or Some otherwise.

This makes parsing of rows much more elegant:

```
import StringImplicits._
def stringToPost(row:String):Post = {
  val r = row.split("~")
  Post(r(0).toIntSafe,
    r(1).toTimestampSafe,
    r(2).toLongSafe,
    r(3),
    r(4).toIntSafe,
    r(5).toTimestampSafe,
    r(6).toIntSafe,
    r(7),
    r(8),
    r(9).toIntSafe,
    r(10).toLongSafe,
    r(11).toLongSafe,
    r(12).toLong)
}
val itPostsDFCase = itPostsRows.map(x => stringToPost(x)).toDF()
```

You first need to import the implicit class you just declared and then parse the individual fields (strings) into objects of appropriate types using the safe methods. Note that the last column (id) can't be null, so a safe method isn't used there.

Now your DataFrame contains the proper types and nullable flags:

```
scala> itPostsDFCase.printSchema
root
 |-- commentCount: integer (nullable = true)
 |-- lastActivityDate: timestamp (nullable = true)
 |-- ownerUserId: long (nullable = true)
 |-- body: string (nullable = true)
 |-- score: integer (nullable = true)
 |-- creationDate: timestamp (nullable = true)
 |-- viewCount: integer (nullable = true)
 |-- title: string (nullable = true)
 |-- tags: string (nullable = true)
 |-- answerCount: integer (nullable = true)
 |-- acceptedAnswerId: long (nullable = true)
 |-- postTypeId: long (nullable = true)
 |-- id: long (nullable = false)
```

Before looking further into the DataFrame API, we'll show you another way of creating DataFrames from RDDs.

CONVERTING RDDS TO DATAFRAMES BY SPECIFYING A SCHEMA

The last method for converting RDDs to DataFrames is to use SparkSession's create-DataFrame method, which takes an RDD containing objects of type Row and a Struct-Type. In Spark SQL, a StructType represents a schema. It contains one or more StructFields, each describing a column. You can construct a StructType schema for the post RDD with the following snippet:

```
import org.apache.spark.sql.types._
val postSchema = StructType(Seq(
  StructField("commentCount", IntegerType, true),
  StructField("lastActivityDate", TimestampType, true),
  StructField("ownerUserId", LongType, true),
  StructField("body", StringType, true),
  StructField("score", IntegerType, true),
  StructField("creationDate", TimestampType, true),
  StructField("viewCount", IntegerType, true),
  StructField("title", StringType, true),
  StructField("tags", StringType, true),
  StructField("answerCount", IntegerType, true),
  StructField("acceptedAnswerId", LongType, true),
  StructField("postTypeId", LongType, true),
  StructField("id", LongType, false))
  )
```

Supported data types

DataFrame takes columns of the usual types supported by major relational databases: strings, integers, shorts, floats, doubles, bytes, dates, timestamps, and binary values (in relational databases, called BLOBs). But it can also contain complex data types:

- Arrays contain several values of the same type.
- Maps contain key-value pairs, where the key is a primitive type.
- Structs contain nested column definitions.

You'll find Scala data type objects that you can use when constructing StructType objects in the org.apache.spark.sql.types package.

The Row class for your RDD needs to contain elements of various types, so you can construct its objects by specifying all the elements or by passing in a Seq or a Tuple. You can change the stringToPost function used previously to a stringToRow function just by changing the Post type to Row (you'll find the stringToRow function in our online repository). But because Spark in version 2.0 doesn't handle Scala Option objects well when constructing DataFrames in this way, you need to use real Java null values. In other words:

```
def stringToRow(row:String):Row = {
    val r = row.split("~")
    Row(r(0).toIntSafe.getOrElse(null),
        r(1).toTimestampSafe.getOrElse(null),
        r(2).toLongSafe.getOrElse(null),
        r(3),
        r(4).toIntSafe.getOrElse(null),
        r(5).toTimestampSafe.getOrElse(null),
        r(6).toIntSafe.getOrElse(null),
        r(7),
        r(8),
        r(9).toIntSafe.getOrElse(null),
        r(10).toLongSafe.getOrElse(null),
        r(11).toLongSafe.getOrElse(null),
        r(12).toLong)
}
```

Then you can create an RDD and the final `DataFrame` like this:

```
val rowRDD = itPostsRows.map(row => stringToRow(row))
val itPostsDFStruct = spark.createDataFrame(rowRDD, postSchema)
```

GETTING SCHEMA INFORMATION

You can verify that the schema of `itPostsDFStruct` is equivalent to that of `itPosts-DFCase` by calling the `printSchema` method. You can also access the schema `Struct-Type` object through the `DataFrame`'s schema field.

Two additional `DataFrame` functions can give you some information about the `Data-Frame`'s schema. The `columns` method returns a list of column names, and the `dtypes` method returns a list of tuples, each containing the column name and the name of its type. For the `itPostsDFCase` `DataFrame`, the results looks like this:

```
scala> itPostsDFCase.columns
res0: Array[String] = Array(commentCount, lastActivityDate, ownerUserId,
  body, score, creationDate, viewCount, title, tags, answerCount,
  acceptedAnswerId, postTypeId, id)

scala> itPostsDFStruct.dtypes
res1: Array[(String, String)] = Array((commentCount,IntegerType),
  (lastActivityDate,TimestampType), (ownerUserId,LongType),
  (body,StringType), (score,IntegerType), (creationDate,TimestampType),
  (viewCount,IntegerType), (title,StringType), (tags,StringType),
  (answerCount,IntegerType), (acceptedAnswerId,LongType),
  (postTypeId,LongType), (id,LongType))
```

5.1.2 DataFrame API basics

Now that you have your `DataFrame` loaded (no matter which method you used to load the data), you can start exploring the rich `DataFrame` API. `DataFrames` come with a DSL for manipulating data, which is fundamental to working with Spark SQL. Spark's machine learning library (ML) also relies on `DataFrames`. They've become a corner-stone of Spark, so it's important to get acquainted with their API.

`DataFrame`'s DSL has a set of functionalities similar to the usual SQL functions for manipulating data in relational databases. `DataFrames` work like RDDs: they're immu-table and lazy. They inherit their *immutable nature* from the underlying RDD architec-ture. You can't directly change data in a `DataFrame`; you have to transform it into another one. They're *lazy* because most `DataFrame` DSL functions don't return results. Instead, they return another `DataFrame`, similar to RDD transformations.

In this section, we'll give you an overview of basic `DataFrame` functions and show how you can use them to select, filter, map, group, and join data. All of these functions have their SQL counterparts, but we'll get to that in section 5.2.

SELECTING DATA

Most of the `DataFrame` DSL functions work with `Column` objects. When using the `select` function for selecting data, you can pass column names or `Column` objects to it, and it will return a new `DataFrame` containing only those columns. For example (first rename the `DataFrame` variable to `postsDf` to make it shorter):

```
scala> val postsDf = itPostsDFStruct
scala> val postsIdBody = postsDf.select("id", "body")
postsIdBody: org.apache.spark.sql.DataFrame = [id: bigint, body: string]
```

Several methods exist for creating `Column` objects. You can create columns using an existing `DataFrame` object and its `col` function:

```
val postsIdBody = postsDf.select(postsDf.col("id"), postsDf.col("body"))
```

or you can use some of the implicit methods that you imported in section 5.1.1. One of them indirectly converts Scala's `Symbol` class to a `Column`. `Symbol` objects are some-times used in Scala programs as identifiers instead of `Strings` because they're *interned* (at most one instance of an object exists) and can be quickly checked for equality. They can be instantiated with Scala's built-in quote mechanism or with Scala's `apply` function, so the following two statements are equivalent:

```
val postsIdBody = postsDf.select(Symbol("id"), Symbol("body"))
val postsIdBody = postsDf.select('id, 'body)
```

Another implicit method (called $) converts strings to `ColumnName` objects (which inherit from `Column` objects, so you can use `ColumnName` objects as well):

```
val postsIdBody = postsDf.select($"id", $"body")
```

`Column` objects are important for `DataFrame` DSL, so all this flexibility is justified.

That's how you specify which columns to select. The resulting `DataFrame` contains only the specified columns. If you need to select all the columns *except* a single one, you can use the `drop` function, which takes a column name or a `Column` object and returns a new `DataFrame` with the specified column missing. For example, to remove the body column from the `postsIdBody` DataFrame (and thus leave only the `id` column), you can use the following line:

```
val postIds = postsIdBody.drop("body")
```

FILTERING DATA

You can filter `DataFrame` data using the `where` and `filter` functions (they're synonymous). They take a `Column` object or an expression string. The variant taking a string is used for parsing SQL expressions. Again, we'll get to that in section 5.2.

Why do you pass a `Column` object to a filtering function, you ask? Because the `Column` class, in addition to representing a column name, contains a rich set of SQL-like operators that you can use to build expressions. These expressions are also represented by the `Column` class.

For example, to see how many posts contain the word *Italiano* in their body, you can use the following line:

```
scala> postsIdBody.filter('body contains "Italiano").count
res0: Long = 46
```

To select all the questions that don't have an accepted answer, use this expression:

```
scala> val noAnswer = postsDf.filter(('postTypeId === 1) and
  ('acceptedAnswerId isNull))
```

Here, the filter expression is based on two columns: the post type ID (which is equal to 1 for questions) and the accepted answer ID columns. Both expressions yield a `Column` object, which is then combined into a third one using the `and` operator. You need to use the extra parenthesis to help the Scala parser find its way.

These are just some of the available operators. We invite you to examine the complete set of operators listed in the official documentation at http://mng.bz/a2Xt. Note that you can use these column expressions in `select` functions as well.

You can select only the first *n* rows of a `DataFrame` with the `limit` function. The following will return a `DataFrame` containing only the first 10 questions:

```
scala> val firstTenQs = postsDf.filter('postTypeId === 1).limit(10)
```

ADDING AND RENAMING COLUMNS

In some situations, you may want to rename a column to give it a shorter or a more meaningful name. That's what the `withColumnRenamed` function is for. It accepts two strings: the old and the new name of the column. For example:

```
val firstTenQsRn = firstTenQs.withColumnRenamed("ownerUserId", "owner")
```

To add a new column to a `DataFrame`, use the `withColumn` function and give it the column name and the `Column` expression. Let's say you're interested in a "views per score point" metric (in other words, how many views are needed to increase score by one), and you want to see the questions whose value of this metric is less than some threshold (which means if the question is more successful, it gains a higher score with fewer views). If your threshold is 35 (which is the actual average), this can be accomplished with the following expression:

```
scala> postsDf.filter('postTypeId === 1).
  withColumn("ratio", 'viewCount / 'score).
  where('ratio < 35).show()
```

The output is too wide to print on this page, but you can run the command yourself and see that the output contains the extra column called ratio.

SORTING DATA

DataFrame's orderBy and sort functions sort data (they're equivalent). They take one or more column names or one or more Column expressions. The Column class has asc and desc operators, which are used for specifying the sort order. The default is to sort in ascending order.

As an exercise, try to list the 10 most recently modified questions. (You'll find the solution in our online repository.)

5.1.3 *Using SQL functions to perform calculations on data*

All relational databases today provide SQL functions for performing calculations on data. Spark SQL also supports a large number of them. SQL functions are available through the DataFrame API and through SQL expressions. In this section, we'll cover their use through the DataFrame API.

SQL functions fit into four categories:

- *Scalar functions* return a single value for each row based on calculations on one or more columns.
- *Aggregate functions* return a single value for a group of rows.
- *Window functions* return several values for a group of rows.
- *User-defined functions* include custom scalar or aggregate functions.

USING BUILT-IN SCALAR AND AGGREGATE FUNCTIONS

Scalar functions return a single value for each row based on values in one or more columns in the same row. Scalar functions include abs (calculates the absolute value), exp (computes the exponential), and substring (extracts a substring of a given string). Aggregate functions return a single value for a group of rows. They are min (returns the minimum value in a group of rows), avg (calculates the average value in a group of rows), and so on.

Scalar and aggregate functions reside within the object org.apache.spark .sql.functions. You can import them all at once (note that they're automatically imported in Spark shell, so you don't have to do this yourself):

```
import org.apache.spark.sql.functions._
```

Spark offers numerous scalar functions to do the following:

- *Math calculations*—abs (calculates absolute value), hypot (calculates hypotenuse based on two columns or scalar values), log (calculates logarithm), cbrt (computes cube root), and others
- *String operations*—length (calculates length of a string), trim (trims a string value left and right), concat (concatenates several input strings), and others
- *Date-time operations*—year (returns the year of a date column), date_add (adds a number of days to a date column), and others

Aggregate functions are used in combination with groupBy (explained in section 5.1.4) but can also be used on the entire dataset in the select or withColumn method. Spark's aggregate functions include min, max, count, avg, and sum. These are so common that we believe no special explanation is necessary.

As an example, let's find the question that was active for the largest amount of time. You can use the lastActivityDate and creationDate columns for this and find the difference between them (in days) using the datediff function, which takes two arguments: end date column and start date column. Here goes:

```scala
scala> postsDf.filter('postTypeId === 1).
  withColumn("activePeriod", datediff('lastActivityDate, 'creationDate)).
  orderBy('activePeriod desc).head.getString(3).
  replace("&lt;","<").replace("&gt;",">")
res0: String = <p>The plural of <em>braccio</em> is <em>braccia</em>, and
the plural of <em>avambraccio</em> is <em>avambracci</em>.</p><p>Why are
the plural of those words so different, if they both are referring to parts
of the human body, and <em>avambraccio</em> derives from
<em>braccio</em>?</p>
```

You use the head DataFrame function to locally retrieve the first Row from the DataFrame and then select its third element, which is the column body. The column body contains HTML-formatted text, so we unescaped it for better readability.

As another example, let's find the average and maximum score of all questions and the total number of questions. Spark SQL makes this easy:

```scala
scala> postsDf.select(avg('score), max('score), count('score)).show
+-----------------+----------+------------+
|      avg(score) |max(score)|count(score)|
+-----------------+----------+------------+
|4.159397303727201|        24|        1261|
+-----------------+----------+------------+
```

WINDOW FUNCTIONS

Window functions are comparable to aggregate functions. The main difference is that they don't group rows into a single output row per group. They let you define a "moving group" of rows, called *frames*, which are somehow related to the current row and can be used in calculations on the current row. You can use window functions to calculate moving averages or cumulative sums, for example. These are calculations that typically require subselects or complex joins to accomplish. Window functions make them much simpler and easier.

When you want to use window functions, start by constructing a `Column` definition with an aggregate function (`min`, `max`, `sum`, `avg`, `count`) or with one of the functions listed in table 5.1. Then build a window specification (`WindowSpec` object) and use it as an argument to the column's `over` function. The `over` function defines a column that uses the specified window specification.

Table 5.1   Ranking and analytic functions that can be used as window functions

Function name	Description
`first (column)`	Returns the value in the first row in the frame.
`last (column)`	Returns the value in the last row in the frame.
`lag (column, offset, [default])`	Returns the value in the row that is `offset` rows behind the row in the frame. Use `default` if such a row doesn't exist.
`lead (column, offset, [default])`	Returns the value in the row that is `offset` rows before the row in the frame. Use `default` if such a row doesn't exist.
`ntile (n)`	Divides the frame into n parts and returns the part index of the row. If the number of rows in the frame isn't divisible by n and division gives a number between x and x+1, the resulting parts will contain x or x+1 rows, with parts containing x+1 rows coming first.
`cumeDist`	Calculates the fraction of rows in the frame whose value is less than or equal to the value in the row being processed.
`rank`	Returns the rank of the row in the frame (first, second, and so on). Rank is calculated by the value.
`denseRank`	Returns the rank of the row in the frame (first, second, and so on), but puts the rows with equal values in the same rank.
`percentRank`	Returns the rank of the row divided by the number of rows in the frame.
`rowNumber`	Returns the sequential number of the row in the frame.

The window specification is built using the static methods in the `org.apache.spark` `.sql.expressions.Window` class. You need to specify one or more columns that define the partition (the same principles apply as with aggregate functions) using the `partitionBy` function, or specify ordering in the partition (assuming the partition is the entire dataset) using the `orderBy` function, or you can do both.

You can further restrict which rows appear in frames by using the `rowsBetween(from, to)` and `rangeBetween(from, to)` functions. The `rowsBetween` function restricts rows by their row index, where index 0 is the row being processed, -1 is the previous row, and so on. The `rangeBetween` function restricts rows by their values and includes only those rows whose values (in the defined column to which the window specification applies) fall in the defined range.

This is a lot of information, so we'll illustrate with two examples using the `postsDf` DataFrame. First, you'll display the maximum score of all user questions (post type ID 1), and for each question, how much its score is below the maximum score for that user. As you can probably imagine, without window functions, this would require a complicated query.

To use window functions, first import the `Window` class:

```
import org.apache.spark.sql.expressions.Window
```

If you filter the posts by type, then you can select the maximum score among other columns. When using the window specification for partitioning rows by the question owner, the `max` function applies only to user questions in the current row. You can then add a column (called `toMax` in the example) to display the difference in points between the current question's score and the user's maximum score:

```
scala> postsDf.filter('postTypeId === 1).
  select('ownerUserId, 'acceptedAnswerId, 'score, max('score).
    over(Window.partitionBy('ownerUserId)) as "maxPerUser").
  withColumn("toMax", 'maxPerUser - 'score).show(10)
+-----------+----------------+-----+----------+-----+
|ownerUserId|acceptedAnswerId|score|maxPerUser|toMax|
+-----------+----------------+-----+----------+-----+
|        232|            2185|    6|         6|    0|
|        833|            2277|    4|         4|    0|
|        833|            null|    1|         4|    3|
|        235|            2004|   10|        10|    0|
|        835|            2280|    3|         3|    0|
|         37|            null|    4|        13|    9|
|         37|            null|   13|        13|    0|
|         37|            2313|    8|        13|    5|
|         37|              20|   13|        13|    0|
|         37|            null|    4|        13|    9|
+-----------+----------------+-----+----------+-----+
```

For the second example, you'll display, for each question, the `id` of its owner's next and previous questions by creation date. Again, first filter posts by their type to get only the questions. Then use the `lag` and `lead` functions to reference the previous and the next rows in the frame. The window specification is the same for both columns: partitioning needs to be done by user, and the questions in the frame need to be ordered by creation date. Finally, order the entire dataset by owner user ID and question ID to make the results clearly apparent:

```
scala> postsDf.filter('postTypeId === 1).
  select('ownerUserId, 'id, 'creationDate,
    lag('id, 1).over(
      Window.partitionBy('ownerUserId).orderBy('creationDate)) as "prev",
    lead('id, 1).over(
```

```
        Window.partitionBy('ownerUserId).orderBy('creationDate)) as "next").
    orderBy('ownerUserId, 'id).show(10)
+-----------+----+--------------------+----------+
|ownerUserId|  id|        creationDate|prev| next|
+-----------+----+--------------------+----------+
|          4|1637|2014-01-24 06:51:...|null| null|
|          8|   1|2013-11-05 20:22:...|null|  112|
|          8| 112|2013-11-08 13:14:...|   1| 1192|
|          8|1192|2013-11-11 21:01:...| 112| 1276|
|          8|1276|2013-11-15 16:09:...|1192| 1321|
|          8|1321|2013-11-20 16:42:...|1276| 1365|
|          8|1365|2013-11-23 09:09:...|1321| null|
|         12|  11|2013-11-05 21:30:...|null|   17|
|         12|  17|2013-11-05 22:17:...|  11|   18|
|         12|  18|2013-11-05 22:34:...|  17|   19|
+-----------+----+--------------------+----+-----+
```

If you need to write a similar SQL query, we're confident you'll know how to appreciate the power and simplicity of window functions.

In the previous sections, we covered only some of the SQL functions Spark supports. We encourage you to explore all the available functions at http://mng.bz/849V.

USER-DEFINED FUNCTIONS

In many situations, Spark SQL may not provide the specific functionality you need in a particular moment. UDFs let you extend the built-in functionalities of Spark SQL.

For example, there's no built-in function that can help you find how many tags each question has. Tags are stored as concatenated tag names surrounded by angle brackets. The angle brackets are encoded so they appear as < and > instead of < and > (for example, the translation tag appears as <translation>). You can calculate the number of tags by counting occurrences of the string "<" in the tags column, but there are no built-in functions for this.

UDFs are created using the udf function (accessible from the functions object) by passing to it the function with the required logic. Each UDF takes zero or more columns (the maximum is 10) and returns the final value. In this case, all occurrences of a string in another one can be found with Scala's regular expressions (r.findAllMatchIn):

```
scala> val countTags = udf((tags: String) =>
  "&lt;".r.findAllMatchIn(tags).length)
countTags: org.apache.spark.sql.UserDefinedFunction = ...
```

Another way of accomplishing the same thing is using the SparkSession.udf.register function:

```
scala> val countTags = spark.udf.register("countTags",
    (tags: String) => "&lt;".r.findAllMatchIn(tags).length)
```

This way, the UDF gets registered with a name that can be also used in SQL expressions (covered in section 5.2).

Now that the `countTags` UDF is defined, it can be used to produce a `Column` definition for the `select` statement (the output was truncated to fit on the page):

```
scala> postsDf.filter('postTypeId === 1).
  select('tags, countTags('tags) as "tagCnt").show(10, false)
+----------------------------------------------------------------+------+
|tags                                                            |tagCnt|
+----------------------------------------------------------------+------+
|&lt;word-choice&gt;                                             |1     |
|&lt;english-comparison&gt;&lt;translation&gt;&lt;phrase-request&gt|3     |
|&lt;usage&gt;&lt;verbs&gt;                                      |2     |
|&lt;usage&gt;&lt;tenses&gt;&lt;english-comparison&gt;           |3     |
|&lt;usage&gt;&lt;punctuation&gt;                                |2     |
|&lt;usage&gt;&lt;tenses&gt;                                     |2     |
|&lt;history&gt;&lt;english-comparison&gt;                       |2     |
|&lt;idioms&gt;&lt;etymology&gt;                                 |2     |
|&lt;idioms&gt;&lt;regional&gt;                                  |2     |
|&lt;grammar&gt;                                                 |1     |
+----------------------------------------------------------------+------+
```

The `false` flag tells the `show` method not to truncate the strings in columns (the default is to truncate them to 20 characters).

5.1.4 *Working with missing values*

Sometimes you may need to clean your data before using it. It might contain `null` or empty values, or equivalent string constants (for example, "N/A" or "unknown"). In those instances, the `DataFrameNaFunctions` class, accessible through the `DataFrames` na field, may prove useful. Depending on your case, you can choose to *drop* the rows containing `null` or `NaN` (the Scala constant meaning "not a number") values, to *fill* null *or* NaN *values* with constants, or to *replace certain values* with string or numeric constants.

Each of these methods has several versions. For example, to remove all the rows from `postsDf` that contain `null` or `NaN` values in at least one of their columns, call drop with no arguments:

```
scala> val cleanPosts = postsDf.na.drop()
scala> cleanPosts.count()
res0: Long = 222
```

This is the same as calling `drop("any")`, which means `null` values can be in any of the columns. If you use `drop("all")`, it removes rows that have `null` values in all of the columns. You can also specify column names. For example, to remove the rows that don't have an accepted answer ID, you can do this:

```
postsDf.na.drop(Array("acceptedAnswerId"))
```

With the `fill` function, you can replace `null` and `NaN` values with a constant. The constant can be a double or a string value. If you specify only one argument, that argument is used as the constant value for all the columns. You can also specify the columns in the second argument. There is a third option: to specify `Map`, mapping column names to replacement values. For example, you can replace `null` values in the `viewCount` column with zeroes using the following expression:

```
postsDf.na.fill(Map("viewCount" -> 0))
```

Finally, the `replace` function enables you to replace certain values in specific columns with different ones. For example, imagine there was a mistake in your data export and you needed to change post ID 1177 to 3000. You can do that with the `replace` function:

```
val postsDfCorrected = postsDf.na.
    replace(Array("id", "acceptedAnswerId"), Map(1177 -> 3000))
```

5.1.5 *Converting DataFrames to RDDs*

You've seen how to create a `DataFrame` from an RDD. Now we'll show you how to do the reverse. `DataFrame`s are based on RDDs, so getting an RDD from a `DataFrame` isn't complicated. Every `DataFrame` has the lazily evaluated `rdd` field for accessing the underlying RDD:

```
scala> val postsRdd = postsDf.rdd
postsRdd: org.apache.spark.rdd.RDD[org.apache.spark.sql.Row] = ...
```

The resulting RDD contains elements of type `org.apache.spark.sql.Row`, the same class used in section 5.1.1 to convert an RDD to a `DataFrame` by specifying a schema (`stringToRow` function). `Row` has various `get*` functions for accessing column values by column indexes (`getString(index)`, `getInt(index)`, `getMap(index)`, and so forth. It also has a useful function for converting rows to strings (mimicking a similar function available for Scala sequences): `mkString(delimiter)`.

Mapping `DataFrame`'s data and partitions with `map`, `flatMap`, and `mapPartitions` transformations is done directly on the underlying `rdd` field. Naturally, they return a new RDD and not a `DataFrame`. Everything we said about those transformations in the last chapter applies here also, with an additional constraint that the functions you pass to them need to work with `Row` objects.

These transformations can change the `DataFrame`'s (RDD's) schema. They can change the order, number, or type of the columns. Or they can convert `Row` objects to some other type. So, automatic conversion back to a `DataFrame` isn't possible. If you don't change the `DataFrame`'s schema, you can use the old schema to create a new `DataFrame`.

As an exercise, let's replace those nasty-looking `&lt;` and `&gt;` strings with `<` and `>` symbols in the `body` (index 3) and `tags` (index 8) columns. You can map each row to a `Seq` object, use the `Seq` object's `updated` method to replace its elements, map the `Seq` back to a `Row` object, and finally use the old schema to create a new `DataFrame`. The following lines accomplish this:

```
val postsMapped = postsDf.rdd.map(row => Row.fromSeq(
  row.toSeq.
    updated(3, row.getString(3).replace("&lt;","<").replace("&gt;",">")).
    updated(8, row.getString(8).replace("&lt;","<").replace("&gt;",">")))))
val postsDfNew = spark.createDataFrame(postsMapped, postsDf.schema)
```

Typically there's no need to convert DataFrames to RDDs and back because most data-mapping tasks can be done with built-in DSL and SQL functions and UTFs.

5.1.6   *Grouping and joining data*

Grouping data is straightforward with DataFrames. If you understand the SQL GROUP BY clause, you'll have no trouble understanding grouping data with DataFrames. It starts with the groupBy function, which expects a list of column names or a list of Column objects and returns a GroupedData object.

GroupedData represents groups of rows that have the same values in the columns specified when calling groupBy, and it offers standard aggregation functions (count, sum, max, min, and avg) for aggregating across the groups. Each of these functions returns a DataFrame with the specified columns and an additional column containing the aggregated data.

To find the number of posts per author, associated tags, and the post type, use the following (treating each combination of tags as a unique value):

```
scala> postsDfNew.groupBy('ownerUserId, 'tags,
    'postTypeId).count.orderBy('ownerUserId desc).show(10)
+-----------+--------------------+----------+-----+
|ownerUserId|                tags|postTypeId|count|
+-----------+--------------------+----------+-----+
|        862|                    |         2|    1|
|        855|         <resources>|         1|    1|
|        846|<translation><eng...|         1|    1|
|        845|<word-meaning><tr...|         1|    1|
|        842|  <verbs><resources>|         1|    1|
|        835|    <grammar><verbs>|         1|    1|
|        833|                    |         2|    1|
|        833|           <meaning>|         1|    1|
|        833|<meaning><article...|         1|    1|
|        814|                    |         2|    1|
+-----------+--------------------+----------+-----+
```

You can perform several aggregations on different columns with the agg function. It can take one or more column expressions using aggregate functions from org.apache.spark.sql.functions (which you used in section 5.1.3) or a map with column names to function name mappings. To find the last activity date and the maximum post score per user, you can use the following two expressions, which accomplish the same result:

```
scala> postsDfNew.groupBy('ownerUserId).
  agg(max('lastActivityDate), max('score)).show(10)
scala> postsDfNew.groupBy('ownerUserId).
  agg(Map("lastActivityDate" -> "max", "score" -> "max")).show(10)
```

They both show the same output:

```
+-----------+--------------------+----------+
|ownerUserId|max(lastActivityDate)|max(score)|
+-----------+--------------------+----------+
|        431| 2014-02-16 14:16:...|         1|
|        232| 2014-08-18 20:25:...|         6|
|        833| 2014-09-03 19:53:...|         4|
|        633| 2014-05-15 22:22:...|         1|
|        634| 2014-05-27 09:22:...|         6|
|        234| 2014-07-12 17:56:...|         5|
|        235| 2014-08-28 19:30:...|        10|
|        435| 2014-02-18 13:10:...|        -2|
|        835| 2014-08-26 15:35:...|         3|
|         37| 2014-09-13 13:29:...|        23|
+-----------+--------------------+----------+
```

The former method is more powerful, however, because it enables you to chain column expressions. For example:

```
scala> postsDfNew.groupBy('ownerUserId).
  agg(max('lastActivityDate), max('score).gt(5)).show(10)
+-----------+--------------------+---------------+
|ownerUserId|max(lastActivityDate)|(max(score) > 5)|
+-----------+--------------------+---------------+
|        431| 2014-02-16 14:16:...|          false|
|        232| 2014-08-18 20:25:...|           true|
|        833| 2014-09-03 19:53:...|          false|
|        633| 2014-05-15 22:22:...|          false|
|        634| 2014-05-27 09:22:...|           true|
|        234| 2014-07-12 17:56:...|          false|
|        235| 2014-08-28 19:30:...|           true|
|        435| 2014-02-18 13:10:...|          false|
|        835| 2014-08-26 15:35:...|          false|
|         37| 2014-09-13 13:29:...|           true|
+-----------+--------------------+---------------+
```

USER-DEFINED AGGREGATE FUNCTIONS

In addition to the built-in aggregate functions, Spark SQL lets you define your own. We don't elaborate much on this because the scope of this chapter doesn't allow us to go into detail. A general approach is to create a class that extends the abstract class `org.apache.spark.sql.expressions.UserDefinedAggregateFunction`, then define input and buffer schemas, and finally implement the initialize, update, merge, and evaluate functions. For details, see the official documentation at http://mng.bz/Gbt3 and a Java example at http://mng.bz/5bOb.

ROLLUP AND CUBE

Data grouping and aggregation can be done with two additional flavors called `rollup` and `cube`. You saw that `groupBy` calculates aggregate values for all combinations of data values in the selected columns; `cube` and `rollup` also calculate the aggregates for subsets of the selected columns. The difference between the two is that `rollup` respects the hierarchy of the input columns and always groups by the first column.

An example will make this much clearer. You'll select a subset of the dataset because the difference between these functions isn't obvious on a large dataset. Begin by selecting the posts from only a couple of users:

```scala
scala> val smplDf = postsDfNew.where('ownerUserId >= 13 and 'ownerUserId <= 15)
```

Counting the posts by owner, tags, and post type (by chance, all the tags are empty and all the post types are 2) gives the following result:

```scala
scala> smplDf.groupBy('ownerUserId, 'tags, 'postTypeId).count.show()
+-----------+----+----------+-----+
|ownerUserId|tags|postTypeId|count|
+-----------+----+----------+-----+
|         15|    |         2|    2|
|         14|    |         2|    2|
|         13|    |         2|    1|
+-----------+----+----------+-----+
```

The `rollup` and `cube` functions, used just like `groupBy`, are also accessible from the `DataFrame` class. The `rollup` function returns the same results but adds subtotals per owner (tags and post type are `null`), per owner and tags (post type is `null`), and the grand total (all `null` values):

```scala
scala> smplDf.rollup('ownerUserId, 'tags, 'postTypeId).count.show()
+-----------+----+----------+-----+
|ownerUserId|tags|postTypeId|count|
+-----------+----+----------+-----+
|         15|    |         2|    2|
|         13|    |      null|    1|
|         13|null|      null|    1|
|         14|    |      null|    2|
|         13|    |         2|    1|
|         14|null|      null|    2|
|         15|    |      null|    2|
|         14|    |         2|    2|
|         15|null|      null|    2|
|       null|null|      null|    5|
+-----------+----+----------+-----+
```

The `cube` function returns all of these results, but also adds other possible subtotals (per post type, per tags, per post type and tags, per post type and user). We'll omit the results here for brevity, but you can find them in our online repository, and you can produce them in your Spark shell yourself.

Configuring Spark SQL

How to configure Spark SQL is essential when working with `DataFrame`s DSL or using SQL commands. You'll find details about configuring Spark in general in chapter 10. Although Spark's main configuration can't be changed during runtime, the Spark SQL configuration can. Spark SQL has a separate set of parameters that affect the execution of `DataFrame` operations and SQL commands.

You can set Spark SQL parameters with the SQL command `SET` (`SET <parameter _name>=<parameter_value>`) or by calling the `set` method of the `RuntimeConfig` object available from `SparkSession`'s `conf` field. `set` accepts a single parameter name and a value (a String, Boolean, or Long). So, these two lines are equivalent:

```
spark.sql("SET spark.sql.caseSensitive=true")
spark.conf.set("spark.sql.caseSensitive", "true")
```

By the way, this parameter enables case sensitivity for query analysis (table and column names), which is something Hive doesn't support natively but Spark SQL does, even when using Hive support.

Another configuration parameter to note is `spark.sql.eagerAnalysis`, which tells Spark whether to evaluate `DataFrame` expressions eagerly. If set to `true`, Spark throws an exception as soon as you mention a non-existent column in a `DataFrame`, instead of waiting for you to perform an action on the `DataFrame` that fetches the results.

We mention several more important parameters in the following sections.

5.1.7 Performing joins

Often you may have related data in two `DataFrame`s that you want to join so the resulting `DataFrame` contains rows from both `DataFrame`s with values common to both. We showed you how to perform joins on RDDs in the previous chapter. Performing them with `DataFrame`s isn't much different.

When calling the `join` function, you need to provide the `DataFrame` to be joined and one or more column names or a column definition. If you use column names, they need to be present in both `DataFrame`s. If they aren't, you can always use column definitions. When using a column definition, you can also pass a third argument specifying the join type (`inner`, `outer`, `left_outer`, `right_outer`, or `leftsemi`).

An important note about performance

One hidden but important parameter is `spark.sql.shuffle.partitions`, which determines the number of partitions a `DataFrame` should have after a shuffle is performed (for example, after a join). As of Spark 1.5.1, the default is 200, which could be too much or too little for your use case and your environment. For the examples in this book, you don't need more than 5 to 10 partitions. But if your dataset is huge, 200 may be too small. If you wish to change the number of partitions, you can set this parameter before performing the action that will trigger the shuffle.

> **(continued)**
> This isn't an ideal situation, however, because the number of DataFrame partitions
> shouldn't be fixed, but should depend on the data and runtime environment instead.
> There are two JIRA tickets (https://issues.apache.org/jira/browse/SPARK-9872 and
> https://issues.apache.org/jira/browse/SPARK-9850) documenting this and propos-
> ing solutions, so the situation will probably change in a future Spark release.

As an example, load the italianVotes.csv file from our online GitHub repository
(which should already be cloned in the first-edition folder), and load it into a Data-
Frame with the following code:

```
val itVotesRaw = sc.textFile("first-edition/ch05/italianVotes.csv").
  map(x => x.split("~"))
val itVotesRows = itVotesRaw.map(row => Row(row(0).toLong, row(1).toLong,
  row(2).toInt, Timestamp.valueOf(row(3))))
val votesSchema = StructType(Seq(
  StructField("id", LongType, false),
  StructField("postId", LongType, false),
  StructField("voteTypeId", IntegerType, false),
  StructField("creationDate", TimestampType, false)) )
val votesDf = spark.createDataFrame(itVotesRows, votesSchema)
```

Joining the two DataFrames on the postId column can be done like this:

```
val postsVotes = postsDf.join(votesDf, postsDf("id") === 'postId)
```

This performs an inner join. You can perform an outer join by adding another
argument:

```
val postsVotesOuter = postsDf.join(votesDf,
  postsDf("id") === 'postId, "outer")
```

If you examine the contents of the postsVotesOuter DataFrame, you'll notice there
are some rows with all null values in the votes columns. These are the posts that have
no votes. Note that you have to tell Spark SQL exactly which id column you're referencing by creating the Column object from the DataFrame object. postId is unique
across both DataFrames, so you can resort to the simpler syntax and create the Column
object by using implicit conversion from Scala's Symbol.

If you'd like to experiment more, you can use other CSV files from the Italian language dataset in our online repository. They contain data about badges, comments,
post history, post links, tags, and users.

5.2 *Beyond DataFrames: introducing DataSets*

DataSets, introduced in Spark 1.6.0 as an experimental feature, graduated into a
pivotal construct in Spark 2.0. The idea behind DataSets "is to provide an API that
allows users to easily express transformations on domain objects, while also

providing the performance and robustness advantages of the Spark SQL execution engine" (https://issues.apache.org/jira/browse/SPARK-9999). That essentially means that you can store ordinary Java objects in `DataSets` and take advantage of Tungsten and Catalyst optimizations.

`DataSets` represent a competition to `RDDs` in a way because they have overlapping functions. Another path the Spark community could have taken was to change the RDD API to include the new features and optimizations. But that would break the API and too many existing applications would need to be changed, so it was decided against that.

`DataFrames` are now simply implemented as `DataSets` containing `Row` objects.

To convert a `DataFrame` to a `DataSet`, you use `DataFrame`'s as method:

```
def as[U : Encoder]: Dataset[U]
```

As you can see, you need to provide an `Encoder` object, which tells Spark how to interpret the `DataSet`'s contents. Most Java and Scala primitive types, such as `String`, `Int`, and so on, are implicitly converted to `Encoders`, so you don't need to do anything special to create a `DataSet` containing `Strings` or `Doubles`:

```
val stringDataSet = spark.read.text("path/to/file").as[String]
```

You can write your own encoders or you can use encoders for ordinary Java bean classes. Fields of the bean class need to be primitive types (or their boxed versions, such as `Integer` or `Double`), `BigDecimals`, `Date` or `Timestamp` objects, arrays, lists, or nested Java beans.

You can manipulate `DataSet`'s columns, as you did with `DataFrames` in this chapter. If you look at `DataSet` documentation {http://mng.bz/3EQc} you will also see many transformations and actions familiar from both `RDD` and `DataFrame` APIs.

`DataSets` will surely improve in future versions of Spark and will integrate more fully with other parts of Spark. So keep an eye on them.

5.3   *Using SQL commands*

The `DataFrame` DSL functionalities presented in the previous sections are also accessible through SQL commands as an alternative interface for programming Spark SQL. Writing SQL is probably easier and more natural to users who are used to working with relational databases, or distributed databases, such as Hive.

When you write SQL commands in Spark SQL, they get translated into operations on `DataFrames`. Because SQL is so widespread, using SQL commands opens Spark SQL and `DataFrames` for use by users who have only an SQL interface at their disposal. They can connect to Spark from their applications through standard JDBC or ODBC protocols by connecting to Spark's Thrift server (we'll talk about it in a bit). In this section, you'll learn how to perform SQL queries referencing your `DataFrames` and how you can enable users to connect to your Spark cluster through the Thrift server.

Spark supports two SQL dialects: Spark's SQL dialect and Hive Query Language (HQL). The Spark community recommends HQL (Spark 1.5) because HQL has a richer set of functionalities. To use Hive functionalities, you need a Spark distribution built with Hive support (which is the case with archives downloaded from the main Spark download page). In addition to bringing a more powerful SQL parser, Hive support lets you access existing Hive tables and use existing, community-built Hive UDFs.

Hive functionalities are enabled in Spark by calling enableHiveSupport() on a Builder object while constructing a SparkSession. If you're using a Spark distribution with Hive support, the Spark shell automatically detects this and enables Hive functionality. In your programs, you would enable it yourself:

```
val spark = SparkSession.builder().
    enableHiveSupport().
    getOrCreate()
```

5.3.1 *Table catalog and Hive metastore*

As you probably know, most SQL operations operate on tables referenced by name. When executing SQL queries using Spark SQL, you can reference a DataFrame by its name by registering the DataFrame as a table. When you do that, Spark stores the table definition in the *table catalog*.

For Spark without Hive support, a table catalog is implemented as a simple in-memory map, which means that table information lives in the driver's memory and disappears with the Spark session. SparkSession with Hive support, on the other hand, uses a Hive metastore for implementing the table catalog. A Hive metastore is a persistent database, so DataFrame definitions remain available even if you close the Spark session and start a new one.

REGISTERING TABLES TEMPORARILY

Hive support still enables you to create temporary table definitions. In both cases (Spark with or without Hive support), the createOrReplaceTempView method registers a temporary table. You can register the postsDf DataFrames like this:

```
postsDf.createOrReplaceTempView("posts_temp")
```

Now you'll be able to query data from postsDf DataFrame using SQL queries referencing the DataFrame by the name posts_temp. We'll show you how to do that in a jiffy.

REGISTERING TABLES PERMANENTLY

As we said, only SparkSession with Hive support can be used to register table definitions that will survive your application's restarts (in other words, they're persistent). By default, HiveContext creates a Derby database in the local working directory under the metastore_db subdirectory (or it reuses the database if it already exists). If you wish to change where the working directory is located, set the hive.metastore.warehouse.dir property in your hive-site.xml file (details shortly).

To register a `DataFrame` as a permanent table, you need to use its `write` member. Using the `postsDf` and `votesDf` DataFrames as an example again:

```
postsDf.write.saveAsTable("posts")
votesDf.write.saveAsTable("votes")
```

After you save DataFrames to a Hive metastore like this, you can subsequently use them in SQL expressions.

WORKING WITH THE SPARK TABLE CATALOG

Since version 2.0, Spark provides a facility for managing the table catalog. It is implemented as the `Catalog` class, accessible through `SparkSession`'s `catalog` field. You can use it to see which tables are currently registered:

```
scala> spark.catalog.listTables().show()
+----------+--------+-----------+---------+-----------+
|      name|database|description|tableType|isTemporary|
+----------+--------+-----------+---------+-----------+
|     posts| default|       null|  MANAGED|      false|
|     votes| default|       null|  MANAGED|      false|
|posts_temp|    null|       null|TEMPORARY|       true|
+----------+--------+-----------+---------+-----------+
```

You can use the `show()` method here because `listTables` returns a `DataSet` of `Table` objects. You can immediately see which tables are permanent and which are temporary (`isTemporary` column). The MANAGED table type means that Spark also manages the data for the table. The table can also be EXTERNAL, which means that its data is managed by another system, for example a RDBMS.

Tables are registered in metastore "databases." The default database, called "default," stores managed tables in the spark_warehouse subfolder in your home directory. You can change that location by setting the `spark.sql.warehouse.dir` parameter to the desired value.

You can also use the `Catalog` object to examine the columns of a specific table:

```
scala> spark.catalog.listColumns("votes").show()
+------------+-----------+---------+--------+-----------+--------+
|        name|description| dataType|nullable|isPartition|isBucket|
+------------+-----------+---------+--------+-----------+--------+
|          id|       null|   bigint|    true|      false|   false|
|      postid|       null|   bigint|    true|      false|   false|
|   votetypeid|      null|      int|    true|      false|   false|
|creationdate|       null|timestamp|    true|      false|   false|
+------------+-----------+---------+--------+-----------+--------+
```

To get a list of all available SQL functions call:

```
scala> spark.catalog.listFunctions.show()
```

You can also manage which tables are cached in memory, and which are not, with the `cacheTable`, `uncacheTable`, `isCached`, and `clearCache` methods.

CONFIGURING A REMOTE HIVE METASTORE

You can also configure Spark to use a remote Hive metastore database. This can be a metastore database of an existing Hive installation or a new database to be used exclusively by Spark. This configuration is done by placing the Hive configuration file hive-site.xml, with the appropriate configuration parameters, in Spark's conf directory. This will override the `spark.sql.warehouse.dir` parameter.

The hive-site.xml file must contain a `configuration` tag with `property` tags in it. Each `property` tag has `name` and `value` subtags. For example:

```
<?xml version="1.0"?>
<?xml-stylesheet type="text/xsl" href="configuration.xsl"?>
<configuration>
<property>
  <name>hive.metastore.warehouse.dir</name>
  <value>/hive/metastore/directory</value>
</property>
</configuration>
```

To configure Spark to use a remote Hive metastore, these properties need to be in the hive-site.xml file:

- `javax.jdo.option.ConnectionURL`—JDBC connection URL
- `javax.jdo.option.ConnectionDriverName`—Class name of the JDBC driver
- `javax.jdo.option.ConnectionUserName`—Database username
- `javax.jdo.option.ConnectionPassword`—Database user password

The connection URL must point to an existing database containing Hive tables. To initialize the metastore database and create the necessary tables, you can use Hive's `schematool`. Please consult the Hive official documentation (http://mng.bz/3HJ5) on how to use it.

The JDBC driver you specify must be in the classpath of the driver and all executors. The easiest way to do this is to supply JAR files with the `--jars` option while submitting your application or starting your Spark shell.

5.3.2 Executing SQL queries

Now that you have a `DataFrame` registered as a table, you can query its data using SQL expressions. This is done with `SparkSession`'s `sql` function. In a Spark shell, it's automatically imported (`import spark.sql`), so you can use it directly for writing SQL commands:

```
val resultDf = sql("select * from posts")
```

The result is again a `DataFrame`. All the data manipulations performed with `DataFrame` DSL in the previous sections can also be done through SQL, but Spark SQL offers more options. When using a `SparkSession` with Hive support, which is the recommended Spark SQL engine, the majority of Hive commands and data types are supported. For example, with SQL you can use DDL commands, such as `ALTER TABLE` and `DROP TABLE`. You can find the complete list of supported Hive features in the Spark documentation (http://mng.bz/8AFz). We won't list them here, but you can find the details in the Hive language manual (http://mng.bz/x7k2).

USING THE SPARK SQL SHELL

In addition to the Spark shell, Spark also offers an SQL shell in the form of the `spark-sql` command, which supports the same arguments as the `spark-shell` and `spark-submit` commands (for details, see chapters 10 and 11) but adds some of its own. When run without arguments, it starts an SQL shell in local mode. At the shell prompt, you can enter the same SQL commands you would using the `sql` command you used in the previous sections.

For example, to show the titles (cropped to 70 characters so they fit on this page) of the three most recent questions from the posts table you permanently saved earlier, enter the following at the Spark SQL shell prompt (you'll need to stop your Spark shell first to avoid locking on the same Derby metastore):

```
spark-sql> select substring(title, 0, 70) from posts where
  postTypeId = 1 order by creationDate desc limit 3;
Verbo impersonale che regge verbo impersonale: costruzione implicita?
Perch?Š si chiama &quot;saracinesca&quot; la chiusura metallica scorren
Perch?Š a volte si scrive l'accento acuto sulla &quot;i&quot; o sulla &
Time taken: 0.375 seconds, Fetched 3 row(s)
```

> **NOTE** In the SQL shell, you need to terminate SQL expressions with semicolons (`;`).

You can also run a single SQL query without entering the shell with the `-e` argument. In this case, you don't need a semicolon. For example:

```
$ spark-sql -e "select substring(title, 0, 70) from posts where
➥ postTypeId= 1 order by creationDate desc limit 3"
```

And to run a file with SQL commands, specify it with the `-f` argument. The i argument enables you to specify an initialization SQL file to run before any other SQL command. Again, you can use the data files in our online repository to play around with Spark SQL and further examine the API.

5.3.3 Connecting to Spark SQL through the Thrift server

In addition to executing SQL queries directly from your programs or through a SQL shell, Spark also lets you run SQL commands remotely, through a JDBC (and ODBC) server called Thrift.[3] JDBC (and ODBC) is a standard way of accessing relational

---

[3] Spark's Thrift server is based on Hive's server of the same name.

databases, which means the Thrift server opens Spark for use by any application capable of communicating with relational databases.

The Thrift server is a special Spark application, capable of accepting JDBC and ODBC connections from multiple users and executing their queries in a Spark SQL session. It runs in a Spark cluster, like any Spark application. SQL queries get translated to `DataFrames` and, finally, RDD operations (as we discussed previously), and the results are sent back over the JDBC protocol. `DataFrames` referenced by the queries must be permanently registered in the Hive metastore used by the Thrift server.

STARTING A THRIFT SERVER

You start a Thrift server with the `start-thriftserver.sh` command from Spark's sbin directory. You can pass to it the same arguments as those accepted by the `spark-shell` and `spark-submit` commands (for details, see chapters 10 and 11). If you set up a remote metastore database, you can tell the Thrift server where to find the JAR with the JDBC driver to access the database using the `--jars` argument. If your remote metastore database is PostgreSQL, you can start the Thrift server like this:

```
$ sbin/start-thriftserver.sh --jars /usr/share/java/postgresql-jdbc4.jar
```

This script starts a Thrift server in the background and then exits. The default Thrift server port is 10000. You can change the listening port and host name of the Thrift server either with the environment variables `HIVE_SERVER2_THRIFT_PORT` and `HIVE_SERVER2_THRIFT_BIND_HOST` (both are needed) or with the `hive.server2 .thrift.port` and `hive.server2.thrift.bind.host` Hive configuration variables, which you specify using the `--hiveconf` parameters when starting the server.

CONNECTING TO THE THRIFT SERVER WITH BEELINE

Beeline is Hive's command-line shell for connecting to a Thrift server, available in Spark's bin directory. You can use it to test the connection to the Thrift server you just started. You need to provide the JDBC URL to the server and, optionally, a username and a password:

```
$ beeline -u jdbc:hive2://<server_name>:<port> -n <username> -p <password>
Connecting to jdbc:hive2://<server_name>:<port>
Connected to: Spark SQL (version 1.5.0)
Driver: Spark Project Core (version 1.5.0)
Transaction isolation: TRANSACTION_REPEATABLE_READ
Beeline version 1.5.0 by Apache Hive
0: jdbc:hive2://<server_name>:<port>>
```

Once connected to the server, Beeline shows its command prompt, where you can enter HQL commands for interacting with the tables in your Hive metastore.

CONNECTING FROM THIRD-PARTY JDBC CLIENTS

As an example of a JDBC client, we'll use Squirrel SQL, an open source Java SQL client. We're using Squirrel SQL to show you the typical steps and configuration needed for connecting to Spark's Thrift server, but you can use any other JDBC client.

Figure 5.2   Defining a Hive driver in Squirrel SQL as an example of a JDBC client connecting to Spark's Thrift server. You need to provide the driver name and classpath. hive-jdbc-<version>-standalone.jar and hadoop-common-<version>.jar are the only JAR files needed for a successful connection.

To connect to your Thrift server from Squirrel SQL, you define a Hive *driver* and an *alias*. Driver definition parameters are shown in figure 5.2. The two JAR files needed in the classpath are hive-jdbc-<version>-standalone.jar and hadoop-common-<version>.jar. The former is part of the Hive distribution (from the lib folder), and the latter can be found in the Hadoop distribution (in the share/hadoop/common folder).

The next step is to define an alias using the defined Hive driver. Figure 5.3 shows the parameters needed: alias name, URL, username, and password. The URL needs to be in the format jdbc:hive2://<*hostname*>:<*port*>.

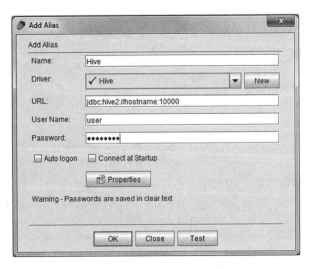

Figure 5.3   Defining an alias for the Thrift server connection in Squirrel SQL as an example of a JDBC client. You need to select the driver defined previously and enter a URL in the format jdbc:hive:// <*hostname*>:<*port*>, a username, and a password.

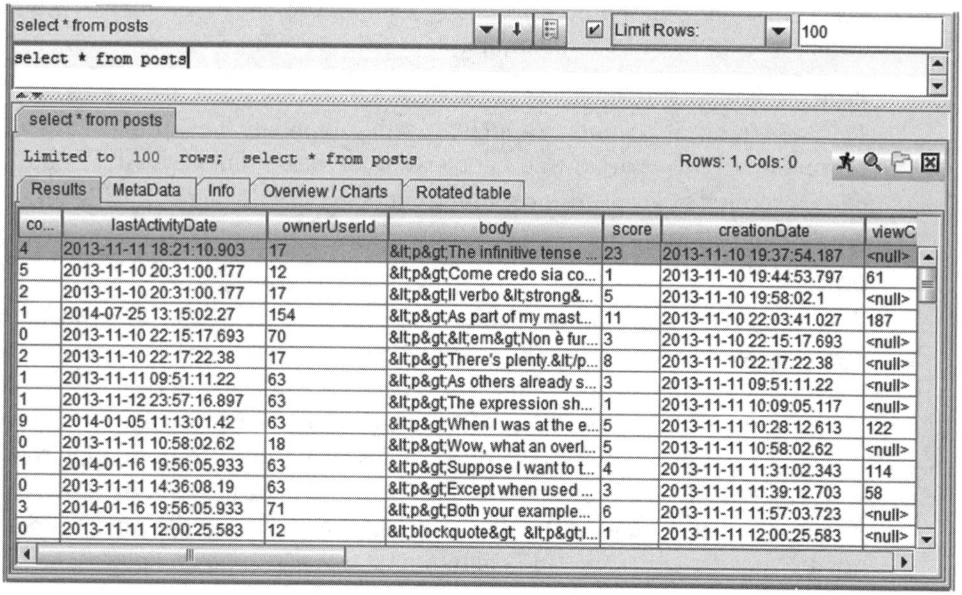

Figure 5.4   Selecting the contents of the `posts` table through the Thrift server using Squirrel SQL, an open source JDBC client program

And that's all the configuration you need. When you connect to the Thrift server, you can enter SQL queries in the SQL tab. An example is shown in figure 5.4. This is a convenient way of connecting your usual visualization and analytical tools to your distributed data through Spark.

5.4   Saving and loading DataFrame data

Spark has built-in support for several file formats and databases (generally called data sources in Spark). These include JDBC and Hive, which we mentioned earlier, and the JSON, ORC, and Parquet file formats. For relational databases, Spark specifically supports *dialects* (meaning data-type mappings) for the MySQL and PostgreSQL databases.

Data sources are pluggable, so you can add your own implementations. And you can download and use some external data, such as the CSV (https://github.com/databricks/spark-csv), Avro (https://github.com/databricks/spark-avro), and Amazon Redshift (https://github.com/databricks/spark-redshift) data sources.

Spark uses the metastore, which we covered in the previous section, to save information about where and how the data is stored. It uses data sources for saving and loading the actual data.

5.4.1   Built-in data sources

Before explaining how to save and load `DataFrame` data, we'll first say a few words about the data formats that Spark supports out of the box. Each has its strengths and weaknesses, and you should understand when to use one or another. The built-in data formats are JSON, ORC, and Parquet.

JSON

The JSON format is commonly used for web development and is popular as a lightweight alternative to XML. Spark can automatically infer a JSON schema, so it can be a great solution for receiving data from and sending data to external systems, but it's not an efficient permanent data-storage format. It's simple, easy to use, and human-readable.

ORC

The optimized row columnar (ORC) file format was designed to provide a more efficient way to store Hive data (http://mng.bz/m6Mn), compared to an RCFile, which was previously the standard format for storing data in Hadoop.

The ORC format is columnar, which means data from a single column is physically stored in close proximity, unlike row formats, where data from a single row is stored sequentially. ORC files consist of groups of row data, called *stripes*, a *file footer*, and a *postscript* area at the end of the file. The file footer contains the list of stripes in a file, number of rows per stripe, and column data types. The postscript area contains compression parameters and the size of the file footer.

Stripes are typically 250 MB, and they contain index data, row data, and a stripe footer. Index data contains minimum and maximum values for each column and row position in columns. Index data can also include a Bloom filter (https://en.wikipedia.org/wiki/Bloom_filter), which can be used for quick testing if the stripe contains a certain value. Index data can speed up table scans because, in this way, certain stripes can be skipped and not read at all.

ORC uses type-specific serializers, which can take advantage of a certain type's specifics to store the data more efficiently. On top of that, stripes are compressed with Zlib or Snappy. The complete ORC file format specification can be found at http://mng.bz/0Z5B.

PARQUET

Unlike the ORC file format, the Parquet format (http://mng.bz/3IOo) started outside Hive and was later integrated with it. Parquet was designed to be independent of any specific framework and free of unnecessary dependencies. This is why it's more popular in the Hadoop ecosystem than the ORC file format.

Parquet is also a columnar file format and also uses compression, but it allows compression schemes to be specified per column. It pays special attention to nested complex data structures, so it works better than the ORC file format on these types of datasets. It supports the LZO, Snappy, and GZIP compression libraries. Furthermore, it keeps min/max statistics about column chunks, so it can also skip some of the data when querying. Parquet is the default data source in Spark.

5.4.2 Saving data

DataFrame's data is saved using the `DataFrameWriter` object, available as `DataFrame`'s `write` field. You already saw an example of using `DataFrameWriter` in section 5.3.1:

```
postsDf.write.saveAsTable("posts")
```

In addition to the `saveAsTable` method, data can be saved using the `save` and `insertInto` methods. `saveAsTable` and `insertInto` save data into Hive tables and use the metastore in the process; `save` doesn't. In case you're not using Spark session with Hive support, the `saveAsTable` and `insertInto` methods create (or insert into) temporary tables. You can configure all three methods with `DataFrameWriter`'s configuration functions (explained next).

CONFIGURING THE WRITER

`DataFrameWriter` implements the builder pattern (https://en.wikipedia.org/wiki/Builder_pattern), which means its configuration functions return objects with configuration fragments so you can stack them up one after another and build the desired configuration incrementally. The configuration functions are the following:

- `format`—Specifies the file format for saving data (the data source name), which can be one of the built-in data sources (`json`, `parquet`, `orc`) or a named custom data source. When no format is specified, the default is `parquet`.
- `mode`—Specifies the save mode when a table or a file already exists. Possible values are `overwrite` (overwrites the existing data), `append` (appends the data), `ignore` (does nothing), and `error` (throws an exception); the default is `error`.
- `option` and `options`—Adds a single parameter name and a value (or a parameter-value map) to the data source configuration.
- `partitionBy`—Specifies partitioning columns.

The Spark SQL parameter `spark.sql.sources.default` determines the default data source. Its default value is `parquet`. (We'll describe the Parquet file format in section 5.3.3.)

As we said, you can stack these functions one after another to build a `DataFrameWriter` object:

```
postsDf.write.format("orc").mode("overwrite").option(...)
```

USING THE SAVEASTABLE METHOD

As we said, `saveAsTable` saves data to a Hive table and registers it in the Hive metastore if you're using Hive support, which we recommend. If you aren't using Hive support, the `DataFrame` is registered as a temporary table.

`saveAsTable` takes only the table name as an argument. If the table already exists, then the `mode` configuration parameter determines the resulting behavior (default is to throw an exception).

The embedded Hive libraries take care of saving the table data if you're saving it in a format for which Hive SerDe (serialization/deserialization class) exists. If no Hive SerDe exists for the format, Spark chooses the format for saving the data (for example, text for JSON).

For example, you can save `postsDf` DataFrame in JSON format with the following line:

```
postsDf.write.format("json").saveAsTable("postsjson")
```

This saves posts data as the postsjson file in the Spark's metastore warehouse directory. Each line in the file contains a complete JSON object. You can now query the table from the Hive metastore:

```
scala> sql("select * from postsjson")
```

USING THE INSERTINTO METHOD

When using the `insertInto` method, you need to specify a table that already exists in the Hive metastore and that has the same schema as the `DataFrame` you wish to save. If the schemas aren't the same, Spark throws an exception. Because the table's format is already known (the table exists), the `format` and `options` configuration parameters will be ignored. If you set the `mode` configuration parameter to `overwrite`, the table's contents will be deleted and replaced with the `DataFrame`'s contents.

USING THE SAVE METHOD

The save method doesn't use a Hive metastore; rather, it saves data directly to the filesystem. You pass to it a direct path to the destination, whether HDFS, Amazon S3, or a local path URL. If you pass in a local path, the file is saved locally on every executor's machine.

USING THE SHORTCUT METHODS

`DataFrameWriter` has three shortcut methods for saving data to the built-in data sources: `json`, `orc`, and `parquet`. Each first calls `format` with the appropriate data-source name and then calls `save`, passing in the input path argument. This means these three methods don't use the Hive metastore.

SAVING DATA TO RELATIONAL DATABASES WITH JDBC

You can save the contents of a `DataFrame` with `DataFrameWriter`'s `jdbc` method. It takes three parameters: a URL string, a table name, and a `java.util.Properties` object containing connection properties, usually `user` and `password`. For example, to save the posts data into a PostgreSQL table named `posts` in the database `mydb` on the server `postgresrv`, you can use the following:

```
val props = new java.util.Properties()
props.setProperty("user", "user")
props.setProperty("password", "password")
postsDf.write.jdbc("jdbc:postgresql://postgresrv/mydb", "posts", props)
```

All of `postsDf`'s partitions connect to the database to save the data, so you have to make sure the `DataFrame` doesn't have too many partitions or you may overwhelm your database. You also have to make sure the required JDBC driver is accessible to your executors. This can be done by setting the `spark.executor.extraClassPath` Spark configuration parameter (for details, see chapter 10).

5.4.3 Loading data

You load data with an `org.apache.spark.sql.DataFrameReader` object, accessible through `SparkSession`'s read field. It functions analogously to `DataFrameWriter`. You can configure it with the `format` and `option`/`options` functions and additionally with the `schema` function. The `schema` function specifies the schema of the `DataFrame`. Most data sources automatically detect the schema, but you can speed it up by specifying the schema yourself.

Similarly to `DataFrameWriter`'s save method, the `load` method loads data directly from the configured data source. Three shortcut methods—`json`, `orc`, and `parquet`—analogously call `format` and then `load`.

You can use the `table` function to load a `DataFrame` from a table registered in the Hive metastore. For example, instead of executing the `SELECT * FROM POSTS` command, as you did previously, you can load the `posts` table like this

```
val postsDf = spark.read.table("posts")
```

or

```
val postsDf = spark.table("posts")
```

LOADING DATA FROM RELATIONAL DATABASES USING JDBC

`DataFrameReader`'s `jdbc` function is similar to `DataFrameWriter`'s `jdbc` function but has several differences. At a minimum it accepts a URL, a table name, and a set of properties (in a `java.util.Properties` object). But you can also narrow the dataset to be retrieved with a set of *predicates* (expressions that can go into a `where` clause).

For example, to load all posts with more than three views from the example PostgreSQL table you created in the previous section, you can use the following:

```
val result = spark.read.jdbc("jdbc:postgresql://postgresrv/mydb",
  "posts", Array("viewCount > 3"), props)
```

LOADING DATA FROM DATA SOURCES REGISTERED USING SQL

An alternative way of registering temporary tables lets you use SQL to reference existing data sources. You can accomplish (almost) the same result as in the previous example with the following snippet:

```
scala> sql("CREATE TEMPORARY TABLE postsjdbc "+
  "USING org.apache.spark.sql.jdbc "+
  "OPTIONS ("+
    "url 'jdbc:postgresql://postgresrv/mydb',"+
    "dbtable 'posts',"+
```

```
    "user 'user',"+
    "password 'password')")
scala> val result = sql("select * from postsjdbc")
```

The method isn't quite the same, though, because this way you can't specify predicates (viewCount > 3). As an example of another built-in data source, to register a Parquet file and load its contents, this is what you can do:

```
scala> sql("CREATE TEMPORARY TABLE postsParquet "+
    "USING org.apache.spark.sql.parquet "+
    "OPTIONS (path '/path/to/parquet_file')")
scala> val resParq = sql("select * from postsParquet")
```

5.5   *Catalyst optimizer*

The Catalyst optimizer is the brain behind DataFrames and DataSets, and is responsible for converting DataFrame DSL and SQL expressions into low-level RDD operations. It can be easily extended, and additional optimizations can be added.

Catalyst first creates a *parsed logical plan* from DSL and SQL expressions. Then it checks the names of tables, columns, and qualified names (called *relations*) and creates an *analyzed logical plan*. In the next step, Catalyst tries to optimize the plan by rearranging and combining the lower-level operations. It might decide to move a filter operation before a join so as to reduce the amount of data involved in the join, for example. This step produces an *optimized logical plan*. A *physical plan* is then calculated from the optimized plan. Future Spark versions will implement the generation of several physical plans and the selection of the best one based on a cost model. Figure 5.5 shows all of these steps.

Logical optimization means Catalyst tries to push predicates down to data sources so that subsequent operations work on as small a dataset as possible. During physical planning, instead of performing a shuffle join, for example, Catalyst may decide to broadcast one of the two datasets if it's small enough (smaller than 10 MB).

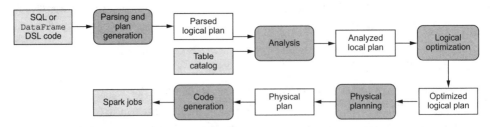

Figure 5.5   The steps of transforming SQL and DSL expressions into RDD operations include analysis, logical optimization, physical planning, and code generation.

EXAMINING THE EXECUTION PLAN

You can see the results of optimizations and examine the generated plans in two ways: by using `DataFrame`'s `explain` method or by consulting the Spark Web UI. Let's again use `postsDf` as an example. Consider the expression you used in section 5.1.2 to filter posts by "views per score point" less than 35:

```
scala> val postsFiltered = postsDf.filter('postTypeId === 1).
  withColumn("ratio", 'viewCount / 'score).where('ratio < 35)
```

You can examine `DataFrame`'s calculated logical and physical plans by calling `explain(true)`. If called without an argument (which is the same as calling it with `false`), `explain` displays only the physical plan. For `postsFiltered`, `explain` returns the following (the output has been truncated for easier viewing; you can find the full output in our online repository):

```
scala> postsFiltered.explain(true)
== Parsed Logical Plan ==
'Filter ('ratio < 35)
 Project [...columns ommitted..., ...ratio expr... AS ratio#21]
  Filter (postTypeId#11L = cast(1 as bigint))
   Project [...columns ommitted...]
    Subquery posts
     Relation[...columns ommitted...] ParquetRelation[path/to/posts]

== Analyzed Logical Plan ==
...columns ommitted...
Filter (ratio#21 < cast(35 as double))
 Project [...columns ommitted..., ...ratio expr... AS ratio#21]
  Filter (postTypeId#11L = cast(1 as bigint))
   Project [...columns ommitted...]
    Subquery posts
     Relation[...columns ommitted...] ParquetRelation[path/to/posts]

== Optimized Logical Plan ==
Project [...columns ommitted..., ...ratio expr... AS ratio#21]
 Filter ((postTypeId#11L = 1) && ((cast(viewCount#6 as double) /
cast(score#4 as double)) < 35.0))
  Relation[...columns ommitted...] ParquetRelation[path/to/posts]

== Physical Plan ==
Project [...columns ommitted..., ...ratio expr... AS ratio#21]
 Filter ((postTypeId#11L = 1) && ((cast(viewCount#6 as double) /
cast(score#4 as double)) < 35.0))
  Scan ParquetRelation[path/to/posts][...columns ommitted...]
```

As you can see, the parsed logical plan looks like the original Scala expression, if you read it from bottom upward. `ParquetRelation` in the last line (the first step of the parsed logical plan) means the data is to be read from a Parquet file. `Project` (the second step) is an internal Spark class that shows which columns are to be selected. The first filter step (in the `Filter` line) filters by the post type, then the next project step adds the `ratio` column, and the last filter step filters by the `ratio` column.

Compare that to the physical plan at the end of the output. The two filters were merged into a single filter, and the `ratio` column isn't added until the last step in the plan.

Beginning with Spark 1.5, you can get the same output using the Spark web UI, available at port 4040 on the machine where your Spark driver is running (for more information about the Spark web UI, see chapter 10). The SQL tab shows completed SQL queries. For each, you can click the +Details link in the Details column and get output similar to the one shown previously.

TAKING ADVANTAGE OF PARTITION STATISTICS

The Catalyst optimizer examines the contents of a `DataFrame`'s partitions, calculates statistics of its columns (such as lower and upper bounds, number of `NULL` values, and so forth), and then uses this data to skip some partitions while filtering, which adds additional performance benefits. These statistics are automatically calculated when `DataFrames` are cached in memory, so there's nothing special you need to do to enable this behavior. Just remember to cache `DataFrames`.

5.6   *Performance improvements with Tungsten*

Spark 1.5 also introduced the Tungsten project. Tungsten presents a complete overhaul of Spark memory management and other performance improvements in sorting, aggregating, and shuffling. Beginning with Spark 1.5, Tungsten is enabled by default (Spark SQL configuration parameter `spark.sql.tungsten.enabled`). Since Spark 2.0, its improvements were extended from structured data in `DataFrames` to unstructured data in `DataSets`.

Tungsten's memory-management improvements are based on binary encoding of the objects (integers, strings, tuples, and so on) and directly referencing them in memory. Two modes are supported: off-heap and on-heap allocation. *On-heap allocation* stores binary-encoded objects in large, JVM-managed arrays of longs. *Off-heap allocation* mode uses the `sun.misc.Unsafe` class to directly allocate (and free) memory by address, similar to how it's done in the C language.

Off-heap mode still uses arrays of `longs` for storing binary-encoded objects, but these arrays are no longer allocated and garbage-collected by JVM. They're directly managed by Spark. A new class, `UnsafeRow`, is used to internally represent rows backed by directly managed memory. Off-heap allocation is disabled by default, but you can enable it by setting the `spark.unsafe.offHeap` Spark configuration parameter (not Spark SQL parameter) to `true`.

Binary-encoded objects take up much less memory than their Java representations. Storing them in arrays of `Long` (on-heap mode) significantly reduces garbage collection. Allocating those arrays (off-heap mode) removes the need for garbage collection entirely. Tungsten's binary encoding also includes several tricks so that the data can be more efficiently cached in a CPU's L1 and L2 caches.

Project Tungsten also improves shuffle performance. Prior to Spark 1.5, only sort-based and hash-based shuffle managers were available. Now you can use a new Tungsten shuffle manager. It's also sort-based but uses binary encoding (mentioned earlier). You can enable it by setting Spark's `spark.shuffle.manager` parameter to `tungsten-sort`. Future Spark versions will bring more performance improvements by further implementing Tungsten's binary encoding in Spark components.

5.7 *Summary*

- `DataFrames` translate SQL code and DSL expressions into optimized, low-level RDD operations.
- `DataFrames` have become one of the most important features in Spark and have made Spark SQL the most actively developed Spark component.
- Three ways of creating `DataFrames` exist: by converting existing RDDs, by running SQL queries, or by loading external data.
- You can use `DataFrame` DSL operations to select, filter, group, and join data.
- `DataFrames` support scalar, aggregate, window, and user-defined functions.
- With the `DataFrameNaFunctions` class, accessible through `DataFrame`'s na field, you can deal with missing values in the dataset.
- SparkSQL has its own configuration method.
- Tables can be registered temporarily and permanently in the Hive metastore, which can reside in a local Derby database or in a remote relational database.
- The Spark SQL shell can be used to directly write queries referencing tables registered in the Hive metastore.
- Spark includes a Thrift server that clients can connect to over JDBC and ODBC and use to perform SQL queries.
- Data is loaded into `DataFrames` through `DataFrameReader`, available through `SparkSession`'s read field.
- Data is saved from `DataFrames` through `DataFrameWriter`, available through `DataFrame`'s write field.
- Spark's built-in data sources are JSON, ORC, Parquet, and JDBC. Third-party data sources are available for download.
- Catalyst optimizer (the brain behind `DataFrames`) can optimize logical plans and create physical execution plans.

- The Tungsten project introduced numerous performance improvements through binary, cache-friendly encoding of objects, on-heap and off-heap allocation, and a new shuffle manager.
- DataSets are an experimental feature similar to DataFrames, but they enable you to store plain Java objects instead of generic Row containers.

Ingesting data
with Spark Streaming

Real-time data ingestion, in today's high-paced, interconnected world, is getting increasingly important. There is much talk today about the so-called *Internet of Things* or, in other words, a world of devices in use in our daily lives, which continually stream data to the internet and to each other and make our lives easier (in theory, at least). Even without those micro-devices overwhelming our networks with their data, many companies today need to receive data in real-time, learn from it, and act on it immediately. After all, time is money, as they say.

It isn't hard to think of professional fields that might (and do) profit from real-time data analysis: traffic monitoring, online advertising, stock market trading, unavoidable social networks, and so on. Many of these cases need scalable and fault-tolerant systems for ingesting data, and Spark boasts all of those features. In addition to enabling scalable analysis of high-throughput data, Spark is also a unifying platform, which means you can use the same APIs from streaming and batch programs. That way, you can build both speed and batch layers of the lambda architecture (the name and the design of lambda architecture come from Nathan Marz; check out his book *Big Data* [Manning, 2015]).

Spark Streaming has connectors for reading data from Hadoop-compatible filesystems (such as HDFS and S3) and distributed systems (such as Flume, Kafka, and Twitter). In this chapter, you'll first stream data from files and write the results back to files. You'll then expand on that and use Kafka, the scalable and distributed message-queuing system, as the source and destination for the data. The same principles you'll learn there can be applied to other sources as well. At the end of the chapter, we'll show you how to ensure good performance for your streaming applications.

In chapter 13, you'll find a successful application of Spark Streaming to the problem of real-time log analysis. Methods and concepts taught in this chapter will be applied there.

6.1 Writing Spark Streaming applications

As you saw in previous chapters, Spark is great for working with structured and unstructured data. And as you already may have concluded, Spark is batch processing–oriented. But how are Spark's batch-processing features applied to real-time data?

The answer is that Spark uses *mini-batches*. This means Spark Streaming takes blocks of data, which come in specific time periods, and packages them as RDDs. Figure 6.1 illustrates this concept.

As shown in the figure, data can come into a Spark Streaming job from various external systems. These include filesystems and TCP/IP socket connections, but also other distributed systems, such as Kafka, Flume, Twitter, and Amazon Kinesis. Different Spark Streaming *receiver* implementations exist for different sources (data from some data sources is read without using receivers, but let's not complicate things too early). Receivers know how to connect to the source, read the data, and forward it further into Spark Streaming. Spark Streaming then splits the incoming data into mini-batch RDDs, one mini-batch RDD for one time period, and then the Spark application processes it according to the logic built into the application. During mini-batch processing, you're free to use other parts of the Spark API, such as machine learning and SQL. The results of computations can be written to filesystems, relational databases, or to other distributed systems.

6.1.1 Introducing the example application

For purposes of learning Spark Streaming concepts, imagine you need to build a dashboard application for a brokerage firm. Clients of the firm use their internet application to place market orders (for buying or selling securities[1]), and brokers

---

[1] *Securities* are tradable financial assets, such as bonds, stocks, and the infamous derivatives.

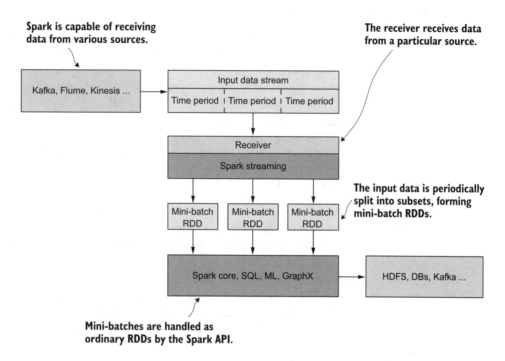

Spark is capable of receiving data from various sources.

The receiver receives data from a particular source.

The input data is periodically split into subsets, forming mini-batch RDDs.

Mini-batches are handled as ordinary RDDs by the Spark API.

Figure 6.1   **The concept of processing streaming data in Apache Spark. Spark Streaming is splitting the input data stream into time-based mini-batch RDDs, which are then processed using other Spark components, as usual.**

need to carry out the orders in the market. The dashboard application you need to build will calculate the number of selling and buying orders per second, the top five clients as measured by the total amounts bought or sold, and the top five securities bought or sold during the last hour.

For starters, to make things simpler, you'll read the data from an HDFS file and write the results back to HDFS. In section 6.2, we'll expand on this and show you how to connect to Kafka, a distributed message-passing system.

Similarly, in order to use simpler functionalities first, the implementation of the first version will only count the number of selling and buying orders per second. Later, you'll add calculations for the top five clients and top five securities.

One more thing to note: everything in this chapter will be done using your Spark shell. We'll point out any differences between running Spark Streaming from the Spark shell and from a standalone application. If you went through chapter 3 successfully, you should be able to apply the principles learned there and embed the code from this chapter into a standalone application, which you would submit to a cluster as a JAR archive.

6.1.2 Creating a streaming context

If you'd like to follow along, now is the time to start up your Spark shell. You can start a local cluster in the spark-in-action VM or connect to a Spark standalone, YARN, or Mesos cluster, if it's available to you (for details, please see chapter 10, 11, or 12). In any case, make sure to have more than one core available to your executors, because each Spark Streaming receiver has to use one core (technically, it's a thread) for reading the incoming data, and at least one more core needs to be available for performing the calculations of your program.

For example, to run a local cluster, you can issue the following command:

```
$ spark-shell --master local[4]
```

Once your shell is up, the first thing you need to do is to create an instance of `StreamingContext`. From your Spark shell, you instantiate it using the `SparkContext` object (available as variable `sc`) and a `Duration` object, which specifies time intervals at which Spark Streaming should split the input stream data and create mini-batch RDDs. The mini-batch intervals depend on the use case (how important it is to see the latest data) and on the performance requirements and capacity of your cluster. We'll have more to say about this later. For now, use an interval of five seconds:

```
scala> import org.apache.spark._
scala> import org.apache.spark.streaming._
scala> val ssc = new StreamingContext(sc, Seconds(5))
```

> **NOTE** Instead of `Seconds`, you can use the `Milliseconds` and `Minutes` objects to specify duration.

The previous `StreamingContext` constructor reuses an existing `SparkContext`, but `SparkStreaming` can also start a new `SparkContext` if you give it a Spark configuration object:

```
val conf = new SparkConf().setMaster("local[4]").setAppName("App name")
val ssc = new StreamingContext(conf, Seconds(5))
```

You could use this snippet from your standalone application, but it wouldn't work if you ran it from your shell because you can't instantiate two Spark contexts in the same JVM.

6.1.3 Creating a discretized stream

As we said, for starters, you'll stream the data from a file. Let's first see what the data will look like.

DOWNLOADING THE DATA TO BE STREAMED

We prepared a file containing 500,000 lines representing buy and sell orders. The data was randomly generated. Each line contains the following comma-separated elements:

- *Order timestamp*—Format `yyyy-mm-dd hh:MM:ss`
- *Order ID*—Serially incrementing integer
- *Client ID*—Integer randomly picked from the range 1 to 100
- *Stock symbol*—Randomly picked from a list of 80 stock symbols
- *Number of stocks to be bought or sold*—Random number from 1 to 1,000
- *Price at which to buy or sell*—Random number from 1 to 100
- *Character* `B` *or* `S`—Whether the event is an order to buy or sell

You can find an archive containing this file in our online repository. You should have already cloned the repository into the /home/spark folder, so you should be able to unzip the file with the following commands:

```
$ cd first-edition/ch06
$ tar xvfz orders.tar.gz
```

This is the data that will be arriving into your streaming application.

For streaming the incoming textual data directly from files, `StreamingContext` provides the `textFileStream` method, which monitors a directory (any Hadoop-compliant directory, such as HDFS, S3, GlusterFS, and local directories) and reads each newly created file in the directory. The method takes only one argument: the name of the directory to be monitored.

Newly created means it won't process the files that already exist in the folder when the streaming context starts, nor will it react to data that's added to a file. It will process only the files copied to the folder after processing starts.

Because it's unrealistic that all 500,000 events will arrive to your system all at once, we also prepared a Linux shell script named `splitAndSend.sh`, which splits the unzipped file (orders.txt) into 50 files, each containing 10,000 lines. It then periodically moves the splits to an HDFS directory (supplied as an argument), waiting for three seconds after copying each split. This is similar to what would happen in a real environment.

The user you're logged in as needs to have access to the `hdfs` command. If you don't have access to HDFS (which you should, if you're using the spark-in-action VM), you can specify a local folder and add an argument: `local`. The script will then periodically move the splits to the specified local folder.

No need to start the script yet. You'll do that later.

CREATING A DSTREAM OBJECT

You should choose a folder (HDFS or a local one) where the splits will be copied to and from where your streaming application will read them (for example, /home/spark/ch06input). Then specify that folder as an argument to the `textFileStream` method:

```
scala> val filestream = ssc.textFileStream("/home/spark/ch06input")
```

The resulting `fileDstream` object is an instance of class `DStream`. `DStream` (which stands for "discretized stream") is the basic abstraction in Spark Streaming, representing a sequence of RDDs, periodically created from the input stream. Needless to say, `DStreams` are lazily evaluated, just like RDDs. So when you create a `DStream` object, nothing happens yet. The RDDs will start coming in only after you start the streaming context, which you'll do in section 6.1.6.

6.1.4 Using discretized streams

Now that you have your `DStream` object, you need to use it to calculate the number of selling and buying orders per second. But how do you do that?

Well, similarly to RDDs, `DStreams` have methods that transform them to other `DStreams`. You can use those methods to filter, map, and reduce data in a `DStream`'s RDDs and even combine and join different `DStreams`.

PARSING THE LINES

For your task, you should first transform each line into something more manageable, like a Scala case class. Let's do that now. First, let's create the `Order` class, which will hold order data:

```scala
scala> import java.sql.Timestamp
scala> case class Order(time: java.sql.Timestamp, orderId:Long,
    clientId:Long, symbol:String, amount:Int, price:Double, buy:Boolean)
```

You use `java.sql.Timestamp` to represent time because it's supported by Spark Data-Frames so you won't have any trouble using this class for constructing DataFrames, in case you need them.

Now you need to parse the lines from the `filestream` `DStream` and thus obtain a new `DStream` containing `Order` objects. There are several ways you can accomplish this. Let's use the `flatMap` transformation, which operates on all elements of all RDDs in a `DStream`. The reason to use `flatMap` and not `map` transformation is that you'd like to ignore any lines that don't match the format we expect. If the line can be parsed, the function returns a list with a single element and an empty list otherwise.

This is the snippet you need:

Each line is first split by commas.

Java's SimpleDateFormat is used for parsing timestamps.

```scala
import java.text.SimpleDateFormat
val orders = filestream.flatMap(line => {
    val dateFormat = new SimpleDateFormat("yyyy-MM-dd hh:mm:ss")
    val s = line.split(",")
    try {
        assert(s(6) == "B" || s(6) == "S")
        List(Order(new Timestamp(dateFormat.parse(s(0)).getTime()),
            s(1).toLong, s(2).toLong, s(3), s(4).toInt,
            s(5).toDouble, s(6) == "B"))
    }
```

The seventh field should be equal to "B" (buy) or "S" (sell).

Constructs an Order object from the parsed fields

> **If anything goes wrong during parsing, the error is logged (to System.out only, in this example), along with the complete line that caused it.**

```
    catch {
        case e : Throwable => println("Wrong line format ("+e+"): "+line)
        List()
    }
})
```

> **If a line can't be parsed, an empty list is returned, ignoring the problematic line.**

Each RDD from the orders DStream now contains Order objects.

COUNTING THE NUMBERS OF BUY AND SELL ORDERS

The task is to count the number of buy and sell orders per second. For this, you'll use the PairDStreamFunctions object. Similar to RDDs, which get implicitly converted to instances of the PairRDDFunctions object if they contain two-element tuples, DStreams containing two-element tuples get automatically converted to PairDStreamFunctions objects. In that way, functions such as combineByKey, reduceByKey, flatMapValues, various joins, and other functions you may recognize from chapter 4, become available on DStream objects.

If you map orders to tuples that contain the order type as the key and the count as the value, you can use reduceByKey (there is no countByKey function in Pair-DStreamFunctions); for example, for counting occurrences of each order type (buy or sell). This is how to do this:

```
scala> val numPerType = orders.map(o => (o.buy, 1L)).
  reduceByKey((c1, c2) => c1+c2)
```

This should be familiar to you from chapter 4. reduceByKey here just sums different values per key, which are all initially equal to 1. Each RDD in the resulting numPerType DStream will contain at most two (Boolean, Long) tuples: one for buy orders (true) and one for sell orders (false).

6.1.5 Saving the results to a file

To save the results of your computation to a file, you can use DStream's saveAsTextFiles method. It takes a String prefix and an optional String suffix and uses them to construct the path at which the data should be periodically saved. Each mini-batch RDD is saved to a folder called *<your_prefix>-<time_in_milliseconds>.<your_suffix>*, or just *<your_prefix>-<time_in_milliseconds>* if a suffix isn't supplied. This means that every 5 seconds (in this example), a new directory is created. Each of these directories contains one file, named part-*xxxxx*, for each partition in the RDD (where *xxxxx* is the partition's number).

To create only one part-*xxxxx* file per RDD folder, you'll repartition the DStream to only one partition before saving it to a file. We've shown that each RDD will contain at most two elements, so you can be certain that putting all the data into one partition won't cause any memory problems. So this is what you can do:

```
scala> numPerType.repartition(1).saveAsTextFiles(
  "/home/spark/ch06output/output", "txt")
```

The output file can again be a local file (if you're running a local cluster) or a file on a distributed Hadoop-compatible filesystem, such as HDFS.

NOTE When developing a streaming application, DStream's print(n) method may prove useful. It prints out the first *n* elements (10 by default) of each mini-batch RDD.

But even after you execute this last command, still nothing happens. That's because you still haven't started the streaming context.

6.1.6 *Starting and stopping the streaming computation*

Finally, you get to see the fruit of your labor. Start the streaming computation by issuing the following command:

```
scala> ssc.start()
```

This starts the streaming context, which evaluates the DStreams it was used to create, starts their receivers, and starts running the programs the DStreams represent. In the Spark shell, this is all you need to do to run the streaming computation of your application. Receivers are started in separate threads, and you can still use your Spark shell to enter and run other lines of code in parallel with the streaming computation.

NOTE Although you can construct several StreamingContext instances using the same SparkContext object, you can't start more than one StreamingContext in the same JVM at a time.

But if you were to start a streaming context like this in a standalone application, although the receiver threads would be started, the main thread of your driver would exit, unless you added the following line:

```
ssc.awaitTermination()
```

This line tells Spark to wait for the Spark Streaming computation to stop. You can also use the awaitTerminationOrTimeout(<timeout in milliseconds>) method, which will wait the specified maximum number of seconds for streaming to finish and will return false, if the timeout occurred, or true, if the streaming computation was stopped before the timeout.

SENDING DATA TO SPARK STREAMING

Now your Spark Streaming application is running, but it doesn't have any data to process. So let's give it some data using the splitAndSend.sh script that we mentioned previously. You might first need to make the script executable:

```
$ chmod +x first-edition/ch06/splitAndSend.sh
```

Then, from your command prompt, start the script and specify the input folder you used in the Spark Streaming code (we assume you used /home/spark/ch06input).

Make sure the unzipped orders.txt file is in /home/spark/first-edition/ch06, and don't forget to add the `local` argument if the streaming input folder is a local one:

```
$ cd first-edition/ch06
$ ./splitAndSend.sh /home/spark/ch06input local
```

This will start copying parts of the orders.txt file to the specified folder, and the application will automatically start counting buy and sell orders in the copied files.

STOPPING THE SPARK STREAMING CONTEXT

You can wait for all the files to be processed (which will take about 2.5 minutes), or you can stop the running streaming context right from your shell. Just paste this line in the shell, and the streaming context will stop:

```
scala> ssc.stop(false)
```

The argument `false` tells the streaming context not to stop the Spark context, which it would do by default. You can't restart a stopped streaming context, but you can reuse the existing Spark context to create a new streaming context. And because the Spark shell allows you to overwrite the previously used variable names, you can paste all the previous lines in your shell and run the whole application again (if you wish to do so).

EXAMINING THE GENERATED OUTPUT

As we said earlier, `saveAsTextFiles` creates one folder per mini-batch. If you look at your output folders, you'll find two files in each of them, named part-00000 and _SUCCESS. _SUCCESS means writing has finished successfully, and part-00000 contains the counts that were calculated. The contents of the part-00000 file might look something like this:

```
(false,9969)
(true,10031)
```

Reading data from all these folders might seem difficult, but it's simple using the Spark API. You can read several text files in one go using asterisks (*) when specifying paths for `SparkContext`'s `textFile` method. To read all the files you just generated into a single RDD, you can use the following expression:

```
val allCounts = sc.textFile("/home/spark/ch06output/output*.txt")
```

The asterisk in this case replaces the generated timestamps.

6.1.7 *Saving the computation state over time*

You've seen how to do basic calculations with Spark Streaming, but how to do the rest of the required calculations still isn't clear. You have to find the top five clients as measured by the total amounts bought or sold, and the top five securities bought or sold during the last hour.

The previous calculations only needed the data from the current mini-batch, but these new numbers have to be obtained by also taking into account the data from previous mini-batches. To calculate the top five clients, you have to keep track of the total dollar amount bought or sold by each client. In other words, you have to keep track of a state that persists over time and over different mini-batches.

This principle is illustrated in figure 6.2. New data periodically arrives over time in mini-batches. Each DStream is a program that processes the data and produces results. By using Spark Streaming methods to update state, DStreams can combine the persisted data from the state with the new data from the current mini-batch. The results are much more powerful streaming programs. Let's see which methods from Spark Streaming let you do this.

KEEPING TRACK OF THE STATE USING UPDATESTATEBYKEY

In addition to window operations, which will be covered in section 6.1.9, Spark provides two main methods for performing calculations while taking into account the previous state of the computation: updateStateByKey and mapWithState. We'll first show you how to use updateStateByKey. Both methods are accessible from PairDStream-Functions; in other words, they're only available for DStreams containing key-value tuples. Therefore, before using these methods, you have to create such a DStream.

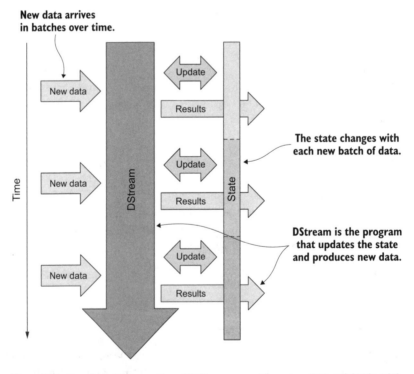

Figure 6.2 Keeping state over time. A DStream combines new data arriving in mini-batches with the data from state persisted over time, produces results, and updates the state.

You'll reuse the `orders` DStream you created previously and expand the previous example by adding and changing a few lines. Creating `orders` and `numPerType` DStreams remains the same as in the previous example. You'll just add the calculation of the state and change the way the results are saved. The complete listing will be given at the end of the section.

Let's first create a `DStream` that contains client IDs as keys and order dollar amounts as values (number of stocks bought or sold multiplied by their price):

```scala
scala> val amountPerClient = orders.map(o => (o.clientId, o.amount * o.price))
```

Now you can use the `updateStateByKey` method. There are two basic versions of `updateStateByKey`. The first one, which you'll use in this example, lets you work with a DStream's values. The second version lets you also work with, and potentially change, a DStream's keys. Both versions return a new `state` DStream, which contains a state value for each key.

The first version, at minimum, takes as an argument a function with this signature:

```
(Seq[V], Option[S]) => Option[S]
```

The first argument of this function is a `Seq` object with new values of a key that came in the current mini-batch. The second argument is the state value of the key, or `None` if the state for that key hasn't been calculated yet. If the state for the key has been calculated, but no new values for the key were received in the current mini-batch, the first argument will be an empty `Seq`. The function should return the new value for the key's state.

This function is the only required argument for the `updateStateByKey` method, but you can also specify the number of partitions or a `Partitioner` object to be used for the resulting DStream. That could become important if you have lots of keys to keep track of and large state objects.

To apply this to the example and create a `state` DStream from the `amountPerClient` DStream, you can use the following snippet:

If state for this key already exists, sum it up with the sum of new values.

```scala
val amountState = amountPerClient.updateStateByKey((vals,
    totalOpt) => {
  totalOpt match {
    case Some(total) => vals.sum + total
    case None => vals.sum
  }
})
```

Otherwise, only return the sum of new values.

Now, to find the top five clients by amounts of their orders, you need to sort each RDD in the `amountState` DStream and leave in each RDD only the first five elements. To leave only the top elements in an RDD, the following will do the job: add an index to each RDD's element using `zipWithIndex`, filter out only the elements with the first five indices, and remove the indices using `map`. The whole snippet looks like this:

```scala
val top5clients = amountState.transform(_.sortBy(_._2, false).
  zipWithIndex.filter(x => x._2 < 5).map(x => x._1))
```

COMBINING TWO DSTREAMS USING UNION

In order to write both calculated results (the top five clients and numbers of buy and sell orders you calculated previously) only once per batch interval, you first have to combine them in a single DStream. Two DStreams can be combined by key using various join methods or the cogroup method, or they can be merged using union. We'll do the latter.

To merge two DStreams, their elements have to be of the same type. You'll transform the top5clients and numPerType DStreams' elements to tuples whose first elements are keys describing the metric ("BUYS" for the number of buy orders, "SELLS" for the number of sell orders, and "TOP5CLIENTS" for the list of top five clients) and whose second elements are lists of strings. They need to be lists because the top-five-clients metric is a list. You'll convert all values to strings in order to be able to add a list of top stocks (their symbols) later.

Converting numPerType to the new format isn't difficult. If the key is true, the value represents the number of buy orders, and the number of sell orders otherwise:

```
val buySellList = numPerType.map(t =>
  if(t._1) ("BUYS", List(t._2.toString))
  else ("SELLS", List(t._2.toString)) )
```

To convert the top5clients DStream, you'll first make sure that all five clients are in the same partition by calling repartition(1). Then you remove the amounts and leave just the client IDs (converted to strings, as we said) and call glom to group all the client IDs in the partition in a single array. Finally, you map that array to a tuple with a key equal to the metric name:

```
val top5clList = top5clients.repartition(1).   ← Makes sure all the data is in a single partition
  map(x => x._1.toString).                      ← Leaves only client IDs
  glom().                                        ← Puts all client IDs into a single array
  map(arr => ("TOP5CLIENTS", arr.toList))       ← Adds the metric key
```

Now you can union the two DStreams together:

```
val finalStream = buySellList.union(top5clList)
```

You save the combined DStream same as previously:

```
finalStream.repartition(1).
  saveAsTextFiles("/home/spark/ch06output/output", "txt")
```

SPECIFYING THE CHECKPOINTING DIRECTORY

You need to do one more thing before starting the streaming context, which is to specify a checkpointing directory:

```
scala> sc.setCheckpointDir("/home/spark/checkpoint")
```

As you may recall from chapter 4, checkpointing saves an RDD's data and its complete DAG (an RDD's calculation plan), so that if an executor fails, the RDD doesn't have to be recomputed from scratch. It can be read from disk. This is necessary for DStreams resulting from the updateStateByKey method, because updateStateByKey expands RDD's DAG in each mini-batch, and that can quickly lead to stack overflow exceptions. By periodically checkpointing RDDs, their calculation plan's dependence on previous mini-batches is broken.

STARTING THE STREAMING CONTEXT AND EXAMINING THE NEW OUTPUT

Finally, you can start the streaming context. The complete code, which you can paste into your Spark shell, is shown in the following listing.

Listing 6.1 Calculating the number of sell/buy orders and finding the top five clients

```
import org.apache.spark._
import org.apache.spark.streaming._
import java.text.SimpleDateFormat

val ssc = new StreamingContext(sc, Seconds(5))

val filestream = ssc.textFileStream("/home/spark/ch06input")

import java.sql.Timestamp
case class Order(time: java.sql.Timestamp, orderId:Long, clientId:Long,
  symbol:String, amount:Int, price:Double, buy:Boolean)

val orders = filestream.flatMap(line => {
  val dateFormat = new SimpleDateFormat("yyyy-MM-dd hh:mm:ss")
  val s = line.split(",")
  try {
    assert(s(6) == "B" || s(6) == "S")
    List(Order(new Timestamp(dateFormat.parse(s(0)).getTime()),
      s(1).toLong,s(2).toLong,s(3),s(4).toInt,s(5).toDouble,s(6) == "B"))
  }
  catch {
    case e : Throwable => println("Wrong line format ("+e+"): "+line)
    List()
  }
})
val numPerType = orders.map(o => (o.buy, 1L)).
  reduceByKey((c1, c2) => c1+c2)

val amountPerClient = orders.map(o => (o.clientId, o.amount*o.price))
val amountState = amountPerClient.updateStateByKey((vals,
  totalOpt:Option[Double]) => {
  totalOpt match {
    case Some(total) => Some(vals.sum + total)
    case None => Some(vals.sum)
  }
})
val top5clients = amountState.transform(_.sortBy(_._2, false).map(_._1).
  zipWithIndex.filter(x => x._2 < 5))
```

```
val buySellList = numPerType.map(t =>
  if(t._1) ("BUYS", List(t._2.toString))
  else ("SELLS", List(t._2.toString)) )
val top5clList = top5clients.repartition(1).
  map(x => x._1.toString).glom().map(arr => ("TOP5CLIENTS", arr.toList))
val finalStream = buySellList.union(top5clList)
finalStream.repartition(1).
➥ saveAsTextFiles("/home/spark/ch06output/output", "txt")

sc.setCheckpointDir("/home/spark/checkpoint ")

ssc.start()
```

After you start the streaming context, start the `splitAndSend.sh` script as you did previously. After a couple of seconds, a part-00000 file in one of your output folders may look like this:

```
(SELLS,List(4926))
(BUYS,List(5074))
(TOP5CLIENTS,List(34, 69, 92, 36, 64))
```

You're making progress, but you still need to find the top-traded securities during the last hour. But before doing that, we have to describe the `mapWithState` method, which we previously skipped.

USING THE MAPWITHSTATE METHOD

The `mapWithState` method is newer than `updateStateByKey` and contains several performance and functional improvements. It's been available since Spark 1.6.

The main difference compared to `updateStateByKey` is that it lets you maintain a state of one type and return data of another. Let us show you what we mean.

`mapWithState` takes only one argument: an instance of class `StateSpec`, which is used for building the actual parameters. You can instantiate a `StateSpec` object by giving it a function with this signature (the first `Time` argument is optional):

```
(Time, KeyType, Option[ValueType], State[StateType]) => Option[MappedType]
```

Similar to `updateStateByKey` and the function you gave to it, the function you pass to `StateSpec` (and to `mapWithState` afterward) will be called for each key's new values (keys are of type `KeyType` and values of type `ValueType`) and for each key's existing state (of type `StateType`). The resulting `DStream` will have elements of type `MappedType`, unlike `updateStateByKey`, whose resulting `DStream` has elements equal to the maintained state.

The `State` object that the provided function receives holds the key's state and has several useful methods for manipulating it:

- `exists`—Returns `true` if the state is defined
- `get`—Obtains the state value

- `remove`—Removes the state for a key
- `update`—Updates or sets the new state value for a key

For example, the following function, used with `mapWithState`, would allow you to obtain the same `amountState` DStream as you did with `updateStateByKey` previously:

Sets the new state value to the new incoming value, if it exists; to zero otherwise

Increments the new state's value by the value of the existing state

```
val updateAmountState = (clientId:Long, amount:Option[Double],
                         state:State[Double]) => {
    var total = amount.getOrElse(0.toDouble)
    if(state.exists())
      total += state.get()
    state.update(total)
    Some((clientId, total))
}
```

Updates the state with the new value

Returns a tuple with the client ID and the new state value

You use this function like this:

```
val amountState = amountPerClient.mapWithState(StateSpec.
  function(updateAmountState)).stateSnapshots()
```

Without that last method, `stateSnapshots`, you'd get a `DStream` with client IDs and their total amounts, but only for the clients whose orders arrived during the current mini-batch. `stateSnaphots` gives you a `DStream` with the whole state (all clients), just like `updateStateByKey`.

When building a `StateSpec` object, in addition to specifying the state mapping function, you can specify the number of desired partitions, a `Partitioner` object to be used, an RDD with initial state values, and a timeout. An RDD with initial state values could be useful in situations when you would like to persist the state and reuse it after you restart the streaming job. In this example, at the end of the day, just after the stock exchange is closed, you could save the list of clients and the amounts they traded, and tomorrow continue where you left off today.

The timeout parameter is also interesting. You can use it to make Spark Streaming remove particular values from the state once the values expire. This can be applied to calculating session timeouts, for example, which has to be done manually when using `updateStateByKey`.

Finally, you can chain all those parameters one after another.

```
StateSpec.function(updateAmountState).numPartitions(10).
  timeout(Minutes(30))
```

These were functional improvements, but `mapWithState` also brings some performance improvements. It can keep 10 times more keys in the maintained state than `updateStateByKey` can, and it can be 6 times faster[2] (mostly by avoiding processing when no new keys have arrived).

---

[2] These numbers are based on measurements done by people at Databricks: http://mng.bz/42QD.

6.1.8   *Using window operations for time-limited calculations*

Let's continue with the example. There is one last task left to do: find the top five most-traded securities during the last hour. This is different than the previous task because it's time-limited. In Spark Streaming, this type of calculation is accomplished using *window operations*.

The main principle is shown in figure 6.3. As you can see, window operations operate on a sliding window of mini-batches. Each *windowed* DStream is determined by window duration and the slide of the window (how often the window data is recomputed), both multiples of the mini-batch duration.

SOLVING THE FINAL TASK WITH WINDOW OPERATIONS

In our example, the window duration is one hour (you need the top five most-traded securities during the last hour). But the slide duration is the same as the mini-batch duration (five seconds), because you want to report the top five most-traded securities in every mini-batch, together with other metrics.

To create a windowed DStream, you can use one of the window methods. For this task, you'll use the reduceByKeyAndWindow method. You need to specify the reduce function

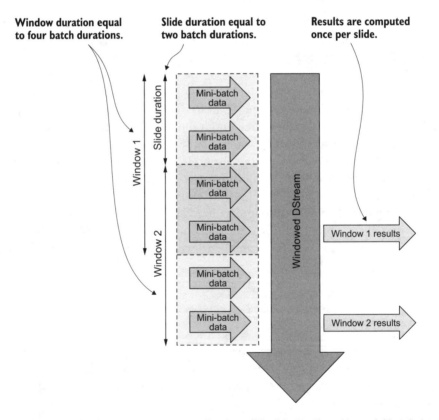

Figure 6.3   Windowed DStream processing data with slide duration of two mini-batch durations, and with window duration of four mini-batch durations. Results are computed once per slide.

and the window duration (you can also specify the slide duration if it's different than the mini-batch duration), and it will create a windowed DStream and reduce it using your reduce function. So, to calculate the amounts traded per stock and per window, you can use this snippet (put this before the finalStream variable initialization):

```
val stocksPerWindow = orders.
  map(x => (x.symbol, x.amount)).window(Minutes(60)).
  reduceByKey((a1:Int, a2:Int) => a1+a2)
```

The rest is the same as what you did for top clients:

```
val topStocks = stocksPerWindow.transform(_.sortBy(_._2, false).map(_._1).
  zipWithIndex.filter(x => x._2 < 5)).repartition(1).
    map(x => x._1.toString).glom().
    map(arr => ("TOP5STOCKS", arr.toList))
```

And you need to add this result to the final DStream:

```
val finalStream = buySellList.union(top5clList).union(topStocks)
```

The rest is the same as before:

```
finalStream.repartition(1).
➥ saveAsTextFiles("/home/spark/ch06output/output", "txt")
sc.setCheckpointDir("/home/spark/checkpoint/")
ssc.start()
```

Now, when you start your streaming application, the resulting part-00000 files may contain results like these:

```
(SELLS,List(9969))
(BUYS,List(10031))
(TOP5CLIENTS,List(15, 64, 55, 69, 19))
(TOP5STOCKS,List(AMD, INTC, BP, EGO, NEM))
```

EXPLORING THE OTHER WINDOW OPERATIONS

The window method isn't the only window operation available. There are a number of others, which can be useful in many situations. Some of them are available for ordinary DStreams and others only for pair DStreams (byKey functions). Table 6.1 lists them all.

Table 6.1 Window operations available in Spark Streaming

Window operation	Description
window(winDur, [slideDur])	Generates RDDs every slideDur with elements that appeared in this DStream during the sliding window of winDur duration. slideDur is equal to the mini-batch duration by default.
countByWindow(winDur, slideDur)	Every slideDur generates single-element RDDs containing the number of elements that appeared in this DStream during the sliding window of winDur duration.

Table 6.1   Window operations available in Spark Streaming *(continued)*

Window operation	Description
countByValueAndWindow(winDur, slideDur, [numParts])	Counts distinct elements in the window (determined by the winDur and slideDur parameters). numParts enables you to change the default number of partitions used.
reduceByWindow(reduceFunc, winDur, slideDur)	Every slideDur generates single-element RDDs containing the elements from the window of winDur duration reduced using the reduceFunc function.
reduceByWindow(reduceFunc, invReduceFunc, winDur, slideDur)	More efficient than reduceByWindow. Every slideDur generates single-element RDDs containing the elements from the window of winDur duration reduced using the reduceFunc function, but subtracts the elements that are leaving the window using the invReduceFunc.
groupByKeyAndWindow(winDur, [slideDur], [numParts/partitioner])	Groups elements from the window (determined by the winDur and slideDur parameters; slideDur is optional) by key. You can also specify the number of partitions *or* a partitioner to be used.
reduceByKeyAndWindow(reduceFunc, winDur, [slideDur], [numParts/partitioner])	Reduces elements from the window (determined by the winDur and slideDur parameters; slideDur is optional) by key. You can also specify the number of partitions *or* a partitioner to be used.
reduceByKeyAndWindow(reduceFunc, invReduceFunc, winDur, [slideDur], [numParts], [filterFunc])	A more efficient version that also uses the inverse reduce function to subtract the elements leaving the window. filterFunc is an optional function specifying the condition that key-value pairs need to satisfy to remain in the DStream.

As you've probably noticed, instead of using the reduceByKeyAndWindow method in the previous example, you could have also used the window method and then the reduceByKey method.

6.1.9   *Examining the other built-in input streams*

Before continuing, let's see what other options you have for receiving data using built-in input streams. Spark Streaming has several more methods for creating DStreams, in addition to the textFileStream method you used previously. We'll briefly explain how to use them.

FILE INPUT STREAMS

To read data from files, there are also the binaryRecordsStream method and the more general fileStream method. They both monitor a folder for newly created files, just like textFileStream, but they can read files of different types.

binaryRecordsStream reads binary files in records of a specified size (you pass to it a folder name and the records' size) and returns a DStream containing arrays of bytes (Array[Byte]). Using fileStream is more involved and requires you to parameterize it with classes for key type, value type, and input format (a subclass of Hadoop's `NewInputFormat`) for reading HDFS files. The resulting `DStream` will contain tuples with two elements of the specified key and value types.

In addition to these classes, you need to provide the path to the folder to be monitored, and you can specify several optional arguments:

- `filter` function that for each `Path` (a Hadoop class representing a file) object determines whether to process it (returns a Boolean)
- `newFilesOnly` flag determining whether to process only newly created files in the monitored folder or all files
- Hadoop `Configuration` object containing additional configuration options for reading HDFS files

Details about reading files with Hadoop API are beyond the scope of this book, but good information can be found in *Hadoop in Practice* by Alex Holmes (Manning, 2014).

SOCKET INPUT STREAMS

You can use Spark Streaming to receive data directly from a TCP/IP socket. You can use `socketStream` and `socketTextStream` methods for this. As you'd expect, `socketTextStream` returns a `DStream` whose elements are UTF8-encoded lines, delimited by newline characters. It needs a hostname and a port number to connect to and an optional `StorageLevel` (the default is `StorageLevel.MEMORY_AND_DISK_SER_2`, which means memory and disk with replication factor of 2). `StorageLevel` determines where the data will be kept and whether it will be replicated.

The `socketStream` method also needs a function for converting Java `InputStream` objects (for reading binary data) into target objects that will be elements of the resulting `DStream`. When you start a socket stream, its receiver runs in an executor on one of the worker nodes.

6.2 Using external data sources

We've shown you how to use the built-in data sources: files and sockets. Now it's time to connect to external data sources, which don't come bundled with Spark. Official Spark connectors exist for the following external systems and protocols:

- *Kafka* (https://kafka.apache.org)—A distributed, fast, scalable publish-subscribe messaging system. It persists all messages and is capable of acting as a replay queue.
- *Flume* (https://flume.apache.org)—A distributed, reliable system for collecting, aggregating, and transferring large amounts of log data.
- *Amazon Kinesis* (https://aws.amazon.com/en/kinesis)—An AWS streaming platform similar to Kafka.
- *Twitter* (https://dev.twitter.com/overview/documentation)—The popular social network's API service.
- *ZeroMQ* (http://zeromq.org)—A distributed messaging system.
- *MQTT* (http://mqtt.org)—A lightweight publish-subscribe messaging protocol.

NOTE   The source code of all of these data sources, except Kafka and Amazon Kinesis, was moved out of the Spark project into the *Spark packages* project at https://github.com/spark-packages.

These are interesting systems that have much to offer, but covering them all in this book isn't possible. So we'll concentrate on (arguably) the most popular among them: Apache Kafka. If you don't know much about Kafka, we invite you to first read the official introduction at http://kafka.apache.org/documentation.html#introduction.

In this section, instead of reading sell and buy orders from files, as you did previously, you'll use a shell script we wrote to send the orders to a Kafka topic. The Spark Streaming job will read orders from this topic and write the computed metrics to a different Kafka topic. You'll then use the Kafka console consumer script to receive and display the results.

6.2.1   *Setting up Kafka*

Examples in this section use Kafka, which is already installed in the spark-in-action VM. If you aren't using our VM, and you wish to follow the examples in this section, you'll need to install and configure Kafka.

To set up Kafka, you first need to download it (from the official download page: http://kafka.apache.org/downloads.html). You should choose the release compatible with your version of Spark[3] (for example, the kafka_2.10-0.8.2.1.tgz archive for Spark 2.0). Next, unpack the archive to a folder on your hard drive:

```
$ tar -xvfz kafka_2.10-0.8.2.1.tgz
```

In the VM, Kafka has been installed for you in the folder /usr/local/kafka.

Kafka requires Apache ZooKeeper, an open source server for reliable, distributed process coordination (https://zookeeper.apache.org/), so you should start it before starting Kafka:

```
$ cd /usr/local/kafka
$ bin/zookeeper-server-start.sh config/zookeeper.properties &
```

This will start the ZooKeeper process on port 2181 and leave ZooKeeper working in the background. Next, you can start the Kafka server:

```
$ bin/kafka-server-start.sh config/server.properties &
```

Finally, you need to create topics that will be used for sending orders and metrics data:

```
$ bin/kafka-topics.sh --create --zookeeper localhost:2181
➥ --replication-factor 1 --partitions 1 --topic orders
$ bin/kafka-topics.sh --create --zookeeper localhost:2181
➥ --replication-factor 1 --partitions 1 --topic metrics
```

---

[3] You can check which version of Kafka to use for your version of Spark at http://mng.bz/Df88.

Now you're ready to update the Spark Streaming program from the previous section so that it reads and writes data to Kafka, instead of a filesystem.

6.2.2 *Changing the streaming application to use Kafka*

If you still have your Spark shell open, you'll need restart it at this point and add the Kafka library and Spark Kafka connector library to its classpath. You can download the required JAR files manually, or you can use the packages parameter[4] and have Spark download the files for you (don't execute this yet, though; you'll do that later):

```
$ spark-shell --master local[4] --packages org.apache.spark:spark-
➥ streaming-kafka-0-8_2.11:1.6.1,org.apache.kafka:kafka_2.11:0.8.2.1
```

The names between the colons in the packages parameter are the group ID, the artifact ID, and the version of the Spark Kafka connector artifact from the central Maven repository. The version depends on the version of Spark you're using. If you were building the application as a Maven project, you'd accomplish the same thing by adding the following dependencies to your pom.xml file:

```
<dependency>
  <groupId>org.apache.spark</groupId>
  <artifactId>spark-streaming-kafka-0-8_2.11</artifactId>
  <version>2.0.0</version>
</dependency>
<dependency>
  <groupId>org.apache.kafka</groupId>
  <artifactId>kafka_2.11</artifactId>
  <version>0.8.2.1</version>
</dependency>
```

USING THE SPARK KAFKA CONNECTOR

There are two versions of the Kafka connector. The first one is a receiver-based connector, and the second one is the newer *direct connector*. When using the receiver-based connector, in some circumstances, the same message may be consumed multiple times; the direct connector makes it possible to achieve exactly-once processing of incoming messages. The receiver-based connector is also less efficient (it requires a write-ahead log to be set up, which slows down the computation). You'll use the direct connector in this section.

To create a DStream that reads data from a Kafka topic, you need to set up a parameter map containing, at minimum, the metadata.broker.list parameter, which points to addresses of Kafka brokers in your cluster. Instead of a metadata.broker.list parameter, you can also specify the bootstrap.servers parameter with the same value. If you're running a single Kafka server on the same machine as your Spark shell, you just set it to the VM's address (192.168.10.2) and the default port, which is 9092:

```
val kafkaReceiverParams = Map[String, String](
  "metadata.broker.list" -> "192.168.10.2:9092")
```

---

[4] In some situations, the download may fail repeatedly. In that case, try to clear the Ivy cache: delete everything under .ivy/cache in your home directory.

Then you pass the parameter map to the `KafkaUtils.createDirectStream` method, along with a reference to the streaming context and a set of topic names to which you wish to connect. The `createDirectStream` method needs to be parameterized with classes to be used for message keys and values, and key and value decoders. In the case of this example, keys and values are strings, and you use Kafka's `StringDecoder` classes to decode them:

```
import org.apache.spark.streaming.kafka.KafkaUtils
val kafkaStream = KafkaUtils.
  createDirectStream[String, String, StringDecoder, StringDecoder](ssc,
  kafkaReceiverParams, Set("orders"))
```

The receiver-based consumer saves the last consumed message offset in ZooKeeper. The direct consumer doesn't use ZooKeeper but stores offsets in the Spark checkpoint directory. The `auto.offset.reset` parameter, which you can place in the parameter map, determines which messages to consume if the offset of the last consumed message isn't available. If it's set to `smallest`, it will start consuming from the smallest offset. By default, it consumes the latest messages.

The created `kafkaStream` can now be used the same way you used `fileStream` previously. The only difference is that `fileStream` had elements that were strings, whereas `kafkaStream` contains tuples with two strings: a key and a message. We'll skip that part of the code for now and first show you how to write messages back to Kafka. The complete code listing will be given at the end of this section.

WRITING MESSAGES TO KAFKA

Previously, you wrote the calculated metrics from the `finalStream` DStream to files. We'll now change that to write to Kafka's `metrics` topic instead. This is accomplished with the DStream's useful `foreachRDD` method, which we didn't mention earlier. You can use it to perform an arbitrary action on each RDD in a DStream. It has two versions:

```
def foreachRDD(foreachFunc: RDD[T] => Unit): Unit
def foreachRDD(foreachFunc: (RDD[T], Time) => Unit): Unit
```

Both versions take only a function as an argument, which receives an RDD and returns `Unit` (which is equal to `void` in Java). The difference is that the second function also receives a `Time` object, so it can make decisions based on the moment the RDD data was received.

To write messages to Kafka, you use Kafka's `Producer` object, which connects to a Kafka broker and sends messages represented as `KeyedMessage` objects. A `Producer` needs to be configured using a `ProducerConfig` object.

`Producer` objects aren't serializable: they open a connection to Kafka, and you can't serialize a connection, deserialize it in another JVM, and continue to use it. So you need to create `Producer` objects in the code that runs in executors. A first naïve attempt at sending messages to Kafka might look like this:

```
import kafka.producer.Producer
import kafka.producer.KeyedMessage
import kafka.producer.ProducerConfig
finalStream.foreachRDD((rdd) => {
  val prop = new java.util.Properties
  prop.put("metadata.broker.list", "192.168.10.2:9092")
  rdd.foreach(x => {
    val p = new Producer[Array[Byte], Array[Byte]](
      new ProducerConfig(prop))
    p.send(new KeyedMessage(topic, x.toString.toCharArray.map(_.toByte)))
    p.close()
  })
})
```

The bold part of the snippet is executed in executors, and the rest is executed in the driver. But this code creates a new `Producer` for each message! That's not good.

You can optimize this by using `foreachPartition` and creating a single `Producer` per RDD partition:

```
finalStream.foreachRDD((rdd) => {
  val prop = new java.util.Properties
  prop.put("metadata.broker.list", "192.168.10.2:9092")
  rdd.foreachPartition((iter) => {
    val p = new Producer[Array[Byte], Array[Byte]](
      new ProducerConfig(prop))
    iter.foreach(x => p.send(new KeyedMessage("metric",
      x.toString.toCharArray.map(_.toByte))))
    p.close()
  })
})
```

That's better but still not ideal. The best way would be to create a singleton object that initializes a `Producer` object only once per JVM. You'll create a singleton object as a companion object of the `KafkaProducerWrapper` class (we hope you remember companion objects from chapter 4). This is the code:

```
import kafka.producer.Producer
import kafka.producer.KeyedMessage
import kafka.producer.ProducerConfig
case class KafkaProducerWrapper(brokerList: String) {
  val producerProps = {
    val prop = new java.util.Properties
    prop.put("metadata.broker.list", brokerList)
    prop
  }
  val p = new Producer[Array[Byte], Array[Byte]](new         ◁──┐ Producer
    ProducerConfig(producerProps))                               object
  def send(topic: String, key: String, value: String) {   ◁──┐ Method for sending
    p.send(new KeyedMessage(topic, key.toCharArray.map(_.toByte),  messages
      value.toCharArray.map(_.toByte)))
  }
}
```

```
object KafkaProducerWrapper {                    ⟵——— Companion object
  var brokerList = ""
  lazy val instance = new KafkaProducerWrapper(brokerList)   ⟵┐ Lazily instantiated
}                                                             │ instance
```

As you may recall from chapter 4, companion objects have to be declared in the same file as the class of the same name. To avoid serialization and instantiation problems in Spark shell, you compile the KafkaProducerWrapper class into a JAR file, which should already be downloaded in the VM in the first-edition/ch06/ directory. Download the JAR file and start your Spark shell, adding the JAR to your Spark's classpath using the --jars parameter. Including the --packages parameter we mentioned before, the complete command for starting the Spark shell now looks like this:

```
$ spark-shell --master local[4] --packages org.apache.spark:spark-
➥ streaming-kafka_2.11:2.0.0,org.apache.kafka:kafka_2.11:0.8.2.1 --jars
{CA} first-edition/ch06/kafkaProducerWrapper.jar
```

Running the Python version

To run the Python version of the program, you'll only need the first package:

```
$ pyspark --master local[4] --packages org.apache.spark:spark-streaming-
➥ kafka_2.10:1.6.1
```

But you'll also need to install the kafka-python Python package (https://github.com/dpkp/kafka-python), which isn't installed in the spark-in-action VM by default. And you need to install pip:

```
$ sudo apt-get install python-pip
$ sudo pip install kafka-python
```

The complete Scala program (the Python version is in the repository), which you can paste into your Spark shell and which calculates all the metrics from this chapter and sends them to Kafka, is given in the following listing. In it, we combined all the code you've seen so far. There isn't much left to do but to execute it.

Listing 6.2 Complete code for calculating metrics and sending the results to Kafka

```
import org.apache.spark._
import kafka.serializer.StringDecoder
import kafka.producer.Producer
import kafka.producer.KeyedMessage
import kafka.producer.ProducerConfig
import org.apache.spark.streaming._
import org.apache.spark.streaming.kafka._

val ssc = new StreamingContext(sc, Seconds(5))

val kafkaReceiverParams = Map[String, String](
  "metadata.broker.list" -> "192.168.10.2:9092")
```

```scala
val kafkaStream = KafkaUtils.
  createDirectStream[String, String, StringDecoder, StringDecoder](ssc,
    kafkaReceiverParams, Set("orders"))

import java.sql.Timestamp
case class Order(time: java.sql.Timestamp, orderId:Long, clientId:Long,
  symbol:String, amount:Int, price:Double, buy:Boolean)
import java.text.SimpleDateFormat
val orders = kafkaStream.flatMap(line => {
  val dateFormat = new SimpleDateFormat("yyyy-MM-dd hh:mm:ss")
  val s = line._2.split(",")
  try {
    assert(s(6) == "B" || s(6) == "S")
    List(Order(new Timestamp(dateFormat.parse(s(0)).getTime()),
    s(1).toLong, s(2).toLong, s(3), s(4).toInt, s(5).toDouble, s(6) == "B"))
  }
  catch {
    case e : Throwable => println("Wrong line format ("+e+"): "+line._2)
    List()
  } })
val numPerType = orders.map(o => (o.buy, 1L)).reduceByKey((c1, c2) =>
  c1+c2)
val buySellList = numPerType.map(t =>
  if(t._1) ("BUYS", List(t._2.toString))
  else ("SELLS", List(t._2.toString)) )

val amountPerClient = orders.map(o => (o.clientId, o.amount*o.price))
val amountState = amountPerClient.updateStateByKey((vals,
    totalOpt:Option[Double]) => {
  totalOpt match {
    case Some(total) => Some(vals.sum + total)
    case None => Some(vals.sum)
  } })
val top5clients = amountState.transform(_.sortBy(_._2, false).map(_._1).
  zipWithIndex.filter(x => x._2 < 5))
val top5clList = top5clients.repartition(1).map(x => x._1.toString).
  glom().map(arr => ("TOP5CLIENTS", arr.toList))

val stocksPerWindow = orders.map(x => (x.symbol, x.amount)).
  reduceByKeyAndWindow((a1:Int, a2:Int) => a1+a2, Minutes(60))
val topStocks = stocksPerWindow.transform(_.sortBy(_._2, false).map(_._1).
  zipWithIndex.filter(x => x._2 < 5)).repartition(1).
    map(x => x._1.toString).glom().
    map(arr => ("TOP5STOCKS", arr.toList))

val finalStream = buySellList.union(top5clList).union(topStocks)

import org.sia.KafkaProducerWrapper
finalStream.foreachRDD((rdd) => {
  rdd.foreachPartition((iter) => {
    KafkaProducerWrapper.brokerList = "192.168.10.2:9092"
    val producer = KafkaProducerWrapper.instance
    iter.foreach({ case (metric, list) =>
      producer.send("metrics", metric, list.toString) })
  }) })
sc.setCheckpointDir("/home/spark/checkpoint")
ssc.start()
```

To see the program in action, you need to open two more Linux shells. We prepared a script that streams lines from the orders.txt file (a line every 0.1 seconds) and sends them to the `orders` Kafka topic. You can find the `streamOrders.sh` script in our online repository (which you should have cloned by now) and start it in the first Linux shell. You may first need to set its execution flag:

```
$ chmod +x streamOrders.sh
```

The script expects the orders.txt file to be present in the same directory and also needs to have the Kafka bin directory in the PATH (it will invoke the `kafka-console-producer.sh` script). You can give it the broker list as an argument (the default is `192.168.10.2:9092`):

```
$ ./streamOrders.sh 192.168.10.2:9092
```

In the second Linux shell, start the `kafka-console-consumer.sh` script, and have it consume messages from the `metrics` topic to see the output from your streaming program:

```
$ kafka-console-consumer.sh --zookeeper localhost:2181 --topic metrics
TOP5CLIENTS, List(62, 2, 92, 25, 19)
SELLS, List(12)
BUYS, List(20)
TOP5STOCKS, List(CHK, DOW, FB, SRPT, ABX)
TOP5CLIENTS, List(2, 62, 87, 52, 45)
TOP5STOCKS, List(FB, CTRE, AU, PHG, EGO)
SELLS, List(28)
BUYS, List(21)
SELLS, List(37)
BUYS, List(12)
TOP5STOCKS, List(FB, CTRE, SDLP, AU, NEM)
TOP5CLIENTS, List(14, 2, 81, 43, 31)
```

And there you have it. Your Spark Streaming program is sending its calculated metrics back through Kafka.

6.3 *Performance of Spark Streaming jobs*

You generally want your streaming applications to

- Process each input record as fast as possible (low latency)
- Keep up with increases in the flow of incoming data (scalability)
- Keep ingesting data and not lose any data in case of a node failure (fault tolerance)

There are a few parameters worth mentioning when it comes to tuning performance for Spark Streaming jobs and ensuring that they're fault-tolerant.

6.3.1 Obtaining good performance

With Spark Streaming, the first parameter you need to decide on is the mini-batch duration. There is no exact method of determining its value, because it depends on the type of processing the job is performing and the capacity of your cluster. What can help you with that is the Streaming page of the Spark web UI, which automatically starts for each Spark application. You can access the Spark web UI on port 4040, by default.

The Streaming tab automatically appears on the web UI if you're running a Spark Streaming application (`StreamingContext`). It shows several useful graphs, shown in figure 6.4, with the following metrics:

- *Input Rate*—Number of incoming records per second
- *Scheduling Delay*—Time the new mini-batches spend waiting for their jobs to be scheduled
- *Processing Time*—Time required to process the jobs of each mini-batch
- *Total Delay*—Total time taken to handle a batch

The total processing time per mini-batch (the total delay) should be lower than the mini-batch duration, and it should be more or less constant. If it keeps increasing, the computation isn't sustainable in the long run, and you'll have to decrease the processing time, increase parallelism, or limit the input rate.

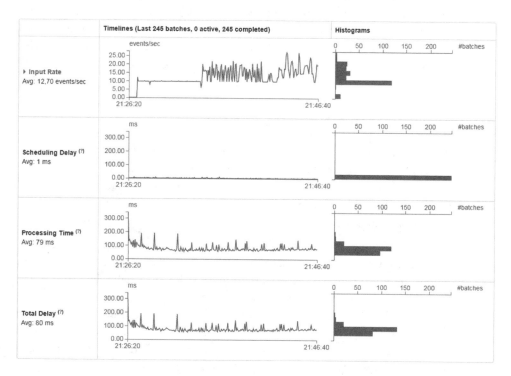

Figure 6.4 Streaming page of the Spark web UI, showing various metrics: Input Rate, Scheduling Delay, Processing Time, and Total Delay

LOWERING THE PROCESSING TIME

If you start seeing scheduling delays, the first step is to try to optimize your program and decrease the processing time per batch. Methods in this book will help with that. You need to avoid unnecessary shuffles, as we discussed in chapter 4. If you're sending data to external systems, you need to reuse connections within partitions and use some kind of connection pooling, as we discussed in this chapter.

You can also try to increase the mini-batch duration, because Spark Streaming job-scheduling, task-serialization, and data-shuffling times will even out on larger datasets and thus decrease the processing time per record. But setting the mini-batch duration too high will increase memory requirements for each mini-batch; in addition, lower output frequency may not satisfy your business requirements.

Additional cluster resources can also help to decrease the processing time. Adding memory may lower the garbage-collection rate, for example, and adding CPU cores may increase processing speed.

INCREASING PARALLELISM

But in order to use all CPU cores efficiently and get more throughput, you need to increase parallelism. You can increase it on several levels. First, you can do so at the input source. For example, Kafka has the concept of *partitions*, which determine the level of parallelism that can be achieved by the consumer. If you're using a Kafka direct connector, it will handle parallelism automatically and match the number of consuming threads in Spark Streaming to the number of partitions in Kafka.

But if you're using a receiver-based connector, you can increase consumer parallelism by creating several DStreams and using them together:

```
val stream1 = ...
val stream2 = ...
val stream = stream2.union(stream2)
```

At the next level, parallelism can be increased by explicitly repartitioning DStreams to a higher number of partitions (by using the repartition method). A general rule of thumb is that the number of receivers shouldn't exceed the number of cores available or the number of executors.

LIMITING THE INPUT RATE

Finally, if you can't decrease the processing time or increase parallelism, and you still experience increasing scheduling delays, you may need to limit the rate at which data is ingested. There are two parameters for manually limiting the ingestion rate: spark.streaming.receiver.maxRate for receiver-based consumers and spark.streaming.kafka.maxRatePerPartition for the Kafka direct consumer. The former limits the number of records per receiver-based stream, and the latter the number of records per Kafka partition (more than one Kafka partition can be read by a single direct Kafka stream). Both represent the number of records per second and aren't set by default.

You can also enable the *backpressure* feature by setting the `spark.streaming` `.backpressure.enabled` parameter to `true`. It will automatically limit the maximum number of messages that can be received by your application if scheduling delays start to appear. But the rate will never exceed the values of the previous two parameters, if they're set.

6.3.2 *Achieving fault-tolerance*

Streaming applications are usually long-running applications, and failures of driver and executor processes are to be expected. Spark Streaming makes it possible to survive these failures with zero data loss.

RECOVERING FROM EXECUTOR FAILURES

Data received through receivers running in executors is replicated in the cluster. If an executor running a receiver fails, the driver will restart the executor on a different node, and the data will be recovered. You don't need to enable this behavior specifically. Spark does this automatically.

RECOVERING FROM DRIVER FAILURES

In the case of a failure of the driver process, the connection to the executors is lost, and the application needs to be restarted. As we'll discuss in chapters 11 and 12, the cluster manager can automatically restart the driver process (if submitted with the `--supervise` option when running in a Spark Standalone cluster, by using cluster mode in YARN, or by using Marathon in Mesos).

Once the driver process is restarted, Spark Streaming can recover the state of the previous streaming application by reading the checkpointed state of the streaming context. Spark's `StreamingContext` has a special method of initialization to take advantage of this feature. The method is `StreamingContext.getOrCreate()`, and it takes a checkpoint directory and a function for initializing the context. The function needs to perform all the usual steps to instantiate your streams and initialize a `StreamingContext` object. The `getOrCreate` method first checks the checkpoint directory to see if any state exists there. If so, it loads the previous checkpointed state and skips the `StreamingContext` initialization. Otherwise, it calls the initialization function.

To use this in the example from this chapter, you need to rearrange the code a bit:

```
def setupStreamContext(): StreamingContext {
  val ssc = new StreamingContext(sc, Seconds(5))
  val kafkaReceiverParams = Map[String, String]("metadata.broker.list" ->
  "192.168.10.2:9092")
  //...
  //perform all other DStream computations
  //...
  ssc.checkpoint("checkpoint_dir")
  ssc
}
val ssc = StreamingContext("checkpoint_dir", setupStreamContext)
ssc.start()
```

`ssc.checkpoint` tells the Streaming context to periodically save the state of the streams to the specified directory. And that's it. In case of a driver restart, your application will be able to continue from where it left off.

One more thing is required to prevent loss of data in case of a driver restart. Spark Streaming receivers can write all the data they receive to the write-ahead log, before the data is processed. They acknowledge to the input source (if the input source allows messages to be acknowledged) that the message was received only after it was written to the write-ahead log. If a receiver (and its executor) is restarted, it reads all the unprocessed data from the write-ahead logs, so no data loss occurs. The Kafka direct connector doesn't need write-ahead logs to prevent data loss, because Kafka provides that functionality.

Write-ahead logs aren't enabled by default. You need to explicitly enable them by setting `spark.streaming.receiver.writeAheadLog.enable` to `true`.

6.4   Structured Streaming

In Spark 2.0, an experimental new streaming API was introduced called *structured streaming*. The idea behind it is to make the streaming API similar to the batch API by obscuring the details that are involved in making streaming operations fault-tolerant and consistent.

Structured streaming operations work directly on `DataFrames` (or rather `DataSets`). There is no longer a concept of a "stream." There are only streaming and ordinary `DataFrames`. Streaming `DataFrames` are implemented as append-only tables. Queries on streaming data return new `DataFrames` and you work with them similarly as you would in a batch program.

6.4.1   Creating a streaming DataFrame

To create a streaming DataFrame, instead of calling `read` on a `SparkSession`, you call `readStream`. It will return a `DataStreamReader`, with almost the same methods as `DataFrameReader`. The crucial difference is that it works on data that is continuously arriving.

As an example, let's load the files from the `ch06input` folder, as you did in the beginning of this chapter, but using the structured streaming API. You will first need the `DataFrame` implicits:

```
import spark.implicits._
```

Then use `DataStreamReader`'s text method to load the files:

```
scala> val structStream = spark.readStream.text("ch06input")
structStream: org.apache.spark.sql.DataFrame = [value: string]
```

As you can see, the resulting object is a `DataFrame` with a single column called "value." You can check if it's a streaming `DataFrame` by calling its `isStreaming` method:

```
scala> structStream.isStreaming
res0: Boolean = true
```

You can also examine the execution plan:

```
scala> structStream.explain()
== Physical Plan ==
StreamingRelation FileSource[ch06input], [value#263]
```

6.4.2 *Outputting streaming data*

The `structStream` will monitor the input folder for new files and periodically process them. You still didn't tell it how to process them, though. To do anything useful with a streaming `DataFrame`, and to start the streaming computation, you have to use `Data-Frame`'s `writeStream` method, which give you an instance of `DataStreamWriter` class. It can also be configured using the *builder* pattern, which means that you can chain configuration functions one after another. Some of the available functions are:

- `Trigger`–Use it to specify the interval at which execution is triggered. You need to use `ProcessingTime.create` function to construct interval descriptions. For example: `ProcessingTime.create("5 seconds")`.
- `format`–Specify the output format. Only `"parquet"`, `"console"`, and `"memory"` are supported in Spark 2.0. The first one writes to Parquet files, the second one prints the `DataFrames` to the console (using `show()`), and the third one keeps the data as a table in the driver's memory, which you can query interactively.
- `outputMode`—Specify the output mode.
- `option`—Specify other specific parameters.
- `foreach`—Use it to perform computations on individual `DataFrames`. You have to specify a class implementing the `ForeachWriter` interface.
- `queryName` - used with the "memory" format.

Only two output modes are currently (Spark 2.0) supported:

- `append`—Output only the data that was received after the last output.
- `complete`—Output all available data every time. Can only be used with aggregations.

After you specify all the configuration options you want, call `start()` to start the streaming computation. To print the first 20 rows of each file arriving into the ch06input folder every five seconds, run this:

```
scala> import org.apache.spark.sql.streaming.ProcessingTime
scala> val streamHandle = structStream.
    writeStream.
    format("console").
    trigger(ProcessingTime.create("5 seconds")).
    start()
```

To see the results in your console, start the `splitAndSend.sh` script in a separate Linux console, as you did at the beginning of this chapter:

```
$ cd first-edition/ch06
$ ./splitAndSend.sh /home/spark/ch06input local
```

You should now see the contents of the files in your Spark shell.

6.4.3   *Examining streaming executions*

`start()` returns a `StreamingQuery` object, which acts as a handle to the streaming execution. You can use it to check execution's status with the `isActive()` method, stop the execution with the `stop()` method, block until the execution is over with the `awaitTermination()` method, examine an exception (in case it occurred) with the `exception()` method, or get execution's ID from the `id` field.

SparkSession also provides the means of querying streaming executions. `SparkSession.streams.active` returns an array of active streaming executions, `SparkSession.streams.get(id)` enables you to get a streaming handle using its ID, and `SparkSession.streams.awaitAnyTermination` blocks until any of the streaming executions finishes.

6.4.4   *Future direction of structured streaming*

While still an experimental feature in Spark 2.0, structured streaming is proving to be a powerful concept. It enables true unification of batch and streaming computations and joining of streaming with batch data, a feature not many streaming engines can boast. On top of that, it brings Tungsten performance improvements to Spark streaming.

The Spark community has big plans with structured streaming. Community members want to extend it to all other Spark components: to train machine-learning algorithms on streaming data and to perform ETL transformations using streaming concepts, which could lower capacity requirements. What other improvements await us, remains to be seen.

This was a short overview of structured streaming. You can find more information about structured streaming as it develops in the official Structured Streaming Programming Guide (http://mng.bz/bxF9) and in its original design document (http://mng.bz/0ipm).

6.5   *Summary*

- Spark Streaming applies Spark's batch-processing features to real-time data by using mini-batches.
- Spark can ingest data from filesystems and TCP/IP socket connections, but also from other distributed systems, such as Kafka, Flume, Twitter, and Amazon Kinesis.
- The mini-batch duration is set when initializing a Spark Streaming context. It determines the interval at which input data will be split and packaged as an RDD. It has a big influence on your system's performance.
- `DStream` (which stands for *discretized stream*) is the basic abstraction in Spark Streaming, representing a sequence of RDDs, periodically created from the input stream. You can't write Spark Streaming programs without them.

- `DStreams` have methods that transform them to other `DStreams`. You can use those methods to filter, map, and reduce data in `DStream`'s RDDs and even combine and join different `DStreams`.

- `DStream`'s `saveAsTextFiles` method takes a `String` prefix and an optional `String` suffix and uses them to construct the path at which the data should be periodically saved. You can use it to save the results of your computations to the filesystem.

- You can use the `updateStateByKey` and `mapWithState` methods to perform calculations while taking into account the previous state of the computation.

- The `mapWithState` method lets you maintain a state of one type and return data of another. It also brings performance improvements.

- Checkpointing is necessary when saving the streaming state, because otherwise the RDD lineage will get too long; this will eventually result in stack-overflow errors.

- Window operations operate on a sliding window of mini-batches, determined by the window duration and the slide of the window. You can use them to maintain a time-bounded state and perform calculations on the data contained in them.

- Before using external sources, their Maven packages need to be added to the Spark classpath.

- Spark has two Kafka connectors: a receiver-based connector and a direct connector. The direct connector enables exactly-once processing.

- The best way to write a message to Kafka is to create a singleton object that initializes a `Producer` object only once per JVM. That way, a single connection per executor can be reused throughout the lifetime of your streaming application.

- The Streaming page of the Spark Web UI contains useful graphs that can help you determine the ideal mini-batch duration.

- Scheduling delays in streaming applications can be reduced by decreasing processing time, increasing parallelism, adding more resources, or limiting the input rate.

- Jobs can be made fault-tolerant by enabling automatic restart of the driver process, initializing the `StreamingContext` with `StreamingContext.getOrCreate`, and enabling write-ahead logs for receiver-based connectors.

7
Getting smart with MLlib

Machine learning is a scientific discipline that studies the use and development of algorithms that make computers accomplish complicated tasks without explicitly programming them. That is, the algorithms eventually learn how they can solve a given task. These algorithms include methods and techniques from statistics, probability, and information theory.

Today, machine learning is ubiquitous. Examples include online stores that offer you similar items that other users have viewed or bought, email clients that automatically move emails to spam, advances in autonomous driving recently developed by several car manufacturers, and speech and video recognition. It's also becoming a big part of online business: finding hidden relationships in user habits and actions (and learning from them) can bring critical added value to existing products and services.

But with the advent of companies handling huge amounts of data (known as *big data*), more scalable machine-learning packages are needed. Spark provides distributed and scalable implementations of various machine-learning algorithms and makes it possible to handle those continuously growing datasets.[1]

Spark offers distributed implementations of the most important and most often-used machine-learning algorithms, and new implementations are constantly being added. Spark's distributed nature helps you apply machine-learning algorithms on very large datasets with adequate speed. Spark, as a unifying platform, lets you perform most of the machine-learning tasks (such as data collection, preparation, analysis, model training, and evaluation) all in the same system and using the same API.

In this chapter, you'll use *linear regression* to predict Boston housing prices. *Regression analysis* is a statistical process of modeling relationships between variables, and *linear regression*, as a special type of the regression analysis, assumes those relationships to be linear. It's historically one of the most widely used and most simple regression methods in statistics.

While using linear regression to predict housing prices, you'll learn about linear regression itself, how to prepare the data, train the model, use the model to make predictions, and evaluate the model's performance and optimize it. We'll begin with a short introduction to machine learning and a primer on using linear regression in Spark.

First, a disclaimer. Machine learning is such a vast subject that it's impossible to fully cover it here. To learn more about machine learning in general, check out *Real-World Machine Learning*, by Henrik Brink and Joseph W. Richards (Manning, 2016 [est.]), and *Machine Learning in Action*, by Peter Harrington (Manning, 2012). A sea of other resources can be found online; Stanford's "Machine Learning" course by Andrew Ng (http://mng.bz/K6XZ) is an excellent starting point.

7.1 Introduction to machine learning

Let's start with an example of using machine learning in real life. Let's say you're running a website that lets people sell their cars online. And let's say you'd like your system to automatically propose to your sellers reasonable starting prices when they post their ads. You know that regression analysis can be used for that purpose by taking data of previous sales, analyzing characteristics of the cars and their selling prices, and modeling the relation between them. But you don't have enough ads in your database, so you decide to get car prices from publicly available sources. You find a lot of

---

[1] Spark isn't the only framework that provides a distributed machine-learning package. There are other frameworks, such as GraphLab, Flink, and TensorFlow.

interesting car sale records online, but most of the data is available in CSV files, and large parts of it are PDF and Word documents (containing car sale offers).

You first parse PDFs and Word documents to identify and match similar fields (manufacturer, model, make, and so on). You know that a regression-analysis model can't handle string values of various fields ("automatic" and "manual," for example), so you come up with a way to convert these values to numeric ones. Then you notice that important fields are missing from some of the records (year manufactured, for example) and you decide to remove those records from your dataset.

When you finally have the data cleaned up and stored somewhere, you start examining various fields—how they're correlated and what their distributions look like (this is important for understanding the hidden dependencies of the data). Then you decide which regression-analysis model to use.

Let's say you choose linear regression, because, based on the correlations you calculated, you assume the main relations to be linear. Before building a model, you normalize and scale the data (more on how and why this is done soon) and split it into training and validation datasets. You finally train your model using the training data (you use the historical data to set weights of the model to predict the future data where the price isn't known; we'll explain this later), and you get a usable linear-regression model. But when you test it on your validation dataset, the results are horrible. You change some of the parameters used for training the model, test it again, and repeat the process until you get a model with acceptable performance. Finally, you incorporate the model in your web application and start getting emails from your clients wondering how you're doing that (or from clients complaining about bad predictions).

What this example illustrates is that a machine-learning project consists of multiple steps. Although typical steps are shown in figure 7.1, the entire process can usually be broken down into the following:

1 *Collecting data*—First the data needs to be gathered from various sources. The sources can be log files, database records, signals coming from sensors, and so on. Spark can help load the data from relational databases, CSV files, remote services, and distributed file systems like HDFS, or from real-time sources using Spark Streaming.

2 *Cleaning and preparing data*—Data isn't always available in a structured format appropriate for machine learning (text, images, sounds, binary data, and so forth), so you need to devise and carry out a method of transforming this unstructured data into numerical features. Additionally, you need to handle missing data and the different forms in which the same values can be entered (for example, *VW* and *Volkswagen* are the same carmaker). Often, data also needs to be scaled so that all dimensions are of comparable ranges.

3 *Analyzing data and extracting features*—Next you analyze the data, examine its correlations, and visualize them (using various tools) if necessary. (The number of dimensions may be reduced in this step if some of them don't bring any extra information: for example, if they're redundant.) You then choose the

appropriate machine-learning algorithm (or set of algorithms) and split the data into training and validation subsets—this is important because you'd like to see how the model behaves on the data not seen during the training phase. Or you decide on a different cross-validation method, where you continuously split the dataset into different training and validation datasets and average the results over the rounds.

4 *Training the model*—You train a model by running an algorithm that *learns* a set of algorithm-specific parameters from the input data.

5 *Evaluating the model*—You then put the model to use on the validation dataset and evaluate its performance according to some criteria. At this point, you may decide that you need more input data or that you need to change the way features were extracted. You may also change the feature space or switch to a different model. In any of these cases, you go back to step 1 or step 2.

6 *Using the model*—Finally, you deploy the built model to the production environment of your website.

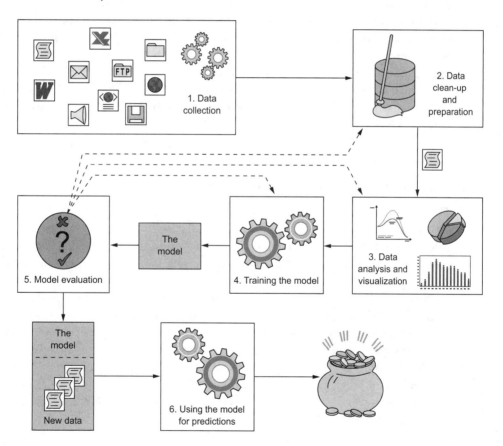

Figure 7.1 Typical steps in a machine-learning project

The mechanics of using an API (Spark or some other machine-learning library) to train and test the models is only the last and the shortest part of the process. Equally important are collection, preparation, and analysis of data, where knowledge about the problem domain is needed. Therefore, this and the following chapter on machine learning are mostly about steps 4 and 5, as described previously.

7.1.1   *Definition of machine learning*

Machine learning is one of the largest research areas in *artificial intelligence,* a scientific field that studies algorithms for simulating intelligence. Ron Kohavi and Foster Provost, in their article "Glossary of Terms," describe machine learning in these words:

> *Machine learning is a scientific discipline that explores the construction and study of algorithms that can learn from and make predictions on data.*[2]

This is in contrast to traditional programming methods where what an algorithm needs to do (like parsing an XML file with a certain structure) is explicitly programmed into it. Such traditional methods can't be easily expanded to cover similar tasks, like parsing XML files with a similar structure. As another example, making a speech-recognition program that recognizes different accents and voices would be impossible by explicitly programming it, because the sheer number of variations in the way a single word can be pronounced would necessitate that many versions of the program.

Instead of incorporating the explicit knowledge about the problem area in the program itself, machine learning relies on methods from the fields of statistics, probability, and information theory to discover and use the knowledge inherent in data and then change the behavior of a program accordingly in order to be able to solve the initial task (such as recognizing speech).

7.1.2   *Classification of machine-learning algorithms*

The most basic classification of machine-learning algorithms divides them into two classes: *supervised* and *unsupervised learners.* A dataset for supervised learning is prelabeled (information about the expected prediction output is provided with the data), whereas one for unsupervised learning contains no labels, and the algorithm needs to determine them itself.

Supervised learning is used for many practical machine-learning problems today, such as spam detection, speech and handwriting recognition, and computer vision. A spam-detection algorithm, for example, is trained on examples of emails manually marked as spam or not spam (labeled data) and learns how to classify future emails.

Unsupervised learning is also a powerful tool that is widely used. Among other purposes, it's used for discovering structure within data—for example, groups of similar items known as *clusters)*—anomaly detection, image segmentation, and so on.

---

[2] Ron Kohavi and Foster Provost, "Glossary of Terms," Special Issue on Applications of Machine Learning and the Knowledge Discovery Process, *Machine Learning,* vol. 30 (1998): 271–274.

CLASSIFICATION OF SUPERVISED AND UNSUPERVISED ALGORITHMS

In supervised learning, an algorithm is given a set of known inputs and matching outputs, and it has to find a function that can be used to transform the given inputs to the true outputs, even in the case of input data not seen during the training phase. The same function can then be used to predict outputs of any future input. The typical supervised learning tasks are regression and classification.

Regression attempts to predict the values of continuous output variables based on a set of input variables. *Classification* aims to classify sets of inputs into two or more classes (discrete output variables). Both regression and classification models are trained based on a set of inputs with known outputs—where known outputs are the output variables, values, or classes, which are supervised problems.

In the case of unsupervised learning, the output isn't known in advance, and the algorithm has to find some structure in the data without additional information being provided. A typical unsupervised learning task is clustering. With clustering, the goal of the algorithm is to discover dense regions, called clusters, in the input data by analyzing similarities between the input examples. There are no known classes used as a reference.

For an example of the differences between supervised and unsupervised learning, consider figure 7.2. It shows the often-used Iris flower dataset[3] created in 1936. The dataset contains widths and lengths of petals and sepals[4] of 150 flowers of three iris species: *Iris setosa, Iris versicolor,* and *Iris virginica* (50 flowers of each species). For the sake of simplicity, only sepal length and width are given in figure 7.2. That way, you can plot the dataset in two dimensions.

Sepal length and sepal width are *features* (or *dimensions*) of the input, and the flower species is the output (or *target variable,* a *label*). You'd like your algorithm to find a mapping function that correctly maps sepal length and sepal width to flower species for existing and future examples.

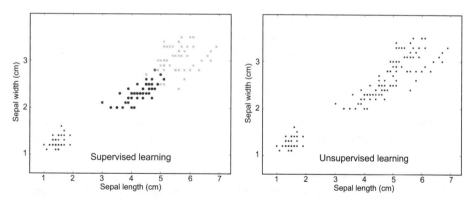

Figure 7.2 Supervised and unsupervised learning in the Iris flower dataset. The dataset for supervised learning is prelabeled, whereas the one for unsupervised learning contains no labels because the algorithm needs to determine them itself.

---

[3] Iris flower dataset, Wikipedia (http://en.wikipedia.org/wiki/Iris_flower_data_set).

[4] A *sepal* is the part of a flower that supports its petals and protects the flower in bud.

NOTE   For historical reasons, and because of many possible application areas, a single concept in machine learning can have several different names. Inputs are also called *examples, points, data samples, observations,* or *instances*. In Spark, training examples for supervised learning are called *labeled points*. Features (sepal length and sepal width in the Iris dataset, for example) are also called *dimensions, attributes, variables,* or *independent variables*.

In the graph on the left in figure 7.2, flower species corresponding to each input are marked with dots, circles, and Xes, which means the flower species are known in advance. We call this the *training set* because it can be used to train (or *fit*) the parameters of the machine-learning model to determine the mapping function. You then test the accuracy of your trained model using a *test set* containing a different set of labeled examples. If satisfied with its performance, you then let it predict labels for real data.

The graph on the right in figure 7.2 shows clustering (a form of unsupervised learning), which requires the algorithm to find the mapping function *and* the categories. As you can see, all the examples are marked with the same symbol (a dot), and the algorithm needs to find the most likely grouping system for the given examples.

In the graph showing clustering, there is obviously a clear separation between the group of examples in the lower-left corner of the graph and the rest of the examples, but the separation between the other two categories isn't that clear. You can probably already guess that an unsupervised learning algorithm will be less successful in correctly separating this dataset into the three flower categories, because the supervised learning algorithm has much more data to learn from.

ALGORITHM CLASSIFICATION BASED ON THE TYPE OF TARGET VARIABLE

In addition to classifying machine-learning algorithms as supervised and unsupervised, we can also classify them according to the type of the target variable into *classification* and *regression* algorithms. The Iris dataset mentioned in the last section is an example of a *classification* problem because target variables are *categorical* (or *qualitative*), which means they can take on a limited number of values (*discrete* values). In classification algorithms, the target variable is also called a *label, class,* or *category*, and the algorithm itself is called a *classifier, recognizer,* or *categorizer*. In the case of regression algorithms, the target variable is *continuous* or *quantitative* (a real number).

Both regression and classification are plainly supervised learning algorithms because the estimation function is fitted according to a priori known values. Figure 7.3 shows an example of linear regression with only one feature, shown on the X axis. The output value is shown on the Y axis.

The goal of regression is to find, based on a set of examples, a mathematical function that is as close an approximation of the relationship between features and the target variable as possible. The regression in figure 7.3 is a simple linear regression because there is only one independent variable (making it simple), and the hypothesis function is modeled as a linear function (a straight line). If there were two variables, you could plot the estimation function in 3D space as a plane. When there are more features, the function becomes a *hyperplane*.

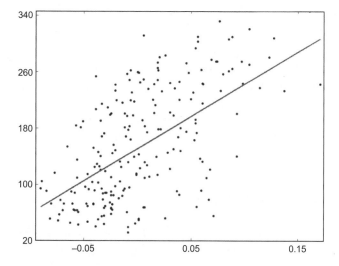

Figure 7.3 Example of a simple linear-regression problem

7.1.3 *Machine learning with Spark*

All the advantages of Spark extend to machine learning, too. The most important aspect of Spark is its distributed nature. It enables you to train and apply machine-learning algorithms on very large datasets with adequate speed.

The second advantage is Spark's unifying nature; it offers a platform for performing most tasks. You can collect, prepare, and analyze the data and train, evaluate, and use the model—all in the same system and using the same API.

Spark offers distributed implementations of the most popular machine-learning algorithms, and new ones are constantly added. Spark's primary machine learning API is called MLlib. It's based on the MLbase project in Berkeley, CA. Since its inclusion in Spark 0.8, MLlib has been expanded and developed by the open source community.

Spark 1.2 introduced a new machine learning API called Spark ML. The idea behind Spark ML is to provide a generalized API that can be used for training and tuning different algorithms in the same way. It also provides *pipelines,* sequences of machine-learning-related processing steps that are collected and handled as a unit.

The new Spark ML API is being developed in parallel with the "old" Spark MLlib API. Spark MLlib will continue to be supported and expanded.

Spark relies on several low-level libraries for performing optimized linear algebra operations. These are Breeze and jblas for Scala and Java and NumPy for Python. Refer to the official documentation (http://mng.bz/417O) for how to configure these. We'll use the default Spark build, but that decision shouldn't influence the functional aspects described in this chapter.

7.2 *Linear algebra in Spark*

Linear algebra is a branch of mathematics focusing on vector spaces and linear operations and mappings between them expressed mainly by matrices. Linear algebra is essential for understanding the math behind most machine-learning algorithms, so if you don't know much about vectors and matrices, you should have a peek at appendix C for a primer on linear algebra.

Matrices and vectors in Spark can be manipulated locally (in the driver or executor processes) or in a distributed manner. Implementations of distributed matrices in Spark enable you to perform linear algebra operations on huge amounts of data, spanning numerous machines. For local linear algebra operations, Spark uses the very fast Breeze and jblas libraries (and NumPy in Python), and it has its own implementations of distributed ones.

Sparse and dense vectors and matrices

Spark supports *sparse* and *dense* vectors and matrices. A vector or matrix is sparse if it contains mostly zeros. It's more efficient to represent such data with pairs of indices and values at those indices. A sparse vector or matrix can be likened to a map (or dictionary in Python).

Conversely, a dense vector or matrix contains all the data—values at all index positions not storing the indices, similar to an array or a list.

7.2.1 *Local vector and matrix implementations*

Local vector and matrix implementations in Spark are located in the package `org.apache.spark.mllib.linalg`. We'll examine Spark's linear algebra API with a set of examples you can run in your Spark shell. To start the shell in local mode, use the command `spark-shell --master local[*]`. We'll assume you're running Spark in the spark-in-action VM.

GENERATING LOCAL VECTORS

Local vectors in Spark are implemented with two classes—`DenseVector` and `SparseVector`—implementing a common interface called `Vector`, making sure both implementations support exactly the same set of operations. The main class for creating vectors is the `Vectors` class and its `dense` and `sparse` method. The `dense` method has two versions: it can take all elements as inline arguments or it can take an array of elements. For the `sparse` method, you need to specify a vector size, an array with indices, and an array with values. The following three vectors (dv1, dv2, and sv) contain the same elements and, hence, represent the same mathematical vectors:

```
import org.apache.spark.mllib.linalg.{Vectors,Vector}
val dv1 = Vectors.dense(5.0,6.0,7.0,8.0)
val dv2 = Vectors.dense(Array(5.0,6.0,7.0,8.0))
val sv = Vectors.sparse(4, Array(0,1,2,3), Array(5.0,6.0,7.0,8.0))
```

> **NOTE** Make sure to always use sorted indices for constructing your sparse vectors (the second argument of the `sparse` method). Otherwise, you may get unexpected results.

You can access a specific element in the vector by its index like this:

```
scala> dv2(2)
res0: Double = 7.0
```

You can get the size of the vector with the `size` method:

```
scala> dv1.size
res1: Int = 4
```

To get all elements of a vector as an array, you can use the `toArray` method:

```
scala> dv2.toArray
res2: Array[Double] = Array(5.0, 6.0, 7.0, 8.0)
```

LINEAR ALGEBRA OPERATIONS ON LOCAL VECTORS

Linear algebra operations on local vectors can be done using the Breeze library, which Spark uses internally for the same purposes. `toBreeze` functions exist in Spark vector and matrix local implementations, but they're declared as private. The Spark community has decided not to allow end users access to this library, because they don't want to depend on a third-party library. But you'll most likely need a library for handling local vectors and matrices.

An alternative would be to create your own function for converting Spark vectors to Breeze classes, which isn't that hard to do. We propose the following solution:

```
import org.apache.spark.mllib.linalg.{DenseVector, SparseVector, Vector}
import breeze.linalg.{DenseVector => BDV,SparseVector => BSV,Vector => BV}
def toBreezeV(v:Vector):BV[Double] = v match {
    case dv:DenseVector => new BDV(dv.values)
    case sv:SparseVector => new BSV(sv.indices, sv.values, sv.size)
}
```

Now you can use this function (`toBreezeV`) and the Breeze library to add vectors and calculate their dot products. For example:

```
scala> toBreezeV(dv1) + toBreezeV(dv2)
res3: breeze.linalg.Vector[Double] = DenseVector(10.0, 12.0, 14.0, 16.0)
scala> toBreezeV(dv1).dot(toBreezeV(dv2))
res4: Double = 174.0
```

The Breeze library offers more linear algebra operations, and we invite you to examine its rich set of functionalities. You should note that the names of Breeze classes conflict with the names of Spark classes, so be careful when using both in your code. One solution is to change the class names during import, as in the preceding `toBreezeV` function example.

GENERATING LOCAL DENSE MATRICES

Similar to the `Vectors` class, the `Matrices` class also has the methods `dense` and `sparse` for creating matrices. The `dense` method expects number of rows, number of columns, and an array with the data (elements of type `Double`). The data should be specified column-wise, which means the elements of the array will be used sequentially to populate columns. For example, to create the following matrix as a `DenseMatrix`

$$M = \begin{bmatrix} 5 & 0 & 1 \\ 0 & 3 & 4 \end{bmatrix}$$

use a code snippet similar to this one:

```
scala> import org.apache.spark.mllib.linalg.{DenseMatrix, SparseMatrix,
Matrix, Matrices}
scala> import breeze.linalg.{DenseMatrix => BDM,CSCMatrix => BSM,Matrix =>
    BM}
scala> val dm = Matrices.dense(2,3,Array(5.0,0.0,0.0,3.0,1.0,4.0))
dm: org.apache.spark.mllib.linalg.Matrix =
5.0   0.0   1.0
0.0   3.0   4.0
```

A `Matrices` object provides shortcut methods for quickly creating identity and diagonal matrices and matrices with all zeros and ones. The `eye(n)` method[5] creates a dense identity matrix of size $n \times n$. The method `speye` is the equivalent for creating a sparse identity matrix. The methods `ones(m, n)` and `zeros(m, n)` create dense matrices with all ones or zeros of size $m \times n$. The `diag` method takes a `Vector` and creates a diagonal matrix (its elements are all zeros, except the ones on its main diagonal) with elements from the input `Vector` placed on its diagonal. Its dimensions are equal to the size of the input `Vector`.

Additionally, you can generate a `DenseMatrix` filled with random numbers in a range from 0 to 1 using the `rand` and `randn` methods of the `Matrices` object. The first method generates numbers according to a uniform distribution, and the second according to Gaussian distribution. (Gaussian distribution, also known as *normal* distribution, has that familiar bell-shaped curve.) Both distributions take the number of rows, the number of columns, and an initialized `java.util.Random` object as arguments. The `sprand` and `sprandn` methods are equivalent methods for generating `SparseMatrix` objects.

NOTE These methods (`eye`, `rand`, `randn`, `zeros`, `ones`, and `diag`) aren't available in Python.

GENERATING LOCAL SPARSE MATRICES

Generating sparse matrices is a bit more involved than generating dense ones. You also pass the number of rows and columns to the `sparse` method, but the nonzero element values (in sparse matrices only, nonzero elements are needed) are specified

---

[5] Identity matrices are usually denoted with the letter *I*, pronounced the same as "eye"; hence the pun in the method name.

in compressed sparse column (CSC) format.[6] CSC format is made of three arrays, containing column pointers, row indices, and the nonzero elements. A row indices array contains the row index of each element in the elements array. The column pointers array contains ranges of indices of elements that belong to the same column.

NOTE `SparseMatrix` isn't available in Python.

For the previous *M* matrix example (the same matrix used previously), the arrays for specifying the matrix in CSC format are as follows:

```
colPtrs = [0 1 2 4], rowIndices = [0 1 0 1], elements = [5 3 1 4]
```

The `colPtrs` array tells us that the elements from index 0 (inclusive) to 1 (non-inclusive), which is only element 5, belong to the first column. Elements from index 1 to 2, which is only element 3, belong to the second column. Finally, elements from index 2 to 4 (elements 1 and 4) belong to the third column. The row index of each element is given in the `rowIndices` array.

To create the `SparseMatrix` object corresponding to the matrix *M*, you use this line of code:

```
val sm = Matrices.sparse(2,3,Array(0,1,2,4), Array(0,1,0,1), Array(5.,3.,1.,4.))
```

(Note that the indices are specified as `Int`s and the values as `Double`s.)

You can convert `SparseMatrix` to `DenseMatrix` and vice versa with the corresponding `toDense` and `toSparse` methods. But you'll need to explicitly cast the `Matrix` object to the appropriate class:

```
scala> import org.apache.spark.mllib.linalg. {DenseMatrix,SparseMatrix}
scala> sm.asInstanceOf[SparseMatrix].toDense
res0: org.apache.spark.mllib.linalg.DenseMatrix =
5.0  0.0  1.0
0.0  3.0  4.0
scala> dm.asInstanceOf[DenseMatrix].toSparse
2 x 3 CSCMatrix
(0,0) 5.0
(1,1) 3.0
(0,2) 1.0
(1,2) 4.0
```

LINEAR ALGEBRA OPERATIONS ON LOCAL MATRICES

Similar to vectors, you can access specific elements of a matrix by indexing it like this:

```
scala> dm(1,1)
res1: Double = 3.0
```

---

[6] Jack Dongarra et al., Compressed Column Storage (CCS), http://mng.bz/Sajv.

You can efficiently create a transposed matrix using the `transpose` method:

```
scala> dm.transpose
res1: org.apache.spark.mllib.linalg.Matrix =
5.0   0.0
0.0   3.0
1.0   4.0
```

For other local matrix operations similar to vectors, conversion to Breeze matrices is necessary. The online repository contains the `toBreezeM` and `toBreezeD` functions that you can use for converting local and distributed matrices to Breeze objects.

Once converted to Breeze matrices, you can use operations like element-wise addition and matrix multiplication. We leave it up to you to further explore the Breeze API.

7.2.2   *Distributed matrices*

Distributed matrices are necessary when you're using machine-learning algorithms on huge datasets. They're stored across many machines, and they can have a large number of rows and columns. Instead of using `Int`s to index rows and columns, for distributed matrices you use `Long`s. There are four types of distributed matrices in Spark, defined in the package `org.apache.spark.mllib.linalg.distributed`: `RowMatrix`, `IndexedRowMatrix`, `BlockMatrix`, and `CoordinateMatrix`.

ROWMATRIX

`RowMatrix` stores the rows of a matrix in an RDD of `Vector` objects. This RDD is accessible as the `rows` member field. The number of rows and columns can be obtained with `numRows` and `numCols`. `RowMatrix` can be multiplied by a local matrix (producing another `RowMatrix`) using the method `multiply`. `RowMatrix` also provides other useful methods, not available for other distributed implementations. We'll describe those later.

Every other type of Spark distributed matrix can be converted to a `RowMatrix` using the built-in `toRowMatrix` methods, but there are no methods for converting a `RowMatrix` to other distributed implementations.

INDEXEDROWMATRIX

`IndexedRowMatrix` is an RDD of `IndexedRow` objects, each containing an index of the row and a `Vector` with row data. Although there is no built-in method for converting a `RowMatrix` to an `IndexedRowMatrix`, it's fairly easy to do:

```
import org.apache.spark.mllib.linalg.distributed.IndexedRowMatrix
import org.apache.spark.mllib.linalg.distributed.IndexedRow
val rmind = new IndexedRowMatrix(rm.rows.zipWithIndex().map(x =>
IndexedRow(x._2, x._1)))
```

COORDINATEMATRIX

`CoordinateMatrix` stores its values as an RDD of `MatrixEntry` objects, which contain individual entries and their (i,j) positions in the matrix. This isn't an efficient way of storing data, so you should use `CoordinateMatrix` only for storing sparse matrices. Otherwise, it could consume too much memory.

BLOCKMATRIX

`BlockMatrix` is the only distributed implementation with methods for adding and multiplying other distributed matrices. It stores its values as RDDs of tuples $((i,j),$ *Matrix*). In other words, `BlockMatrix` contains local matrices (blocks) referenced by their position in the matrix. Sub-matrices take up blocks of the same sizes (of rows-per-block and columns-per-block dimensions), except for the last sub-matrices, which can be smaller (to allow the total matrix to be of any dimensions). The `validate` method checks whether all blocks are of the same size (except the last ones).

LINEAR ALGEBRA OPERATIONS WITH DISTRIBUTED MATRICES

Linear algebra operations with distributed matrix implementations are somewhat limited, so you'll need to implement some of these yourself. For example, element-wise addition and multiplication of distributed matrices is available only for `BlockMatrix` matrices. The reason is that only `BlockMatrices` offer a way to efficiently handle these operations for matrices with many rows and columns.

Transposition is available only for `CoordinateMatrix` and `BlockMatrix`. The other operations, like matrix inverse, for example, have to be done manually.

7.3 *Linear regression*

Now you finally get to do some machine learning. In this section, you'll learn how linear regression works and how to apply it on a sample dataset. In the process, you'll learn how to analyze and prepare the data for linear regression and how to evaluate your model's performance. You'll also learn important concepts such as bias-variance tradeoff, cross-validation, and regularization.

7.3.1 *About linear regression*

Historically, linear regression has been one of the most widely used regression methods and one of the basic analytical methods in statistics, and it's still widely used today. That's because modeling linear relationships is much easier than modeling nonlinear ones. Interpretation of the resulting models is also easier. The theory behind linear regression also forms the basis for more advanced methods and algorithms in machine learning.

Like other types of regression, linear regression lets you use a set of independent variables to make predictions about a target variable and quantify the relationship between them. Linear regression makes an assumption that there is a *linear* relationship (hence the name) between the independent and target variables. Let's see what this means when you have only one independent and one target variable, which is also called *simple linear regression*. Using simple linear regression, you can plot the problem in two dimensions: the X-axis is the independent variable, and the Y-axis is the target variable. Later, you'll expand this into a model with more independent variables, which is called *multiple linear regression*.

7.3.2   *Simple linear regression*

As an example, let's use the UCI Boston housing dataset.[7] Although the dataset is rather small and, as such, doesn't represent a big-data problem, it's nevertheless appropriate for explaining machine-learning algorithms in Spark. Besides, this enables you to use it on your local machine if you want to do so.

The dataset contains mean values of owner-occupied homes in the suburbs of Boston and 13 features that can be used to predict home values. These features include the crime rate, number of rooms per dwelling, accessibility to highways, and so on.

For the simple linear-regression example, you'll predict home prices based on the average number of rooms per dwelling. You might not need to use linear regression to find out that the price of a house probably rises if there are more rooms in it. That's obvious and intuitive. But linear regression does enable you to quantify that relationship—to say what the expected price is for a certain number of rooms. If you were to plot the average number of rooms on the X-axis and the average price on the Y-axis, you'd get output similar to that shown in figure 7.4.

There is obviously a correlation between the two variables: almost no expensive houses have a small number of rooms, and no inexpensive houses have a large number of rooms. Linear regression enables you to find a line that goes through the middle of these data points and, in that way, to approximate the most likely home price you could expect given an average number of rooms. We've already calculated this line, as shown in figure 7.4. Let's see what the method is for finding it.

Generally, if you want to draw a line in two-dimensional space, you need two values: the *slope* of the line and the value at which the line intersects the Y-axis, also called the *intercept*. If you denote the number of rooms as *x*, the function for calculating the

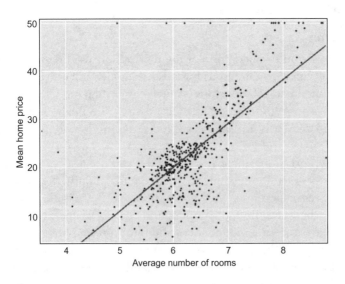

Figure 7.4   **Mean home prices in Boston by average number of rooms per dwelling. Linear regression was used to find a best-fit line for this data (shown on the graph).**

[7]   Housing Data Set, *UCI Machine Learning Repository*, https://archive.ics.uci.edu/ml/datasets/Housing.

home price as h (which stands for *hypothesis*), and the intercept and slope as w_0 and w_1, respectively, the line can be described with the following formula:

$$h(x) = w_0 + w_1x$$

The goal is to find the *weights* w_0 and w_1 that best fit the data. Linear regression's method for finding appropriate weight values is to minimize the so-called *cost function*. The cost function returns a single value that can be used as a measure of how well the line, determined by weights, fits all examples in a dataset. Different cost functions can be used. The one used in linear regression is the mean of the squared differences between predicted and real values of the target variable for all m examples in the dataset (mean squared error). The cost function (we call it C in the equation) can be written like this:

$$C(w_0, w_1) \;=\; \frac{1}{2m} \sum_{i=1}^{m} \left(h(x^{(i)}) - y^{(i)} \right)^2 \;=\; \frac{1}{2m} \sum_{i=1}^{m} \left(w_0 + w_1 x^{(i)} - y^{(i)} \right)^2$$

If you give this function a set of m examples $x^{(1)}$ to $x^{(m)}$ (with matching target values $y^{(1)}$ to $y^{(m)}$) and the weights w_0 and w_1, which you think would be most appropriate for the data, the function will give you a single error value. If this value is lower than a second one, obtained for a different set of weights, that means the first model (determined by chosen weights w_0 and w_1) better fits the dataset.

But how do you get the best-fit weights? You can find the minimum of the cost function. If you plot the cost function with respect to weights w_0 and w_1, it forms a curved plane in a three-dimensional space, similar to the one in figure 7.5. The shape

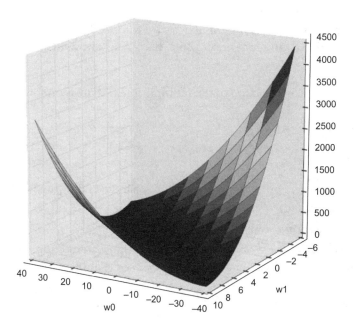

Figure 7.5 The cost function of the housing dataset, depending on weights w_0 and w_1. The valley in the middle shows that many combinations of w_0 and w_1 can fit the data equally well.

of the cost function depends on your dataset. In this example, the cost function has a valley along which many points correspond to low error values. That means you could draw many lines (defined by weights w_0 and w_1) in figure 7.4 that would fit the dataset equally well.

The mean-squared-error cost function is used in linear regression because it offers certain benefits: the squares of individual deviations can't cancel each other out (they're always positive), even though the corresponding deviations may be negative; the function is convex, which means there are no local minima, only a global minimum; and an analytical solution for finding its minimum exists.

7.3.3   *Expanding the model to multiple linear regression*

There is a nice vectorized solution for finding the minimum of the cost function C, but let's first expand the model to use multiple linear regression. As we said previously, expanding the model to use multiple linear regression means examples will have more *dimensions* (independent variables). In this example, you need to add the remaining 12 dimensions of the housing dataset. This adds additional information to the dataset and enables the model to make better predictions based on that additional information. It also means, from this point on, you won't be able to plot the data or the cost function, because the linear-regression solution now becomes a 13-dimensional hyperplane (instead of a line in 2 dimensions).

After adding the remaining 12 dimensions to the dataset, the hypothesis function becomes

$$h(x) = w_0 + w_1 x_1 + \ldots + w_n x_n = \boldsymbol{w}^T \boldsymbol{x}$$

where n, in this example, is equal to 12. On the right side, you can see the vectorized version of the same expression. To be able to introduce the vectorized notation (because the intercept value w_0 is multiplied by 1), you need to extend the original vector x with an additional component, x_0, which has a constant value of 1:

$$x^T = [1 \ x_1 \ \ldots \ xn]$$

You can now rewrite the cost function of the multiple linear-regression model like this:

$$C(\boldsymbol{w}) = \frac{1}{2m} \sum_{i=1}^{m} (\boldsymbol{w}^T \boldsymbol{x}^{(i)} - y^{(i)})^2$$

This is also a vectorized version of the cost function (as indicated by the bold letters in this equation).

FINDING THE MINIMUM WITH THE NORMAL EQUATION METHOD

The vectorized solution to the problem of minimizing the cost function, in respect to the weights w_0 to w_n, is given by the *normal equation method* formula:

$$\boldsymbol{w} = (X^T X)^{-1} X^T \boldsymbol{y}$$

X here is a matrix with m rows (m examples) and $n + 1$ columns (n dimensions plus 1s for x_0). w and y are vectors with $n + 1$ weights and m target values, respectively. Unfortunately, the scope of this book doesn't allow us to explain the math behind this formula.

FINDING THE MINIMUM WITH GRADIENT DESCENT

Directly solving this equation with the previous formula can be very expensive and not easy to do (because of the matrix multiplications and matrix-inversion calculations required), especially if there is a large number of dimensions and rows in the dataset. So we'll use the *gradient-descent method*, which is more commonly employed—and you can use it in Spark, too.

Gradient-descent algorithms work iteratively. It starts from a certain point, representing a best guess of the weight parameters' values (this point can also be randomly chosen), and for each weight parameter w_j, calculates a partial derivative of the cost function with respect to that weight parameter. The partial derivative tells the algorithm how to change the weight parameter in question to descend to the minimum of the cost function as quickly as possible. The algorithm then updates the weight parameters according to the calculated partial derivatives and calculates the value of the cost function at the new point. If the new value is less than some *tolerance* value, we say that the algorithm has *converged*, and the process stops. See figure 7.6 for an illustration.

As an example of a gradient-descent algorithm, let's return to the simple linear-regression example and its cost function, shown in figure 7.6. The dots on the white line in the figure are points the algorithm visits in each step. The white line is the shortest path from the starting point to the minimum of the cost function.

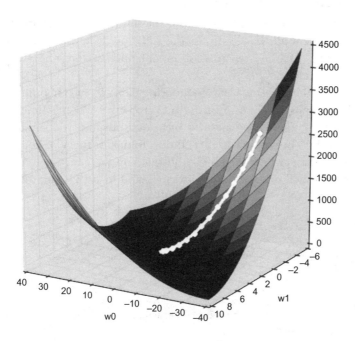

Figure 7.6 A gradient-descent algorithm determines the minimum value for the cost function in the simple linear-regression model for the housing dataset. The white line connects the points the algorithm visits in each step.

The partial derivative of the cost function C, with respect to any weight parameter w_j, is given by this formula:

$$\frac{\partial}{\partial w_i} C(w) = \frac{1}{m} \sum_{i=1}^{m} (h(x^{(i)}) - y^{(i)}) x_j^{(i)}$$

(Please note that x_0 is equal to 1 for all examples, as mentioned previously.)

If the partial derivative is negative, the cost function *decreases* with an *increase* of the weight parameter w_j. You can now use this value to update the weight parameter w_j to *decrease* the value of the cost function. And you do it for all weight parameters as part of a single step:

$$w_j := w_j - \gamma \frac{\partial}{\partial w_j} C(w) = w_j - \gamma \frac{1}{m} \sum_{i=1}^{m} (h(x^{(i)}) - y^{(i)}) x_j^{(i)}, \textit{for every } j$$

After updating all weight parameters, you calculate the cost function again (the second point along the black line in figure 7.6), and if it's still unacceptably high, you update the weights again using partial derivatives. You repeat this process until *convergence* (the value of the cost function remains stable).

Parameter γ (Greek letter *gamma*) is the *step-size parameter* that helps stabilize the algorithm. We'll have more to say about the step-size parameter later.

7.4 *Analyzing and preparing the data*

That was a good dose of theoretical background for the linear-regression example. Now it's time to implement all that using Spark's API. You'll download the housing dataset, prepare the data, fit a linear-regression model, and use the model to predict target values of some examples.

To begin, download the housing dataset (housing.data) from our online repository (use our GitHub repository[8] and not the one from the UCI machine learning repository because we changed the dataset a bit). We'll assume you've cloned the GitHub repository to the /home/spark/first-edition folder in the VM. You can find the description of the dataset in the file ch07/housing.names.

First, start the Spark shell in your home directory, and load the data with the following code:

```
import org.apache.spark.mllib.linalg.Vectors
val housingLines = sc.textFile("first-edition/ch07/housing.data", 6)
val housingVals = housingLines.map(x =>
Vectors.dense(x.split(",").map(_.trim().toDouble)))
```

---

[8] Find the housing dataset here: https://github.com/spark-in-action/first-edition/blob/master/ch07/housing.data.

We're using six partitions for the `housingLines` RDD, but you can choose another value, depending on your cluster environment.[9]

Now you have your data parsed and available as `Vector` objects. But before doing anything useful with it, acquaint yourself with the data. The first step when dealing with any machine-learning problem is to analyze the data and notice its distribution and interrelationships among different variables.

7.4.1 *Analyzing data distribution*

To get a feeling for the data you just loaded, you can calculate its multivariate statistical summary. You can obtain that value from the corresponding `RowMatrix` object like this

```
import org.apache.spark.mllib.linalg.distributed.RowMatrix
val housingMat = new RowMatrix(housingVals)
val housingStats = housingMat.computeColumnSummaryStatistics()
```

or you can use the `Statistics` object for the same purpose:

```
import org.apache.spark.mllib.stat.Statistics
val housingStats = Statistics.colStats(housingVals)
```

You can now use the obtained `MultivariateStatisticalSummary` object to examine the average (the `mean` method), maximum (the `max` method), and minimum (the `min` method) values in each column of the matrix. For example, the minimum values in the columns are these:

```
scala> housingStats.min
res0: org.apache.spark.mllib.linalg.Vector = [0.00632,0.0,0.46,0.0,0.385,
3.561,2.9,1.1296,1.0,187.0,12.6,0.32,1.73,5.0]
```

You can also get the L1 norm (sum of absolute values of all elements per column) and L2 norm (also called *Euclidian norm*; equal to the length of a vector/column) for each column, with the methods `normL1` and `normL2`. The variance of each column can be obtained with the `variance` method.

> **DEFINITION**   *Variance* is a measure of dispersion of a dataset and is equal to the average of the squared deviations of values from their mean value. The *standard deviation* is calculated as the square root of the variance. The *covariance* is a measure of how much two variables change relative to each other.

All of this can be useful when examining data for the first time, especially when deciding whether feature scaling (described shortly) is necessary.

---

[9] If you need more information about the number of partitions required, chapter 4 is a good place to look.

7.4.2 *Analyzing column cosine similarities*

Understanding column cosine similarities is another thing that helps when analyzing data. *Column cosine similarities* represent an angle between two columns, viewed as vectors. A similar procedure can be used for other purposes as well (for example, for finding similar products, or similar articles).

You obtain column cosine similarities from the `RowMatrix` object:

```
val housingColSims = housingMat.columnSimilarities()
```

> **PYTHON** The `columnSimilarities` method isn't available in Python.

The resulting object is a distributed `CoordinateMatrix` containing an upper-triangular matrix (*upper-triangular matrices* contain data only above their diagonal). The value at the i-th row and j-th column in the resulting `housingColSims` matrix gives a measure of similarity between the i-th column and j-th column in the `housingMat` matrix. The values in the `housingColSims` matrix can go in value from –1 to 1. A value of –1 means the two columns have completely opposite orientations (directions), a value of 0 means they're orthogonal to one another, and a value of 1 means the two columns (vectors) have the same orientation.

The easiest way to see the contents of this matrix is to convert it to a Breeze matrix using the `toBreezeD` method and then print the output with the utility method `printMat` that you can find in our repository listing, which we omit due to brevity. To do this, first paste the `printMat` method definition into your shell and execute the following:

```
printMat(toBreezeD(housingColSims))
```

This will pretty-print the contents of the matrix (you can also find the expected output in our online repository). If you look at the last column of the result, it gives you a measure of how well each dimension in the dataset corresponds to the target variable (average price). The last column reads: 0.224, 0.528, 0.693, 0.307, 0.873, 0.949, 0.803, 0.856, 0.588, 0.789, 0.897, 0.928, 0.670, 0.000. The biggest value here is the sixth value (0.949), which corresponds to the column containing the average number of rooms. Now you can see that it was no coincidence that we chose that column for the previous simple linear-regression example—it has the strongest similarity with the target value and thus represents the most appropriate candidate for simple linear regression.

7.4.3 *Computing the covariance matrix*

Another method for examining similarities between different columns (dimensions) of the input set is the *covariance matrix*. It's important in statistics for modeling linear correspondence between variables. In Spark, you compute the covariance matrix similarly to column statistics and column similarities, using the `RowMatrix` object:

```
val housingCovar = housingMat.computeCovariance()
printMat(toBreezeM(housingCovar))
```

PYTHON The `computeCovariance` method isn't available in Python.

The expected output is also available in our online repository. Notice that there is a large range of values in the matrix and that some of them are negative and some are positive. You'll also probably notice that the matrix is symmetric (that is, each (i, j) element is the same as a (j, i) element).

This is because the variance-covariance matrix contains the variance of each column on its diagonal and the covariance of the two matching columns on all other positions. If a covariance of two columns is zero, there is no linear relationship between them. Negative values mean the values in the two columns move in opposite directions from their averages, whereas the opposite is true for positive values.

Spark also offers two other methods for examining the correlations between series of data: Spearman's and Pearson's methods. An explanation of those methods is beyond the scope of this book. You can access them through the `org.apache.spark.mllib` `.stat.Statistics` object.

7.4.4 *Transforming to labeled points*

Now that you've examined the dataset, you can go on to preparing the data for linear regression. First you have to put each example in the dataset in a structure called a `LabeledPoint`, which is used in most of Spark's machine-learning algorithms. It contains the target value and the vector with the features. `housingVals` containing `Vector` objects with all variables, and the equivalent `housingMat RowMatrix` object, were useful when you were examining the dataset as a whole (in the previous sections), but now you need to separate the target variable (the label) from the features.

To do that, you can transform the `housingVals` RDD (the target variable is in the last column):

```
import org.apache.spark.mllib.regression.LabeledPoint
val housingData = housingVals.map(x => {
  val a = x.toArray
  LabeledPoint(a(a.length-1), Vectors.dense(a.slice(0, a.length-1)))
})
```

7.4.5 *Splitting the data*

The second important step is splitting the data into training and validation sets. A *training* set is used to train the model, and a *validation* set is used to see how well the model performs on data that wasn't used to train it. The usual split ratio is 80% for the training set and 20% for the validation set.

You can split the data easily in Spark with the RDD's built-in `randomSplit` method:

```
val sets = housingData.randomSplit(Array(0.8, 0.2))
val housingTrain = sets(0)
val housingValid = sets(1)
```

The method returns an array of RDDs, each containing approximately the requested percentage of orginal data.

7.4.6   *Feature scaling and mean normalization*

We're not done with data preparation yet. As you probably noticed when you were examining distribution of the data, there are large differences in data spans between the columns. For example, the data in the first column goes from 0.00632 to 88.9762, and the data in the fifth column from 0.385 to 0.871.

Interpreting results from a linear-regression model trained with data like this can be difficult and can render some data transformations (which you're going to perform in the coming sections) problematic. It's often a good idea to standardize the data first, which can't hurt your model. There are two ways you can do this: with feature scaling and with mean normalization.

Feature scaling means the ranges of data are scaled to comparable sizes. *Mean normalization* means the data is translated so that the averages are roughly zero. You can do both in a single pass, but you need a `StandardScaler` object to do that. In the constructor, you specify which of the standardization techniques you want to use (you'll use both) and then fit it according to some data:

```
import org.apache.spark.mllib.feature.StandardScaler
val scaler = new StandardScaler(true, true).
  fit(housingTrain.map(x => x.features))
```

Fitting finds column-summary statistics of the input data and uses these statistics (in the next step) to do the scaling. You fitted the scaler according to the training set, and you'll then use the same statistics to scale both the training and validation sets (only data from the training set should be used for fitting the scaler):

```
val trainScaled = housingTrain.map(x => LabeledPoint(x.label,
➥ scaler.transform(x.features)))
val validScaled = housingValid.map(x => LabeledPoint(x.label,
➥ scaler.transform(x.features)))
```

Now you're finally ready to use the housing dataset for linear regression.

7.5   *Fitting and using a linear regression model*

A linear regression model in Spark is implemented by the class `LinearRegression-Model` in the package `org.apache.spark.mllib.regression`. It's produced by fitting a model and holds the fitted model's parameters. When you have fitted a `Linear-RegressionModel` object, you can use its `predict` method on individual `Vector` examples to predict the corresponding target variables. You construct the model using the `LinearRegressionWithSGD` class, which implements the algorithm used for training the model. You can do this in two ways. The first is the standard Spark way of invoking the static `train` method:

```
val model = LinearRegressionWithSGD.train(trainScaled, 200, 1.0)
```

Unfortunately, this doesn't allow you to find the intercept value (only the weights), so use the second, nonstandard method:

Sets the option to find the intercept value

Instantiates object

Sets the number of iterations to run

```
import org.apache.spark.mllib.regression.LinearRegressionWithSGD
val alg = new LinearRegressionWithSGD()
alg.setIntercept(true)
alg.optimizer.setNumIterations(200)
trainScaled.cache()
validScaled.cache()
val model = alg.run(trainScaled)
```

Caching input data is important.

Starts training the model

Within a few seconds of executing this code, you'll have your Spark linear-regression model ready to use for predictions. The datasets are cached, which is important for iterative algorithms, such as machine learning ones, because they tend to reuse the same data many times.

7.5.1 *Predicting the target values*

You can now use the trained model to predict the target values of vectors in the validation set by running `predict` on every element. The validation set contains labeled points, but you only need the features. You also need the predictions together with the original labels, so you can compare them. This is how you can map labeled points to pairs of predicted and original values:

```
val validPredicts = validScaled.map(x => (model.predict(x.features),
x.label))
```

The moment of truth has arrived. You can see how well your model is doing on the validation set by examining the contents of `validPredicts`:

```
scala> validPredicts.collect()
res123: Array[(Double, Double)] = Array((28.250971806168213,33.4),
(23.050776311791807,22.9), (21.278600156174313,21.7),
(19.067817892581136,19.9), (19.463816495227626,18.4), ...
```

Some predictions are close to original labels, and some are further off. To quantify the success of your model, calculate the root mean squared error (the root of the cost function defined previously):

```
scala> math.sqrt(validPredicts.map{case(p,l) => math.pow(p-l,2)}.mean())
res0: Double = 4.775608317676729
```

The average value of the target variables (home prices) is 22.5—which you learned earlier when you were calculating column statistics—so a root mean squared error (RMSE) of 4.78 seems rather large. But if you take into account that the variance of home prices is 84.6, the number suddenly looks much better.

7.5.2   *Evaluating the model's performance*

This isn't the only way you can evaluate the performance of your regression model. Spark offers the `RegressionMetrics` class for this purpose. You give it an RDD with pairs of predictions and labels, and it returns several useful evaluation metrics:

```
scala> import org.apache.spark.mllib.evaluation.RegressionMetrics
scala> val validMetrics = new RegressionMetrics(validPredicts)
scala> validMetrics.rootMeanSquaredError
res1: Double = 4.775608317676729
scala> validMetrics.meanSquaredError
res2: Double = 22.806434803863162
```

In addition to the root mean squared error that you previously calculated yourself, `RegressionMetrics` gives you the following:

- `meanAbsoluteError`—Average absolute difference between a predicted and real value (3.044 in this case).
- `r2`—Coefficient of determination R^2 (0.71 in this case) is a value between 0 and 1 and represents the *fraction of variance explained*. It's a measure of how much a model accounts for the variation in the target variable (predictions) and how much of it is "unexplained." A value close to 1 means the model explains a large part of variance in the target variable.
- `explainedVariance`—A value similar to R^2 (0.711 in this case).

All of these are used in practice, but the coefficient of determination can give you somewhat misleading results (it tends to rise when the number of features increases, whether or not they're relevant). For that reason, you'll use the RMSE from now on.

7.5.3   *Interpreting the model parameters*

The set of weights the model has learned can tell you something about the influence of individual dimensions on the target variable. If a particular weight is near zero, the corresponding dimension doesn't contribute to the target variable (price of housing) in a significant way (assuming the data has been scaled—otherwise even low-range features might be important).

You can inspect absolutes of the individual weights with the following snippet of code:

```
scala> println(model.weights.toArray.map(x => x.abs).
  | zipWithIndex.sortBy(_._1).mkString(", "))
(0.112892822124492423,6), (0.163296952677502576,2),
(0.588838584855835963,3), (0.939646889835077461,0),
(0.994950411719257694,11), (1.263479388579985779,1),
(1.660835069779720992,9), (2.030167784111269705,4),
(2.072353314616951604,10), (2.419153951711214781,8),
(2.794657721841373189,5), (3.113566843160460237,7),
(3.323924359136577734,12)
```

The model's `weights` Vector is first converted to a Scala `Array`, then the absolute values are calculated, an index is attached to each weight using the Scala's `zipWithIndex` method, and, finally, the weights are sorted by their values.

You can see that the most influential dimension of the dataset is the one with index 12, which corresponds to the LSTAT column, or the "percentage of lower status of the population." (You can find the column descriptions in the housing.names file in the book's online repository.) The second-most influential dimension is the column with index 7, or "weighted distances to five Boston employment centers," and so on.

The two least influential dimensions are the "proportion of owner-occupied units built prior to 1940" and the "proportion of non-retail business acres per town." Those dimensions can be removed from the dataset without influencing the model's performance significantly. In fact, that might even improve it a bit because in that way, the model would be move focused on the important features.

7.5.4 *Loading and saving the model*

Because training a model using lots of data can be an expensive and lengthy operation, Spark offers a way to save the model to a filesystem as a Parquet file (covered in chapter 5) and load it later, when needed. Most Spark MLlib models can be saved using the `save` method. You just pass a `SparkContext` instance and a filesystem path to it, similar to this:

```
model.save(sc, "chapter07output/model")
```

Spark uses the path for creating a directory and creates two Parquet files in it: data and metadata.

In the case of linear-regression models, the metadata file contains the model's implementation class name, the implementation's version, and the number of features in the model. The data file contains the weights and the intercept of the linear regression model.

To load the model, use the corresponding `load` method, again passing to it a `Spark-Context` instance and the path to the directory with the saved model. For example:

```
import org.apache.spark.mllib.regression.LinearRegressionModel
val model = LinearRegressionModel.load(sc, "ch07output/model")
```

The model can then be used for predictions.

7.6 *Tweaking the algorithm*

In section 7.3.3, you saw the gradient descent formula:

$$w_j := w_j - \gamma \frac{\partial}{\partial w_j} C(w) = w_j - \gamma \frac{1}{m} \sum_{i=1}^{m} (h(x^{(i)}) - y^{(i)})x_j^{(i)}, \textit{for every } j$$

Parameter γ (Greek letter *gamma*) in the formula is the *step-size parameter*, which helps to stabilize the gradient descent algorithm. But it can be difficult to find the optimal value for this parameter. If it's too small, the algorithm will take too many small steps to converge. If it's too large, the algorithm may never converge. The right value depends on the dataset.

It's similar with the number of iterations. If it's too large, fitting the model will take too much time. If it's too small, the algorithm may not reach the minimum.

Although you only set the number of iterations for the previous run of the linear-regression algorithm (the step size you used had the default value of 1.0), you can set both of these parameters when using `LinearRegressionWithSGD`. But you can't tell Spark to "iterate until the algorithm converges" (which would be ideal). You have to find the optimal values for these two parameters yourself.

7.6.1   *Finding the right step size and number of iterations*

One way to find satisfactory values for these two parameters is to experiment with several combinations and find the one that gives the best results. We put together a function that can help you do this. Find the `iterateLRwSGD` function in our online repository (in the ch07-listings.scala and ch07-listings.py files), and paste it into your Spark shell. This is the complete function:

```
import org.apache.spark.rdd.RDD
def iterateLRwSGD(iterNums:Array[Int], stepSizes:Array[Double],
    train:RDD[LabeledPoint], test:RDD[LabeledPoint]) = {
  for(numIter <- iterNums; step <- stepSizes) {
    val alg = new LinearRegressionWithSGD()
    alg.setIntercept(true).optimizer.setNumIterations(numIter).
        setStepSize(step)
    val model = alg.run(train)
    val rescaledPredicts = train.map(x =>
        (model.predict(x.features), x.label))
    val validPredicts = test.map(x => (model.predict(x.features), x.label))
    val meanSquared = math.sqrt(rescaledPredicts.map(
        {case(p,l) => math.pow(p-l,2)}).mean())
    val meanSquaredValid = math.sqrt(validPredicts.map(
        {case(p,l) => math.pow(p-l,2)}).mean())
    println("%d, %5.3f -> %.4f, %.4f".format(numIter,
        step, meanSquared, meanSquaredValid))
  }
}
```

The `iterateLRwSGD` function takes two arrays, containing different numbers of iterations and step-size parameters, and two RDDs, containing training and validation data. For each combination of step size and number of iterations in the input arrays, the function returns the RMSE of the training and validation sets. Here's what the printout should look like:

```
scala> iterateLRwSGD(Array(200, 400, 600), Array(0.05, 0.1, 0.5, 1, 1.5, 2,
➥ 3), trainScaled, validScaled)
200, 0.050 -> 7.5420, 7.4786
200, 0.100 -> 5.0437, 5.0910
200, 0.500 -> 4.6920, 4.7814
200, 1.000 -> 4.6777, 4.7756
200, 1.500 -> 4.6751, 4.7761
200, 2.000 -> 4.6746, 4.7771
200, 3.000 -> 108738480856.3940, 122956877593.1419
400, 0.050 -> 5.8161, 5.8254
400, 0.100 -> 4.8069, 4.8689
400, 0.500 -> 4.6826, 4.7772
400, 1.000 -> 4.6753, 4.7760
400, 1.500 -> 4.6746, 4.7774
400, 2.000 -> 4.6745, 4.7780
400, 3.000 -> 25240554554.3096, 30621674955.1730
600, 0.050 -> 5.2510, 5.2877
600, 0.100 -> 4.7667, 4.8332
600, 0.500 -> 4.6792, 4.7759
600, 1.000 -> 4.6748, 4.7767
600, 1.500 -> 4.6745, 4.7779
600, 2.000 -> 4.6745, 4.7783
600, 3.000 -> 4977766834.6285, 6036973314.0450
```

You can see several things from this output. First, the testing RMSE is always greater than the training RMSE (except for some corner cases). That's to be expected. Furthermore, for every number of iterations, both errors decline rapidly as step size increases, following some inverse exponential function. That makes sense because for smaller numbers of iterations and smaller step sizes, there weren't enough iterations to get to the minimum.

Then the error values flatten out, more quickly for larger numbers of iterations. This also makes sense because there are some limitations to how well you can fit a dataset. And models fitted with larger numbers of iterations will perform better. For a step size value of 3, the error values explode. This step size value is too large, and the algorithm misses the minimum. It seems that a step size of 0.5 or 1.0 gives the best results if the number of iterations stays the same.

You may also have noticed that running more iterations doesn't help much. For example, a step size of 1.0 with 200 iterations gives you almost the same training RMSE as with 600 iterations.

7.6.2 Adding higher-order polynomials

It seems that the testing RMSE of 4.7760 is the lowest error you can get for the housing dataset. You can do better (when we added higher-order polynomials, the model changes and it is not "the model" any longer). Often, data doesn't follow a simple linear formula (a straight line in a two-dimensional space) but may be some kind of a curve. Curves can often be described with functions containing higher-order polynomials.

For example:

$$h(x) = w_0 x^3 + w_1 x^2 + w_2 x + w_3$$

This hypothesis is capable of matching data governed by a nonlinear relationship. You'll see an example of this in the next section.

Spark doesn't offer a method of training a nonlinear regression model that includes higher-order polynomials, such as the preceding hypothesis. Instead, you can employ a little trick and do something that has a similar effect: you can expand your dataset with additional features obtained by multiplying the existing ones. For example, if you have features x_1 and x_2, you can expand the dataset to include x_1^2 and x_2^2. Adding the *interaction term* $x_1 x_2$ helps in cases when x_1 and x_2 influence the target variable together.

Let's do that now with this dataset. You'll use a simple function to map each Vector in the dataset to include the square of each feature:

```
def addHighPols(v:Vector): Vector =                        Adds squares
{                                                          to a Vector
  Vectors.dense(v.toArray.flatMap(x => Array(x, x*x)))
}
val housingHP = housingData.map(x => LabeledPoint(x.label,   Maps the original
addHighPols(x.features)))                                   dataset
```

The `housingHP` RDD now contains `LabeledPoints` from the original `housingData` RDD, but expanded with additional features containing second-order polynomials. You now have 26 features instead of the previous 13:

```
scala> housingHP.first().features.count()
res0: Int = 26
```

Next it's necessary to once again go through the process of splitting the dataset for training and testing subsets and to scale the data the same way you did previously:

```
val setsHP = housingHP.randomSplit(Array(0.8, 0.2))
val housingHPTrain = setsHP(0)
val housingHPValid = setsHP(1)
val scalerHP = new StandardScaler(true, true)
scalerHP.fit(housingHPTrain.map(x => x.features))
val trainHPScaled = housingHPTrain.map(x => LabeledPoint(x.label,
➥ scalerHP.transform(x.features)))
val validHPScaled = housingHPValid.map(x => LabeledPoint(x.label,
➥ scalerHP.transform(x.features)))
trainHPScaled.cache()
validHPScaled.cache()
```

You can see how the new model behaves with different numbers of iterations and step sizes:

```
iterateLRwSGD(Array(200, 400), Array(0.4, 0.5, 0.6, 0.7, 0.9, 1.0, 1.1, 1.2,
      1.3, 1.5), trainHPScaled, validHPScaled)
```

As you can see from the results (omitted for brevity, but available in our online repository), the RMSE explodes for a step size of 1.3, and you get the best results for a step size of 1.1. The error values are lower than before. The best RMSE is 3.9836 (for 400 iterations), compared to 4.776 before. You can conclude that adding higher-order polynomials helped the linear-regression algorithm find a better-performing model.

But is this the lowest RMSE you can get with this dataset? Let's see what happens if you increase the number of iterations (and use the best-performing step size of 1.1):

```scala
scala> iterateLRwSGD(Array(200, 400, 800, 1000, 3000, 6000), Array(1.1),
➥ trainHPScaled, validHPScaled)
200, 1.100 -> 4.1605, 4.0108
400, 1.100 -> 4.0378, 3.9836
800, 1.100 -> 3.9438, 3.9901
1000, 1.100 -> 3.9199, 3.9982
3000, 1.100 -> 3.8332, 4.0633
6000, 1.100 -> 3.7915, 4.1138
```

With more iterations, the testing RMSE is even starting to increase. (Depending on your dataset split, you may get different results.) So which step size should you choose? And why is the RMSE increasing?

7.6.3   *Bias-variance tradeoff and model complexity*

The situation where the testing RMSE is increasing while the training RMSE is decreasing is known as *overfitting*. What happens is that the model gets too attuned to the "noise" in the training set and becomes less accurate when analyzing new, real-world data that doesn't possess the same properties as the training set. There is also an opposite term—*underfitting*—where the model is too simple and is incapable of adequately capturing the complexities of the data. Understanding these phenomena is important for correctly using machine-learning algorithms and getting the most out of your data.

Figure 7.7 shows a sample dataset (circles) following a quadratic function. The linear model (graph on the left) isn't capable of properly modeling the data. The quadratic function in the middle is just about right, and the function with higher-order polynomials on the right overfits the dataset.

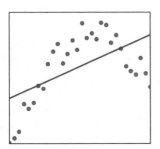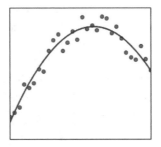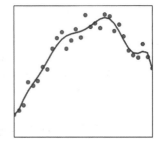

Figure 7.7   The linear model (left) underfits the dataset, a model with higher-order polynomials (right) overfits it, and a quadratic model (middle) fits nicely.

You normally want your model to fit the data in your training dataset, but also to be expandable to some other, presently unknown data. It's not necessarily possible to do both perfectly.

And that leads us to the *bias-variance tradeoff*. Bias here pertains to the model. For example, the linear model on the left in figure 7.7 has a high bias: it's assuming the linear relationship between the independent and target variables, so it's biased. The model on the right side has a high variance because the values it predicts are oscillating more. Bias-variance tradeoff says that you can't necessarily have both at the same time and that you need to seek an equilibrium, or middle ground.

How do you know if your model has high bias (it's underfitted) or high variance (it's overfitted)? Let's return to the example. Generally, overfitting occurs when the ratio of model complexity and training-set size gets large. If you have a complex model but also a relatively large training set, overfitting is less likely to occur. You saw that the RMSE on the validation set started to rise when you added higher-order polynomials and trained the model with more iterations. Higher-order polynomials bring more complexity to the model, and more iterations overfit the model to the data while the algorithm is converging. Let's see what happens if you try even more iterations:

```
scala> iterateLRwSGD(Array(10000, 15000, 30000, 50000), Array(1.1),
➥ trainHPScaled, validHPScaled)
10000, 1.100 -> 3.7638, 4.1553
15000, 1.100 -> 3.7441, 4.1922
30000, 1.100 -> 3.7173, 4.2626
50000, 1.100 -> 3.7039, 4.3163
```

You can see that the training RMSE continues to decrease while the testing RMSE continues to rise. And that's typical for an overfitting situation: the training error falls and then plateaus (which would happen for even more iterations), and the testing error falls and then starts to rise, meaning the model learns training set–specific properties instead of characteristics representative of the whole population. If you were to plot this, you'd get a graph similar to figure 7.8.

To answer the question of which values for the number of iterations and step size to choose: choose the values corresponding to the minimum of the testing RMSE curve, at the point before it starts to rise. In this case, 400 iterations and a step size of 1.1 give very good results (testing RMSE of 3.98).

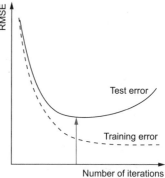

Figure 7.8   Error as a function of the number of iterations used. The test RMSE falls but then starts to rise at a certain point. Parameters corresponding to that point should be chosen for the model, because the model is beginning to overfit the data.

7.6.4   *Plotting residual plots*

But how can you tell if you need to keep adding higher-order polynomials, or if you need to add any in the first place? And where do you stop? Examining *residual plots* can help you answer those questions.

The *residual* is the difference between the predicted and actual values of the target variable. In other words, for a single example in the training dataset, the residual is the difference between its label's value and what the model says the label's value should be. Residual plots have residuals on the Y-axis and the predicted values on the X-axis.

A residual plot should show no noticeable patterns—it should have the same height at all points on the X-axis, and if you plot a best-fit line (or a curve) through the plotted values, the line should stay flat. If it shows a shape similar to the letter *u* (or inverted *u*), that means a nonlinear model would be more appropriate for some of the dimensions.

The two residual plots for the two models (the original linear-regression model and the one with added second-order polynomials) are shown in figure 7.9. The one on the left shows a shape of an inverted *u*-curve. The one on the right, although still not perfect, shows an improvement: the shape is more balanced.

As we said, the new residual plot still isn't perfect, and further dimension transformations might help, but probably not much. A line in the lower-right part of both figures is also visible. This is due to several *outliers*, or points that represent some kind of exceptions. In this case, there are several instances of expensive houses ($50,000) that should otherwise be not as expensive. This could also be caused by a missing variable—

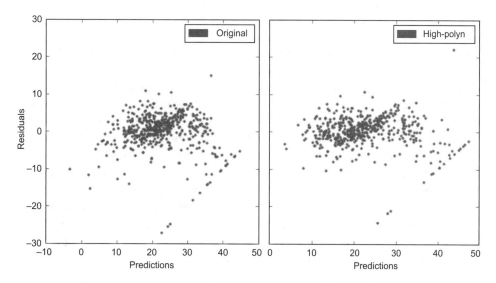

Figure 7.9   Residual plots for two linear-regression models. The model on the left was fitted using the original housing dataset and shows an inverted *u*-curve shape. The one on the right was fitted using the dataset with added second-order polynomials and shows a more balanced pattern.

some factor making a house expensive (aesthetics, for example), but not present in the dataset.

Residual plots can also help you in a number of other situations. If the plot shows a *fan-in* or a *fan-out* shape (the residuals show greater variance at one end of the plot than at the other, a phenomenon called *heteroscedasticity*[10]), one solution in addition to adding higher-order polynomials may be to transform the *target variable* logarithmically so that your model predicts log(*y*) (or some other function) and not *y*.

Further discussion of this important topic is beyond the scope of this book. The main thing to remember is that you should always spend time studying residual plots to get further information about how your model is actually doing.

7.6.5 Avoiding overfitting by using regularization

Let's get back to overfitting. You've seen how it decreases the model's performance. You can avoid overfitting using a method called *regularization,* which increases the bias of your model and decreases variance by penalizing large values in the model parameters.

Regularization adds an additional element (we denote it as β) to the cost function that penalizes complexity in the model. There are different regularization types. The most common ones are L1 and L2 regularizations (named after L1 and L2 norms discussed in section 7.4.2), and they're the ones available in Spark. Linear regression with L1 regularization is called *Lasso regression,* and the one with L2 regression is called *Ridge regression.*

The cost function with the regularization element β looks like this:

$$C(w) = \frac{1}{2m} \sum_{i=1}^{m} (w^T x^{(i)} - y^{(i)})^2 + \beta = \frac{1}{2m} \sum_{i=1}^{m} (w^T x^{(i)} - y^{(i)})^2 + \lambda \|x\|_{I/(II)}$$

β is a product of two elements: λ, the regularization parameter, and L1 ($\|w\|_i$) or L2 ($\|w\|_{ii}$) norm of the weight vector. As we said in section 7.4.2, the L1 norm is the sum of the absolute values of the vector's elements, and the L2 norm is the square root of the sum of squares of the vector's elements, which is equal to the length of the vector.

The regularization increases the error in proportion to absolute weight values. In that way, the optimization function tries to deemphasize individual dimensions and slow the algorithm as the weights get larger. L1 regularization (Lasso regression) is more aggressive in this process. It's capable of reducing individual weights to zero and thus completely removing some of the features from the dataset.

In addition, both L1 and L2 regularizations in Spark decrease the step size in proportion to the number of iterations. This means the longer the algorithm runs, the smaller steps it takes. (This isn't related to regularization per se but is part of L1 and L2 regularization implementations in Spark.)

---

[10] For further information, see https://en.wikipedia.org/wiki/Heteroscedasticity.

Regularization can help you in situations where you're overfitting the model to the dataset. By increasing the regularization parameter (β), you can decrease overfitting. In addition, regularization can help you get to lower error values more quickly, when you have many dimensions, because it decreases the influence of dimensions that have less impact on performance. But the downside is that regularization requires you to configure an extra parameter, which adds complexity to the process.

Using Lasso and Ridge regressions in Spark

In Spark, you can set Lasso and Ridge regressions manually by changing the `regParam` and `updater` properties of the `LinearRegressionWithSGD.optimizer` object or by using the `LassoWithSGD` and `RidgeRegressionWithSGD` classes. The latter is what we did.

You can find two additional methods in our online repository: `iterateLasso` and `iterateRidge`. They're similar to the `iterateLRwSGD` method you used before, but they take an additional `regParam` argument and train different models.

You can try these two methods and see the RMSE values Lasso and Ridge regression give on the dataset with the second-order polynomials you used earlier (`trainHP-Scaled` and `validHPScaled`) with the same step size as before and with the value of regression parameter of 0.01, which gives the best results:

```
iterateRidge(Array(200, 400, 1000, 3000, 6000, 10000), Array(1.1), 0.01,
trainHPScaled, validHPScaled)
iterateLasso(Array(200, 400, 1000, 3000, 6000, 10000), Array(1.1), 0.01,
trainHPScaled, validHPScaled)
```

The results (available in our repository online) show that Ridge gives a lower RMSE than Lasso regression and that Ridge is better even than the ordinary least squares (OLS) regression used previously (3.966 for 1,000 iterations instead of 3.984 for 400 iterations). Note that the increase in test RMSE, which was happening for numbers of iterations larger than 400 and which was the effect of overfitting, also happens for Ridge and Lasso regressions. The overfitting kicks in later for Ridge regressions. If you were to increase the regularization parameter, you would see RMSE increase later, but the RMSE levels would be greater.

Which regularization method and which regularization parameter you should choose is difficult to say because it depends on your dataset. You should apply an approach similar to the one you used for finding the number of iterations and the step size (train several models with different parameters and pick the ones with the lowest error). The most common method for doing this is k-fold cross-validation.

7.6.6 K-fold cross-validation

K-fold cross-validation is a method of model validation. It consists of dividing the dataset into *k* subsets of roughly equal size and training *k* models, excluding a different subset each time. The excluded subsets are used as the validation set and the union of all the remaining subsets as the training set.

For each set of parameters you want to validate, train all *k* models and calculate the mean error across all *k* models. Finally, you choose the set of parameters giving you the smallest average error.

Why is this important? Because fitting a model depends very much on the training and validation sets used. If you take the housing dataset, split it randomly into training and validation sets again, and then go through all the actions you did in this chapter, you'll notice that the results and parameters will be different, maybe even dramatically so. K-fold cross-validation can help you decide which of the parameter combinations to choose. We'll have more to say about k-fold cross-validation when we talk about Spark's new ML Pipeline API in the next chapter.

7.7   *Optimizing linear regression*

We have a couple more things to say about linear-regression optimization. As you saw in earlier examples, `LinearRegressionSGD` (and its parent class `GeneralizedLinear-Algorithm`) has an `optimizer` member object you can configure. You previously used the default `GradientDescent` optimizer and configured it with the number of iterations and the step size.

There are two additional methods you can employ to make linear regression find the minimum of the cost function more quickly. The first is to configure the `Gradient-Descent` optimizer as a mini-batch stochastic gradient descent. The second is to use Spark's LBFGS optimizer (see section 7.7.2).

7.7.1   *Mini-batch stochastic gradient descent*

As explained in section 7.3.3, gradient descent updates the weights in each step by going through the entire dataset. If you recall, the formula used for updating each weight parameter is this:

$$w_j := w - y \frac{1}{m} \sum_{i=1}^{m} (h(x^{(i)}) - y^{(i)}) x_j^{(i)}$$

This is also called *batch gradient descent* (BGD). In contrast, the mini-batch stochastic gradient descent uses only a subset of the data in each step; and instead of *i* going from 1 to *m* (the entire dataset), it only goes from 1 to *k* (as some fraction of *m*). If *k* is equal to 1—which means the algorithm considers only one example in each step—the optimizer is called the *stochastic gradient descent* (SGD).

Mini-batch SGD is much less computationally expensive, especially when parallelized, but it compensates for this parallelization with more iterations. It has more difficulties to converge, but it gets to the minimum close enough (except in some rare cases). If the mini-batch size (*k*) is small, the algorithm is more *stochastic,* meaning it has a more random route toward the cost function minimum. If *k* is larger, the algorithm is more stable. In both cases, though, it reaches the minimum and can get very close to BGD results.

Let's see how to use mini-batch SGD in Spark. The same `GradientDescent` optimizer you used before is used for mini-batch SGD, but you need to specify an additional parameter (`miniBatchFraction`). `miniBatchFraction` takes a value between 0 and 1. If it's equal to 1 (the default), a mini-batch SGD becomes a BGD because the entire dataset is considered in each step.

Parameters for mini-batch SGD can be chosen similarly to how you did it previously, only now there is one more parameter to be configured. If a step-size parameter worked on BGD, that doesn't mean it will work on mini-batch SGD, so the parameter's value has to be chosen the same way you did it before—or, preferably, using k-fold cross-validation.

A good starting point for the mini-batch fraction parameter is 0.1, but it will probably have to be fine-tuned. The number of iterations can be chosen so that the dataset as a whole is iterated about 100 times in total (and sometimes even less). For example, if the fraction parameter is 0.1, specifying 1,000 iterations guarantees that elements in the dataset are taken into account 100 times (on average). For performance reasons, to balance computation and communication between nodes in the cluster, the mini-batch size (absolute size, not the fraction parameter) must typically be at least two orders of magnitude larger than the number of machines in the cluster.[11]

In our online repository, you'll find the method `iterateLRwSGDBatch`, which is a variation of `iterateLRwSGD` with one additional line:

```
alg.optimizer.setMiniBatchFraction(miniBFraction)
```

The signature of the method is also different because its parameter takes three arrays: in addition to number of iterations and step sizes, an array with mini-batch fractions. The method tries all combinations of the three values and prints the results (training and testing RMSE). You can try it out on the dataset expanded with feature squares (`trainHPScaled` and `validHPScaled` RDDs). First, to get a feeling for the step-size parameter in the context of the other two, execute this command:

```
iterateLRwSGDBatch(Array(400, 1000), Array(0.05, 0.09, 0.1, 0.15, 0.2, 0.3,
0.35, 0.4, 0.5, 1), Array(0.01, 0.1), trainHPScaled, validHPScaled)
```

The results (available online) show that a step size of 0.4 works best. Now use that value and see how the algorithm behaves when you change other parameters:

```
iterateLRwSGDBatch(Array(400, 1000, 2000, 3000, 5000, 10000), Array(0.4),
➥ Array(0.1, 0.2, 0.4, 0.5, 0.6, 0.8), trainHPScaled, validHPScaled)
```

The results (again, available online) show that 2,000 iterations are enough to get the best RMSE of 3.965, which is slightly better even than the previous best RMSE of 3.966 (for Ridge regression). The results also show that with more than 5,000 iterations, you

---

[11] Chenxin Ma et al., "Adding vs. Averaging in Distributed Primal-Dual Optimization," www.cs.berkeley.edu/~vsmith/docs/cocoap.pdf.

get into overfitting territory. This lowest RMSE was accomplished with a mini-batch fraction of 0.5.

If your dataset is huge, a mini-batch fraction of 0.5 may be too large to get good performance results. You should try lower mini-batch fractions and more iterations. Some experimenting will be needed.

We can conclude that mini-batch SGD can give the same RMSE as BGD. Because of its performance improvements, you should prefer it to BGD.

7.7.2   LBFGS optimizer

LBFGS is a limited-memory approximation of the Broyden-Fletcher-Goldfarb-Shanno (BFGS) algorithm for minimizing multidimensional functions. The classic BFGS algorithm calculates an approximate inverse of the so-called *Hessian matrix*, which is a matrix of second-degree derivatives of a function, and keeps an $n \times n$ matrix in memory, where n is the number of dimensions. LBFGS keeps fewer than 10 of the last-calculated corrections and is more memory efficient, especially for larger numbers of dimensions.

PYTHON   An LBFGS regression optimizer isn't available in Python.

LBFGS can give good performance. And it's much simpler to use, because instead of requiring the number of iterations and the step size, its stopping criterion is the convergence-tolerance parameter. It stops if the RMSE after each iteration changes less than the value of the convergence-tolerance parameter. This is a much more natural and more simple criterion.

You also need to give it the maximum number of iterations to run (in case it doesn't converge), the number of corrections to keep (this should be less than 10, which is the default), and the regularization parameter (it gives you freedom to use L1 or L2 regularization).

You can find the `iterateLBFGS` method in our online repository and paste it into your Spark Scala shell to try it out like this—but before running it, you might want to set the Breeze library logging level to `WARN` (the snippet is available online):

```
iterateLBFGS(Array(0.005, 0.007, 0.01, 0.02, 0.03, 0.05, 0.1), 10, 1e-5,
➥ trainHPScaled, validHPScaled)
0.005, 10 -> 3.8335, 4.0383
0.007, 10 -> 3.8848, 4.0005
0.010, 10 -> 3.9542, 3.9798
0.020, 10 -> 4.1388, 3.9662
0.030, 10 -> 4.2892, 3.9996
0.050, 10 -> 4.5319, 4.0796
0.100, 10 -> 5.0571, 4.3579
```

Now, wasn't that fast? It flew by. And it was simple, too. The only parameter you needed to tweak is the regularization parameter, because the other two don't influence the algorithm much, and these defaults can be used safely. Obviously, a regularization parameter of 0.02 gives the best RMSE of 3.9662. And that's almost the same as the previous best RMSE, which took great effort to get to.

7.8 *Summary*

- Supervised learning uses labeled data for training. Unsupervised-learning algorithms discover the inner structure of unlabeled data through model fitting.

- Regression and classification differ by the type of target variable: continuous (a real number) for regression and categorical (a set of discreet numbers) for classification.

- Before using data for linear regression, it's a good idea to analyze its distribution and similarities. You should also normalize and scale the data and split it into training and validation datasets.

- A root mean squared error (RMSE) is commonly used for evaluating a linear-regression model's performance.

- The learned parameters of a linear-regression model can give you insight into how each feature affects the target variable.

- Adding higher-order polynomials to the dataset enables you to apply linear regression to nonlinear problems and can yield better results on some datasets.

- Increasing a model's complexity can lead to overfitting. The bias-variance tradeoff says that you can either have high bias or high variance, but not both.

- Ridge and Lasso regularizations help reduce overfitting for linear regression.

- Mini-batch stochastic gradient descent optimizes performance of the linear-regression algorithm.

- The LBFGS optimizer in Spark takes much less time to train and offers great performance.

ML: classification and clustering

In the previous chapter, you got acquainted with Spark MLlib (Spark's machine learning library), with machine learning in general, and linear regression, the most important method of regression analysis. In this chapter, we'll cover two equally important fields in machine learning: classification and clustering.

Classification is a subset of supervised machine learning algorithms, where the *target* variable is a *categorical* variable, which means it takes only a limited set of values. So the task of classification is to categorize input examples into several classes. Recognizing handwritten letters is a classification problem, for example, because each input image needs to be labeled as one of the letters in an alphabet. Recognizing a sickness a patient may have, based on their symptoms, is a similar problem.

Clustering also groups input data into classes (called *clusters*), but as an unsupervised learning method, it has no properly labeled data to learn from and has to figure out on its own what constitutes a cluster. You could, for example, use clustering for grouping clients by their habits or characteristics (client segmentation) or recognizing different topics in news articles (text categorization).

For classification tasks in Spark, you have *logistic regression, naïve Bayes, support vector machines* (*SVM*), *decision trees*, and *random forests* at your disposal. They all have their pluses and minuses and different logic and theory behind them. We'll cover logistic regression, decision trees, and random forests in this chapter, as well as k-means clustering, the most-often-used clustering algorithm.

We don't have enough space in this book to cover naïve Bayes, SVM, and other Spark clustering algorithms such as power iteration clustering, Gaussian mixture model, and latent Dirichlet allocation. We'll also have to skip other machine learning methods, such as recommendations with alternating least squares, text feature extraction, and frequent item sets. We'll keep those for some other book and some other time.

As you may remember from the previous chapter, Spark has two machine learning libraries: MLlib, which you used in chapter 7, and the new ML library. They're both being actively developed, but currently the focus of development is more on the ML library. For the most part, you'll use the ML library in this chapter to see how it's used and how it differs from MLlib.

In section 8.1, we'll give you an overview of the ML library; in section 8.2 you'll use it for classification with logistic regression, a well-known classification algorithm. In section 8.3, you'll learn how to use Spark's decision tree and random forest, two algorithms that can be used for both classification and clustering. In section 8.4, you'll use a k-means clustering algorithm for clustering sample data. We'll be explaining theory behind these algorithms along the way. Let's get started.

8.1 Spark ML library

The Spark ML library was introduced in Spark 1.2. The motivation for a new machine library came from the fact that MLlib wasn't scalable and extendable enough, nor was it sufficiently practical for use in real machine learning projects. The goal of the new Spark ML library is to generalize machine learning operations and streamline machine learning processes. Influenced by the Python's *scikit-learn* library,[1] it introduces several new abstractions—estimators, transformers, and evaluators—that can be combined to form pipelines. All four can be parameterized with ML parameters in a general way.

Spark ML ubiquitously uses `DataFrame` objects to present datasets. This is why the old MLlib algorithms can't be simply upgraded: the Spark ML architecture requires structural changes, so new implementations of the same algorithms are necessary. At the time of writing, the old MLlib library still offers a richer set of algorithms than ML,

---

[1] For more information, see the Spark "Pipelines and Parameters" design document at http://mng.bz/22lY and the corresponding JIRA ticket at https://issues.apache.org/jira/browse/SPARK-3530.

but that is bound to change soon. Because estimators, transformers, evaluators, ML parameters, and pipelines are the main components of Spark ML, let's examine them more closely.

8.1.1   *Estimators, transformers, and evaluators*

In Spark, you use *transformers* (no, not *those* Transformers) to implement machine learning components that convert one dataset to another. Machine learning models in Spark ML are transformers because they transform datasets by adding predictions. The main method for this is `transform`, which takes a `DataFrame` and an optional set of parameters.

Estimators produce transformers by fitting on a dataset. A linear regression algorithm produces a linear regression model with fitted weights and an intercept, which is a transformer. The main method for using estimators is `fit`, which also takes a `DataFrame` and an optional set of parameters.

Evaluators evaluate the performance of a model based on a single metric. For instance, regression evaluators can use RMSE and R^2 as metrics. Figure 8.1 shows the operations of transformers, estimators, and evaluators graphically. You'll see examples of transformers, estimators, and evaluators throughout this chapter.

8.1.2   *ML parameters*

Specifying parameters for estimators and transformers is generalized in Spark ML, so all parameters can be specified the same way with the `Param`, `ParamPair`, and `Param-Map` classes. `Param` describes parameter types: it holds the parameter name, its class

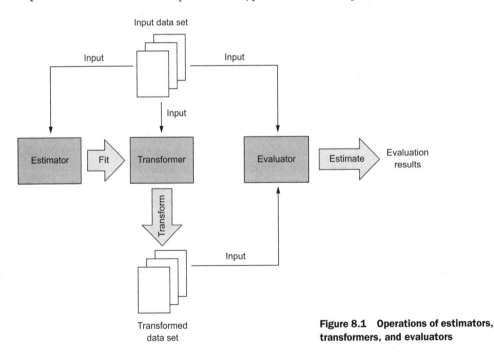

Figure 8.1   Operations of estimators, transformers, and evaluators

type, a parameter description, a function for validating the parameter, and an optional default value. `ParamPair` contains a parameter type (a `Param` object) and its value. `ParamMap` contains a set of `ParamPair` objects.

You pass `ParamPair` or `ParamMap` objects to the `fit` or `transform` methods of estimators and transformers, or you can set the parameters using the specific, named setter methods. You can, for example, call `setRegParam(0.1)` on a `LinearRegression` object named `linreg`, or you can pass a `ParamMap(linreg.regParam -> 0.1)` object to its `fit` method.

8.1.3 *ML pipelines*

As you saw in chapter 7, in machine learning, the same steps are often repeated in the same sequence over and over again with slightly different parameters to find those that yield the best results (lowest error or some other metric). In chapter 7 you trained a linear regression model several times, each time with a different set of parameters. Then you added higher-order polynomials to the dataset and trained the model several times again.

Instead of doing this manually each time, Spark ML lets you create a `Pipeline` object with two stages. The first stage transforms the dataset by adding higher-order polynomials. The `PolynomialExpansion` transformer in the ML library does this using the polynomial degree as a parameter. The second stage performs linear regression analysis, and then it lets you treat the entire pipeline as a single estimator, which produces a `PipelineModel`. The `PipelineModel` also has two stages: a polynomial expansion step and the fitted linear regression model. You can use it on the validation data to see how well it performs.

Each time you fit the pipeline, you give it a different set of parameters (a `ParamMap` that contains parameters for both stages) and then choose the set that gives you the best results. This is much simpler when you have several steps in the process.

This was a brief description of the ML API. You'll see full examples in the following sections.

8.2 *Logistic regression*

As you may remember, your goal in chapter 7 was to predict median home prices in Boston suburbs. That is a typical example of regression analysis because the goal is to find a single value based on a set of input variables. The goal of classification, on the other hand, is to classify input examples (consisting of input variables' values) into two or more classes.

You can easily transform the problem of predicting median home prices into a classification problem if you want to predict whether the mean price is greater than some fixed amount (let's say $30,000[2]). Then the target variable takes only two possible

---

[2] $30,000 may seem inexpensive, but bear in mind that the Boston housing dataset was created in 1978.

values: 1, if the price is greater than $30,000; or 0, if it's less than $30,000. This is called a *binary response* because there are only two possible classes.

Logistic regression outputs probabilities that a certain example belongs to a certain class. The binary-response example is an example of a binary logistic regression. We'll describe its model in the next section and then show you how to train and use a logistic-regression model in Spark. We'll also talk about how to evaluate classification results in general, using logistic regression as an example. At the end of this section, we'll expand a logistic regression model to a multiclass logistic regression, which can classify examples into more than two classes.

8.2.1   *Binary logistic regression model*

A linear regression model trained on the home prices dataset gives you a single number that you can then treat either as a 1 (if it's larger than some threshold) or as a 0 (if it's smaller than the threshold). Linear regression can give you very good results in binary-classification problems like this one, but it wasn't designed for predicting categorical variables. Again, classification methods such as logistic regression output a probability $p(x)$ that an example x (a vector) belongs to a specific category.

Probabilities lie in the range from 0 to 1 (corresponding to 0% and 100% probabilities), but linear regression outputs values outside of these boundaries. So, in logistic regression, instead of modeling the probability $p(x)$ with the linear equation

$$p(x) = w_0 + w_1 x_1 + \ldots + w_n x_n = w^T x$$

it's modeled with the so-called *logistic function* (from which logistic regression gets its name):

$$p(x) = \frac{e^{w^T x}}{1 + e^{w^T x}} = \frac{1}{1 + e^{-w^T x}}$$

The result of plotting this function for two different sets of weights w is shown in figure 8.2. The plot on the left side of the figure shows the basic logistic function, where $w0$ is 0 and $w1$ is 1. The one on the right corresponds to a different set of weights, where $w0$ is 4 and $w1$ is -2. You can see that the weight parameter $w0$ moves the step of the function left or right along the X-axis, and the weight parameter $w1$ changes the slope of the step and also influences the horizontal position of it. Because the logistic function always gives values between 0 and 1, it's better suited for modeling probabilities.

By further manipulating the logistic function, you can arrive at the following:

$$\frac{p(x)}{1 - p(x)} = e^{w^T x}$$

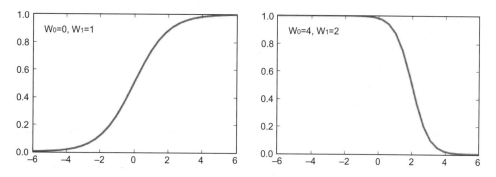

Figure 8.2 A logistic function gives values in the range from 0 to 1 for any input value. This is ideal for modeling probabilities. The plot on the left is a logistic function with weights w_0 of 0 and w_1 of 1. The plot on the right corresponds to the weights w_0 of 4 and w_1 of -2.

The expression on the left side of this equation is known as the *odds*. You may have heard a gambler say something similar to "the odds are three to one." This is expressed by the odds formula: the probability of an event happening divided by the probability of the opposite. After taking the natural logarithm of the equation, you arrive at the following expression:

$$ln\frac{p(x)}{1-p(x)} = w^T x$$

The expression on the left side of the equation becomes the *logit* (or *log-odds*) of the logistic function; and, as you can see, it linearly depends on x. Note that the vector *w* contains an intercept w_0 and that x_0 equals 1.

If you think about it, $p(x)$ is actually the probability that input example x belongs to category 1 (mean home price is greater than \$30,000), so $1 - p(x)$ equals the probability of the opposite case (mean home price is less than \$30,000). This can be written in the following way, using conditional-probability notation:

$$p(x) = p(y = 1|x;w)$$
$$1 - p(x) = p(y = 0|x;w)$$

The right side of the first equation can be read as "probability that category is *1*, given the example x and parameterized by the vector of weights *w*."

Optimal values for weight parameters in logistic regression are determined by maximizing the so-called *likelihood function*, which gives you the *joint probability* (the probability that a set of events happens in the same time) of correctly predicting the labels of all examples from the dataset. You want the predicted probability (given by the logistic function and parameterized by weight values) to be as close as possible to 1 for the examples that are labeled as such, and as close as possible to 0 for those that aren't. Expressing this mathematically yields the following equation:

$$L(w) = \prod_{i:y_i = 1} p(x_i) \prod_{j:y_j = 0} (1 - p(x_j)) = p(y_1|x_1;w)p(y_2|x_2;w)...p(y_n|x_n;w)$$

Taking a natural logarithm of the last expression gives you the log-likelihood function (or *log-loss*), which is easier to maximize, so it's used as the cost function for logistic regression:

$$L(w) = ln\, p(y_1|x_1;w) + p(y_2|x_2;w) + ... + p(y_n|x_n;w)$$

If you work out the math, the log-likelihood function gets reduced to the following:

$$l(w) = \sum_{i = 1}^{m} y_i w^T x_i - ln\left(1 - e^{w^T x_i}\right)$$

Now that you have the cost function, gradient descent can be applied to finding its minimum, similar to how it's done in linear regression as described in chapter 7. In fact, many of the methods you used for linear regression in the previous chapter, such as L1 and L2 regularizations and LBFGS optimization, can be used for logistic regression, too.

The partial derivative of the log-likelihood function, with respect to the *j*-th weight parameter w_j (necessary for performing gradient descent), is the following:

$$\frac{\partial}{\partial w_j} l(w) = \sum_{i = 1}^{m} \left(y_i - \frac{e^{w^T x_i}}{1 + e^{w^T x_i}} \right) x_{ij}$$

But that's more math than you need in order to use logistic regression in Spark. Let's see how to do that.

8.2.2   Preparing data to use logistic regression in Spark

In this section, you'll load an example dataset, clean up the data, and package it so that it's usable by the Spark ML API. In the next section, you'll use this data to train a logistic-regression model.

The example dataset that you'll use for logistic regression is the well-known adult dataset (http://archive.ics.uci.edu/ml/datasets/Adult), extracted from the 1994 United States census data. It contains 13 attributes[3] with data about a person's sex,

---

[3] We removed the education-num column because it's a transformation of the education column and as such contains no extra information.

age, education, marital status, race, native country, and so on, and the target variable (income). The goal is to predict whether a person earns more or less than $50,000 per year (the income column contains only values 1 and 0).

The first step is to download the dataset (you'll find the adult.raw file in our online repository, which you should have cloned by now) and load it into your Spark shell. Start your Spark shell on a local cluster, taking all the available CPU cores (you can also run it on Mesos or YARN, if you want, but we'll assume you're running a local cluster in the spark-in-action VM):

```
$ cd /home/spark
$ spark-shell --master local[*]
```

Load the dataset with the following command (the third line converts to doubles all values that can be converted; others are left as strings):

```
val census_raw = sc.textFile("first-edition/ch08/adult.raw", 4).
  map(x => x.split(", ")).
  map(row => row.map(x => try { x.toDouble }
    catch { case _ : Throwable => x }))
```

Let's first examine the data by loading it into a DataFrame (DataFrames should be familiar to you from chapter 5).

```
val adultschema = StructType(Array(
    StructField("age",DoubleType,true),
    StructField("workclass",StringType,true),
    StructField("fnlwgt",DoubleType,true),
    StructField("education",StringType,true),
    StructField("marital_status",StringType,true),
    StructField("occupation",StringType,true),
    StructField("relationship",StringType,true),
    StructField("race",StringType,true),
    StructField("sex",StringType,true),
    StructField("capital_gain",DoubleType,true),
    StructField("capital_loss",DoubleType,true),
    StructField("hours_per_week",DoubleType,true),
    StructField("native_country",StringType,true),
    StructField("income",StringType,true)
))
val dfraw = sqlContext.createDataFrame(census_raw.map(Row.fromSeq(_)),
    adultschema)
```

DEALING WITH MISSING VALUES

There are several small problems (let's call them "challenges") here. First, if you examine the data (by listing the first 20 rows with dfraw.show(), for example), you'll see that some columns have missing values (marked as "?"). You have several options for dealing with missing data:

- If a lot of data is missing from a column, you can remove the entire column from the dataset because that column (feature) can negatively affect the results.
- You can remove the individual examples (rows) from the dataset if they contain too many missing values.
- You can set the missing data to the most common value in the column.
- You can train a separate classification or regression model and use it to predict the missing values.

The last option is obviously the most involved and time-consuming, so you'll implement the third option by counting all the values and using the most frequent ones.

Missing values occur only in these three columns: workclass, occupation, and native _country. Let's examine the count of individual values in the workclass column:

```
scala> dfraw.groupBy(dfraw("workclass")).count().rdd.foreach(println)
[?,2799]
[Self-emp-not-inc,3862]
[Never-worked,10]
[Self-emp-inc,1695]
[Federal-gov,1432]
[State-gov,1981]
[Local-gov,3136]
[Private,33906]
[Without-pay,21]
```

You can see that the value Private occurs the most often in the workclass column. For the occupation column, the value Prof-specialty is the most common. For the native_country column it is, not surprisingly, United-States. You can now use this information to *impute* (which is the official term) the missing values with the Data-FrameNaFunctions class, available through the DataFrame's na field:

```
val dfrawrp = dfraw.na.replace(Array("workclass"),
  Map("?" -> "Private"))
val dfrawrpl = dfrawrp.na.replace(Array("occupation"),
  Map("?" -> "Prof-specialty"))
val dfrawnona = dfrawrpl.na.replace(Array("native_country"),
  Map("?" -> "United-States"))
```

The replace method takes an array of column names and replaces values as specified by the map in the second argument. DataFrameNaFunctions can also fill missing (null) values with several versions of the fill method and drop rows if they contain a certain number of missing values (implemented by several versions of the drop method).[4]

DEALING WITH CATEGORICAL VALUES

That's settled now, but you still have a challenge: most of the values in the dfrawnona data frame are string values, and classification algorithms can't handle them. So you first need to transform the data to numeric values. But even after you do that, you'll

---

4 For further information, check the official documentation at http://mng.bz/X3Zg.

still have a problem because a numeric encoding ranks categories by their numeric values, and it's often not clear how they should be ranked. If you encode the `marital status` field's values (`separated`, `divorced`, `never married`, `widowed`, `married`[5]) with integer values from 0 to 4, would that be a realistic interpretation of their meanings? Is `never married` "greater than" `separated`? No, it isn't. So a technique known as *one-hot encoding* is more commonly used.

In one-hot encoding, a column is expanded to as many columns as there are distinct values in it so that, for a single row, only one of the columns contains a 1 and all the others contain 0s. For the `marital status` column example (shown in figure 8.3), the column gets expanded to 5 columns (values from 0 to 4), and if a row contains the value `married`, the new columns contain values 0, 0, 0, 0, 1. In this way, all possible values become equally important.

Marital status		Married	Divorced	Separated	Widowed	Never Married
Separated		0	0	1	0	0
Divorced		0	1	0	0	0
Widowed		0	0	0	1	0
Married	→	1	0	0	0	0
Widowed		0	0	0	1	0
Separated		0	0	1	0	0
Never married		0	0	0	0	1
Married		1	0	0	0	0

Figure 8.3 One-hot encoding of the `marital status` column. It gets expanded into five new columns, each containing only ones and zeros. Each row contains only one 1 in the column corresponding to the original column value.

Three classes in the new Spark ML library can help you deal with categorical values:

- `StringIndexer`
- `OneHotEncoder`
- `VectorAssembler`

USING STRINGINDEXER

`StringIndexer` helps you convert `String` categorical values into integer indexes of those values. `StringIndexer` takes a `DataFrame` and fits a `StringIndexerModel`, which is then used for transformations of a column. You have to fit as many `StringIndexerModels` as there are columns you want to transform. We wrote a method that does this for you:

```
import org.apache.spark.sql.DataFrame
def indexStringColumns(df:DataFrame, cols:Array[String]):DataFrame = {
  var newdf = df
  for(col <- cols) {
    val si = new StringIndexer().setInputCol(col).setOutputCol(col+"-num")
```

[5] We omit a few other possible values here.

For each column in the cols
argument, fits a StringIndexerModel

Creates a DataFrame by
putting the transformed
values in the new column
with suffix "-num"; drops
the old column

```
    val sm:StringIndexerModel = si.fit(newdf)
    newdf = sm.transform(newdf).drop(col)
    newdf = newdf.withColumnRenamed(col+"-num", col)
  }
  newdf
}
val dfnumeric = indexStringColumns(dfrawnona, Array("workclass",
  "education", "marital_status", "occupation", "relationship", "race",
  "sex", "native_country", "income"))
```

Renames the new column
to have the old name

Transforms columns of the dfrawnona
DataFrame to numeric values

`StringIndexerModel` also adds metadata to the columns it transforms. This metadata contains information about the type of values a column contains (binary, nominal, numeric). Some algorithms depend on this metadata.

ENCODING THE DATA WITH ONEHOTENCODER

The second class that helps with data preparation is `OneHotEncoder`, which one-hot-encodes a column and puts the results into a new column as a one-hot-encoded sparse `Vector`. Here, we provide the method `oneHotEncodeColumns` that you can use to one-hot-encode an arbitrary number of columns. You provide a `DataFrame` object and a list of numeric columns, and it will replace each column with a `Vector` with one-hot-encoded values:

Creates OneHotEncoder
for each specified column

```
def oneHotEncodeColumns(df:DataFrame, cols:Array[String]):DataFrame = {
    var newdf = df
    for(c <- cols) {
        val onehotenc = new OneHotEncoder().setInputCol(c)
        onehotenc.setOutputCol(c+"-onehot").setDropLast(false)
        newdf = onehotenc.transform(newdf).drop(c)
        newdf = newdf.withColumnRenamed(c+"-onehot", c)
    }
    newdf
}
val dfhot = oneHotEncodeColumns(dfnumeric, Array("workclass", "education",
  "marital_status", "occupation", "relationship", "race", "native_country"))
```

Renames
the new
column
to the
old name

Creates the new
column and drops
the old column

MERGING THE DATA WITH VECTORASSEMBLER

The final step is to merge all these new `Vectors` and the original columns into a single `Vector` column containing all the features. Spark ML algorithms work with two columns named `features` and `label`, by default. If you recall from chapter 7, MLlib algorithms work with RDDs containing `LabeledPoint` objects. If you convert an RDD containing a `LabeledPoint` into a `DataFrame` (using the `toDF` method), the resulting `DataFrame` contains two columns: `features` and `label`. So, we can say this is the `DataFrame` equivalent of `LabeledPoint`.

This is where a third helpful class, VectorAssembler, comes into play. It takes a number of column names (as the inputCols parameter), an output column name (as the outputCol parameter), and a DataFrame and then assembles the values from all input columns into the output column.

The final step is to use VectorAssembler. The input columns are all the columns of the dfhot DataFrame, minus the income column:

```
val va = new VectorAssembler().setOutputCol("features").
  setInputCols(dfhot.columns.diff(Array("income")))
```

After the transformation, you still need to rename the income column label:

```
val lpoints = va.transform(dfhot).select("features", "income").
  withColumnRenamed("income", "label")
```

VectorAssembler also adds metadata about features it assembles. Again, some algorithms depend on these. Now that you have a data frame with labeled points, you can finally move on to fitting a logistic regression model.

8.2.3 *Training the model*

As with any machine learning model, you have to train it on the prepared data. This means the algorithm needs to find the model with parameters that correspond to the data as much as possible.

Logistic-regression models in Spark can be trained with the MLlib classes LogisticRegressionWithSGD and LogisticRegressionWithLBFGS (this gives you an MLlib LogisticRegressionModel object), and with the new ML API class LogisticRegression (this gives you an ML LogisticRegressionModel object). As we said, you'll use the new ML API in this chapter.

You'll use the same principle of dividing the dataset into training and validation sets that you used in the previous chapter. DataFrames also provide a randomSplit method for this purpose, the same as RDDs:

```
val splits = lpoints.randomSplit(Array(0.8, 0.2))
val adulttrain = splits(0).cache()
val adultvalid = splits(1).cache()
```

You'll use the training set to fit your models and then use the validation set to test the performance of the models. Notice that the sets are cached in memory: this is important for machine learning algorithms that are iterative in nature and reuse the same dataset many times.

To train a logistic-regression model, set the parameters on a LogisticRegression object and call its fit method, passing in a DataFrame:

```
val lr = new LogisticRegression
lr.setRegParam(0.01).setMaxIter(500).setFitIntercept(true)
val lrmodel = lr.fit(adulttrain)
```

As we said in section 8.1, you can also set the parameters with the `fit` method:

```
val lrmodel = lr.fit(adulttrain, ParamMap(lr.regParam -> 0.01,
  lr.maxIter -> 500, lr.fitIntercept -> true))
```

Logistic regression in Spark ML uses the LBFGS algorithm (which you encountered in chapter 7) to minimize the loss function because it converges quickly and is easier to use. The logistic-regression implementation in Spark also automatically scales the features.

INTERPRETING THE MODEL PARAMETERS

You can now inspect the model parameters that the algorithm found:

```
scala> lrmodel.weights
res0: org.apache.spark.mllib.linalg.Vector =
[0.02253347752531383,5.79891265368467E-7,1.4056502945663293E-4,
5.405187982713647E-4,0.025912049724868744,-0.5254963078098936,
0.060803010946022244,-0.3868418367509028,...
scala> lrmodel.intercept
res1: Double = -4.396337959898011
```

Your results may be somewhat different. What do these numbers mean?

In the previous chapter, the trained linear regression model gave you weights whose magnitude directly corresponded to the importance of particular features: in other words, to the influence they had on the target variable. In logistic regression, we're interested in the probability that a sample is in a certain category, but a model's weights don't linearly influence that probability. Instead, they linearly influence the log-odds given by this equation (repeated from section 8.2.1):

$$ln\frac{p(x)}{1-p(x)} = w^{T}x$$

From the *log-odds* equation, the equation for calculating the *odds* follows:

$$\frac{p(x)}{1-p(x)} = e^{w^{T}x}$$

To see how individual weight parameters influence the probability, let's see what happens if you increase a single feature (let's say x_1) by 1 and leave all other values the same. It can be shown this is equal to multiplying the odds by e^{w}_1.

If you take the age dimension as an example, the corresponding weight parameter is 0.0225335 (rounded). $e^{0.0225335}$ equals 1.0228, which means increasing age by 1 increases the odds of the person earning more than $50,000 per year by 2.28%. That is, in a nutshell, the way to interpret logistic-regression parameters.

8.2.4 Evaluating classification models

Now that you have a trained model, you can see how well it performs on the training dataset. First, you use the linear regression model `lrmodel`, which is a `Transformer`, to transform the validation dataset; and then you use `BinaryClassificationEvaluator` to evaluate the model's performance:

```
val validpredicts = lrmodel.transform(adultvalid)
```

The `validpredicts` DataFrame now contains the `label` and `features` columns from the `adultvalid` DataFrame, along with a few additional columns:

```
scala> validpredicts.show()
+--------------------+-----+-----------------+-----------------+----------+
|            features|label|    rawPrediction|      probability|prediction|
+--------------------+-----+-----------------+-----------------+----------+
|(103,[0,1,2,4,5,6...|  0.0|[1.00751014104...|[0.73253259721...|       0.0|
|(103,[0,1,2,4,5,6...|  0.0|[0.41118861448...|[0.60137285202...|       0.0|
|(103,[0,1,2,4,5,6...|  0.0|[0.39603063020...|[0.59773360388...|       0.0|
...
```

The `probability` column contains vectors with two values: the probability that the sample isn't in the category (the person is making less than $50,000) and the probability that it is. These two values always add up to 1. The `rawPrediction` column also contains vectors with two values: the log-odds that a sample doesn't belong to the category and the log-odds that it does. These two values are always opposite numbers (they add up to 0). The `prediction` column contains 1s and 0s, which indicates whether a sample is likely to belong to the category. A sample is likely to belong to the category if its probability is greater than a certain threshold (0.5 by default).

The names of all these columns (including `features` and `label`) can be customized using parameters (for example, `outputCol`, `rawPredictionCol`, `probabilityCol`, and so on).

USING BINARYCLASSIFICATIONEVALUATOR

To evaluate the performance of your model, you can use the `BinaryClassification-Evaluator` class and its `evaluate` method:

```
scala> val bceval = new BinaryClassificationEvaluator()
bceval: org.apache.spark.ml...
scala> bceval.evaluate(validpredicts)
res0: Double = 0.9039934862200736
```

But what does this result mean, and how is it calculated? You can check the metric the `BinaryClassificationEvaluator` used by calling the `getMetricName` method:

```
scala> bceval.getMetricName
res1: String = areaUnderROC
```

This metric is known as "area under receiver operating characteristic curve." `Binary-ClassificationEvaluator` can also be configured to calculate "area under precision-recall curve" by setting `setMetricName("areaUnderPR")`.

Great: you know the names of the metrics, but you don't know what they mean yet. To understand what these terms mean, you first need to understand precision and recall.

PRECISION AND RECALL

In chapter 7, you used the RMSE to evaluate the performance of linear regression. When evaluating classification results, which are nominal values, this method isn't appropriate. Instead, you use metrics based on counting good and bad predictions.

To evaluate your model's performance, you can count *true positives* (TP), which is the number of your model's predictions that it correctly classified as positives, and *false positives* (FP), which are those that it predicted as positives but are actually negatives. Analogously, there are *true negatives* (TN) and *false negatives* (FN).

From these four numbers, *precision* (P) and *recall* (R) measures are calculated like this:

$$P = \frac{TP}{TP + FP}, R = \frac{TP}{TP + FN}$$

In other words, precision is the percentage of true positives out of all positives your model has labeled as such. Recall is the percentage of all positives that your model identified (or *recalled*). Recall is also called *sensitivity*, *true positive rate* (TPR), and *hit rate*.

So, if your model predicts only 0s, it has both precision and recall equal to 0, because there are no true or false positives. But if it predicts only 1s, recall is equal to 1 and precision will depend on the dataset: if there is a large percentage of positives in the dataset, precision will also be close to 1, which is misleading.

This is why a measure called *f-measure*, or *f1-score*, is more commonly used. It's calculated as the harmonic mean of precision and recall:

$$f_1 = \frac{2PR}{P + R}$$

The f1-score will be 0 if any of the two (precision or recall) is 0, and it will be close to 1 if both of them are.

PRECISION-RECALL CURVE

A precision-recall (PR) curve is obtained when you gradually change the probability threshold at which your model determines whether a sample belongs to a category (say, from 0 to 1), and at each point, you calculate precision and recall. Then you plot the obtained values on the same graph (precision on the Y-axis and recall on the X-axis).

If you increase the probability threshold, there will be fewer false positives, so precision will go up; but recall will go down, because fewer positives in the dataset will be identified. If you decrease the threshold, precision will go down because many more positives (true and false) will be identified, but recall will go up.

PYTHON The `BinaryClassificationMetrics` class in Python doesn't provide methods for calculating precision and recall values at different threshold values. It does provide `areaUnderPR` and `areaUnderROC` metrics, though.

You can change the threshold of your model using the `setThreshold` method. A class `BinaryClassificationMetrics` from the MLlib library can calculate precision and recall for an RDD containing tuples with predictions and labels. We wrote a small method called `computePRCurve` (you can find it in our online repository) that outputs precision and recall for 11 values of threshold from 0 to 1. The results are available in our online repository. The resulting plot of the PR curve is shown in figure 8.4.

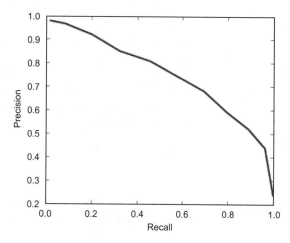

Figure 8.4 The precision-recall curve for the example model

Finally, the area under the PR curve is one of two metrics available when using the `BinaryClassificationEvaluator` class we mentioned previously. In this case, the area under the PR curve is 0.7548, which isn't a bad result.

RECEIVER OPERATING CHARACTERISTIC CURVE

When using `BinaryClassificationEvaluator`, the second available metric (and the default one) is area under the receiver operating characteristic (ROC) curve. The ROC curve is similar to the PR curve, but it has recall (TPR) plotted on its Y-axis and the false positive rate (FPR) plotted on its X-axis. FPR is calculated as the percentage of false positives out of all negative samples:

$$FPR = \frac{FP}{FP + TN}$$

In other words, FPR measures the percentage of all negative samples that your model wrongly classified as positives. The ROC curve for the example model is shown in figure 8.5. The data for it was generated using the `computeROCCurve` method in our online repository.

An ideal model would have a low FPR (low number of false positives) and a high TPR (low number of false negatives), and the matching ROC curve would pass close to the upper-left corner. A ROC curve close to the diagonal is a sign of a model giving almost random results. If the model places FPR and TPR values in the bottom-right corner, the model can be inverted to get it to output more correct results.

The ROC curve shown in figure 8.5 is pretty good. As you've already seen, the matching area under the curve is 0.904, which is pretty high.

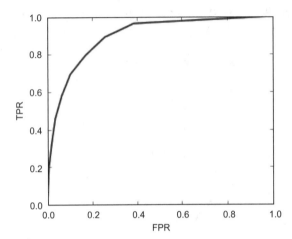

Figure 8.5   The ROC curve for the example model

PR curves can give more relevant results than ROC curves when your dataset has a small percentage of positive samples. Both ROC curves and PR curves are used to compare different models.

8.2.5   *Performing k-fold cross-validation*

We briefly touched on k-fold cross-validation in chapter 7, and we promised we would say more about it later. Here's where we do that. In general, using cross-validation helps you validate the performance of your model more reliably because it validates the model several times and returns the average as the final result. In this way, it's less likely to overfit one particular view of the data.

As we said in the last chapter, k-fold cross-validation consists of dividing the dataset into *k* subsets of equal sizes and training *k* models excluding a different subset each time. The excluded subset is used as the validation set, and all other subsets are used together as the training set. This is shown in figure 8.6.

For each set of parameters you want to validate, you train all *k* models and then calculate the mean error across all *k* models (as in figure 8.6). Finally, you choose the set of parameters giving you the smallest average error.

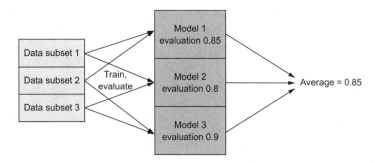

Figure 8.6   An example three-fold cross-validation. The dataset is divided into three subsets that are used to train three models with the same parameters. The average evaluation result is taken as a measure of the model's performance with the selected parameters.

The `CrossValidator` class in Spark ML can automate this for you. You give it an estimator (a `LogisticRegression` object, for example) and an evaluator (`Binary-ClassificationEvaluator`) and then set the number of folds it is to use (default is 3):

```
val cv = new CrossValidator().setEstimator(lr).
  setEvaluator(bceval).setNumFolds(5)
```

`CrossValidator` takes several sets of parameters (an array of `ParamMaps`) in the `set-EstimatorParamMaps` method. It performs k-fold cross-validation for each of those `ParamMap` objects. Another class, `ParamGridBuilder`, makes it easy to generate combinations of parameters as an array of `ParamMaps`. You add grids with sets of values for individual parameters and then build the complete grid, like this:

```
scala> val paramGrid = new ParamGridBuilder().
  addGrid(lr.maxIter, Array(1000)).
  addGrid(lr.regParam, Array(0.0001, 0.001, 0.005, 0.01, 0.05, 0.1)).
  build()
```

To perform logistic regression with LBFGS, only the regularization parameter is relevant, so only the `regParam` parameter is varied in the parameter grid, and the maximum number of iterations is kept constant at 1,000. Finally, the parameter grid is fed to the `CrossValidator`:

```
scala> cv.setEstimatorParamMaps(paramGrid)
```

When you call the `fit` method of the `cv CrossValidator`, it fits the necessary models and returns the best one, as measured by the `bceval` evaluator (this may take some time):

```
scala> val cvmodel = cv.fit(adulttrain)
```

The returned model is of type CrossValidatorModel, and you can access the selected logistic-regression model through the bestModel field:

```
scala> cvmodel.bestModel.asInstanceOf[LogisticRegressionModel].coefficients
res0: org.apache.spark.mllib.linalg.Vector =
      [0.0248435418248564,7.555156155398289E-7,3.1447428691767557E-4,
6.176181173588984E-4,0.027906992593851074,-0.7258527114344593,...
```

Furthermore, to find out which regularization parameter was selected as best, you can access the bestModel's parent (you can't do this in Python):

```
scala>cvmodel.bestModel.parent.asInstanceOf[LogisticRegression].getRegParam
res1: Double = 1.0E-4
```

The regularization parameter of 0.0001 gives the best results. You can now test its performance on the validation dataset:

```
scala> new BinaryClassificationEvaluator().
  evaluate(cvmodel.bestModel.transform(adultvalid))
res2: Double = 0.9073005687252869
```

As you can see, CrossValidatorModel makes it simple to perform k-fold cross-validation. Although you can't use it for model comparison across different algorithms, it speeds up comparison across different sets of parameters.

8.2.6   *Multiclass logistic regression*

As we said earlier, multiclass classification means a classifier categorizes input examples into several classes. Spark ML's logistic regression doesn't support multiclass classification at this time, but you can use MLlib's LogisticRegressionWithLBFGS to perform it. We don't have space to get into LogisticRegressionWithLBFGS here,[6] but we'll show you another method for performing multiclass classification using binary classification models. It's called the *one vs. rest* strategy.

When using the one vs. rest strategy, you train one model per class, each time treating all other classes (*the rest*) as negatives. Then, when classifying new samples, you classify them using all the trained models and pick the class corresponding to the model that gives the highest probability.

Spark ML provides the OneVsRest class precisely for this purpose. It produces a OneVsRestModel that you can use for dataset transformation. Because the multiclass evaluator in the Spark ML library doesn't exist in Spark at the time of writing, you'll use the MulticlassMetrics class from MLlib.

We'll show you how to use these classes on an example dataset containing data extracted from scaled images of handwritten numbers. It's a public dataset available from the UCI machine learning repository,[7] containing 10,992 samples of handwritten digits from 0 to 9. Each sample contains 16 pixels with intensity values of 0–100.

---

[6] You can find an example in the official Spark configuration: http://mng.bz/Ab91.
[7] You can find it at http://mng.bz/9jHs.

PYTHON `OneVsRest` isn't available in Python.

To begin, download the penbased.dat file from our online repository and load it into Spark in much the same way you did the adult dataset (see section 8.2.2):

```
StructField("pix1",IntegerType,true), StructField("pix2",IntegerType,true),
StructField("pix3",IntegerType,true), StructField("pix4",IntegerType,true),
StructField("pix5",IntegerType,true), StructField("pix6",IntegerType,true),
StructField("pix7",IntegerType,true), StructField("pix8",IntegerType,true),
StructField("pix9",IntegerType,true), StructField("pix10",IntegerType,true),
StructField("pix11",IntegerType,true),StructField("pix12",IntegerType,true),
StructField("pix13",IntegerType,true), IntegerType ("pix14",IntegerType,true),
StructField("pix15",IntegerType,true),StructField("pix16",IntegerType,true),
StructField("label",IntegerType,true)))
val pen_raw = sc.textFile("first-edition/ch08/penbased.dat", 4).
  map(x => x.split(", ")).
  map(row => row.map(x => x.toDouble.toInt))
import org.apache.spark.sql.Row
val dfpen = spark.createDataFrame(pen_raw.map(Row.fromSeq(_)), penschema)
import org.apache.spark.ml.feature.VectorAssembler
val va = new VectorAssembler().setOutputCol("features")
va.setInputCols(dfpen.columns.diff(Array("label")))
val penlpoints = va.transform(dfpen).select("features", "label")
```

You already know that you need to split the dataset into training and validation sets:

```
val pensets = penlpoints.randomSplit(Array(0.8, 0.2))
val pentrain = pensets(0).cache()
val penvalid = pensets(1).cache()
```

Now you're ready to use the dataset. First you'll specify a classifier for `OneVsRest`. Here, you'll use a logistic-regression classifier (but you could also use some other classifier):

```
val penlr = new LogisticRegression().setRegParam(0.01)
val ovrest = new OneVsRest()
ovrest.setClassifier(penlr)
```

Finally, you'll fit it on the training set to obtain the model:

```
val ovrestmodel = ovrest.fit(pentrain)
```

The one vs. rest model you just obtained contains 10 logistic-regression models (one for each digit). You can now use it to predict classes of samples from the validation dataset:

```
val penresult = ovrestmodel.transform(penvalid)
```

As we said, Spark ML still has no multiclass evaluator, so you'll use the `Multiclass-Metrics` class from Spark MLlib; but it requires an RDD with tuples containing predictions and labels. So you first need to convert the `penresult` DataFrame to an RDD:

```
val penPreds = penresult.select("prediction", "label").
  rdd.map(row => (row.getDouble(0), row.getDouble(1)))
```

And finally, you'll construct a `MulticlassMetrics` object:

```
val penmm = new MulticlassMetrics(penPreds)
```

Recall and precision are equal for multiclass classifiers because the sum of all false positives is equal to the sum of all false negatives. In this case, they're equal to 0.90182. `MulticlassMetrics` can also give you precision, recall, and f-measure per individual class:

```
scala> penmm.precision(3)
res0: Double = 0.9026548672566371
scala> penmm.recall(3)
res1: Double = 0.9855072463768116
scala> penmm.fMeasure(3)
res2: Double = 0.9422632794457274
```

It can also show you the confusion matrix, which has rows and columns that correspond to classes. Each element on the *i*th row and *j*th column shows how many elements from the *i*th class were classified as the *j*th class:

```
scala> penmm.confusionMatrix
res3: org.apache.spark.mllib.linalg.Matrix =
228.0  1.0    0.0    0.0    1.0    0.0    1.0    0.0    10.0   1.0
0.0    167.0  27.0   3.0    0.0    19.0   0.0    0.0    0.0    0.0
0.0    11.0   217.0  0.0    0.0    0.0    0.0    2.0    0.0    0.0
0.0    0.0    0.0    204.0  1.0    0.0    0.0    1.0    0.0    1.0
0.0    0.0    1.0    0.0    231.0  1.0    2.0    0.0    0.0    2.0
0.0    0.0    1.0    9.0    0.0    153.0  9.0    0.0    9.0    34.0
0.0    0.0    0.0    0.0    1.0    0.0    213.0  0.0    2.0    0.0
0.0    14.0   2.0    6.0    3.0    1.0    0.0    199.0  1.0    0.0
7.0    7.0    0.0    1.0    0.0    4.0    0.0    1.0    195.0  0.0
1.0    9.0    0.0    3.0    3.0    7.0    0.0    1.0    0.0    223.0
```

The values on the diagonal correspond to the correctly classified samples. You can see that this model performs rather well. Let's now see how decision trees and random forests handle this dataset.

8.3   *Decision trees and random forests*

In this section, we'll show you how to use decision trees and random forests, simple but powerful algorithms that can be used for both classification and regression. We'll follow the same approach we used for other algorithms in these two chapters: we'll explain their theoretical background and then show you how to use them in Spark. We'll do that first for decision trees and then for random forests.

A decision-trees algorithm uses a tree-like set of user-defined or learned rules to classify input examples based on their feature values. It's simple to use and easy to understand because it isn't based on complicated math. It can perform classification and regression analysis using simple decision rules, learned from a training dataset. The learned decision rules can be visualized, and they offer an intuitive explanation of inner workings of the algorithm. Furthermore, decision trees don't require data normalization, they can handle numeric and categorical data, and they can work with missing values.

They're prone to overfitting (covered in chapter 7), though, and are very sensitive to the input data. Small changes in the input dataset can drastically change the decision rules. Training an optimal decision tree is *NP-complete*[8] (no efficient way to find a solution is known), so existing practical solutions find locally optimal solutions at each node, which aren't guaranteed to be globally optimal.

Random forests train a certain number of decision trees on data randomly sampled from the original dataset. Methods that use several trained models are generally called *ensemble learning methods,* and the procedure of using randomly sampled data for training the models and then averaging their results is called *bagging.* Bagging helps in reducing variance and, thus, reducing overfitting. That isn't all there is to say about a random-forest algorithm, and we'll get to that later. Let's first examine decision trees.

8.3.1 Decision trees

How does a decision-tree algorithm work? It starts by testing how well each feature classifies the entire training dataset. The metrics used for this are called *impurity* and *information gain* (we'll say more about this later). The best feature is selected as a node, and new branches leaving the node are created according to possible values of the selected feature. If a feature contains continuous values, it's binned into subranges (or bins). A parameter decides how many bins will be used per feature.

Spark creates only binary decision trees; that is, each node has only two branches leaving it. The dataset is divided according to the branches (the selected feature's values), and the entire procedure is repeated for each branch. If a branch contains only a single class, or if a certain tree depth for the branch is reached, the branch becomes a *leaf node* and the procedure for that branch stops.

AN ILLUMINATING EXAMPLE

This may sound complicated, so let's illustrate it with an example. To create an example dataset, we took the housing dataset used in the previous chapter and simplified it a bit. We selected only the features age, education, sex, hours worked per week, and the target variable income and converted the income values to categorical labels (1 if a person earns more than $50,000 and 0 otherwise). Then we sampled the data to obtain only 16 samples. The resulting dataset is shown on the left in figure 8.7.

We next used the dataset to train a decision-tree model. The way the algorithm used the original dataset is shown on the right in the figure. In the first step (in the root node of the resulting tree), the algorithm determined that the education feature should be selected first (that is why the education column is shown first in the table on the right). It divided the possible categories of the education feature according to

---

[8] Laurent Hyafil and Ronald L. Rivest, "Constructing Optimal Binary Decision Trees Is NP-Complete," 1976, http://mng.bz/9G3C.

Age	Hours per week	Education	Sex	Income
25.0	40.0	Bachelors	Male	
39.0	40.0	Some college	Male	
27.0	30.0	HS-grad	Female	
51.0	40.0	Some college	Male	>$50k
46.0	40.0	Some college	Female	
52.0	30.0	Prof-school	Female	>$50k
48.0	35.0	10th	Female	
36.0	40.0	HS-grad	Female	
37.0	50.0	1HS-grad	Male	
47.0	35.0	Masters	Male	>$50k
63.0	44.0	1Assoc-voc	Female	
19.0	25.0	Some college	Female	
63.0	60.0	7th-8th	Male	>$50k
59.0	40.0	HS-grad	Male	>$50k
27.0	40.0	HS-grad	Male	
58.0	40.0	Some college	Female	

1st level	2nd level	3rd level		
Education	Age	Sex	Hours per week	Income
Bachelors	25.0	Male	40.0	
Some college	19.0	Female	25.0	
Some college	39.0	Male	40.0	
Some college	46.0	Female	40.0	
Some college	58.0	Female	40.0	
HS-grad	36.0	Female	40.0	
HS-grad	27.0	Male	40.0	
HS-grad	27.0	Female	30.0	
10th	48.0	Female	35.0	
9th	37.0	Male	50.0	
1st-4th	63.0	Female	44.0	
Prof-school	52.0	Female	30.0	
Some college	51.0	Male	40.0	>$50k
HS-grad	59.0	Male	40.0	>$50k
Masters	47.0	Male	35.0	>$50k
7th-8th	63.0	Male	60.0	>$50k

Figure 8.7   The example dataset on the left serves for training of a decision-tree model. The model's algorithm first divides the dataset by education. The resulting left branch (black background) is divided by age, and the resulting right branch (gray background) is divided by sex. The built model (tree) has a depth of three and has seven nodes. Each group of colored cells in a column corresponds to a node, plus the root node not visible in the figure.

target class values (income) into *left categories*, corresponding to the left branch in figure 8.8 and depicted with a dark gray background in figure 8.7; and *right categories*, corresponding to the right branch in figure 8.8 and depicted with a light gray background in figure 8.7. The resulting right branch only contains the positive examples (income is greater than $50,000), so it's declared to be a leaf node (the final node in the tree).

In the next step, the algorithm uses the age feature. It repeats the same process and divides only those column values in the left education branch (because the values in the right education branch became a leaf node) into two sets. Because age is continuous, it uses a threshold value (value 48) and not a set of categories to divide the values. This time the left branch becomes a leaf node (predicting the classification value false). For the right branch, the sex feature is chosen, and the two final leaf nodes result. As you can see, the algorithm never got to use the hours per week feature, so that feature will have no influence on predictions. The corresponding decision tree is shown in figure 8.8.

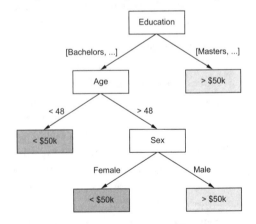

Figure 8.8   The decision tree corresponding to the data shown in figure 8.7. The decision tree has seven nodes and a depth of three. Leaf nodes are depicted with black or gray background, depending on the prediction.

Nodes with a white background in figure 8.8 correspond to the columns used to split the dataset, and the dark gray and light gray arrows correspond to the resulting left and right subsets of the data. The nodes with dark gray and light gray backgrounds are leaf nodes containing final prediction values. The trained decision tree has seven nodes and a depth of three. The decision tree can be used to quickly classify incoming feature vectors.

UNDERSTANDING IMPURITY AND INFORMATION GAIN

We said that the decision-tree algorithm uses impurity and information gain to determine which feature to split. Two measures of impurity are used in decision trees: entropy and Gini impurity. Gini impurity is the default in Spark and in other decision-tree implementations.

Entropy (Shannon entropy) comes from information theory and is a measure of the amount of information contained in a message. The entropy of a dataset D is calculated as:

$$E(D) = \sum_{j=i}^{K} -P(C_j)log_2 P(C_j)$$

where K is the number of target classes and $p(Cj)$ is the proportion of jth class Cj. For the binary-classification example dataset shown in figure 8.7, entropy is equal to

$$E(D) = -\frac{5}{16}log_2\frac{5}{16} - \frac{11}{16}log_2\frac{11}{16} = 0.3125 \cdot 1.678072 + 0.6875 \cdot 0.540568 = 0.896038$$

If only one class is present in a dataset, the entropy is equal to 0. Entropy reaches a maximum if all classes are equally present in the dataset. For a binary classification, this maximum is equal to 1.

Gini impurity is a measure of how often a randomly chosen element from the dataset would be incorrectly labeled if it were randomly labeled according to the distribution of labels in the dataset.[9] It's calculated like this:

$$Gini(D) = 1 - \sum_{j=1}^{K} P(C_j)^2$$

It also reaches a maximum if all classes are equally present in the dataset (equal to 0.5 in the case of two classes) and is equal to 0 if the dataset contains only one class (the value of the target variable). For the example, the dataset in figure 8.8 is equal to 0.4296875.

That's how impurity is calculated. When deciding how to split the dataset, an information-gain metric is used. It represents the expected impurity reduction after splitting the dataset D according to a feature F. It's calculated in the following manner

---

[9] As defined by Wikipedia: https://en.wikipedia.org/wiki/Decision_tree_learning#Gini_impurity.

$$IG(D, F) = I(D) - \sum_{s \varepsilon subsets(F)} \frac{|D_s|}{|D|} I(D_s)$$

where *subsets(F)* are subsets of the feature *F* after the split, $|D_s|$ is the number of elements in the subset s, and $|D|$ is the number of elements in the dataset. In the previous example, when splitting the dataset according to the feature education, the information gain is equal to the following. Note that entropy is used for calculating impurity in this example:

$$IG(D, F_{education}) = 0.896038 - \frac{13}{16}\left(-\frac{2}{13}log_2\frac{2}{13} - \frac{11}{13}log_2\frac{11}{13}\right) - \frac{3}{16}0 = 0.3928$$

If any other split of education categories were chosen, information gain would be lower. This is obvious by examining the education and income columns in figure 8.7. If you move the bachelors feature to the right branch, for example, the right branch would no longer contain a single class (the bachelors row's class is "less than \$50k" and the other two light gray education values—Masters and 7th-8th—have class of ">\$50k"), and its impurity would be greater than zero, thus reducing information gain. The algorithm uses information gain to decide how to split the dataset at each node of the decision tree.

TRAINING A DECISION-TREE MODEL

You'll now train a decision-tree model on the same handwritten digit dataset that you used previously for multiclass logistic regression. But before using the dataset, one extra data-preparation step is necessary. You need to add column metadata, which the decision-tree algorithm needs to determine the number of possible classes. You can use the StringIndexer class (the same class you used in section 8.2.2 to convert categorical string values to integer nominal values) for this because StringIndexer adds the needed metadata information to the transformed column. The penlpoints Data-Frame you loaded in section 8.2.6 contains the dataset, and you can add the metadata information with the following snippet of code:

```
val dtsi = new StringIndexer().setInputCol("label").setOutputCol("label-i")
val dtsm:StringIndexerModel = dtsi.fit(penlpoints)
val pendtlpoints = dtsm.transform(penlpoints).drop("label").
  withColumnRenamed("label-i", "label")
```

As always, splitting the dataset into training and validation sets is necessary:

```
val pendtset = penlpointsf.randomSplit(Array(0.8, 0.2))
val pendttrain = pendtsets(0).cache()
val pendtvalid = pendtsets(1).cache()
```

The decision-tree classification algorithm in Spark ML is implemented by the class DecisionTreeClassifier. A decision tree for regression is implemented by the class

DecisionTreeRegressor, but you won't use it here. It can be configured with several parameters:

- maxDepth determines the maximum tree depth. The default is 5.
- maxBins determines the maximum number of bins created when binning continuous features. The default is 32.
- minInstancesPerNode sets the minimum number of dataset samples each branch needs to have after a split. The default is 1.
- minInfoGain sets the minimum information gain for a split to be valid (otherwise, the split will be discarded). The default is 0.

The default parameters work fine in most cases. For this example, you need to adjust the maximum depth to 20 (because the default depth of 5 levels isn't enough) and train the model by calling fit on the training set:

```
val dt = new DecisionTreeClassifier()
dt.setMaxDepth(20)
val dtmodel = dt.fit(pendttrain)
```

EXAMINING THE DECISION TREE

As we said previously, one of the advantages of decision trees is that the learned decision rules can be visualized, and they can offer an intuitive explanation of the inner workings of the algorithm. How do you examine the learned decision rules of the model in Spark?

You can begin by examining the root node of the tree (note that these results are highly dependent on the way the dataset was split, so your results may be somewhat different):

```
scala> dtmodel.rootNode
res0: org.apache.spark.ml.tree.Node = InternalNode(prediction = 0.0,
impurity = 0.4296875, split = org.apache.spark.ml.tree.
CategoricalSplit@557cc88b)
```

Here you can see the calculated impurity of the root node (equal to 0.4296875). You can also see which feature was used for the split on the first node by examining the featureIndex field of rootNode's split (you'll need to cast the root node to Internal-Node first):

```
scala> dtmodel.rootNode.asInstanceOf[InternalNode].split.featureIndex
res1: Int = 15
```

> **PYTHON** You can't access the root node in Python.

An index of 15 corresponds to the last pixel in the dataset. Using the split field, you can also see which threshold was used to split the values of feature 15:

```
scala> dtmodel.rootNode.asInstanceOf[InternalNode].split.
  asInstanceOf[ContinuousSplit].threshold
res2: Double = 51.0
```

If the feature 15 were a categorical value, the split would be an instance of the `CategoricalSplit` class, and you could access its `leftCategories` and `rightCategories` fields to examine which categories were used for each branch.

Furthermore, you can access the left and right nodes:

```
dtmodel.rootNode.asInstanceOf[InternalNode].leftChild
dtmodel.rootNode.asInstanceOf[InternalNode].rightChild
```

You can continue the procedure for all nodes in the model.

EVALUATING THE MODEL

Now you can transform the validation set and evaluate the model using `MulticlassMetrics`, as you did for multiclass logistic regression:

```
scala> val dtpredicts = dtmodel.transform(pendtvalid)
scala> val dtresrdd = dtpredicts.select("prediction", "label").rdd
  .map(row => (row.getDouble(0), row.getDouble(1)))
scala> val dtmm = new MulticlassMetrics(dtresrdd)
scala> dtmm.precision
res0: Double = 0.951442968392121
scala> dtmm.confusionMatrix
res1: org.apache.spark.mllib.linalg.Matrix =
192.0  0.0    0.0    9.0    2.0    0.0    2.0    0.0    0.0    0.0
0.0    225.0  0.0    1.0    0.0    1.0    0.0    0.0    3.0    2.0
0.0    1.0    217.0  1.0    0.0    1.0    0.0    1.0    1.0    0.0
9.0    1.0    0.0    205.0  5.0    1.0    3.0    1.0    1.0    0.0
2.0    0.0    1.0    1.0    221.0  0.0    2.0    3.0    0.0    0.0
0.0    1.0    0.0    1.0    0.0    201.0  0.0    0.0    0.0    1.0
2.0    1.0    0.0    2.0    1.0    0.0    207.0  0.0    2.0    3.0
0.0    0.0    3.0    1.0    1.0    0.0    1.0    213.0  1.0    2.0
0.0    0.0    0.0    2.0    0.0    2.0    2.0    4.0    198.0  6.0
0.0    1.0    0.0    0.0    1.0    0.0    3.0    3.0    4.0    198.0
```

As you can see, without much preparation the decision tree gives you better results than logistic regression. Precision and recall for logistic regression were 0.90182, and here they're 0.95, which is an increase of 5.5%. But as you'll see, random forests can give you even better results.

8.3.2   *Random forests*

We'll now move to random forests, a powerful classification and regression algorithm that can give excellent results without much tuning. As we said previously, the random-forests algorithm is an ensemble method of training a number of decision trees and selecting the best result by averaging results from all of them. This enables the algorithm to avoid overfitting and to find a global optima that particular decision trees can't find on their own.

Random forests furthermore use *feature bagging*, where only a subset of features is randomly selected in each node of a decision tree and the best split is determined according to that reduced feature set. The reason for doing this is that the error rate of a random-forests model increases when decision trees are correlated (are similar). Feature bagging makes decision trees less similar.

As we mentioned, random forests give better results, reduce overfitting, and are generally easy to train and use, but they aren't as easy to interpret and visualize as decision trees.

USING RANDOM FORESTS IN SPARK

Random forests in Spark are implemented by the classes `RandomForestClassifier` and `RandomForestRegressor`. Because this chapter is about classification, you'll use `RandomForestClassifier`. You can configure it with two additional parameters:

- `numTrees` is the number of trees to train. The default is 20.
- `featureSubsetStrategy` determines how feature bagging is done. Its value can be one of the following: `all` (uses all features), `onethird` (randomly selects one-third of the features), `sqrt` (randomly selects `sqrt` (*number of features*)), `log2` (randomly selects `log2` (*number of features*)), or `auto`, which means `sqrt` for classification and `onethird` for regression. The default is `auto`.

The defaults work fine in most cases. If you want to train a large number of trees, you need to make sure you give enough memory to your driver, because the trained decision trees are kept in the driver's memory.

Training a random-forests classifier model is straightforward:

```
val rf = new RandomForestClassifier()
rf.setMaxDepth(20)
val rfmodel = rf.fit(pendttrain)
```

Having a model available, you can examine the trees it trained by accessing the `trees` field:

```
scala> rfmodel.trees
res0: Array[org.apache.spark.ml.tree.DecisionTreeModel] =
Array(DecisionTreeClassificationModel of depth 20 with 833 nodes,
DecisionTreeClassificationModel of depth 17 with 757 nodes,
DecisionTreeClassificationModel of depth 16 with 691 nodes, ...
```

After transforming the validation set, you can evaluate the model's performance in the usual way, using the `MulticlassMetrics` class:

```
scala> val rfpredicts = rfmodel.transform(pendtvalid)
scala> val rfresrdd = rfpredicts.select("prediction", "label").
  rdd.map(row => (row.getDouble(0), row.getDouble(1)))
scala> val rfmm = new MulticlassMetrics()
scala> rfmm.precision
res1: Double = 0.9894640403114979
scala> rfmm.confusionMatrix
res2: org.apache.spark.mllib.linalg.Matrix =
205.0   0.0     0.0     0.0     0.0     0.0     0.0     0.0     0.0     0.0
0.0     231.0   0.0     0.0     0.0     0.0     0.0     0.0     1.0     0.0
```

```
0.0    0.0    221.0   1.0     0.0     0.0     0.0     0.0     0.0     0.0
5.0    0.0    0.0     219.0   0.0     0.0     2.0     0.0     0.0     0.0
0.0    0.0    0.0     0.0     230.0   0.0     0.0     0.0     0.0     0.0
0.0    1.0    0.0     0.0     0.0     203.0   0.0     0.0     0.0     0.0
1.0    0.0    0.0     1.0     0.0     0.0     216.0   0.0     0.0     0.0
0.0    0.0    1.0     0.0     2.0     0.0     0.0     219.0   0.0     0.0
0.0    0.0    0.0     1.0     0.0     0.0     0.0     1.0     212.0   0.0
0.0    0.0    0.0     0.0     0.0     0.0     2.0     2.0     2.0     204.0
```

Here the precision of the random-forests model is 0.99, which means it has an error rate of only 1%. That's better than the decision tree's precision by 4% and better than logistic regression by 10%. And you didn't need to tune the algorithm at all.

These are excellent results. And it's no wonder. Random forests are one of the most popular algorithms because of their excellent performance and ease of use. They have also been shown to perform equally well on high-dimensional datasets,[10] which isn't true for other algorithms.

8.4   *Using k-means clustering*

The final family of machine learning algorithms that we're going to cover in this book is *clustering*. The task of clustering is to group a set of examples into several groups (clusters), based on some similarity metric. Clustering is an unsupervised learning method, which means unlike classification, the examples aren't labeled prior to clustering: a clustering algorithm learns the labels itself.

For instance, a *classification* algorithm gets a set of images labeled *cats* and *dogs*, and it learns how to recognize cats and dogs on future images. A clustering algorithm can try to spot differences between different images and automatically categorize them into two groups, but not knowing the names for each group. At most it can label them "group 1" and "group 2".

Clustering can be used for many purposes:

- Partitioning data into groups (for example, customer segmentation or grouping customers by similar habits)
- Image segmentation (recognizing different regions in an image)
- Detecting anomalies
- Text categorization or recognizing topics in a set of articles
- Grouping search results (for example, the www.yippy.com search engine automatically groups results by their categories)

The reason labels are missing from clustering datasets may be that it's too expensive and time consuming to label all the data (for example, when grouping search results) or that clusters aren't known in advance (for example, market segmentation) and you want the algorithm to find the clusters for you so you can better understand the data. Spark offers implementations of the following clustering algorithms:

---

[10] Rich Caruana et al., "An Empirical Evaluation of Supervised Learning in High Dimensions," Cornell University, Ithaca, NY.

- K-means clustering
- Gaussian mixture model
- Power-iteration clustering

K-means clustering is the simplest and the most often used of the three. Unfortunately, it has drawbacks: it has trouble handling non-spherical clusters and unevenly sized clusters (uneven by density or by radius). It also can't make efficient use of the one-hot-encoded features you used in section 8.2.2. It's often used for classifying text documents, along with the term frequency-inverse document frequency (TF-IDF) feature-vectorization method.[11]

The Gaussian mixture model (or mixture of Gaussians) is a model-based clustering technique, which means each cluster is represented by a Gaussian distribution, and the model is a mixture of these distributions. It performs *soft clustering* (modeling a probability that an example belongs to a cluster), unlike k-means, which performs *hard clustering* (modeling whether an example belongs to a cluster). Because the Gaussian mixture model doesn't scale well to datasets with many dimensions, we won't cover it here.

Power-iteration clustering is a form of spectral clustering, and the math behind it is too advanced for this chapter. Its implementation in Spark is based on the GraphX library, which we'll cover in the next chapter.

The rest of this section is devoted to k-means clustering. We'll explain how k-means clustering works, and then you'll perform clustering on the handwritten digit dataset you used before.

8.4.1 K-means clustering

Let's see how a k-means clustering algorithm works. Let's say you have a set of examples in a two-dimensional dataset, shown in the top-left graph in figure 8.9, and you'd like to group these examples into two clusters.

In the first step, the k-means clustering algorithm randomly chooses two points as cluster centers. In the next step, distances from each of the centers to all points in the dataset are calculated. The points are then assigned to the cluster they're closest to. Finally, mean points in each cluster are calculated, and these points become the new cluster centers.

Then the distances to all points are calculated again, the points are assigned to the clusters accordingly, and new cluster centers are calculated again. If the new cluster centers didn't move significantly, the process stops.

At the end of this process, you have a set of cluster centers. You can classify each new point as belonging to one of the clusters by calculating its distance from each cluster center and picking the closest one.

---

[11] For more information, see TF-IDF in the Spark documentation: http://mng.bz/4GE3.

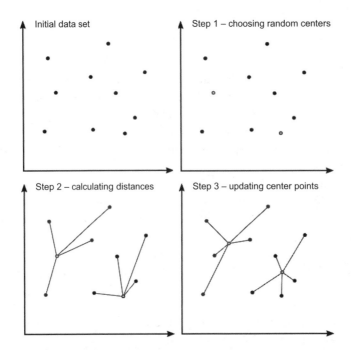

Figure 8.9   Running the k-means clustering algorithm. In the first step, two points are randomly chosen as cluster centers. The distances from these centers to all points in the dataset are calculated in the second step, and the points are assigned to the cluster they're closest to. In the third step, new cluster centers are calculated; the process is repeated until cluster centers don't move significantly.

USING K-MEANS CLUSTERING IN SPARK

As you can see, the algorithm is indeed simple. Let's see how that works in Spark. Each image of handwritten digits, which you'll use for this example, is represented as a series of numbers (dimensions) representing image pixels. As such, each image is a point in an *n*-dimensional space. K-means clustering can group together images that are close in this space. In an ideal case, all of these will be images of the same digit.

To implement k-means, you first have to make sure your dataset is *standardized* (all dimensions are of comparable ranges), because k-means clustering doesn't work well with non-standardized data. The dimensions of the handwritten digit dataset are already standardized (all the values go from 0 to 100), so you can skip this step now.

With clustering algorithms, there's no point in having a validation and a training dataset. So, you'll use the entire dataset contained in the `penlpoints` DataFrame you used before. The `KMeans` estimator can be parameterized with the following parameters:

- `k`—Number of clusters to find (default is 2)
- `maxIter`—Maximum number of iterations to perform (required).
- `predictionCol`—Prediction column name (default is "prediction")

- featuresCol—Features column name (default is "features")
- tol—Convergence tolerance
- seed—Random seed value for cluster initialization

The number of clusters is 10, of course (there are 10 digits in the dataset), and the maximum number of iterations can be set to several hundred. A larger number of iterations usually isn't needed.

If you suspect you need more iterations, turn on the logging of informational messages (check chapter 2 if you need a refresher) and see if the message "KMeans reached the max number of iterations" appears. If you see that message, you need more iterations.

To train a k-means model, use the following lines:

```
import org.apache.spark.ml.clustering.KMeans
val kmeans = new KMeans()
kmeans.setK(10)
kmeans.setMaxIter(500)

val kmmodel = kmeans.fit(penlpoints)
```

EVALUATING THE MODEL

Evaluating clustering models can be difficult because of the nature of the clustering problem: clusters aren't known in advance, and it isn't easy to separate good and bad clusters. There's no silver bullet for solving this problem, but several measures can help: cost value, average distance from the center, and the contingency table.

The *cost value* (a measure also called *distortion*), calculated as the sum of the squared distances from all points to the matching cluster centers, is the main metric for evaluating k-means models.

The KMeansModel class has a computeCost(DataFrame) method you can use to compute the cost on the dataset:

```
scala> kmmodel.computeCost(penlpoints)
res0: Double = 4.517530920539787E7
```

This value is dependent on the dataset and can be used to compare different k-means models on the same dataset, but it doesn't provide an intuitive way of understanding how well the model is doing overall. And how do you put this huge value into context? *Average distance from the center* may be a bit more intuitive. To obtain it, take the square root of the cost divided by the number of examples in the dataset:

```
scala> math.sqrt(kmmodel.computeCost(penlpoints)/penlpoints.count())
res2: Double = 66.5102817068467
```

This way, the value is comparable to the maximum value the features can have (100).

At times, in clustering problems, some of the examples can be manually labeled. If that's the case, you can compare these original labels with the clusters they end up in. With the handwritten digit dataset, you have the labels available, and you can compare them with the predicted labels. But the predicted labels (cluster indexes) were constructed by the k-means clustering algorithm independently of the original labels. Label 4 (handwritten digit 4), for example, doesn't have to correspond to cluster 4. How do you match the two? Well, just find the cluster with the most examples for a particular label in it, and assign the label to that cluster.

We wrote a simple `printContingency` method (you can find it in our online repository) that will print the so-called *contingency table* with the original labels as rows and k-means cluster indexes as columns. The cells in the table contain counts of examples belonging both to the original label and the predicted cluster.

The method takes an RDD containing tuples with predictions and the original labels (both `double` values). Before using the method, you need to obtain an RDD with this information. You can do it like this:

```
val kmpredicts = kmmodel.transform(penlpoints)
```

The `printContingency` method also takes an array of label values it will use for constructing the table (it assumes both cluster indexes and original labels are from the same range). For each original label, the method also finds the cluster where the label is most frequent, prints the mappings found, and calculates *purity*, which is a measure defined as a ratio of correctly classified examples. Finally:

```
printContingency(kmpredicts, 0 to 9)
orig.class|Pred0|Pred1|Pred2|Pred3|Pred4|Pred5|Pred6|Pred7|Pred8|Pred9
----------+-----+-----+-----+-----+-----+-----+-----+-----+-----+-----
        0 |    1|  379|   14|    7|    2|  713|    0|    0|   25|    2
----------+-----+-----+-----+-----+-----+-----+-----+-----+-----+-----
        1 |  333|    0|    9|    1|  642|    0|   88|    0|    0|   70
----------+-----+-----+-----+-----+-----+-----+-----+-----+-----+-----
        2 | 1130|    0|    0|    0|   14|    0|    0|    0|    0|    0
----------+-----+-----+-----+-----+-----+-----+-----+-----+-----+-----
        3 |    1|    0|    0|    1|   24|    0| 1027|    0|    0|    2
----------+-----+-----+-----+-----+-----+-----+-----+-----+-----+-----
        4 |    1|    0|   51| 1046|   13|    0|    1|    0|    0|   32
----------+-----+-----+-----+-----+-----+-----+-----+-----+-----+-----
        5 |    0|    0|    6|    0|    0|    0|  235|  624|    3|  187
----------+-----+-----+-----+-----+-----+-----+-----+-----+-----+-----
        6 |    0|    0| 1052|    3|    0|    0|    0|    1|    0|    0
----------+-----+-----+-----+-----+-----+-----+-----+-----+-----+-----
        7 |  903|    0|    1|    1|  154|    0|   78|    4|    1|    0
----------+-----+-----+-----+-----+-----+-----+-----+-----+-----+-----
        8 |   32|  433|    6|    0|    0|   16|  106|   22|  436|    4
----------+-----+-----+-----+-----+-----+-----+-----+-----+-----+-----
        9 |    9|    0|    1|   88|   82|   11|  199|    0|    1|  664
----------+-----+-----+-----+-----+-----+-----+-----+-----+-----+-----
Purity: 0.6672125181950509
Predicted->original label map: Map(8.0 -> 8.0, 2.0 -> 6.0, 5.0 -> 0.0,
4.0 -> 1.0, 7.0 -> 5.0, 9.0 -> 9.0, 3.0 -> 4.0, 6.0 -> 3.0, 0.0 -> 2.0)
```

Purity is calculated as the sum of the largest values in each column divided by the total number of examples[12] (sum of the values in all cells).

There are some problems with this table. The cluster 0 column has two values that are largest in their rows (labels 2 and 7). That means both labels 2 and 7 are mostly clustered in cluster 0. Because label 2 is more frequent in cluster 0, 2 was chosen to be its label, and now label 7 has no matching cluster. There's also a problem with cluster 1. It holds examples with labels that are more frequent in other tables, so it has no label at all. Similar to cluster 0, cluster 1 also contains two equally frequent labels: label 0 and label 8.

What happened? Well, the algorithm confused 8s with 0s and 7s with 2s. These digits look similar, so it's no surprise the algorithm could have trouble recognizing the differences between them. There isn't much you can do about this. You can only try to "correct" the dataset by creating features from the images of handwritten digits in a different way.

But in a real-life situation, you most likely wouldn't have this option. You would only have a set of cluster centers and sets of clustered samples. Interpreting the meanings of the clusters depends on the nature of the data.

DETERMINING THE NUMBER OF CLUSTERS

In a real-life situation, you'd also have an additional question: what number of clusters should you use? Sometimes you have a rough idea for the number of clusters, but often you don't. In these cases, you can use the *elbow method*.

It goes like this. You gradually increase the number of clusters, train a model for each number, and look at the cost of each model. The cost will inevitably decrease because as the clusters increase in number, they keep getting smaller and smaller, and the distances from the centers decrease. But if you plot the cost as a function of number of clusters K, you may notice a few "elbows" where the slope of the function changes abruptly. K numbers corresponding to these points are good candidates for use.

We plotted the costs of models trained on the pen dataset with the numbers of clusters from 2 to 30. The result is shown in figure 8.10.

The curve on the figure is mostly smooth. The only slight elbow is at the K value of 15 and then at 36. But these aren't so obvious.

There is much debate about how to choose the right number of clusters. Several methods have been proposed, but none of them is available in Spark out of the box. For example, silhouette, information criterion, information theoretic, and cross validation are some of the proposed approaches. A great overview is available in the paper by Trupti M. Kodinariya and Dr. Prashant R. Makwana.[13]

---

[12] Purity is equal to precision (and accuracy), and the contingency table contains the same values as the confusion matrix you used for classification.

[13] Trupti M. Kodinariya and Dr. Prashant R. Makwana, "Review on Determining Number of Cluster in K-means Clustering," *International Journal of Advance Research in Computer Science and Management Studies* 1, no. 6 (November 2013), http://mng.bz/k2up.

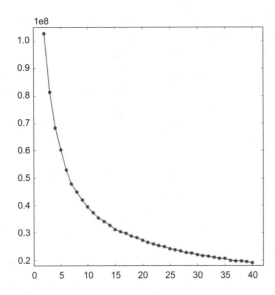

Figure 8.10 Cost of models trained on the pen dataset as a function of the number of clusters

8.5   *Summary*

- The Spark ML library generalizes machine learning operations and streamlines machine learning processes.
- Spark ML introduces several new abstractions—estimators, transformers, and evaluators—that can be combined to form pipelines. All four are parameterized in a general way with ML parameters.
- The goal of classification is to classify input examples into two or more classes.
- Logistic regression outputs probabilities that a certain example belongs to a certain class using a logistic function.
- Missing data can be dealt with by removing columns, by removing rows, by setting missing data to the most common value, or by predicting the missing values using a separate model.
- Categorical values can be one-hot-encoded so that a column is expanded to as many columns as there are distinct values in it; thus, for a single row, only one of the columns contains a 1 and all the others contain 0s.
- `VectorAssembler` combines several columns into one column containing all values in a `Vector`.
- Area under the precision and recall (PR) curve is one of the metrics for evaluating classification models.
- Area under the receiver operating characteristic (ROC) curve is another metric for evaluating classification models.
- K-fold cross-validation validates the performance of models more reliably because it validates the model several times and takes the average as the final result.

- Multiclass logistic regression classifies examples into more than two classes. The results are evaluated with the `MulticlassMetrics` class.
- The decision-trees algorithm uses a tree-like set of user-defined or learned rules to classify input examples based on their features values.
- Impurity and information gain are used in decision trees to decide how to split the dataset.
- The decision-tree structure can be examined and visualized.
- Random forests train a certain number of decision trees on data randomly sampled from the original dataset and averages the results.
- K-means clustering forms clusters by calculating the distances of data points from cluster centers and moving the cluster centers to the average position in the cluster. It stops when the cluster centers stop moving significantly.
- A contingency table can be used to visualize the results of clustering.
- An appropriate number of clusters to use can sometimes be determined using the elbow method.

Connecting
the dots with GraphX

This chapter covers

- Using the GraphX API
- Transforming and joining graphs
- Using GraphX algorithms
- Implementing the A* search algorithm with the GraphX API

This chapter completes your tour of Spark components with an overview of GraphX, Spark's graph-processing API. In this chapter, we'll show you how to use GraphX and give you examples of using graph algorithms in Spark. These include shortest paths, page rank, connected components, and strongly connected components. If you're interested in learning about other algorithms available in Spark (triangle count, LDA, and SVD++), or more about GraphX in general, Michael Malak and Robin East go into much more detail in their book *GraphX in Action* (Manning, 2016), which we highly recommend.

9.1 Graph processing with Spark

A *graph*, as a mathematical concept of linked objects, consists of *vertices* (objects in the graph) and *edges* that connect the vertices (or links between the objects). In Spark, edges are *directed* (they have a source and a destination vertex), and both edges and vertices have property objects attached to them. For example, in a graph containing data about pages and links, property objects attached to the vertices may contain information about a page's URL, title, date, and so on, and property objects attached to the edges may contain a description of the link (contents of an <a> HTML tag).

Once presented as a graph, some problems become easier to solve; they give rise naturally to graph algorithms. For example, presenting hierarchical data can be complicated using traditional data-organization methods, such as relational databases, and can be simplified using graphs. In addition to using them to represent social networks and links between web pages, graph algorithms have applications in biology, computer chip design, travel, physics, chemistry, and other areas.

In this section, you'll learn how to construct and transform graphs using GraphX. You'll build an example graph representing a social network (shown in figure 9.1) consisting of seven vertices and nine edges. In this graph, vertices represent people, and edges represent relationships between them. Each vertex has a vertex ID (a number in a circle) and vertex properties (information about the person's name and age) attached to it. Edge properties contain information about a relation type. It would make sense in this case to also draw edges in the opposite direction (because "married to," for example, works both ways), but we wanted to keep it simple and save some

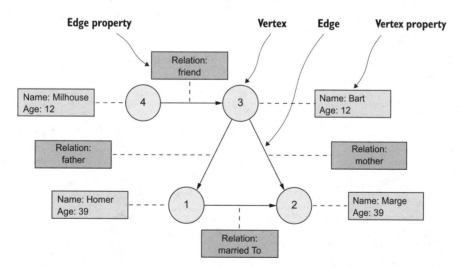

Figure 9.1   An example graph representing a simple social network involving the Simpsons family (before Maggie was born). The numbered circles are graph vertices, and the solid lines connecting them are graph edges. The properties attached to vertices (with the dotted lines) contain information about name and age. The properties attached to edges (also with the dotted lines) describe the type of relationship.

memory space. This isn't a limitation of Spark; Spark allows you to define several edges between the same vertices, and they can be directed both ways. Let's build this graph using the Spark GraphX API.

9.1.1 *Constructing graphs using GraphX API*

`Graph` (http://mng.bz/078M) is the main class in GraphX providing access to vertices and edges and various operations for transforming graphs. Vertices and edges in Spark are realized by two special RDD implementations:

- `VertexRDDs` contain tuples, which consist of two elements: a vertex ID of type `Long` and a property object of an arbitrary type.
- `EdgeRDDs` contain `Edge` objects, which consist of source and destination vertex IDs (`srcId` and `dstId`, respectively) and a property object of an arbitrary type (`attr` field).

CONSTRUCTING THE GRAPH

You can construct graphs with Spark in several ways. One way is to instantiate a `Graph` object using an `RDD` containing tuples, consisting of a vertex ID and a vertex property object, and using an `RDD` containing `Edge` objects. You'll use this method to construct the example graph from figure 9.1. First you need to import the required classes. Open your Spark shell, and paste in the following line:

```
import org.apache.spark.graphx._
```

> **NOTE** You can find the complete code for this chapter in our online repository. But because the Spark GraphX API isn't available in Python or Java, you won't find any Python or Java code there.

The `Person` case class holds properties of the nodes (edge properties are simple strings):

```
case class Person(name:String, age:Int)
```

Next you construct the vertex and edge RDDs with the required vertex and edge objects:

```
val vertices = sc.parallelize(Array((1L, Person("Homer", 39)),
  (2L, Person("Marge", 39)), (3L, Person("Bart", 12)),
  (4L, Person("Milhouse", 12))))
val edges = sc.parallelize(Array(Edge(4L, 3L, "friend"),
  Edge(3L, 1L, "father"), Edge(3L, 2L, "mother"),
  Edge(1L, 2L, "marriedTo")))
```

Finally, you construct the graph object:

```
val graph = Graph(vertices, edges)
```

You can now access the graph's `vertices` and `edges` properties and use other graph-transformation and -manipulation methods that we'll get to later:

```
scala> graph.vertices.count()
res0: Long = 4
scala> graph.edges.count()
res1: Long = 4
```

In section 9.4, we'll show you several more methods for creating graphs in GraphX.

9.1.2　*Transforming graphs*

Let's look at what you can do with graphs and how you can manipulate them. In this section, we'll show you how to *map* edges and vertices in order to add data to property objects attached to them, or to transform them by calculating their new values. Then we'll show you how to send messages throughout a graph by *aggregating* them and by using Spark's implementation of Pregel, Google's system for large-scale graph processing. Finally, we'll show you how to *join* and *filter* graphs.

As we said, the main class for representing graphs in GraphX is `Graph`. But there's also the `GraphOps` class (http://mng.bz/J4jv), whose methods are implicitly added to `Graph` objects. You need to consider both classes when figuring out which methods to use. Some of the methods we'll mention in this section come from `Graph`, and some from `GraphOps`.

MAPPING EDGES AND VERTICES

Let's say you need to change the edges of your `graph` object to make them instances of the `Relationship` class (given in a moment) instead of strings as they are now. This is just an example illustrating the concept, and the `Relationship` class is just a wrapper around the String `relation` property. But you could add more information to the edges this way, and you could later use this information for additional calculations. For example, you could add information about when two people started their relationship and how often they meet.

You can transform edge and vertex property objects with the `mapEdges` and `mapVertices` methods. The `mapEdges` method requires a mapping function, which takes a partition ID and an iterator of edges in the partition and returns the transformed iterator containing a new *edge property object* (not a new edge) for each input edge. The following code will do the job:

```
case class Relationship(relation:String)
val newgraph = graph.mapEdges((partId, iter) =>
    iter.map(edge => Relationship(edge.attr)))
```

`newgraph` now has `Relationship` objects as edge properties:

```
scala> newgraph.edges.collect()
res0: Array[org.apache.spark.graphx.Edge[Relationship]] =
Array(Edge(3,1,Relationship(father)), ...)
```

TIP Another useful method for mapping edges is `mapTriplets`. It also maps edge property objects to new ones, but the mapping function it expects receives an `EdgeTriplet` object. An `EdgeTriplet` object, in addition to containing `srcId`, `dstId`, and `attr` fields as `Edge` does, holds source and destination vertex property objects (`srcAttr` and `dstAttr`). You can use `mapTriplets` when you need to calculate the contents of a new property object as a function of the edge's current property object and the properties of the connected vertices.

Let's say you want to attach to each person in your graph the number of children, friends, and coworkers they have and add a flag indicating whether they're married. You first need to change the vertex property objects so they allow for storage of these new properties. Let's use the `PersonExt` case class for this:

```
case class PersonExt(name:String, age:Int, children:Int=0, friends:Int=0,
    married:Boolean=false)
```

Now you need to change the graph's vertices to use this new property class. The `mapVertices` method maps vertices' property objects and works similarly to `mapEdges`. The mapping function you need to give to it takes a vertex ID and a vertex property object and returns the new property object:

```
val newGraphExt = newgraph.mapVertices((vid, person) =>
    PersonExt(person.name, person.age))
```

Now all vertices in `newGraphExt` have these new properties, but they all default to 0, so no person in the graph is married, has children, or has friends. How do you calculate the right values? That's where the `aggregateMessages` method comes in.

AGGREGATING MESSAGES

The `aggregateMessages` method is used to run a function on each vertex of a graph and optionally send messages to its neighboring vertices. The method collects and aggregates all the messages sent to each vertex and stores them in a new `VertexRDD`. It has the following signature:

```
def aggregateMessages[A: ClassTag](
    sendMsg: EdgeContext[VD, ED, A] => Unit,
    mergeMsg: (A, A) => A,
    tripletFields: TripletFields = TripletFields.All)
  : VertexRDD[A]
```

You need to provide two functions, `sendMsg` and `mergeMsg`, and the `tripletFields` property.

The `sendMsg` function receives an `EdgeContext` object for each edge in the graph and, if necessary, uses the edge context to send messages to vertices. The `EdgeContext` object contains IDs and property objects for source and destination vertices, the property object for the edge, and two methods for sending messages to neighboring vertices:

`sendToSrc` and `sendToDst`. The `sendMsg` function can use the edge context to decide which, if any, message to send to each vertex.

The `mergeMsg` function aggregates messages destined for the same vertex. Finally, the `tripletFields` argument specifies which fields should be provided as part of the edge context. Possible values are static fields in the `TripletFields` class (`None`, `EdgeOnly`, `Src`, `Dst`, and `All`).

Let's use `aggregateMessages` to calculate additional properties in the `PersonExt` objects (number of friends and children and the `married` flag), for each vertex of the `newGraphExt` graph:

```
val aggVertices = newGraphExt.aggregateMessages(
  (ctx:EdgeContext[PersonExt, Relationship,
      Tuple3[Int, Int, Boolean]]) => {
    if(ctx.attr.relation == "marriedTo")
      { ctx.sendToSrc((0, 0, true)); ctx.sendToDst((0, 0, true)); }
    else if(ctx.attr.relation == "mother" || ctx.attr.relation == "father")
      { ctx.sendToDst((1, 0, false)); }
    else if(ctx.attr.relation.contains("friend"))
      { ctx.sendToDst((0, 1, false)); ctx.sendToSrc((0, 1, false));}
  },
  (msg1:Tuple3[Int, Int, Boolean],
      msg2:Tuple3[Int, Int, Boolean]) =>
    (msg1._1+msg2._1, msg1._2+msg2._2, msg1._3 || msg2._3)
)
```

The messages the `sendMsg` function sends to vertices are tuples containing the number of children (an `Int`), the number of friends (an `Int`), and whether the person is married (a `Boolean`). These values are set to 1 (or `true`) only if the edge examined is of an appropriate type. The second function (`mergeMsg`) adds up all the values per vertex so that the resulting tuple contains the sums.

Because the `marriedTo` and `friendOf` relationships are represented with only one edge (to save space) but are in reality bidirectional relationships, `sendMsg` in those cases sends the same message to both source and destination vertices. *Mother* and *father* relationships are unidirectional and are used for counting the number of children, so those messages are sent only once.

The resulting RDD has seven elements as with the original `VertexRDD`, because all the vertices received messages:

```
scala> aggVertices.collect.foreach(println)
(4,(0,1,false))
(2,(1,0,true))
(1,(1,0,true))
(3,(0,1,false))
```

The result is a `VertexRDD`, so your work isn't done because you still don't have the resulting `Graph`. To update the original graph with these newly found values, you'll need to join the old graph with the new vertices.

JOINING GRAPH DATA

To join the original graph and the new vertex messages, use the `outerJoinVertices` function, which has the following signature:

```
def outerJoinVertices[U:ClassTag, VD2:ClassTag](other: RDD[(VertexId, U)])
  (mapFunc: (VertexId, VD, Option[U]) => VD2) : Graph[VD2, ED]
```

You need to provide two arguments: an RDD that contains tuples with vertex IDs and new vertex objects, and a mapping function to combine old vertex property objects (of type `VD`) and new vertex objects from the input RDD (of type `U`). If no object exists in the input RDD for a particular vertex ID, the mapping function receives `None`.

The following statement will join your `newGraphExt` graph with the new information from `aggVertices`:

```
val graphAggr = newGraphExt.outerJoinVertices(aggVertices)(
  (vid, origPerson, optMsg) => { optMsg match {
    case Some(msg) => PersonExt(origPerson.name, origPerson.age,
                                msg._1, msg._2, msg._3)
    case None => origPerson
    }}
)
```

The mapping function copies the summed values from an input message into a new `PersonExt` object, conserving the `name` and `age` properties, if an input message for a vertex exists. It returns the original `PersonExt` object otherwise:

```
scala> graphAggr.vertices.collect().foreach(println)
(4,PersonExt(Milhouse,12,0,1,false))
(2,PersonExt(Marge,39,1,0,true))
(1,PersonExt(Homer,39,1,0,true))
(3,PersonExt(Bart,12,0,1,false))
```

The resulting graph is shown in figure 9.2.

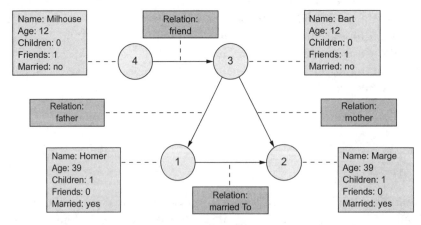

Figure 9.2   The transformed graph with additional vertex properties added. These were obtained using the `aggregateMessages` and `outerJoinVertices` methods.

The previously described Graph methods, `aggregateMessages` and `outerJoinVertices`, along with the mapping functions, are the bread and butter of graph operations in GraphX. You'll find yourself using them often in your GraphX applications.

GraphX's Pregel implementation

Pregel is Google's system for large-scale graph processing.[1] GraphX contains an implementation of a Pregel-like API, which you can use to perform calculations similar to `aggregateMessages`. But Pregel is more powerful, which is why it was used to implement many of the graph algorithms in GraphX.

Pregel works by executing a sequence of iterations called *supersteps*. Each superstep is similar to `aggregateMessages` in that the `sendMsg` function is invoked on edges and the `mergeMsg` function is used to merge messages destined for the same vertex. Additionally, a user-defined vertex program (`vprog`) is invoked for each vertex. The `vprog` function receives the incoming message and computes a new value for the vertex.

The initial superstep is executed on all vertices, and subsequent supersteps are executed only on those vertices that receive a message. `sendMsg` is invoked only for the outgoing edges of the vertices that receive a message. The process stops if no new messages are sent or the maximum number of iterations is attained. GraphX's Pregel API is implemented by the Pregel object, whose `apply` method has the following signature:

```
def apply[VD: ClassTag, ED: ClassTag, A: ClassTag]
  (graph: Graph[VD, ED],
   initialMsg: A,
   maxIterations: Int = Int.MaxValue,
   activeDirection: EdgeDirection = EdgeDirection.Either)
  (vprog: (VertexId, VD, A) => VD,
   sendMsg: EdgeTriplet[VD, ED] => Iterator[(VertexId, A)],
   mergeMsg: (A, A) => A)
  : Graph[VD, ED]
```

These are the parameters the method takes:

- `graph`—Input graph on which to operate.
- `initialMsg`—Message sent to all vertices in the first superstep.
- `maxIterations`—Maximum number of supersteps to perform.
- `activeDirection`—When to invoke the `sendMsg` function: on edges whose source vertex received a message (`EdgeDirection.Out`), on edges whose destination vertex received a message (`EdgeDirection.In`), if either source or destination received a message (`EdgeDirection.Either`), or if both vertices received a message (`EdgeDirection.Both`).
- `vprog`—Vertex program function to invoke on each vertex. It receives the message and potentially changes the content of a vertex.
- `sendMsg`—Function that receives an `EdgeTriplet` and returns an iterator of (vertex ID, message) tuples. These messages are sent to the specified vertices.
- `mergeMsg`—Function to merge messages directed to the same vertex.

---

[1] Grzegorz Malewicz et al., "Pregel: A System for Large-Scale Graph Processing," https://kowshik.github.io/JPregel/pregel_paper.pdf.

SELECTING GRAPH SUBSETS

Another important operation on graphs is selecting only a part of a graph. Here, we'll show you three methods you can use to accomplish this:

- subgraph—Selects vertices and edges based on supplied predicates
- mask—Selects only the vertices present in another graph
- filter—Combination of the previous two

Let's select from graphAggr only those persons who have children. You can use the subgraph method and give it predicates that vertices and edges have to satisfy in order to be selected. This is subgraph's signature:

```
def subgraph(
    epred: EdgeTriplet[VD, ED] => Boolean = (x => true),
    vpred: (VertexId, VD) => Boolean = ((v, d) => true))
  : Graph[VD, ED]
```

As you can see, the edge predicate function (epred) receives an EdgeTriplet object. If it returns true, the particular edge will be included in the resulting graph. The vertex predicate function (vpred) receives a vertex ID and its property object. If you omit the vertex predicate function, the subgraph function keeps all the original vertices in the new graph. Edges whose vertices no longer exist in the new graph are automatically removed.

To select only the persons who have children, you can do this:

> Edges are automatically removed if the source or destination vertex no longer exists.

```
val parents = graphAggr.subgraph(_ => true,
(vertexId, person) => person.children > 0)
```

> Keeps only people with one or more children

If you look at the remaining edges and vertices, you'll see that only Marge and Homer are left, with the single edge that connects them:

```
scala> parents.vertices.collect.foreach(println)
(1,PersonExt(Homer,39,1,0,true))
(2,PersonExt(Marge,39,1,0,true))
scala> parents.edges.collect.foreach(println)
Edge(1,2,Relationship(marriedTo))
```

The mask function is another way to filter a graph in GraphX. With mask, you can project a graph onto another graph and keep only those vertices and edges that also exist in the second graph, not taking into account property objects of either graph. The only argument mask takes is the second graph.

The third function for filtering a graph's contents is filter. It's related to both the subgraph and mask functions. It takes three arguments: a *preprocessing function* and edge and vertex predicate functions (just like subgraph). The preprocessing function lets you transform the original graph into another graph, which will then be pruned using the supplied edge and vertex predicate functions. The resulting graph will be used as a *mask* for the original graph. In other words, `filter` lets you combine two steps into one and is useful only if you don't need the preprocessed graph except for masking the original one.

9.2 Graph algorithms

Graph algorithms are the reason GraphX exists in the first place: the whole point of organizing data into graphs is to be able to use algorithms built specifically for working with graph data. Many problems can be elegantly solved using graph solutions.

In this section, we'll cover several Spark graph algorithms:

- *Shortest paths*—Finds the shortest paths to a set of vertices
- *Page rank*—Calculates the relative importance of vertices in a graph based on the number of edges leading to and from them
- *Connected components*—Finds distinct subgraphs, if they exist in a graph
- *Strongly connected components*—Finds clusters of doubly connected vertices

As we've said, if you're interested in learning about other graph algorithms Spark provides, such as triangle count, SVD++ (a collaborative filtering model), and Latent Dirichlet allocation (LDA, a topic model for text documents), we recommend *Spark GraphX in Action* by Michael Malak and Robin East (Manning, 2016).

9.2.1 Presentation of the dataset

In this section, you'll switch to a different dataset. The dataset you'll use can be obtained from Stanford University.[2] It was prepared by Robert West and Jure Leskovec as part of their project "Human Wayfinding in Information Networks."[3] The dataset is based on an online game called Wikispeedia (http://snap.stanford.edu/data/ wikispeedia.html), also a part of a research project.[4] The game contains a subset of Wikipedia articles and challenges a user to connect two articles with as few links as possible. The dataset archive (http://mng.bz/N2kf) contains several files, but for this section you need only two: articles.tsv and links.tsv. The first contains unique article names (one per line), and the second contains links with source and destination article names separated by a tab character. Both files are available from our GitHub repository (which you cloned in chapter 2).

Using `zipWithIndex`, the following snippet loads article names, removes empty lines and comment lines, and assigns a unique number (ID) to each article name (assuming you're running in your home directory, where you cloned the repository):

---

[2] Wikispeedia Navigation Paths dataset: http://snap.stanford.edu/data/wikispeedia.html.

[3] Robert West and Jure Leskovec, "Human Wayfinding in Information Networks," 21st International World Wide Web Conference (WWW), 2012.

[4] Robert West, Joelle Pineau, and Doina Precup, "Wikispeedia: An Online Game for Inferring Semantic Distances between Concepts," 21st International Joint Conference on Artificial Intelligence (IJCAI), 2009.

```
val articles = sc.textFile("first-edition/ch09/articles.tsv").
  filter(line => line.trim() != "" && !line.startsWith("#")).
  zipWithIndex().cache()
```

Calling `cache` will make article names and IDs available for quick lookup. Loading lines with links is analogous, except you don't need to use `zipWithIndex`:

```
val links = sc.textFile("first-edition/ch09/links.tsv").
  filter(line => line.trim() != "" && !line.startsWith("#"))
```

Parse each link line to obtain the article names, and then replace each name with the article ID by joining names with the `articles` RDD:

```
val linkIndexes = links.map(x => {
    val spl = x.split("\t");
    (spl(0), spl(1)) }).
  join(articles).map(x => x._2).join(articles).map(x => x._2)
```

The resulting RDD contains tuples with source and destination article IDs. You can use it to construct a `Graph` object:

```
val wikigraph = Graph.fromEdgeTuples(linkIndexes, 0)
```

You can see that there's a slight difference in the number of articles and vertices in the graph:

```
scala> wikigraph.vertices.count()
res0: Long = 4592
scala> articles.count()
res1: Long = 4604
```

That's because some articles are missing from the links file. You can check that by counting all the distinct article names in the `linkIndexes` RDD:

```
scala> linkIndexes.map(x => x._1).union(linkIndexes.map(x => x._2)).
  distinct().count()
res2: Long = 4592
```

You're now ready to get acquainted with the graph algorithms available in GraphX.

9.2.2 *Shortest-paths algorithm*

For each vertex in a graph, the shortest-paths algorithm finds the minimum number of edges you need to follow in order to reach the starting vertex. If you have a LinkedIn account, you've undoubtedly seen an example of the shortest-paths algorithm. In the section How You're Connected, LinkedIn shows you the persons whom you can get acquainted with through the person you're looking at.

Spark implements the shortest-paths algorithm with the `ShortestPaths` object. It has only one method, called `run`, which takes a graph and a `Seq` of *landmark* vertex IDs.

The returned graph's vertices contain a map with the shortest path to each of the landmarks, where the landmark vertex ID is the key and the shortest-path length is the value.

One of the challenges Wikispeedia presents is to connect the 14th Century and Rainbow pages. In the paths_finished.tsv file, you'll find examples of successfully completed challenges. Some people finished the challenge with six clicks and some with as few as three clicks. Let's see what Spark says is the minimum number of clicks you need:

First, you need to find the vertex ID of the two pages:

```
scala> articles.filter(x => x._1 == "Rainbow" || x._1 == "14th_century").
  collect().foreach(println)
(14th_century,10)
(Rainbow,3425)
```

Then call `ShortestPaths`'s run method with `wikigraph` and one of the IDs in a Seq as arguments:

```
import org.apache.spark.graphx.lib._
val shortest = ShortestPaths.run(wikigraph, Seq(10))
```

The shortest graph has vertices whose property objects are maps with distances to landmarks. Now you only need to find the vertex corresponding to the Rainbow article:

```
scala> shortest.vertices.filter(x => x._1 == 3425).collect.foreach(println)
(3425,Map(1772 -> 2))
```

The actual minimum number of clicks is two; but `ShortestPaths` doesn't give you the path from one vertex to another, only the number of edges you need to reach it.

To find the vertices on the shortest path, you'd need to write your own implementation of the shortest-paths algorithm, which is beyond the scope of this book. But if you need to take that road, *GraphX in Action*, which we mentioned earlier, can help you. Another thing you can use as a reference is our implementation of the A* algorithm given in section 9.3.

9.2.3 *Page rank*

The page-rank algorithm was invented by Larry Page, cofounder of Google. It determines the importance of vertices in a graph by counting incoming edges. It's been widely used to analyze the relative importance of web pages in a web graph. It starts by assigning each vertex a page rank (PR) value of 1. It divides this PR value by the number of outgoing edges and then adds the result to the PR value of all neighboring vertices. This process is repeated until no PR value changes by more than the tolerance parameter.

Because the PR value of a page is divided by the number of outgoing edges, the page's influence shrinks proportionally to the number of pages it references. The highest-ranked page is the one that has the minimum number of outgoing links and the maximum number of incoming links.

You can run the page-rank algorithm on a graph by calling its `pageRank` method and passing in the tolerance parameter. The tolerance parameter determines the amount the page-rank values can change and still be considered to converge. Smaller values mean more accuracy, but the algorithm will also need more time to converge. The result is a graph whose vertices contain the PR values:

```
val ranked = wikigraph.pageRank(0.001)
```

Let's see the 10 highest-ranked pages in the Wikispeedia subset of Wikipedia pages:

```
val ordering = new Ordering[Tuple2[VertexId,Double]] {
  def compare(x:Tuple2[VertexId, Double], y:Tuple2[VertexId, Double]):Int =
    x._2.compareTo(y._2) }
val top10 = ranked.vertices.top(10)(ordering)
```

The `top10` array now contains vertex IDs and their PR values of the 10 highest-ranked pages, but you still don't know to which pages those IDs belong. You can join this array with the `articles` RDD to find out:

```
scala> sc.parallelize(top10).join(articles.map(_.swap)).collect.
  sortWith((x, y) => x._2._1 > y._2._1).foreach(println)
(4297,(43.064871681422574,United_States))
(1568,(29.02695420077583,France))
(1433,(28.605445025345137,Europe))
(4293,(28.12516457691193,United_Kingdom))
(1389,(21.962114281302206,English_language))
(1694,(21.77679013455212,Germany))
(4542,(21.328506154058328,World_War_II))
(1385,(20.138550469782487,England))
(2417,(19.88906178678032,Latin))
(2098,(18.246567557461464,India))
```

The first element of each tuple in the result is the vertex ID; the second element contains the PR value and the page name. As you can see, the page about the United States is the most influential page in the dataset.

9.2.4   *Connected components*

Finding connected components of a graph means finding subgraphs in which every vertex can be reached from every other vertex by following the edges in the subgraph. A graph is *connected* if it contains only one connected component and all of its vertices can be reached from every other vertex. A graph with two connected components is shown in figure 9.3: vertices from one connected component can't be reached from the other.

Finding connected components is important in many situations. For example, you should check whether your graph is connected before running other algorithms, because that may affect your results and skew your conclusions.

To find connected components on a GraphX graph, you call its `connected-Components` method (implicitly made available from `GraphOps` object). Connected

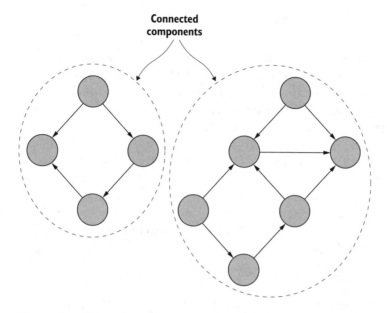

Figure 9.3   A graph with two connected components. Although they belong to the same graph, vertices from one connected component can't be reached from the other.

components are represented by the lowest vertex ID in the connected component. To use the Wikispeedia graph:

```
val wikiCC = wikigraph.connectedComponents()
```

Property objects of the `wikiCC` graph's vertices contain the lowest vertex ID of the connected component to which they belong. To find all the connected components in the graph, you can find the distinct connected component IDs. To find page names of those IDs, you can again join them with the `articles` RDD:

```
scala> wikiCC.vertices.map(x => (x._2, x._2)).
  distinct().join(articles.map(_.swap)).collect.foreach(println)
(0,(0,%C3%81ed%C3%A1n_mac_Gabr%C3%A1in))
(1210,(1210,Directdebit))
```

As you can see, the Wikispeedia graph has two separate clusters of web pages. The first is identified by the vertex ID of the page about Áedán mac Gabráin and the second by the vertex ID of the Direct Debit page.

Let's see how many pages are in each cluster:

```
scala> wikiCC.vertices.map(x => (x._2, x._2)).countByKey().foreach(println)
(0,4589)
(1210,3)
```

The second cluster has only three pages, which means Wikispeedia is well connected.

9.2.5   *Strongly connected components*

Strongly connected components (SCCs) are subgraphs where all vertices are connected to every other vertex in the subgraph (not necessarily directly). All vertices in an SCC need to be reachable from each other (following the direction of the edges). An example is given in figure 9.4, showing a graph with four strongly connected components. Unlike connected components, SCCs can be connected to each other through some of their vertices.

SCCs have many applications in graph theory and other areas. As a practical example, let's consider LinkedIn again. SCCs in a LinkedIn graph are likely to occur in small companies, on teams, or among lifelong friends, but aren't likely to exist across industries, such as IT and construction.

In Spark, the `stronglyConnectedComponents` method is also available from the `GraphOps` object, implicitly added to `Graph` objects. You just need to give it the maximum number of iterations to perform:

```
val wikiSCC = wikigraph.stronglyConnectedComponents(100)
```

As with the connected-components algorithm, the vertices of the graph resulting from the SCC algorithm contain the lowest vertex ID of the strongly connected component to which they belong.

The `wikiSCC` graph contains 519 strongly connected components:

```
scala> wikiSCC.vertices.map(x => x._2).distinct.count
res0: Long = 519
```

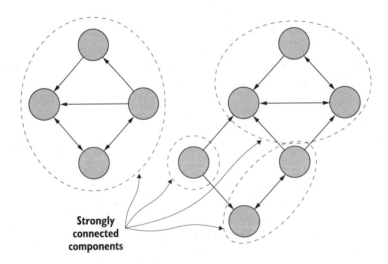

Strongly connected components

Figure 9.4   A graph with four strongly connected components. Every vertex in each component is connected to every other vertex.

Let's see which ones are largest:

```
scala> wikiSCC.vertices.map(x => (x._2, x._1)).countByKey().
  filter(_._2 > 1).toList.sortWith((x, y) => x._2 > y._2).foreach(println)
(6,4051)
(2488,6)
(1831,3)
(892,2)
(1950,2)
(4224,2)
...
```

The largest SCC has 4,051 vertices, which is too many to display here. You can examine the names of the pages belonging to the vertices in several smaller SCCs. For the three next-largest SCCs found, members of the first SCC are lists of countries by continents (those pages were changed in Wikipedia since the Wikispeedia dataset was constructed, and they no longer form an SCC):

```
scala> wikiSCC.vertices.filter(x => x._2 == 2488).
  join(articles.map(x => (x._2, x._1))).collect.foreach(println)
(2490,(2488,List_of_Asian_countries))
(2496,(2488,List_of_Oceanian_countries))
(2498,(2488,List_of_South_American_countries))
(2493,(2488,List_of_European_countries))
(2488,(2488,List_of_African_countries))
(2495,(2488,List_of_North_American_countries))
scala> wikiSCC.vertices.filter(x => x._2 == 1831).
  join(articles.map(x => (x._2, x._1))).collect.foreach(println)
(1831,(1831,HD_217107))
(1832,(1831,HD_217107_b))
(1833,(1831,HD_217107_c))
scala> wikiSCC.vertices.filter(x => x._2 == 892).
  join(articles.map(x => (x._2, x._1))).collect.foreach(println)
(1262,(892,Dunstable_Downs))
(892,(892,Chiltern_Hills))
```

The second SCC contains pages about a star (HD_217107) and its two planets. Members of the third SCC are regions in England.

9.3   *Implementing the A* search algorithm*

In this section, you'll implement the A* (pronounced as *A star*) search algorithm for finding the shortest path between two vertices in a graph. The A* algorithm is widely popular because of its efficiency in path finding. The main reason to implement this algorithm using the GraphX API in this chapter is to help you get a better understanding of GraphX classes and methods.

Through the process, you'll apply graph filtering, message aggregation, and joining vertices—all the methods we talked about in the previous sections—to a real problem. And you'll also learn about the A* search algorithm itself, of course.

9.3.1   *Understanding the A* algorithm*

The A* algorithm may seem complicated initially but is simple once you get the hang of it. You need a start vertex and an end vertex; the A* algorithm finds the shortest path between them. The algorithm works by calculating the cost of each vertex, relative to the start and end vertices, and then selecting the path containing the vertices with the minimum cost.

We'll illustrate how the A* algorithm works using a simple 2D map (see figure 9.5). The map contains a grid with starting and ending squares and a barrier between them. Imagine this 2D map is represented as a graph, where each square is a vertex connected to its neighboring squares by edges. Vertices aren't connected diagonally, only horizontally and vertically.

The cost of each vertex is calculated using two measures, shown in figure 9.5 with a dotted line and a dashed line. The light gray square represents a vertex for which the cost is being calculated. The dotted line is a path between that vertex and the starting node (the path traversed so far). The length of that path is denoted by the letter *G*, and in this example is equal to 2 because the distance between two neighbors is always 1 (each edge has a length, or *weight*, of 1).

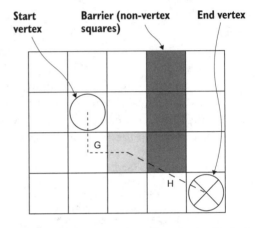

Figure 9.5   **2D map, which will be used to illustrate how the A* algorithm works. Its squares can be represented as nodes of a graph, with edges connecting the neighboring squares. The darker squares are barriers. The goal of the A* algorithm is to find the shortest path between the start and end nodes. The light gray square is the square for which the cost is being calculated. The dotted line is the path between the start vertex and the vertex under consideration. The dashed line is an estimated distance between the vertex under consideration and the end vertex.**

The dashed line is an estimated path between the vertex under consideration and the end vertex. The length of that path is denoted by the letter *H* and is an estimation of how far the end vertex is from the current vertex. In this case, the value *H* is calculated as the length of a straight line from a vertex to the destination, but other estimation functions can be used too.

The final vertex cost, denoted by letter F, is calculated by summing up the *G* and *H* values:

$$F = G + H$$

The estimation function is central to the A* algorithm, and you can't use the A* algorithm on graphs that don't have an option of calculating the estimated distance between two random vertices. The graph from section 9.1 is such a graph because you can't estimate distance between Marge and Milhouse. You can calculate the distance if you know the path between them, but there's no way to estimate it only by examining the two vertices alone.

Figure 9.6 shows the A* algorithm in action. The algorithm holds vertices in the *open* and *closed* groups, and it keeps track of the *current vertex*. Squares in the closed group are denoted with a light gray background. Squares in the open group have a white background with the calculated numbers written on them. The upper two numbers are the G and H values, and the lower number is the final F value (the sum of G and H).

In the first iteration of the algorithm, the starting vertex is the current vertex. Its G value is equal to 0, and its H value isn't used. In each iteration, the A* algorithm puts the current vertex in the closed group and calculates the G, H, and F values of each of its neighbors not in the closed group. If a neighbor already had its F value calculated (which means it was in the open group), the old F value is compared with the new one, and the smaller one is used.

Iteration 1:

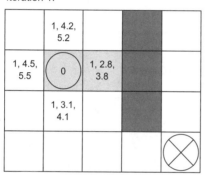

Iteration 2:

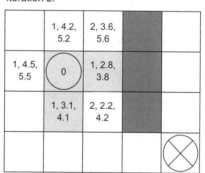

Iteration 3:

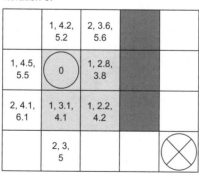

Iteration 4, 5, 6:

Figure 9.6   An A* algorithm finding a path from the starting vertex (square with the circle) to the end vertex (vertex with an X). In each iteration, the algorithm calculates F, G, and H values for neighbors of the current vertex. Once the values are calculated, the vertices belong to the open group. Next, the algorithm selects the vertex from the open group with the lowest F value as the next current vertex and puts it in the closed group (light gray squares). Once the destination vertex is reached, the algorithm constructs the path to the starting vertex by following the lowest F values (darker gray squares). The black squares in the figure are barriers.

Next, a vertex from the open group with the minimum *F* value is selected as the new current vertex. If the new current vertex is the destination vertex, the final path is constructed by going back and following the vertices with minimal *F* values (or by using the vertex parent information, as is the case with our implementation).

In figure 9.6, the final path is shown with the darker gray color. The darkest color denotes the barrier.

9.3.2   Implementing the A* algorithm

Now, let's build an implementation of the A* algorithm using the GraphX API. You'll use here almost all the methods you learned in previous sections.

The complete algorithm is given in the following listing. You can also find it in our online repository. We'll go through it line by line.

Listing 9.1   GraphX implementation of the A* search algorithm

```
object AStar extends Serializable {
  import scala.reflect.ClassTag

  private val checkpointFrequency = 20

  def run[VD: ClassTag, ED: ClassTag](graph:Graph[VD, ED],
    origin:VertexId, dest:VertexId, maxIterations:Int = 100,
    estimateDistance:(VD, VD) => Double,
    edgeWeight:(ED) => Double,
    shouldVisitSource:(ED) => Boolean = (in:ED) => true,
    shouldVisitDestination:(ED) => Boolean = (in:ED) => true):Array[VD] =
  {
    val resbuf = scala.collection.mutable.ArrayBuffer.empty[VD]

    val arr = graph.vertices.flatMap(n => if(n._1 == origin ||
      n._1 == dest) List[Tuple2[VertexId, VD]](n) else List()).collect()
    if(arr.length != 2)
      throw new IllegalArgumentException("Origin or destination not found")
    val origNode = if (arr(0)._1 == origin) arr(0)._2 else arr(1)._2
    val destNode = if (arr(0)._1 == origin) arr(1)._2 else arr(0)._2
    var dist = estimateDistance(origNode, destNode)

    case class WorkNode(origNode:VD, g:Double=Double.MaxValue,
      h:Double=Double.MaxValue, f:Double=Double.MaxValue,
      visited:Boolean=false, predec:Option[VertexId]=None)
    var gwork = graph.mapVertices{ case(ind, node) => {
      if(ind == origin)
        WorkNode(node, 0, dist, dist)
      else
        WorkNode(node)
      }}.cache()

    var currVertexId:Option[VertexId] = Some(origin)
    var lastIter = 0
    for(iter <- 0 to maxIterations
      if currVertexId.isDefined;
```

```scala
    if currVertexId.getOrElse(Long.MaxValue) != dest)
{
  lastIter = iter
  println("Iteration "+iter)
  gwork.unpersistVertices()
  gwork = gwork.mapVertices((vid:VertexId, v:WorkNode) => {
    if(vid != currVertexId.get)
      v
    else
      WorkNode(v.origNode, v.g, v.h, v.f, true, v.predec)
    }).cache()
  if(iter % checkpointFrequency == 0)
    gwork.checkpoint()
  val neighbors = gwork.subgraph(trip => trip.srcId ==
    currVertexId.get || trip.dstId == currVertexId.get)
  val newGs = neighbors.aggregateMessages[Double](ctx => {
      if(ctx.srcId == currVertexId.get &&
          !ctx.dstAttr.visited && shouldVisitDestination(ctx.attr)) {
        ctx.sendToDst(ctx.srcAttr.g + edgeWeight(ctx.attr))
      }
      else if(ctx.dstId == currVertexId.get &&
        !ctx.srcAttr.visited && shouldVisitSource(ctx.attr)) {
          ctx.sendToSrc(ctx.dstAttr.g + edgeWeight(ctx.attr))
      }}
    , (a1:Double, a2:Double) => a1, //never supposed to happen
    TripletFields.All)

  val cid = currVertexId.get
  gwork = gwork.outerJoinVertices(newGs)((nid, node, totalG) =>
    totalG match {
      case None => node
      case Some(newG) => {
        if(node.h == Double.MaxValue) {
          val h = estimateDistance(node.origNode, destNode)
          WorkNode(node.origNode, newG, h, newG+h, false, Some(cid))
        }
        else if(node.h + newG < node.f) //the new f is less than old
        {
          WorkNode(node.origNode, newG, node.h, newG+node.h, false,
            Some(cid))
        }
        else
          node
      }})
  val openList = gwork.vertices.filter(v => v._2.h < Double.MaxValue &&
    !v._2.visited)
  if(openList.isEmpty)
    currVertexId = None
  else {
    val nextV = openList.map(v => (v._1, v._2.f)).
      reduce((n1, n2) => if(n1._2 < n2._2) n1 else n2)
    currVertexId = Some(nextV._1)
  }
}
```

```
    if(currVertexId.isDefined && currVertexId.get == dest) {
      var currId:Option[VertexId] = Some(dest)
      var it = lastIter
      while(currId.isDefined && it >= 0) {
        val v = gwork.vertices.filter(x => x._1 == currId.get).collect()(0)
        resbuf += v._2.origNode
        currId = v._2.predec
        it = it - 1
      }
    }
    else
      println("Path not found!")
    gwork.unpersist()
    resbuf.toArray.reverse
  }
}
```

INITIALIZING THE ALGORITHM

You run the A* algorithm by calling the `run` method of the `AStar` object. The arguments are described here.

- `graph`—Graph on which to run the A*algorithm (required).
- `origin`—Origin vertex ID (required).
- `dest`—Destination vertex ID (required).
- `maxIterations`—Maximum number of iterations to run. Default is 100.
- `estimateDistance`—Function that takes two vertex property objects and estimates the distance between them (required).
- `edgeWeight`—Function that takes an edge property object and calculates its weight: a measure of how costly it would be to include the edge in the path (required).
- `shouldVisitSource`—Function that takes an edge property object and determines whether to visit the source vertex. Defaults to `true` for all edges and vertices. Can be used to simulate a bidirectional graph with unidirectional edges.
- `shouldVisitDestination`—Function that takes an edge property object and determines whether to visit the destination vertex. Defaults to `true` for all edges and vertices. Can be used to simulate a bidirectional graph with unidirectional edges.

The `estimateDistance` function returns an estimated distance between two vertices, determined by their property objects. For example, as shown in figure 9.6, it takes X and Y coordinates of two squares and calculates the distance between them using the Pythagorean formula. The `edgeWeight` function determines the weight for each edge. In figure 9.6, it always returned 1 because squares are connected only to their neighboring squares, which are always one square away. `shouldVisitSource` and `shouldVisitDestination` determine whether to visit the edges' source and destination vertices, respectively. You can use this function to visit both vertices even if the graph is unidirectional, or to determine whether an edge is one-way for only some edges. If your graph has edges going in both directions, then only shouldVisitDestination should return true; shouldVisitSource should return false.

The run method first checks whether the supplied origin and destination vertex IDs exist in the graph and estimates the starting distance to the destination:

```
val arr = graph.vertices.flatMap(n =>
  if(n._1 == origin || n._1 == dest)
    List[Tuple2[VertexId, VD]](n)
  else
    List()).collect()
if(arr.length != 2)
  throw new IllegalArgumentException("Origin or destination not found")
val origNode = if (arr(0)._1 == origin) arr(0)._2 else arr(1)._2
val destNode = if (arr(0)._1 == origin) arr(1)._2 else arr(0)._2
var dist = estimateDistance(origNode, destNode)
```

It then prepares a working graph, which will be used to calculate *F*, *G* and *H* values. The WorkNode case class is used for this purpose:

```
case class WorkNode(origNode:VD,
  g:Double=Double.MaxValue,
  h:Double=Double.MaxValue,
  f:Double=Double.MaxValue,
  visited:Boolean=false,
  predec:Option[VertexId]=None)
```

WorkNode keeps the original node object in the origNode attribute, but it also contains attributes for the *G*, *H*, and *F* values, the visited flag (if visited is true, the vertex is in the closed group), and the ID of the predecessor vertex (predec attribute), used to construct the final path.

The working graph (gwork) is created by mapping vertices to WorkNode objects. The origin vertex's *F*, *G*, and *H* values are also set in the process:

```
var gwork = graph.mapVertices{ case(ind, node) => {
  if(ind == origin)
    WorkNode(node, 0, dist, dist)
  else
    WorkNode(node)
  }}.cache()
```

Finally, the origin is set as the current vertex:

```
var currVertexId:Option[VertexId] = Some(origin)
```

All the prerequisites for the main loop are now complete.

UNDERSTANDING THE MAIN LOOP

The currVertexId will be set to None if there are no more vertices in the open group and the destination hasn't been reached. It will be equal to the destination vertex ID if the destination has been reached. These are the two conditions for staying in the main loop; the third condition is the number of iterations:

```
for(iter <- 0 to maxIterations
  if currVertexId.isDefined;
  if currVertexId.getOrElse(Long.MaxValue) != dest) {
```

In the main loop, the following happens:

1 The current vertex is marked as visited (the equivalent of placing it in the closed group).
2 The *F*, *G*, and *H* values of the current vertex's neighboring vertices are calculated.
3 The next current vertex is selected from the open group.

Because the working graph is reused in the main loop, it's cached, and then its vertices are unpersisted before the next iteration. Edges aren't modified, so they stay cached.

Caching and checkpointing graphs

Many graph algorithms need to reuse the same data repeatedly. It's therefore helpful to have your graph data readily available in memory. Graph's cache method does this for you by caching both vertices and edges. By default, Spark caches vertex and edge data in memory only, but other storage levels can be specified when using the persist method. It takes StorageLevel as an argument, which has several constants defined (DISK_ONLY, MEMORY_AND_DISK, and so on). You can find more information about storage levels at http://mng.bz/pM17.

But if a graph's data is continually changed and cached, it will soon fill the available memory space and force JVM to do garbage collection (GC) often. Spark can free the cached data more efficiently than JVM can, so if you frequently persist graph data, you should also unpersist it. To do this, you can use the unpersist method, which uncaches both edges and vertices; or you can use the unpersistVertices method, which uncaches only vertices. Both methods take a boolean argument that determines whether to block until data is uncached.

MARKING THE CURRENT VERTEX AS VISITED

Because RDDs are immutable, you can't change a vertex's property object. You need to transform the vertices RDD. This in itself is simple:

```
gwork = gwork.mapVertices((vid:VertexId, v:WorkNode) => {
  if(vid != currVertexId.get)
    v
  else
    WorkNode(v.origNode, v.g, v.h, v.f, true, v.predec)
  }).cache()
```

You keep the work nodes of all edges unchanged, except the current vertex, for which only the `visited` property is set to `true`.

CHECKPOINTING THE WORKING GRAPH

The working graph needs to be periodically checkpointed (every 20th iteration) because its RDD DAG grows too large and gradually too expensive for calculation:

```
if(iter % checkpointFrequency == 0)
  gwork.checkpoint()
```

The working graph is continuously transformed, and if too many iterations are performed, that can lead to stack-overflow errors. Periodic checkpointing avoids this by persisting the DAG plan.

CALCULATING F, G, AND H VALUES

The *F*, *G*, and *H* values need to be calculated only for neighboring vertices, so you first create a subgraph of your working graph containing only edges to and from the current vertex:

```
val neighbors = gwork.subgraph(trip => trip.srcId == currVertexId.get ||
  trip.dstId == currVertexId.get)
```

Next, you send a message to each of those neighbors if they haven't already been visited and if the `shouldVisit*` function says you should visit it. The message you send to each node (using `sendToSrc` or `sendToDst`) contains the new *G* value for that vertex, calculated using the provided `edgeWeight` function. The result (`newGs`) is a `VertexRDD` containing only the new *G*s as vertices' values:

```
val newGs = neighbors.aggregateMessages[Double](ctx => {
    if(ctx.srcId == currVertexId.get &&
        !ctx.dstAttr.visited && shouldVisitDestination(ctx.attr)) {
      ctx.sendToDst(ctx.srcAttr.g + edgeWeight(ctx.attr))
    } else if(ctx.dstId == currVertexId.get  && !ctx.srcAttr.visited &&
        shouldVisitSource(ctx.attr)) {
      ctx.sendToSrc(ctx.dstAttr.g + edgeWeight(ctx.attr))
  }}, (a1:Double, a2:Double) => a1,
  TripletFields.All)
```

In the next step, the graph containing the new *G* values is joined with the working graph. If the new *F* value (new *G* plus *H* value) is less than the current *F* value, the vertex is updated, and its `predec` (predecessor) field is set to the current vertex ID. For those vertices that don't have a new *G* value calculated in the `newG` graph (they aren't neighbors of the current vertex), the `totalG` value in the join function will be `None`, and the function leaves the existing vertex object the same:

```
val cid = currVertexId.get
gwork = gwork.outerJoinVertices(newGs)((nid, node, totalG) =>
  totalG match {
    case None => node
```

```
  case Some(newG) => {
    if(node.h == Double.MaxValue) {
      val h = estimateDistance(node.origNode, destNode)
      WorkNode(node.origNode, newG, h, newG+h, false, Some(cid))
    } else if(node.h + newG < node.f) {
    WorkNode(node.origNode, newG, node.h, newG+node.h, false, Some(cid))
    }
    else
      node
} })
```

The new gwork graph now contains the updated *F* values for all vertices in the current open group. All that's left to do is to choose the next current vertex.

SELECTING THE NEXT CURRENT VERTEX

To find the next current vertex, first select only the vertices in the open group:

```
val openList = gwork.vertices.filter(v =>
    v._2.h < Double.MaxValue && !v._2.visited)
```

If the open group is empty, the destination vertex can't be reached. Otherwise, the vertex with the smallest *F* value is found:

```
if(openList.isEmpty)
  currVertexId = None
else {
  val nextV = openList.map(v => (v._1, v._2.f)).
    reduce((n1, n2) => if(n1._2 < n2._2) n1 else n2)
  currVertexId = Some(nextV._1)
}
```

COLLECTING THE FINAL PATH VERTICES

Finally, after the main loop finishes and the destination is reached, the current-VertexId is equal to the destination vertex ID. The A* algorithm then follows the predec fields of each vertex, takes the corresponding vertex property objects, and puts them in the final collection (resbuf, a Scala mutable ArrayBuffer):

```
if(currVertexId.isDefined && currVertexId.get == dest) {
  println("Found!")
  var currId:Option[VertexId] = Some(dest)
  var it = lastIter
  while(currId.isDefined && it >= 0) {
    val v = gwork.vertices.filter(x => x._1 == currId.get).collect()(0)
    resbuf += v._2.origNode
    currId = v._2.predec
    it = it - 1
  }
}
```

The contents of the resbuf is then reversed and returned as the final shortest path:

```
resbuf.toArray.reverse
```

9.3.3 *Testing the implementation*

Let's test the implementation on a simple, easy-to-visualize dataset. The graph you'll use connects points in a three-dimensional space. Each vertex in the graph contains *X*, *Y*, and *Z* coordinates. You'll use the following case class to denote the points:

```
case class Point(x:Double, y:Double, z:Double)
```

And you'll create the graph by specifying the points manually:

```
val vertices3d = sc.parallelize(Array((1L, Point(1,2,4)),
  (2L, Point(6,4,4)), (3L, Point(8,5,1)), (4L, Point(2,2,2)),
  (5L, Point(2,5,8)), (6L, Point(3,7,4)), (7L, Point(7,9,1)),
  (8L, Point(7,1,2)), (9L, Point(8,8,10)),
  (10L, Point(10,10,2)), (11L, Point(8,4,3)) ))
val edges3d = sc.parallelize(Array(Edge(1, 2, 1.0), Edge(2, 3, 1.0),
  Edge(3, 4, 1.0), Edge(4, 1, 1.0), Edge(1, 5, 1.0), Edge(4, 5, 1.0),
  Edge(2, 8, 1.0), Edge(4, 6, 1.0), Edge(5, 6, 1.0), Edge(6, 7, 1.0),
  Edge(7, 2, 1.0), Edge(2, 9, 1.0), Edge(7, 9, 1.0), Edge(7, 10, 1.0),
  Edge(10, 11, 1.0), Edge(9, 11, 1.0 ) ))
val graph3d = Graph(vertices3d, edges3d)
```

The corresponding points and the edges between them are shown in figure 9.7.

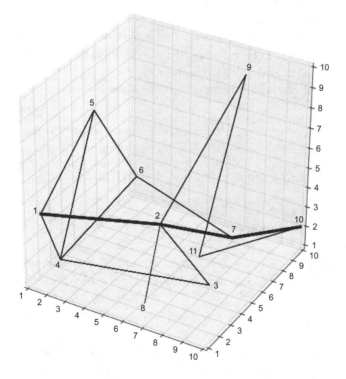

Figure 9.7 The example graph used to test the A* algorithm implementation. The vertices of the graph are points in three-dimensional space. The shortest path from vertex 1 to vertex 10 is shown with a thick line. (The graphic was drawn using Python's matplotlib library.)

The edges of the graph all have a value of 1. The `calcDistance3d` function calculates distances between two points in three-dimensional space:

```
val calcDistance3d = (p1:Point, p2:Point) => {
    val x = p1.x - p2.x
    val y = p1.y - p2.y
    val z = p1.z - p2.z
    Math.sqrt(x*x + y*y + z*z)
}
```

You can use this function to map edges and calculate the real distance between the vertices each edge connects:

```
val graph3dDst = graph3d.mapTriplets(t =>
  calcDistance3d(t.srcAttr, t.dstAttr))
```

Because the A* algorithm uses checkpointing (covered in chapter 4), before running this algorithm, set the Spark checkpointing directory:

```
sc.setCheckpointDir("/spark/checkpoint/directory")
```

Now you can run the A* algorithm on the `graph3dDst` graph. The same `calcDistance3d` function can be used to calculate *H* values (the distance from a vertex to the destination vertex). The function that calculates edge weights can return the property object attached to each vertex (because you just calculated the weight of each edge and `graph3dDst` already contains them).

Let's calculate the shortest path between vertices 1 and 10:

```
scala> AStar.run(graph3dDst, 1, 10, 50, calcDistance3d, (e:Double) => e)
res0: Array[Point] = Array(Point(1.0,2.0,4.0), Point(6.0,4.0,4.0),
Point(7.0,9.0,1.0), Point(10.0,10.0,2.0))
```

The resulting shortest path is shown with a thick line in figure 9.7.

9.4   Summary

- A graph is a mathematical concept of linked objects, used to model relations between them.
- Graphs consist of vertices (nodes in a graph) and edges that connect the vertices. In Spark, edges are directed, and both edges and vertices have property objects attached to them.
- In Spark, vertices and edges are realized by two special RDD implementations: `VertexRDD` and `EdgeRDD`.
- You can construct a graph object with an RDD containing tuples with vertex IDs and vertex property objects, and an RDD containing `Edge` objects.

- You can transform graph objects using the `mapEdges`, `mapVertices`, and `mapTriplets` methods to add more information to the edges and vertices or to transform property objects attached to them.

- Using the `aggregateMessages` method, you can run a function on each vertex of a graph and optionally send messages to its neighboring vertices, collecting and aggregating all the messages sent to each vertex in a new `VertexRDD`.

- You can join two graphs using the `outerJoinVertices` method. `aggregateMessages` and `outerJoinVertices`, along with the mapping functions, are the bread and butter of graph operations in GraphX. You'll use them often in your GraphX applications.

- GraphX contains an implementation of a Pregel-like API. It also functions by sending messages throughout the graph.

- Graphs can be filtered using the `subgraph`, `mask`, and `filter` functions.

- The shortest-paths algorithm finds the shortest paths from a set of vertices to every other vertex in a graph. You can use it for various tasks, such as finding the smallest number of links you need to follow from one page to another.

- Page rank finds the relative importance of a vertex based on the number of edges going in or out of the vertex. You can use it to find the most influential nodes in a graph (such as web pages and the links between them, or people in a social network).

- The connected-components algorithm finds distinct, disjoint subgraphs of a graph.

- The strongly connected components algorithm finds clusters of doubly connected vertices.

- The A* search algorithm is a quick algorithm to find paths. We presented a GraphX implementation of the A* algorithm for educational purposes.

Part 3

Spark ops

Using Spark isn't just about writing and running Spark applications. It's also about configuring Spark clusters and system resources to be used efficiently by applications. The necessary concepts and configuration options for running Spark applications on Spark standalone, Hadoop YARN, and Mesos clusters are explained in this part of the book.

Chapter 10 explores Spark runtime components, Spark cluster types, job and resource scheduling, configuring Spark, and the Spark web UI. These are concepts common to all cluster managers that Spark can run on: the Spark standalone cluster, YARN, and Mesos. The two local modes are also explained in chapter 10.

You'll learn about the Spark standalone cluster in chapter 11: its components, how to start it and run applications on it, and how to use its web UI. Spark History Server, which keeps details about previously run jobs, is also discussed. You'll also learn how to use Spark's scripts to start up a Spark standalone cluster on Amazon EC2.

Chapter 12 goes through the specifics of setting up, configuring, and using YARN and Mesos clusters for running Spark applications.

Running Spark

10

This chapter covers

- Spark runtime components
- Spark cluster types
- Job and resource scheduling
- Configuring Spark
- Spark web UI
- Running Spark on the local machine

In previous chapters, we mentioned different ways to run Spark. In this and the next two chapters, we'll discuss ways to set up a Spark cluster. A Spark *cluster* is a set of interconnected processes, usually running in a distributed manner on different machines. The main cluster types that Spark runs on are YARN, Mesos, and Spark standalone. Two other runtime options, local mode and local cluster mode, although the easiest and quickest methods of setting up Spark, are used mainly for testing purposes. The local mode is a pseudo-cluster running on a single machine, and the local cluster mode is a Spark standalone cluster that's also confined to a single machine. If all this sounds confusing, don't worry. We'll explain these concepts in this chapter one step at a time.

In this chapter, we'll also describe common elements of the Spark runtime architecture that apply to all the Spark cluster types. For example, driver and executor processes, as well as Spark context and scheduler objects, are common to all Spark runtime modes. Job and resource scheduling also function similarly on all cluster types, as do usage and configuration for the Spark web UI, used to monitor the execution of Spark jobs.

We'll also show you how to configure a runtime instance of Spark, which is similar for all cluster types. The number of different configuration options and different runtime modes can be bewildering; we'll explain and list the usage of the most important parameters and configuration options. Familiarity with these common concepts will help you understand specific cluster types in the following two chapters and is very important if you want to control how your Spark programs run.

10.1   *An overview of Spark's runtime architecture*

When talking about the Spark runtime architecture, we can distinguish the specifics of various cluster types and the typical Spark components shared by all. The next two chapters describe the details of Spark standalone, YARN, and Mesos clusters. Here we'll describe typical Spark components that are the same regardless of the runtime mode you choose.

10.1.1   *Spark runtime components*

A basic familiarity with Spark runtime components will help you understand how your jobs work. Figure 10.1 shows the main Spark components running in a cluster: *client, driver,* and *executors.*

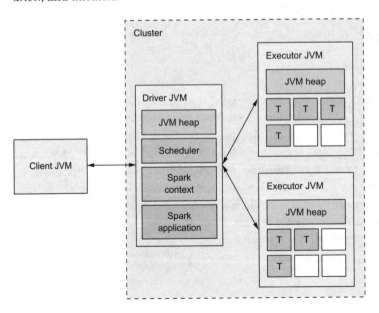

Figure 10.1   Spark runtime components in cluster-deploy mode. Application tasks running in task slots are labeled with a *T.* Unoccupied task slots are in white boxes.

The physical placement of executor and driver processes depends on the cluster type and its configuration. For example, some of these processes could share a single physical machine, or they could all run on different ones. Figure 10.1 shows only the logical components in cluster-deploy mode.

RESPONSIBILITIES OF THE CLIENT-PROCESS COMPONENT

The *client process* starts the driver program. The client process can be a `spark-submit` script for running applications, a `spark-shell` script, or a custom application using Spark API. The client process prepares the classpath and all configuration options for the Spark application. It also passes application arguments, if any, to the application running in the driver.

RESPONSIBILITIES OF THE DRIVER COMPONENT

The *driver* orchestrates and monitors execution of a Spark application. There is always one driver per Spark application. You can think of the driver as a wrapper around the application. The driver and its subcomponents—the Spark context and scheduler—are responsible for the following:

- Requesting memory and CPU resources from cluster managers
- Breaking application logic into stages and tasks
- Sending tasks to executors
- Collecting the results

Chapter 4 describes the logic behind dividing the application's work into stages and tasks.

There are two basic ways the driver program can be run.

- *Cluster-deploy mode* is shown in figure 10.1. In this mode, the driver process runs as a separate JVM process in a cluster, and the cluster manages its resources (mostly JVM heap memory).
- *Client-deploy mode* is shown in figure 10.2. In this mode, the driver is running in the client's JVM process and communicates with the executors managed by the cluster.

The deploy mode you choose affects how you configure Spark and the resource requirements of the client JVM. We'll talk about that in the following chapters.

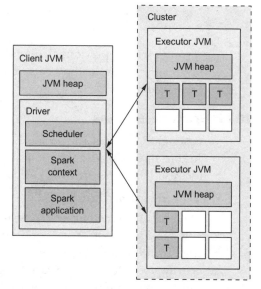

Figure 10.2 Spark runtime components in client-deploy mode. The driver is running in the client's JVM process.

RESPONSIBILITIES OF THE EXECUTORS

The *executors,* which are JVM processes, accept tasks from the driver, execute those tasks, and return the results to the driver. The example drivers in figures 10.1 and 10.2 use only two executors, but you can use a much larger number (some companies today run Spark clusters with tens of thousands of executors).

Each executor has several *task slots* for running tasks in parallel. The executors in the figures have six task slots each. The slots in white boxes are vacant. You can set the number of task slots to a value two or three times the number of CPU cores. Although these task slots are often referred to as *CPU cores* in Spark, they're implemented as threads and don't have to correspond to the number of physical CPU cores on the machine.

CREATION OF THE SPARK CONTEXT

Once the driver is started, it starts and configures an instance of SparkContext. You've seen code examples of this in previous chapters. When running a Spark REPL shell, the shell is the driver program. Your Spark context is already preconfigured and available as an sc variable. When running a standalone Spark application by submitting a JAR file or by using the Spark API from another program, your Spark application starts and configures the Spark context. There can be only one Spark context per JVM.

> **NOTE** Although the configuration option spark.driver.allowMultiple-Contexts exists, it's misleading because using multiple Spark contexts is discouraged. This option is used only for Spark internal tests, and we recommend that you don't use it in your user programs. If you do, you may get unexpected results while running more than one Spark context in a single JVM.

As you've seen in previous chapters, a Spark context comes with many useful methods for creating RDDs, loading data, and so on. It's the main interface for accessing the Spark runtime.

10.1.2   Spark cluster types

Although Spark can run in local mode and in Spark standalone, YARN, and Mesos clusters, one may be more applicable for your environment and use cases. In this section, you'll find the pros and cons of each cluster type.

SPARK STANDALONE CLUSTER

A Spark standalone cluster is a Spark-specific cluster. Because a standalone cluster is built specifically for Spark applications, it doesn't support communication with an HDFS secured with the Kerberos authentication protocol. If you need that kind of security, use YARN to run Spark. A Spark standalone cluster, however, provides faster job startup than those jobs running on YARN. We'll cover Spark standalone clusters in chapter 11.

YARN CLUSTER

YARN is Hadoop's resource manager and execution system. It's also known as *MapReduce 2* because it superseded the MapReduce engine in Hadoop 1 that supported only MapReduce jobs.

Running Spark on YARN has several advantages:

- Many organizations already have YARN clusters of a significant size, along with the technical know-how, tools, and procedures for managing and monitoring them.
- YARN lets you run different types of Java applications, not just Spark, so you can mix legacy Hadoop and Spark applications with ease.
- YARN provides methods for isolating and prioritizing applications among users and organizations, functionality the standalone cluster doesn't have.
- It's the only cluster type that supports Kerberos-secured HDFS.
- You don't have to install Spark on all nodes in the cluster.

MESOS CLUSTER

Mesos is a scalable and fault-tolerant distributed systems kernel written in C++. Running Spark in a Mesos cluster also has advantages. Unlike YARN, Mesos supports C++ and Python applications. And unlike YARN and a standalone Spark cluster, which only schedule memory, Mesos provides scheduling of other types of resources (for example, CPU, disk space, and ports), although these additional resources aren't used by Spark in the current release (1.6). Mesos has additional options for job scheduling that other cluster types don't have (for example, fine-grained mode).

Mesos is a "scheduler of scheduler frameworks" because of its two-level scheduling architecture. The jury is still out on whether YARN or Mesos is better; but now, with the Myriad project (http://myriad.incubator.apache.org/), you can run YARN on top of Mesos to solve the dilemma. We'll discuss YARN and Mesos in chapter 12.

SPARK LOCAL MODES

Spark local mode and Spark local cluster mode are special cases of a Spark standalone cluster running on a single machine. Because these cluster types are easy to set up and use, they're convenient for quick tests, but they shouldn't be used in a production environment.

Furthermore, in these local modes, the workload isn't distributed, thus providing the resource restrictions of a single machine and suboptimal performance. Of course, true high availability isn't possible on a single machine. We'll get into the details in section 10.6.

10.2 *Job and resource scheduling*

Resources for Spark applications are scheduled as executors (JVM processes) and CPU (task slots) and then memory is allocated to them. The cluster manager of the currently running cluster and the Spark scheduler grant resources for execution of Spark jobs.

The cluster manager starts the executor processes requested by the driver and starts the driver process itself when running in cluster-deploy mode. The cluster manager can also restart and stop the processes it has started and can set the maximum number of CPUs that executor processes can use.

Once the application's driver and executors are running, the Spark scheduler communicates with them directly and decides which executors will run which tasks. This is called *job scheduling*, and it affects CPU resource usage in the cluster. Indirectly, it also affects memory use, because more tasks running in a single JVM use more of its heap. The memory, however, isn't directly managed at the task level like CPU is. Spark manages the JVM heap memory allocated by the cluster manager by separating it into several segments, as you'll soon learn.

A set of dedicated executors is allocated for each Spark application running in a cluster. If several Spark applications (and, possibly, applications of other types) run in a single cluster, they compete for the cluster's resources.

Thus, two levels of Spark resource scheduling exist:

- *Cluster resource scheduling* for allocating resources for Spark executors of different Spark applications
- *Spark resource scheduling* for scheduling CPU and memory resources within a single application

10.2.1 *Cluster resource scheduling*

Cluster resource scheduling (dividing cluster resources among several applications running in a single cluster) is the responsibility of the cluster manager. This works similarly on all cluster types supported by Spark, but with minor differences.

All supported cluster managers provide requested resources for each application and free up the requested resources when the application closes. Mesos is unique among the three cluster types: its fine-grained scheduler can allocate resources for each task, instead of for each application. This way, an application can use resources not currently requested by other applications.

For more details, we'll explain standalone clusters in chapter 11 and Mesos and YARN clusters in chapter 12. You'll learn about Spark local modes at the end of this chapter.

10.2.2 *Spark job scheduling*

Once the cluster manager allocates CPU and memory resources for the executors, scheduling of jobs occurs within the Spark application. Job scheduling depends solely on Spark and doesn't rely on the cluster manager. It's implemented by a mechanism for deciding how to split jobs into tasks and how to choose which executors will execute them. As you saw in chapter 4, Spark creates jobs, stages, and tasks based on the RDD's lineage. The scheduler then distributes these tasks to executors and monitors their execution.

It's also possible for several users (multiple threads) to use the same `SparkContext` object simultaneously (`SparkContext` is thread-safe). In that case, several jobs of the same `SparkContext` compete for its executors' resources.

Figures 10.1 and 10.2 showed each driver using a single scheduler for distributing tasks. Actually, several scheduling objects are in play, but all of them can be abstracted as a single one, as shown in the figures.

Spark grants CPU resources in one of two ways: *FIFO* (first-in-first-out) *scheduling* and *fair scheduling*. The Spark parameter `spark.scheduler.mode` sets the scheduler mode, and it takes two possible values: `FAIR` and `FIFO`. (For details on setting Spark parameters, see section 10.3.)

FIFO SCHEDULING

FIFO scheduling functions on the principle of first-come, first-served. The first job that requests resources takes up all the necessary (and available) executor task slots (assume each job consists of only one stage).

If there are 500 task slots in the cluster, and the first job requires only 50, other jobs can use the remaining 450 while the first job runs. But if the first job requires 800 task slots, all the other jobs must wait until the first job's tasks have released executor resources. Figure 10.3 shows another example.

In this example, a driver has 2 executors, each having 6 task slots, and 2 Spark jobs to run. The first job has 15 tasks that need to be executed, 12 of which are currently executing. The second job has 6 tasks, but they need to wait because job 1 was first to request the resources. Compare this figure with the fair scheduler example in figure 10.4. FIFO scheduling is the default scheduler mode, and it works best if your application is a single-user application that is running only one job at a time.

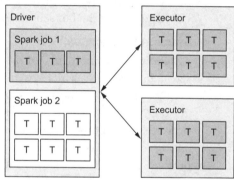

Figure 10.3 FIFO scheduling mode with two jobs and two executors. Tasks from job 2 must wait until all tasks from the job 1 finish executing.

FAIR SCHEDULING

Fair scheduling evenly distributes available resources (executor threads) among competing Spark jobs in a round-robin fashion. It's a better option for multiuser applications running several jobs simultaneously. Spark's fair scheduler was inspired by YARN's fair scheduler (described in chapter 12). Figure 10.4 provides an example.

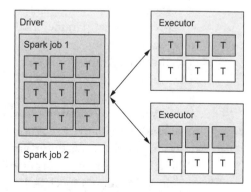

Figure 10.4 Fair scheduling mode with two jobs and two executors. Tasks from job 2 execute in parallel with tasks from job 1, although job 1 was first to request resources.

The number of jobs and tasks in the example is the same as in the FIFO scheduling example, so that you can see the difference between the two scheduling modes. Tasks from job 2 are now executing in parallel with the tasks from job 1. Other tasks from job 1 are waiting for free task slots. In this way, a shorter-running job (job 2) can run immediately without having to wait for the longer-running job (job 1) to finish, although job 2 wasn't the first to request task slots.

The fair scheduler has a concept of *scheduler pools* that is similar to YARN's queues covered in chapter 12. Each pool has *weight* value, which determines the number of resources its jobs have in comparison to jobs from other pools, and a *minimum share* value, which determines the number of CPU cores the pool has at its disposal at all times.

You specify the pool configuration by setting the `spark.scheduler.allocation` `.file` parameter, which must point to an XML configuration file. You can find an example XML configuration in the <SPARK_HOME>/conf/fairscheduler.xml.template file. Using pools with the fair scheduler lets you set priorities for different users or job types.

SPECULATIVE EXECUTION OF TASKS

An additional option for configuring the way Spark dispatches tasks to executors is *speculative execution*, which attempts to solve the problem of *stragglers* (tasks that are taking longer to finish than other tasks at the same stage). One of your executors may get bogged down with some other process, using up all of its CPU resources, which prevents it from finishing your tasks in a timely fashion. In that case, if speculative execution is turned on, Spark may try to run the same task for that partition on some other executor. If that happens and the new task finishes, Spark accepts the results of the new task and discards the old task's results. That way, a single malfunctioning executor doesn't cause the job to stall.

Speculative execution is turned off by default. Turn it on by setting the `spark.speculation` parameter to `true`. When turned on, Spark checks every `spark.speculation.interval` setting to determine whether any of the tasks need to be restarted.

Two additional parameters determine the criteria for selecting which tasks need to be started again. `spark.speculation.quantile` determines the percentage of tasks that need to complete before speculation is started for a stage, and `spark.speculation.multiplier` sets how many times a task needs to run before it needs to be restarted.

For some jobs (for example, those that write to external systems such as relational databases), speculative execution isn't desirable because two tasks can run simultaneously on the same partition and can write the same data to the external system. Although one task may finish earlier than the other, it may be prudent to explicitly disable speculation, especially if you don't have complete control over Spark's configuration affecting your application.

10.2.3 *Data-locality considerations*

Data locality means Spark tries to run tasks as close to the data location as possible. This affects the selection of executors on which to run tasks and is, therefore, related to job scheduling.

Spark tries to maintain a list of preferred locations for each partition. A partition's *preferred location* is a list of hostnames or executors where the partition's data resides so that computation can be moved closer to the data. This information can be obtained for RDDs that are based on HDFS data (HadoopRDD) and for cached RDDs.

In the case of RDDs based on HDFS data, the Hadoop API gets this information from an HDFS cluster. In the case of cached RDDs, Spark itself tracks which executor each partition is cached on.

If Spark obtains a list of preferred locations, the Spark scheduler tries to run tasks on the executors where the data is physically present so that no data transfer is required. This can have a big impact on performance.

There are five levels of data locality:

- PROCESS_LOCAL—Execute a task on the executor that cached the partition.
- NODE_LOCAL—Execute a task on the node where the partition is available.
- RACK_LOCAL—Execute the task on the same rack as the partition if rack information is available in the cluster (currently only on YARN).
- NO_PREF—No preferred locations are associated with the task.
- ANY—Default if everything else fails.

If a task slot with the best locality for the task can't be obtained (that is, all the matching task slots are taken), the scheduler waits a certain amount of time and then tries a location with the second-best locality, and so on. The Locality Level column in the Tasks table (section 10.4.2) on the Stage Details page of the Spark web UI shows the locality level for a specific task.

The amount of time the scheduler waits for each locality level before moving to the next is determined by the spark.locality.wait parameter. The default is 30 seconds. You can also set wait times for specific locality levels with spark.locality.wait.process, spark.locality.wait.node, and spark.locality.wait.rack. If any of these parameters is set to 0, the corresponding level is ignored, and tasks won't be assigned according to that level.

If you set any of these wait times to a much higher value, you'll force the scheduler to always honor the desired locality level by waiting until it becomes available. For example, you can force HDFS data to be always processed on the node where the data resides by increasing spark.locality.wait.node to 10 minutes. This also means a wait of 10 minutes is theoretically possible if something gets stuck on the node in question. Use a high value in situations where data locality is of critical importance (that is, other nodes should not be allowed to process the data).

10.2.4 *Spark memory scheduling*

We'll now move away from CPU resource scheduling and see how Spark schedules memory resources. We said previously that the cluster manager allocates memory for Spark executor JVM processes (and for the driver process, if the driver is running in cluster-deploy mode). Once memory is allocated, Spark schedules and manages its usage with jobs and tasks. Memory problems can be frequent in Spark programs, so it's important to understand how Spark manages memory and how you can configure its management.

MEMORY MANAGED BY THE CLUSTER MANAGER

You set the amount of memory you want allocated for your executors with the `spark.executor.memory` parameter. (Setting Spark parameters is discussed in the next section.) You can use the `g` (for gigabytes) and `m` (for megabytes) suffixes. The default executor memory size is 512 MB (`512m`).

The cluster manager allocates the amount of memory specified with the `spark.executor.memory` parameter. Spark then uses and partitions that memory.

MEMORY MANAGED BY SPARK

Spark reserves parts of that memory for cached data storage and for temporary shuffle data. Set the heap for these with the parameters `spark.storage.memoryFraction` (default 0.6) and `spark.shuffle.memoryFraction` (default 0.2). Because these parts of the heap can grow before Spark can measure and limit them, two additional safety parameters must be set: `spark.storage.safetyFraction` (default 0.9) and `spark.shuffle.safetyFraction` (default 0.8). Safety parameters lower the memory fraction by the amount specified, as shown in figure 10.5.

The actual part of the heap used for storage by default is 0.6×0.9 (safety fraction times the storage memory fraction), which equals 54%. Similarly, the part of the heap used for shuffle data is 0.2×0.8 (safety fraction times the shuffle memory fraction), which equals 16%.

You then have 30% of the heap reserved for other Java objects and resources needed to run tasks. You should, however, count on only 20%.

SETTING THE DRIVER MEMORY

You set the memory for your driver with the `spark.driver.memory` parameter. This parameter applies when you're starting your application with `spark-shell` and `spark-submit` scripts (both in cluster and client-deploy modes).

If you start a Spark context programmatically from another application (client mode), then that application contains

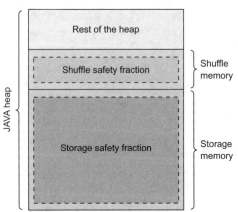

Figure 10.5   Fractions of memory on Spark executors

your driver. Therefore, to increase the memory available to your driver, use the -Xmx Java option to set the maximum size of the Java heap of the containing process.

10.3 Configuring Spark

You affect how Spark runs by setting configuration parameters. For example, you'll most likely need to adjust the memory for the driver and executors (as we discussed in the previous section) or the classpath for your Spark application. Although specifying these settings is straightforward and common to other similar frameworks, a few details aren't so obvious. It is worth spending a few moments to study the different ways of configuring Spark.

Here we'll only describe the *mechanisms* for specifying various runtime parameters and not the specific configuration options themselves. We explain specific parameters throughout the book in the appropriate context. You can check the official documentation (http://spark.apache.org/docs/latest/configuration.html) for a list of currently valid configuration parameters.

You can specify Spark configuration parameters using several methods: on the command line, in Spark configuration files, as system environment variables, and from within user programs. The SparkConf object, accessible through SparkContext, contains all currently applied configuration parameters. Parameters specified with the methods described here all end up in the SparkConf object. As you've seen in previous chapters, when using spark-shell, SparkContext is already instantiated, preconfigured, and available as the variable sc. You can get the SparkConf object with its getConf method:

```
scala> sc.getConf
```

10.3.1 Spark configuration file

You specify default Spark parameters in the <spark_home>/conf/spark-defaults.conf file. If not otherwise specified, the values from this file are applied to your Spark runtime, no matter what method you use to start Spark.

You can override the filename from the command line using the parameter --properties-file. That way, you can maintain a different set of parameters for specific applications and specify a different configuration file for each one.

10.3.2 Command-line parameters

You can use command-line parameters as arguments to the spark-shell and spark-submit commands. These parameters are passed to a SparkConf object in the REPL shell (when using the spark-shell command) or in your program (when using the spark-submit command). They take precedence over arguments specified in the Spark configuration file.

NOTE As you probably recall from chapter 3, you have to specify a JAR file containing your application when using spark-submit. Make sure you specify any arguments you want to pass to your application *after* the JAR filename and any Spark configuration parameters *before* the JAR filename.

The names of Spark command-line parameters are different than their counterparts in Spark's configuration file. Furthermore, only some Spark configuration parameters have command-line versions. For example, these two lines accomplish the same thing (set the driver's memory to 16 GB):

```
spark-shell --driver-memory 16g
spark-shell --conf spark.driver.memory=16g
```

You can get a complete list of command-line parameters by running `spark-shell` (or `spark-submit`) with the `--help` option.

You can also use the `--conf` command-line argument to set any Spark configuration parameter, using its name as it appears in the configuration file. Specify a separate `--conf` argument for each configuration parameter you want to set.

10.3.3 *System environment variables*

Some configuration parameters can be specified in the spark-env.sh file in the <SPARK_HOME>/conf directory. You can also set their defaults as OS environment variables. Parameters specified using this method have the lowest priority of all configuration methods.

Most of these variables have a Spark configuration file counterpart. For example, in addition to the two methods for setting the driver's memory mentioned earlier, you can specify it by setting the `SPARK_DRIVER_MEMORY` system environment variable.

You can speed up creation of the spark-env.sh file by changing the spark-env.sh.template file that Spark provides. In that file, you can find all possible variables that can be used in spark-env.sh.

> **NOTE** If you change spark-env.sh, and you're running the Spark standalone cluster, you should copy the file to all worker machines so that all executors run with the same configuration.

10.3.4 *Setting configuration programmatically*

You can set Spark configuration parameters directly in your program by using the `SparkConf` class. For example:

```
val conf = new org.apache.spark.SparkConf()
conf.set("spark.driver.memory", "16g")
val sc = new org.apache.spark.SparkContext(conf)
```

Note that the Spark configuration can't be changed at runtime using this method, so you need to set up the `SparkConf` object with all the configuration options you need *before* creating the `SparkContext` object. Otherwise, `SparkContext` uses the default Spark configuration, and your options aren't applied. Any parameters set this way have precedence over parameters set with the methods mentioned previously (they have the highest priority).

10.3.5 *The master parameter*

The `master` parameter tells Spark which cluster type to use. When running `spark-shell` and `spark-submit` commands, you define this parameter like this:

```
spark-submit --master <master_connection_url>
```

When specifying it from your application, you can do it in this way

```
val conf = org.apache.spark.SparkConf()
conf.set("spark.master", "<master_connection_url>")
```

or you can use `SparkConf`'s `setMaster` method:

```
conf.setMaster("<master_connection_url>")
```

`<master_connection_url>` varies according to the type of cluster used (which will be duly explained).

If you're submitting your application as a JAR file, it's best not to set the `master` parameter in the application, because doing so reduces its portability. In that case, specify it as a parameter to `spark-submit` so that you can run the same JAR file on different clusters by only changing the `master` parameter. Setting it in your application is an option when you're only embedding Spark as part of other functionalities.

10.3.6 *Viewing all configured parameters*

To see the list of all options explicitly defined and loaded in the current Spark context, call the `sc.getConf.getAll` method in your program (assuming `sc` is the `SparkContext` instance). For example, this snippet prints the current configuration options:

```
scala> sc.getConf.getAll.foreach(x => println(x._1+": "+x._2))
spark.app.id: local-1524799343426
spark.driver.memory: 16g
spark.driver.host: <your_hostname>
spark.app.name: Spark shell
...
```

To see the complete list of configured parameters affecting your Spark application, consult the Environment page of the Spark web UI (see section 10.4.4).

10.4 *Spark web UI*

Each time a `SparkContext` object is initialized, Spark starts a web UI, providing information about the Spark environment and job execution statistics. The web UI default port is 4040, but if that port is already taken (by another Spark web UI, for example), Spark adds to the port number until it finds one that's free.

When starting a Spark shell, you'll see an output line similar to this one (unless you turned off INFO log messages):

```
SparkUI: Started SparkUI at http://svgubuntu01:4040
```

NOTE   You can disable the Spark web UI by setting the `spark.ui.enabled` configuration parameter to `false`. You can change its port with the `spark.ui.port` parameter.

An example Spark web UI Welcome page is shown in figure 10.6. This web UI was started from a Spark shell, so its name is set to Spark shell, as shown in the upper-right corner of the figure. You can change the application name that is displayed in the Spark web UI by programmatically calling the `setAppName` method of your `SparkConf` object. You can also set it on the command line when running the `spark-submit` command with `--conf spark.app.name=<new_name>`, but you can't change the application name when starting a Spark shell. In that case, it always defaults to Spark shell.

10.4.1   Jobs page

The Welcome page of the Spark web UI (figure 10.6) provides statistics about running, completed, and failed jobs. For each job, you see when it started, how long it ran, and how many stages and tasks it ran. (For a refresher on Spark jobs and stages, see section 4.6.2.)

If you click a job description, you see information about its completed and failed stages. Click a stage again in the table to display the Stage Details page.

By clicking the Timeline link, you get a graphical representation of jobs as they executed over the time. An example is shown in figure 10.7. Clicking a job in the timeline view also takes you to the Job Details page, where you can see its completed and failed stages (see figure 10.8).

Figure 10.6   The Spark web UI Jobs page shows information about active, completed, and failed jobs. Column headings describe the information.

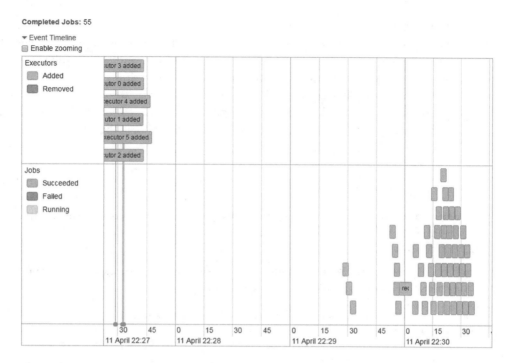

Figure 10.7 Timeline view showing when each job started and when it finished

Stages for All Jobs

Active Stages: 1
Pending Stages: 169
Completed Stages: 426

Active Stages (1)

Stage Id	Description		Submitted	Duration	Tasks: Succeeded/Total	Input	Output	Shuffle Read	Shuffle Write
41164	mapPartitions at VertexRDDImpl.scala:251	(kill) +details	2016/04/11 22:53:44	52 ms	3/6	202.5 KB			47.7 KB

Pending Stages (169)

Stage Id	Description		Submitted	Duration	Tasks: Succeeded/Total	Input	Output	Shuffle Read	Shuffle Write
41037	mapPartitions at VertexRDDImpl.scala:251	+details	Unknown	Unknown	0/6				
41028	mapPartitions at VertexRDDImpl.scala:247	+details	Unknown	Unknown	0/6				
41082	mapPartitions at VertexRDDImpl.scala:247	+details	Unknown	Unknown	0/6				
41046	mapPartitions at VertexRDD.scala:358	+details	Unknown	Unknown	0/6				
41073	mapPartitions at GraphImpl.scala:235	+details	Unknown	Unknown	0/6				

Figure 10.8 Spark web UI Stages page showing stage duration, number of tasks, and amount of data read or written

## 10.4.2	*Stages page*

The Stages page (figure 10.8) provides summary information about job stages. There you can see when each stage started, how long it ran or whether it's still running, how large its input and output were, and shuffle reads and writes.

When you click a Details link, you see a stack trace from the point in the code where the stage started. If you set the `spark.ui.killEnabled` parameter to `true`, an additional option *(Kill)* appears next to the Details link (see figure 10.9).

Description		
foreach at SampleApp.scala:22	+details	(kill)

**Figure 10.9	The option to kill a long-running stage is available after setting the `spark.ui`
`.killEnabled` parameter.**

After you click the Kill link and confirm your choice, the stage is terminated, and a stack trace similar to this one appears in your log file:

```
15/03/20 09:58:25 INFO DAGScheduler: Job 0 failed: foreach at
➥ SampleApp.scala:22, took 59,125413 s
Exception in thread "main" org.apache.spark.SparkException: Job 0 cancelled
➥ because Stage 0 was cancelled
        at org.apache.spark.scheduler.DAGScheduler....
```

To open the Stage Details page (figure 10.10), click a stage description. On the Stage Details page, you can find useful information for debugging the state of your jobs. If you see problems with the duration of your jobs, you can use these pages to quickly drill down to the problematic stages and tasks and narrow the problem.

If, for example, you see excessive GC time, that's a signal to increase the available memory or to increase the number of RDD partitions (which lowers the number of elements in partitions, thus lowering memory consumption). If you see excessive shuffle reads and writes, you may want to change your program logic to avoid unnecessary shuffling. The page also shows the stage timeline graph with details about how long it took to execute each subcomponent of task processing: task serialization, computation, shuffling and so on.

If your Spark job uses accumulators, the appropriate Stage Details page displays a section similar to the one shown in figure 10.11. In the Accumulators section, you can track the value of each accumulator used in your program. As we mentioned in section 4.5.1, you need to use a named accumulator in order for it to appear here.

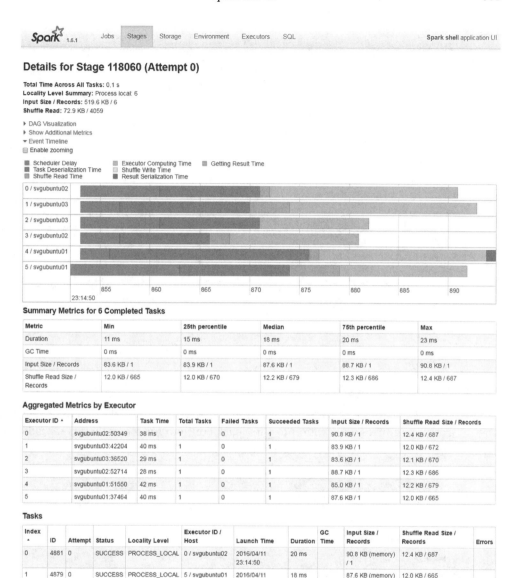

Figure 10.10   Spark web UI Stage Details page showing stage and task metrics useful for debugging the state of Spark jobs

Accumulators

Accumulable	Value
Test accumulator	10000

Figure 10.11   Accumulators section of the Stage Details page showing the current count of your accumulators

10.4.3 Storage page

The Storage page gives you information about your cached RDDs and how much memory, Tachyon storage, or disk space the cached data is consuming. For the example in figure 10.12, several small RDDs are cached in memory.

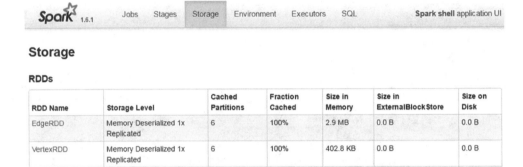

RDD Name	Storage Level	Cached Partitions	Fraction Cached	Size in Memory	Size in ExternalBlockStore	Size on Disk
EdgeRDD	Memory Deserialized 1x Replicated	6	100%	2.9 MB	0.0 B	0.0 B
VertexRDD	Memory Deserialized 1x Replicated	6	100%	402.8 KB	0.0 B	0.0 B
VertexRDD	Memory Deserialized 1x Replicated	8	133%	473.0 KB	0.0 B	0.0 B
ZippedWithIndexRDD	Memory Deserialized 1x Replicated	10	167%	843.0 KB	0.0 B	0.0 B
EdgeRDD	Memory Deserialized 1x	6	100%	2.9 MB	0.0 B	0.0 B

Figure 10.12   Spark web UI Storage page showing cached RDD metrics

10.4.4 Environment page

On the Environment page, you see Java and Scala versions, Java system properties, and classpath entries, in addition to the Spark configuration parameters we talked about previously. An example is shown in figure 10.13.

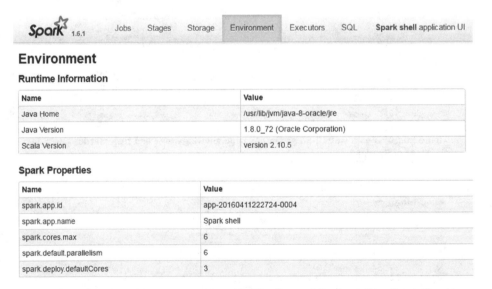

Figure 10.13   Spark web UI Environment page showing Java and Spark configuration parameters

10.4.5 Executors page

The Executors page (see figure 10.14) gives you a list of all executors configured in your cluster (including the driver) with information about available and used memory and other statistics aggregated per executor/driver. The amount of memory shown in the Memory Used column is the amount of storage memory, which by default is equal to 54% of the heap, as described in section 10.2.4.

Click the Thread Dump link to take current stack traces of all threads for a particular executor. This can be useful for debugging purposes when waits and deadlocks are slowing the execution of your program.

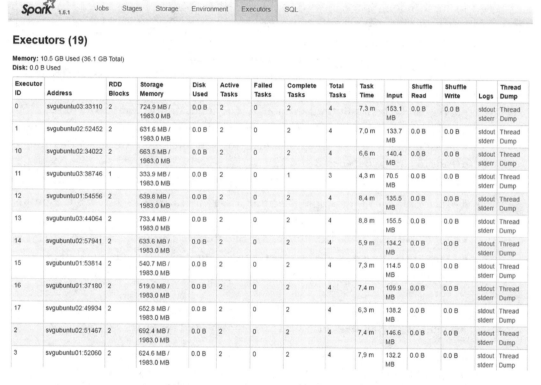

Executors (19)

Memory: 10.5 GB Used (36.1 GB Total)
Disk: 0.0 B Used

Executor ID	Address	RDD Blocks	Storage Memory	Disk Used	Active Tasks	Failed Tasks	Complete Tasks	Total Tasks	Task Time	Input	Shuffle Read	Shuffle Write	Logs	Thread Dump
0	svgubuntu03:33110	2	724.9 MB / 1983.0 MB	0.0 B	2	0	2	4	7.3 m	153.1 MB	0.0 B	0.0 B	stdout stderr	Thread Dump
1	svgubuntu02:52452	2	631.6 MB / 1983.0 MB	0.0 B	2	0	2	4	7.0 m	133.7 MB	0.0 B	0.0 B	stdout stderr	Thread Dump
10	svgubuntu02:34022	2	663.5 MB / 1983.0 MB	0.0 B	2	0	2	4	6.6 m	140.4 MB	0.0 B	0.0 B	stdout stderr	Thread Dump
11	svgubuntu03:38746	1	333.9 MB / 1983.0 MB	0.0 B	2	0	1	3	4.3 m	70.5 MB	0.0 B	0.0 B	stdout stderr	Thread Dump
12	svgubuntu01:54556	2	639.8 MB / 1983.0 MB	0.0 B	2	0	2	4	8.4 m	135.5 MB	0.0 B	0.0 B	stdout stderr	Thread Dump
13	svgubuntu03:44064	2	733.4 MB / 1983.0 MB	0.0 B	2	0	2	4	8.8 m	155.5 MB	0.0 B	0.0 B	stdout stderr	Thread Dump
14	svgubuntu02:57941	2	633.6 MB / 1983.0 MB	0.0 B	2	0	2	4	5.9 m	134.2 MB	0.0 B	0.0 B	stdout stderr	Thread Dump
15	svgubuntu01:53814	2	540.7 MB / 1983.0 MB	0.0 B	2	0	2	4	7.3 m	114.5 MB	0.0 B	0.0 B	stdout stderr	Thread Dump
16	svgubuntu01:37180	2	519.0 MB / 1983.0 MB	0.0 B	2	0	2	4	7.4 m	109.9 MB	0.0 B	0.0 B	stdout stderr	Thread Dump
17	svgubuntu02:49934	2	652.8 MB / 1983.0 MB	0.0 B	2	0	2	4	6.3 m	138.2 MB	0.0 B	0.0 B	stdout stderr	Thread Dump
2	svgubuntu02:51467	2	692.4 MB / 1983.0 MB	0.0 B	2	0	2	4	7.4 m	146.6 MB	0.0 B	0.0 B	stdout stderr	Thread Dump
3	svgubuntu01:52060	2	624.6 MB / 1983.0 MB	0.0 B	2	0	2	4	7.9 m	132.2 MB	0.0 B	0.0 B	stdout stderr	Thread Dump

Figure 10.14 Spark web UI Executors page showing executors' addresses; number of RDD blocks; amount of memory and disk used; number of active, failed, and complete tasks; and other useful metrics

10.5 Running Spark on the local machine

Now that we've acquainted you with the basics of running Spark and its architecture, we can start exploring different Spark runtime modes. To begin, we'll look into two ways of running Spark on a local machine: local mode and local cluster mode.

10.5.1   *Local mode*

We mostly used Spark local mode to run the
examples in the previous chapters. This
mode is convenient for testing purposes
when you don't have access to a full cluster
or you want to try something out quickly.

In local mode, there is only one executor in the same client JVM as the driver, but
this executor can spawn several threads to
run tasks. This is illustrated in figure 10.15.

In local mode, Spark uses your client
process as the single executor in the cluster, and the number of threads specified
determines how many tasks can be executed in parallel. You can specify more
threads than available CPU cores. That way,

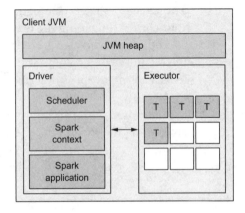

**Figure 10.15   Spark running in local mode.
The driver and the single executor are running
in the same JVM.**

CPU cores can be better utilized. Although it depends on the complexity of your jobs,
multiplying the number of CPU cores by two or three gives you a good starting point
for this parameter (for example, for a machine with quad-core CPUs, set the number
of threads to a value between 8 and 12).

To run Spark in local mode, set the `master` parameter to one of the following values:

- `local[<n>]`—Run a single executor using <n> threads, where <n> is a positive
  integer.
- `local`—Run a single executor using one thread. This is the same as `local[1]`.
- `local[*]`—Run a single executor using a number of threads equal to the number of CPU cores available on the local machine. In other words, use up all CPU
  cores.
- `local[<n>,<f>]`—Run a single executor using <n> threads, and allow a maximum of <f> failures per task. This is mostly used for Spark internal tests.

NOTE   If you use `--master local` with only one thread, you may notice that
your log lines are missing from the driver's output. That's because in Spark
Streaming, for example, that single thread is used to read streaming data
from a source, and the driver wouldn't have any threads left to print out the
results of your program. If you want the output printed to your log file, be
sure to specify at least two threads (`local[2]`).

If you start a `spark-shell` or `spark-submit` script with no `--master` parameter,
(`local[*]`), local mode taking all CPU cores is assumed.

10.5.2 *Local cluster mode*

The second method of running Spark on the local machine is local cluster mode. Local cluster mode is intended mostly for Spark internal tests, but it can be useful for quick tests and demonstrations requiring inter-process communication.

Local cluster mode is a full Spark standalone cluster running on the local machine. The difference between local cluster mode and full standalone cluster is that the master isn't a separate process but runs in the client JVM. Most configuration parameters affecting the Spark standalone cluster can be applied to local cluster mode, too. We'll go into the details of a Spark standalone cluster in the next chapter, so we won't explain them here.

You start Spark in local cluster mode by setting the `master` parameter to the value `local-cluster[<n>,<c>,<m>]` (without spaces). This means that you're running a local Spark standalone cluster with <n> executors, each using <c> threads and <m> megabytes of memory. (Specify memory only as an integer representing megabytes. Don't use the `g` or `m` suffixes here.) Each executor in local cluster mode runs in a separate JVM, which makes it similar to a Spark standalone cluster, covered in the next chapter.

10.6 *Summary*

- Typical components of the Spark runtime architecture are the client process, the driver, and the executors.
- Spark can run in two deploy modes: client-deploy mode and cluster-deploy mode. This depends on the location of the driver process.
- Spark supports three cluster managers: Spark standalone cluster, YARN, and Mesos. Spark local modes are special cases of the Spark standalone cluster.
- The cluster manager manages (schedules) resources for Spark executors of different Spark applications.
- Spark itself schedules CPU and memory resources in a single application in two possible modes: FIFO scheduling and fair scheduling.
- Data locality means Spark tries to run tasks as close to the data location as possible; five locality levels exist.
- Spark directly manages memory available to its executors by partitioning it into storage memory, shuffle memory, and the rest of the heap.
- Spark can be configured through the configuration file, using command-line parameters, using system environment variables, and programmatically.
- The Spark web UI shows useful information about running jobs, stages, and tasks.
- Spark local mode runs the entire cluster in a single JVM and is useful for testing purposes.
- Spark local cluster mode is a full Spark standalone cluster running on the local machine, with the master process running in the client JVM.

11
Running on a
Spark standalone cluster

After describing common aspects of running Spark and examining Spark local modes in chapter 10, now we get to the first "real" Spark cluster type. The Spark standalone cluster is a Spark-specific cluster: it was built specifically for Spark, and it can't execute any other type of application. It's relatively simple and efficient and comes with Spark out of the box, so you can use it even if you don't have a YARN or Mesos installation.

In this chapter, we'll explain the runtime components of a standalone cluster and how to configure and control those components. A Spark standalone cluster comes with its own web UI, and we'll show you how to use it to monitor cluster processes and running applications. A useful component for this is Spark's History Server; we'll also show you how to use it and explain why you should.

Spark provides scripts for quickly spinning up a standalone cluster on Amazon EC2. (If you aren't acquainted with it, Amazon EC2 is Amazon's cloud service, offering virtual servers for rent.) We'll walk you through how to do that. Let's get started.

11.1 Spark standalone cluster components

A standalone cluster comes bundled with Spark. It has a simple architecture and is easy to install and configure. Because it was built and optimized specifically for Spark, it has no extra functionalities with unnecessary generalizations, requirements, and configuration options, each with its own bugs. In short, the Spark standalone cluster is simple and fast.

The standalone cluster consists of master and worker (also called *slave*) processes. A master process acts as the cluster manager, as we mentioned in chapter 10. It accepts applications to be run and schedules worker resources (available CPU cores) among them. Worker processes launch application executors (and the driver for applications in cluster-deploy mode) for task execution. To refresh your memory, a driver orchestrates and monitors execution of Spark jobs, and executors execute a job's tasks.

Both masters and workers can be run on a single machine, essentially becoming Spark in local cluster mode (described in chapter 10), but this isn't how a Spark standalone cluster usually runs. You normally distribute workers across several nodes to avoid reaching the limits of a single machine's resources.

Naturally, Spark has to be installed on all nodes in the cluster in order for them to be usable as slaves. Installing Spark means unpacking a binary distribution or building your own version from Spark source files (for details, please see the official documentation at http://spark.apache.org/docs/latest/building-spark.html).

Figure 11.1 shows an example Spark standalone cluster running on two nodes with two workers:

Step 1. A client process submits an application to the master.

Step 2. The master instructs one of its workers to launch a driver.

Step 3. The worker spawns a driver JVM.

Step 4. The master instructs both workers to launch executors for the application.

Step 5. The workers spawn executor JVMs.

Step 6. The driver and executors communicate independent of the cluster's processes.

Each executor has a certain number of threads (CPU cores) allocated to it, which are task slots for running multiple tasks in parallel. In a Spark standalone cluster, for each application, there can be only one executor per worker process. If you need more executors per machine, you can start multiple worker processes. You may want to do this if your JVM heap is really large (greater than 64 GB) and GC is starting to affect job performance.

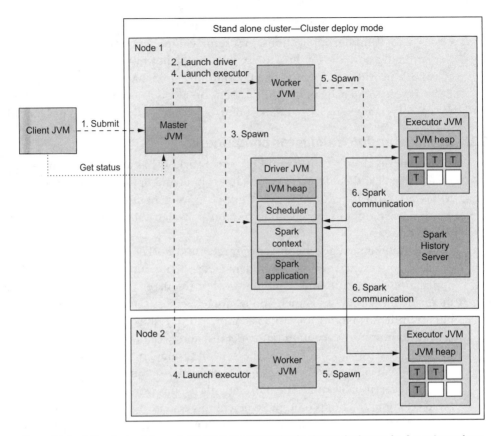

Figure 11.1   A Spark standalone cluster with an application in cluster-deploy mode. A master and one worker are running on Node 1, and the second worker is running on Node 2. Workers are spawning drivers' and executors' JVMs.

The driver in figure 11.1 is running in the cluster or, in other words, in cluster-deploy mode. As we said in chapter 10, it can also run in the client JVM, which is called *client-deploy mode.*

We should also mention that only one application is shown running in this cluster. If there were more, each would have its own set of executors and a separate driver running either in the cluster, like this one, or in its client's JVM (depending on the deploy mode).

An optional History Server is also shown in figure 11.1. It's used for viewing the Spark web UI after the application has exited. We'll explain this feature in more detail in section 11.5.

11.2 *Starting the standalone cluster*

Unlike starting Spark in one of the local cluster modes you saw in chapter 10, you must start a Spark standalone cluster before submitting an application or prior to starting the Spark shell. When the cluster is running, connect your application to the cluster using the master connection URL. A master connection URL for a standalone cluster has the following syntax:

```
spark://master_hostname:port
```

If you have a standby master process running (see section 11.2.4), you can specify several addresses:

```
spark://master1_hostname:port1,master2_hostname:port2
```

To start the standalone cluster, you have two basic options: use Spark-provided scripts or start the components manually.

11.2.1 *Starting the cluster with shell scripts*

Startup scripts are the most convenient way to start Spark. They set up the proper environment and load your Spark default configuration. In order for scripts to run correctly, Spark should be installed at the same location on all the nodes in the cluster.

Spark provides three scripts for starting standalone-cluster components (you can find them in the *SPARK_HOME*/sbin directory):

- `start-master.sh` starts the master process.
- `start-slaves.sh` starts all defined worker processes.
- `start-all.sh` starts both master and worker processes.

Counterpart scripts for stopping the processes are also available: `stop-master.sh`, `stop-slaves.sh`, and `stop-all.sh`.

> **NOTE** On a Windows platform, no scripts for starting and stopping a standalone cluster are provided. The only option is to start and stop the cluster manually, as explained in section 11.2.2.

START-MASTER.SH

`start-master.sh` starts the master process. It takes no arguments and shows just one line when started:

```
$ sbin/start-master.sh
starting org.apache.spark.deploy.master.Master, logging to log_file
```

You can use the log file that the script outputs to find the command used to start the master and the master's runtime messages. The default log file is *SPARK_HOME*/logs/spark-*username*-org.apache.spark.deploy.master.Master-1-*hostname*.out.

To customize the `start-master.sh` script, you can use the system environment variables listed in table 11.1. The best way to apply them is to put them in the spark-env.sh file in the conf folder. (If it doesn't exist, you can use the spark-env.sh.template as a starting point.) The Java parameters in table 11.2 can be specified in the SPARK _MASTER_OPTS variable in this format:

```
-Dparam1_name=param1_value -Dparam2_name=param2_value
```

Table 11.1 System environment variables affecting the behavior of the `start-master.sh` script

System environment variable	Description
SPARK_MASTER_IP	Hostname the master should bind to.
SPARK_MASTER_PORT	Port the master should bind to (default is 7077).
SPARK_MASTER_WEBUI_PORT	Port on which the cluster web UI (described in section 11.4.3) should be started.
SPARK_DAEMON_MEMORY	Amount of heap memory to give the master and worker Java processes (default is 512 MB). The same parameter applies both to worker and master processes. Note that this only affects cluster daemon processes and not the driver or executors.
SPARK_MASTER_OPTS	Lets you pass additional Java parameters to the master process.

Table 11.2 Java parameters you can specify in the `SPARK_MASTER_OPTS` environment variable

Java parameter	Description
spark.deploy.defaultCores	Default maximum number of cores to allow per application. Applications can override this by setting the `spark.cores.max` parameter. If it isn't set, applications take all available cores on the machine.
spark.worker.timeout	Maximum number of seconds the master waits for a heartbeat from a worker before considering it lost (default is 60).
spark.dead.worker.persistence	Amount of time (measured as multiples of `spark.worker.timeout`) to keep dead workers displayed in the master web UI (default is 15).
spark.deploy.spreadOut	If set to `true`, which is the default, the master attempts to spread an application's executors across all workers, taking one core at a time. Otherwise, it starts an application's executors on the first free workers it finds, taking all available cores. Spreading out can be better for data locality when working with HDFS, because applications will run on a larger number of nodes, increasing the likelihood of running where data is stored.
spark.master.rest.enabled	Whether to start the standalone REST server for submitting applications (default is `true`). This is transparent to the end user.
spark.master.rest.port	Listening port for the standalone REST server (default is 6066).
spark.deploy.retainedApplications	Number of completed applications to display in the cluster web UI (default is 200).
spark.deploy.retainedDrivers	Number of completed drivers to display in the cluster web UI (default is 200).

In addition to the Java parameters in table 11.2, in the SPARK_MASTER_OPTS environment variable you can specify parameters for master recovery (which we'll describe in section 11.2.4).

START-SLAVES.SH

The start-slaves.sh script is a bit different. Using the SSH protocol, it connects to all machines defined in the *SPARK_HOME*/conf/slaves file and starts a worker process there. For this to work, Spark should be installed at the same location on all machines in the cluster.

A slaves file (similar to a Hadoop slaves file) should contain a list of worker hostnames, each on a separate line. If there are any duplicates in the file, starting additional workers on those machines will fail due to port conflicts. If you need more workers per machine, you can start them manually; or you can set the SPARK_WORKER_INSTANCES environment variable to the number of workers you want on each machine, and the start-slaves.sh script will start all of them automatically.

By default, the script will try to start all workers in tandem. For this, you need to set up *password-less* SSH. You can override this by defining any value for the SPARK_SSH_FOREGROUND environment variable. In that case, the script will start workers serially and allow you to enter a password for each remote machine.

Similar to the start-master.sh script, start-slaves.sh prints the path to the log file for each worker process it starts. The system environment variables listed in table 11.3 let you customize worker behavior.

Table 11.3   System environment variables affecting the behavior of worker processes

System environment variable	Description
SPARK_MASTER_IP	Hostname of the master process with which the worker should register.
SPARK_MASTER_PORT	Port of the master process with which the worker should register.
SPARK_WORKER_WEBUI_PORT	Port on which the worker web UI should be started (default is 8081).
SPARK_WORKER_CORES	Maximum combined number of CPU cores (task slots) for all executors launched by the worker.
SPARK_WORKER_MEMORY	Maximum combined total size of the Java heap for all executors launched by the worker.
SPARK_WORKER_DIR	Directory for the application's log files (and other application files, such as JAR files).
SPARK_WORKER_PORT	Port to which the worker should bind.
SPARK_WORKER_OPTS	Additional Java parameters to pass to the worker process.

The Java parameters specified in table 11.4 can be specified in the SPARK_WORKER _OPTS environment variable in this format:

```
-Dparam1_name=param1_value -Dparam2_name=param2_value
```

Table 11.4 Java parameters that can be specified in the `SPARK_WORKER_OPTS` environment variable

Java parameter	Description
`spark.worker.timeout`	Worker will be declared dead after this many seconds. Worker will send heartbeats to the master every `spark.worker.timeout` / 4 seconds.
`spark.worker.cleanup.enabled`	Interval for cleanup of old applications' log data and other files from the work directory (default is `false`).
`spark.worker.cleanup.interval`	Interval for cleanup of old applications' data (default is 30 minutes).
`spark.worker.cleanup.appDataTtl`	Time in seconds after which an application is considered old (default is 7 days, in seconds).

START-ALL.SH

The `start-all.sh` script calls `start-master.sh` and then `start-slaves.sh`.

11.2.2 *Starting the cluster manually*

Spark also provides an option to start cluster components manually, which is the only option available on a Windows platform. This can be accomplished by calling the `spark-class` script and specifying the complete Spark master or Spark worker class name as an argument. When starting the worker, you also need to specify the master URL. For example:

```
$ spark-class org.apache.spark.deploy.master.Master
$ spark-class org.apache.spark.deploy.worker.Worker spark://<IPADDR>:<PORT>
```

Both commands accept several optional parameters, listed in table 11.5. (Some of the parameters apply only to worker processes, as specified by the Only Worker column.) Starting the processes this way makes it a bit easier to specify these parameters, but starting with `start-all.sh` is still the most convenient method.

Table 11.5 Optional parameters that can be specified when starting masters or workers manually

Optional parameter	Description	Only worker
`-h HOST` or `--host HOST`	Hostname to listen on. For a master, the same as the `SPARK_MASTER_HOST` environment variable.	
`-p PORT` or `--port PORT`	Port to listen on (default is random). Same as `SPARK_WORKER_PORT` for a worker or `SPARK_MASTER_PORT` for a master.	
`--webui-port PORT`	Port for the web UI. Same as `SPARK_MASTER_WEBUI_PORT` or `SPARK_WORKER_WEBUI_PORT`. Default on a master is 8080 and on a worker is 8081.	

Table 11.5 Optional parameters that can be specified when starting masters or workers manually *(continued)*

Optional parameter	Description	Only worker
`--properties-file FILE`	Path to a custom Spark properties file (default is conf/spark-defaults.conf).	
`-c CORES` or `--cores CORES`	Number of cores to use. Same as the `SPARK_WORKER_CORES` environment variable.	P
`-m MEM` or `--memory MEM`	Amount of memory to use (for example, 1000 MB or 2 GB). Same as the `SPARK_WORKER_MEMORY` environment variable.	P
`-d DIR` or `--work-dir DIR`	Directory in which to run applications (default is `SPARK_HOME/work`). Same as the `SPARK_WORKER_DIR` environment variable.	P
`--help`	Shows help for invoking the script.	

11.2.3 Viewing Spark processes

If you're curious which cluster processes are started, you can use the JVM Process Status Tool (`jps` command) to view them. The `jps` command outputs PIDs and the names of JVM processes running on the machine:

```
$ jps
1696 CoarseGrainedExecutorBackend
403 Worker
1519 SparkSubmit
32655 Master
6080 DriverWrapper
```

Master and worker processes appear as `Master` and `Worker`. A driver running in the cluster appears as `DriverWrapper`, and a driver spawned by the `spark-submit` command (that also includes `spark-shell`) appears as `SparkSubmit`. Executor processes appear as `CoarseGrainedExecutorBackend`.

11.2.4 Standalone master high availability and recovery

A master process is the most important component in the standalone cluster. Because client processes connect to it to submit applications, the master requests resources from the workers on behalf of the clients, and users rely on it to view the state of running applications. If the master process dies, the cluster becomes unusable: clients can't submit new applications to the cluster, and users can't see the state of the currently running ones.

Master high availability means the master process will be automatically restarted if it goes down. Worker processes, on the other hand, aren't critical for cluster availability. This is the case because if one of the workers becomes unavailable, Spark will restart its tasks on another worker.

If the master process is restarted, Spark provides two ways to recover application and worker data that was running before the master died: using the filesystem and using ZooKeeper. ZooKeeper also provides automatic master high availability, as you'll see. With filesystem recovery, though, you have to set up master high availability yourself (if you need it) by using one of the tools available for that purpose (for example, start the master process from `inittab` with the `respawn` option[1]).

> **NOTE**   All parameters mentioned in this section should be specified in the `SPARK_MASTER_OPTS` variable mentioned earlier and not in the spark-defaults.conf file.

FILESYSTEM MASTER RECOVERY

When using filesystem master recovery, a master persists information about registered workers and running applications in the directory specified by the `spark.deploy` `.recoveryDirectory` parameter. Normally, if the master restarts, workers re-register automatically, but the master loses information about running applications. This doesn't affect the applications, but users won't be able to monitor them through the master web UI.

If filesystem master recovery is enabled, the master will restore worker state instantly (no need for them to re-register), along with the state of any running applications. You enable filesystem recovery by setting the `spark.deploy.recoveryMode` parameter to `FILESYSTEM`.

ZOOKEEPER RECOVERY

ZooKeeper is a fast and simple system providing naming, distributed synchronization, and group services. ZooKeeper clients (or Spark, in this case) use it to coordinate their processes and to store small amounts of shared data. In addition to Spark, it's used in many other distributed systems.

ZooKeeper allows client processes to register with it and use its services to elect a leader process. Those processes not elected as leaders become followers. If a leader process goes down, a leader election process starts, producing a new leader.

To set up master high availability, you need to install and configure ZooKeeper. Then you start several master processes, instructing them to synchronize through ZooKeeper. Only one of them becomes a ZooKeeper leader. If an application tries to register with a master that currently isn't a leader, it will be turned down. If the leader fails, one of the other masters will take its place and restore the master's state using ZooKeeper's services.

Similar to filesystem recovery, the master will persist information about registered workers and running applications, but it will persist that information to ZooKeeper. This way, ZooKeeper provides both recovery and high-availability services for Spark master processes. To store the recovery data, ZooKeeper uses the directory specified by the `spark.deploy.zookeeper.dir` parameter on the machines where ZooKeeper is running.

---

[1]   See the Linux man pages: www.manpages.info/linux/inittab.5.html.

You turn on ZooKeeper recovery by setting the `spark.deploy.recoveryMode` parameter to `ZOOKEEPER`. ZooKeeper needs to be accessible to the URLs specified by the `spark.deploy.zookeeper.url` parameter.

11.3 Standalone cluster web UI

When you start a master or a worker process, each starts its own web UI application. This is different than the way the web UI Spark context starts, as discussed in chapter 10. The Spark web UI shows information about applications, stages, tasks, and so on, and the standalone cluster web UI shows information about master and workers. An example master web UI is shown in figure 11.2.

Spark 1.6.1 Spark Master at spark://svgubuntu01:7077

URL: spark://svgubuntu01:7077
REST URL: spark://svgubuntu01:6066 *(cluster mode)*
Alive Workers: 6
Cores in use: 12 Total, 7 Used
Memory in use: 29.0 GB Total, 8.0 GB Used
Applications: 2 Running, 5 Completed
Drivers: 1 Running, 0 Completed
Status: ALIVE

Workers

Worker Id	Address	State	Cores	Memory
worker-20160411215448-192.168.0.87-48481	192.168.0.87:48481	ALIVE	2 (1 Used)	4.8 GB (1024.0 MB Used)
worker-20160411215450-192.168.0.87-55107	192.168.0.87:55107	ALIVE	2 (1 Used)	4.8 GB (2.0 GB Used)
worker-20160411215450-192.168.0.88-51061	192.168.0.88:51061	ALIVE	2 (1 Used)	4.8 GB (1024.0 MB Used)
worker-20160411215450-192.168.0.89-51380	192.168.0.89:51380	ALIVE	2 (1 Used)	4.8 GB (1024.0 MB Used)
worker-20160411215450-192.168.0.89-51848	192.168.0.89:51848	ALIVE	2 (1 Used)	4.8 GB (1024.0 MB Used)
worker-20160411215451-192.168.0.88-58571	192.168.0.88:58571	ALIVE	2 (2 Used)	4.8 GB (2.0 GB Used)

Running Applications

Application ID		Name	Cores	Memory per Node	Submitted Time	User	State	Duration
app-20160412192031-0006	(kill)	Sample App	3	1024.0 MB	2016/04/12 19:20:31	hduser	RUNNING	1,1 min
app-20160412185512-0005	(kill)	Spark shell	3	1024.0 MB	2016/04/12 18:55:12	hduser	RUNNING	26 min

Running Drivers

Submission ID		Submitted Time	Worker	State	Cores	Memory	Main Class
driver-20160412192023-0000	(kill)	Tue Apr 12 19:20:23 CEST 2016	worker-20160411215450-192.168.0.87-55107	RUNNING	1	2.0 GB	SampleApp

Completed Applications

Application ID	Name	Cores	Memory per Node	Submitted Time	User	State	Duration
app-20160411222724-0004	Spark shell	6	1024.0 MB	2016/04/11 22:27:24	hduser	FINISHED	20,5 h
app-20160411222147-0003	Sample App	6	1024.0 MB	2016/04/11 22:21:47	hduser	FINISHED	45 s
app-20160411221956-0002	Sample App	6	1024.0 MB	2016/04/11 22:19:56	hduser	FINISHED	1,7 min
app-20160411221816-0001	Sample App	3	1024.0 MB	2016/04/11 22:18:16	hduser	FINISHED	19 s
app-20160411215752-0000	Sample App	3	1024.0 MB	2016/04/11 21:57:52	hduser	FINISHED	20 min

Figure 11.2 Example Spark master web UI page showing the running workers, running applications and drivers, and the completed applications and drivers

Spark Spark Worker at svgubuntu02:55175

ID: worker-20150303224421-svgubuntu02-55175
Master URL: spark://svgubuntu01:7077
Cores: 2 (2 Used)
Memory: 4.8 GB (4.0 GB Used)
Back to Master

Running Executors (1)

ExecutorID	Cores	State	Memory	Job Details	Logs
2	1	LOADING	2.0 GB	ID: app-20150303224215-0000 Name: Spark shell User: hduser	stdout stderr

Running Drivers (1)

DriverID	Main Class	State	Cores	Memory	Logs	Notes
driver-20150303224234-0000	SampleApp	RUNNING	1	2.0 GB	stdout stderr	

Figure 11.3 Sample Spark worker web UI

On the master web UI pages, you can see basic information about memory and CPU cores used and those available in the cluster, as well as information about workers, applications, and drivers. We'll talk more about these in the next section.

If you click a worker ID, you're taken to the web UI page started by a worker process. A sample UI page is shown in figure 11.3. On the worker web UI page, you can see which executors and drivers the worker is managing, and you can examine their log files by clicking the appropriate links.

If you click an application's name when on the master web UI page, you'll be taken to the Spark web UI page started by that application's Spark context. If you click an application's ID, though, you'll be taken to the application screen of the master web UI (figure 11.4).

Spark 1.6.1 Application: Spark shell

ID: app-20160412185512-0005
Name: Spark shell
User: hduser
Cores: Unlimited (3 granted)
Executor Memory: 1024.0 MB
Submit Date: Tue Apr 12 18:55:12 CEST 2016
State: RUNNING
Application Detail UI

Executor Summary

ExecutorID	Worker	Cores	Memory	State	Logs
2	worker-20160411215450-192.168.0.89-51848	1	1024	RUNNING	stdout stderr
1	worker-20160411215450-192.168.0.89-51380	1	1024	RUNNING	stdout stderr
0	worker-20160411215451-192.168.0.88-58571	1	1024	RUNNING	stdout stderr

Figure 11.4 Sample Spark master web UI application screen

The application screen shows which workers and executors the application is running on. You can access the Spark web UI again by clicking the Application Detail UI link. You can also view the application's logs on each worker machine.

The Spark cluster web UIs (master and workers) and the Spark web UI come with Spark out of the box and offer a way of monitoring applications and jobs. That should be enough in most situations.

11.4 Running applications in a standalone cluster

As with the other cluster types, you can run Spark programs on a standalone cluster by submitting them with the spark-submit command, running them in a Spark shell, or instantiating and configuring a SparkContext object in your own application. We already talked about these options in chapter 10. In all three cases, you need to specify a master connection URL with the hostname and port of the master process.

> **NOTE** When connecting your applications to a Spark standalone cluster, it's important to use the exact hostname in the master connection URL as that used to start the master process (the one specified by the SPARK_MASTER_IP environment variable or your hostname).

You have two basic options when running Spark applications in a standalone cluster, and they differ in the location of the driver process.

11.4.1 Location of the driver

As we said in section 10.1.1, the driver process can run in the client process that was used to launch the application (like spark-submit script), or it can run in the cluster. Running in the client process is the default behavior and is equivalent to specifying the --deploy-mode client command-line argument. In this case, spark-submit will wait until your application finishes, and you'll see the output of your application on the screen.

> **NOTE** The spark-shell script supports only client-deploy mode.

To run the driver in the cluster, you have to specify the --deploy-mode cluster command-line argument. In that case, you'll see output similar to this:

```
Sending launch command to spark://<master_hostname>:7077
Driver successfully submitted as driver-20150303224234-0000
... waiting before polling master for driver state
... polling master for driver state
State of driver-20150303224234-0000 is RUNNING
Driver running on <client_hostname>:55175 (worker-20150303224421-
<client_hostname>-55175)
```

The option --deploy-mode is only used on standalone and Mesos clusters. YARN has a different master URL syntax.

NOTE If you're embedding SparkContext in your application and you're not using the spark-submit script to connect to the standalone cluster, there's currently no way to specify deploy mode. It will default to client-deploy mode, and the driver will run in your application.

In cluster-deploy mode, the cluster manager takes care of the driver's resources and can automatically restart your application if the driver process fails (see section 11.4.5).

If you're submitting your application in cluster-deploy mode using the spark-submit script, the JAR file you specify needs to be available on the worker (at the location you specified) that will be executing the application. Because there's no way to say in advance which worker will execute your driver, you should put your application's JAR file on all the workers if you intend to use cluster-deploy mode, or you can put your application's JAR file on HDFS and use the HDFS URL as the JAR filename.

Log files from the driver running in cluster mode are available from the master and worker web UI pages. Of course, you can also access them directly on the filesystem of the corresponding worker.

NOTE Python applications can't run in cluster-deploy mode on a standalone cluster.

The example web UI page in figure 11.2 (in section 11.3) shows three configured workers and two applications. One application is a Spark shell; the other is a custom application (called *Sample App*) submitted as a JAR file in cluster-deploy mode, so a running driver can also be seen on the web UI page. In cluster-deploy mode, the driver is spawned by one of the worker processes and uses one of its available CPU cores. We show this in figure 11.3 (in section 11.3).

11.4.2 *Specifying the number of executors*

Each of the two applications in figure 11.2 uses three cores out of six available (Sample App is using four cores; its driver is using the fourth one). This is accomplished by setting the parameter spark.deploy.defaultCores in the SPARK_MASTER_OPTS environment variable to 3 (as described previously). You can accomplish the same thing by setting the spark.cores.max parameter for each application you want to prevent from taking all available cores. You can also set the SPARK_WORKER_CORES environment variable to limit the number of cores each application can take *per machine*. If neither spark.cores.max nor spark.deploy.defaultCores were set, a single application would have taken all the available cores, and the subsequent applications would have had to wait for the first application to finish.

To control how many executors are allocated for your application, set spark.cores.max to the total number of cores you wish to use, and set spark.executor.cores to the number of cores per executor (or set their command-line equivalents: --executor-cores and --total-executor-cores). If you wish to use 3 executors with the total of 15 cores, set spark.cores.max to 15 and spark.executor.cores to 5. If you plan to run only one application, leave these settings at the default value, which is *infinite* (`Int.MaxValue`).

11.4.3 *Specifying extra classpath entries and files*

In many situations, it's necessary to modify the classpath of your application or to make other files available to it. For example, your application may need a JDBC driver to access a relational database or other third-party classes not bundled with Spark. This means you need to modify the classpath of executor and driver processes, because that's where your application is executing. Special Spark parameters exist for these purposes, and you can apply them at different levels, as is often the case when configuring Spark.

> **NOTE** Techniques described in this section aren't specific to the standalone cluster and can be used on other cluster types, too.

USING THE **SPARK_CLASSPATH** VARIABLE

You can use the `SPARK_CLASSPATH` environment variable to add additional JAR files to the driver and executors. If you set it on the client machine, the extra classpath entries will be added to both the driver's and workers' classpaths. When using this variable, however, you'll need to manually copy the required files to the same location on all machines. Multiple JAR files are separated by semicolons (;) on Windows and by colons (:) on all other platforms.

USING THE COMMAND-LINE OPTIONS

Another option is to use the Spark configuration parameters `spark.driver.extra-ClassPath` and `spark.executor.extraClassPath` for JAR files, and `spark.driver.extraLibraryPath` and `spark.executor.extraLibraryPath` for native libraries. There are two additional `spark-submit` parameters for specifying driver paths: `--driver-class-path` and `--driver-library-path`. You should use these parameters if the driver is running in client mode, because then `--conf spark.driver.extraClassPath` won't work. JAR files specified with these options will be *prepended* to the appropriate executor classpaths. You'll still need to have these files on your worker machines as well.

USING THE –JARS PARAMETER

This option uses `spark-submit` with the `--jars` parameter, which automatically copies the specified JAR files (separated with commas) to the worker machines and adds them to the executor classpaths. That means the JAR files need not exist on the worker machines before submitting the application. Spark uses the same mechanism to distribute your application's JAR file to worker machines.

When using the `--jars` option, you can fetch the JAR files from different locations, depending on the prefix before the specified filename (a colon at the end of each prefix is required):

- `file:`—The default option described earlier. The file is copied to each worker.
- `local:`—The file exists on all worker machines at the exact same location.
- `hdfs:`—The file path is HDFS, and each worker can access it directly from HDFS.
- `http:`, `https:`, or `ftp:`—The file path is a URI.

NOTE If your application JAR includes classes or JARs also used by Spark itself, and you're experiencing conflicts among class versions, you can set the configuration parameter `spark.executor.userClassPathFirst` or `spark.driver.userClassPathFirst` to `true` to force Spark to load your classes before its own.

You can use a similar option (`--files`) to add ordinary files to workers (files that aren't JAR files or libraries). They can also be local, HDFS, HTTP, or FTP files. To use these files on workers, you need to access them with `SparkFiles.get(<filename>)`.

ADDING FILES PROGRAMMATICALLY

There is a programmatic method of adding JARs and files by calling `SparkContext`'s `addJar` and `addFile` methods. The `--jars` and `--files` options described earlier call these methods, so most things said previously also apply here. The only addition is that you can use `addFile(filename, true)` to recursively add an HDFS directory (the second argument means *recursive*).

ADDING ADDITIONAL PYTHON FILES

For Python applications, extra .egg, .zip, or .py files can be added with the `--py-files` `spark-submit` option. For example:

```
spark-submit --master <master_url> --py-files file1.py,file2.py main.py
```

where main.py is the Python file instantiating a Spark context.

11.4.4 Killing applications

If you submitted your application to the cluster in cluster mode, and the application is taking too long to complete or you want to stop it for some other reason, you can kill it by using the `spark-class` command like this:

```
spark-class org.apache.spark.deploy.Client kill <master_URL> <driver_ID>
```

You can do this only for applications whose driver is running in the cluster (cluster mode). For those applications submitted using the `spark-submit` command in client mode, you can kill the client process. You can still terminate particular stages (and jobs) using the Spark web UI, as described in section 10.4.2.

11.4.5 Application automatic restart

When submitting an application in cluster-deploy mode, a special command-line option (`--supervise`) tells Spark to restart the driver process if it fails (or ends abnormally). This restarts the entire application because it isn't possible to recover the state of a Spark program and continue at the point where it failed.

If the driver is failing every time and keeps getting restarted, you'll need to kill it using the method described in the previous section. Then you need to investigate the problem and change your application so that the driver executes without failing.

11.5 *Spark History Server and event logging*

We mentioned the History Server earlier. What's it for? Let's say you ran your application using `spark-submit`. Everything went smoothly, or so you thought. You suddenly notice something strange and would like to check a detail on the Spark web UI. You use the master's web UI to get to the application page, and you click the Application Detail UI link, but you get the message shown in figure 11.5. Or, even worse, you restarted the master process in the meantime, and your application isn't listed on the master's web UI.

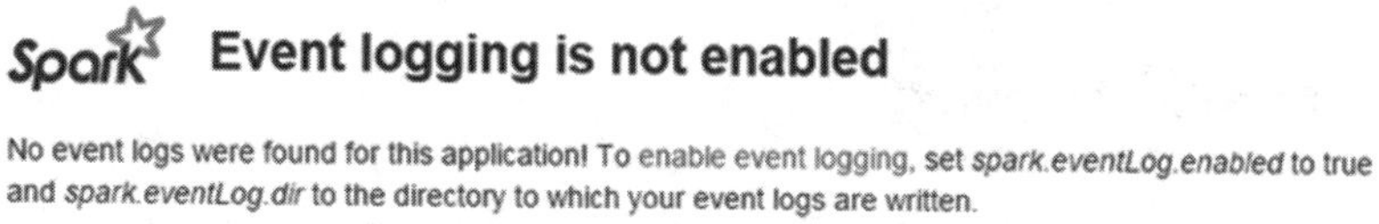

Spark✭ Event logging is not enabled

No event logs were found for this application! To enable event logging, set *spark.eventLog.enabled* to true and *spark.eventLog.dir* to the directory to which your event logs are written.

Figure 11.5   A web UI message showing that event logging isn't enabled

Event logging exists to help with these situations. When enabled, Spark logs events necessary for rendering the web UI in the folder specified by `spark.eventLog.dir`, which is /tmp/spark-events by default. The Spark master web UI will then be able to display this information in a manner identical to the Spark web UI so that data about jobs, stages, and tasks is available even after the application has finished. You enable event logging by setting `spark.eventLog.enabled` to `true`.

If you restarted (or stopped) the master, and your application is no longer available from the master web UI, you can start the Spark History Server, which displays a Spark web UI for applications whose events have been logged in the event log directory.

> **TIP**   Unfortunately, if an application is killed before finishing, it may not appear in the History Server UI because the History Server expects to find a file named APPLICATION_COMPLETE in the application's directory (/tmp/spark-events/<application_id> by default). You can manually create an empty file with that name if it's missing, and the application will appear in the UI.

You start the Spark History Server with the script `start-history-server.sh` in the sbin directory, and you stop it with `stop-history-server.sh`. The default HTTP port is 18080. You can change this with the `spark.history.ui.port` parameter.

An example History Server page is shown in figure 11.6. Click any application ID link to go to the appropriate web UI pages, which we covered in section 11.4.

Spark⭐ History Server

Event log directory: file:/tmp/spark-events

Showing 1-8 of 8

App ID	App Name	Started	Completed	Duration	Spark User	Last Updated
app-20150303232024-0002	Spark shell	2015/03/03 23:20:22	2015/03/03 23:23:34	3,2 min	hduser	2015/03/03 23:23:35
app-20150303224215-0000	Spark shell	2015/03/03 22:42:13	2015/03/03 22:45:25	3,2 min	hduser	2015/03/03 22:45:26
app-20150303223829-0000	Spark shell	2015/03/03 22:38:27	2015/03/03 22:41:29	3,0 min	hduser	2015/03/03 22:41:31
app-20150303223424-0000	Spark shell	2015/03/03 22:34:22	2015/03/03 22:37:57	3,6 min	hduser	2015/03/03 22:37:58
app-20150303222458-0000	Spark shell	2015/03/03 22:24:56	2015/03/03 22:33:47	8,8 min	hduser	2015/03/03 22:33:48
app-20150303215707-0000	Spark shell	2015/03/03 21:57:04	2015/03/03 22:24:15	27 min	hduser	2015/03/03 22:24:16
app-20150303215146-0000	Spark shell	2015/03/03 21:51:43	2015/03/03 21:55:17	3,6 min	hduser	2015/03/03 21:55:18
app-20150303213244-0000	Spark shell	2015/03/03 21:32:41	2015/03/03 21:48:29	16 min	hduser	2015/03/03 21:48:30

Figure 11.6   Spark History Server

You can customize the History Server with several environment variables: use `SPARK_DAEMON_MEMORY` to specify how much memory it should take, `SPARK_PUBLIC_DNS` to set its public address, `SPARK_DAEMON_JAVA_OPTS` to pass additional param-eters to its JVM, and `SPARK_HISTORY_OPTS` to pass to it `spark.history.*` parameters. For the complete list of these parameters, see the official documentation (http://spark.apache.org/docs/latest/configuration.html). You can also set `spark.history.*` parameters in the spark-default.conf file.

11.6   *Running on Amazon EC2*

You can use any physical or virtual machine to run Spark, but in this section, we'll show you how to use Spark's EC2 scripts to quickly set up a Spark standalone cluster in Amazon's AWS cloud. Amazon EC2 is Amazon's cloud service that lets you rent virtual servers to run your own applications. EC2 is just one of the services in Amazon Web Services (AWS); other services include storage and databases. AWS is popular because of its ease of use, broad set of features, and relatively low price. Of course, we don't want to start a flame war about which cloud provider is better. There are other provid-ers and you can manually install Spark on them and set up a standalone cluster as described in this chapter.

To go through this tutorial, we'll use Amazon resources that go outside the free tier, so you should be prepared to spend a buck or two. You'll first obtain secret AWS keys, necessary for connecting to AWS services, and set up basic security. Then you'll use Spark's EC2 scripts to launch a cluster and log in to it. We'll show you how to stop and restart parts of the cluster you created. Finally, you'll destroy the fruit of all that hard work.

11.6.1 Prerequisites

In order to follow along, you should have an Amazon account and obtain these AWS keys: Access Key ID and Secret Access Key. These keys are used for user identification when using the AWS API. You can use the keys of your main user, but this isn't recommended. A better approach would be to create a new user with lower permissions and then generate and use those keys.

OBTAINING THE AWS SECRET KEYS

You create a new user with Amazon's Identity and Access Management (IAM) service. For the purposes of this tutorial, we created a user named *sparkuser* by selecting Services > IAM from the AWS landing page, going to the Users page, and clicking the Create New Users button. We entered a single username and left the option Generate an Access Key for Each User checked. Figure 11.7 shows our keys ready for download. You should store the keys in a safe place right away, because you won't be able to access them later.

Figure 11.7 AWS user created

In order to successfully use this user for the Spark cluster setup, the user has to have adequate permissions. Click the new user's name, and then click the Attach Policy button on the Permissions tab (see figure 11.8). From the list of available policies, choose AmazonEC2FullAccess. This will be enough for your Spark setup.

Figure 11.8 Giving the user adequate permissions

CREATING A KEY PAIR

The next prerequisite is a key pair, which is necessary for securing communication between a client and AWS services. On the EC2 Services page (available from any page through the top menu Services > EC2), under Network & Security, select Key Pairs and then choose your region in the upper-right corner. Choosing the correct region is important because keys generated for one region won't work in another. We chose Ireland (eu-west-1).

Click Create Key Pair, and give the pair a name. The name can be anything you like; we chose SparkKey. After creating the key pair, a private key will be automatically downloaded as a <key_pair_name>.pem file. You should store that file in a secure but accessible place and change its access rights so that only you can read it:

```
chmod 400 SparkKey.pem
```

Just to be sure everything is OK before starting the scripts (you could have made a mistake in pasting its contents), check that the key is valid using this command:

```
openssl rsa -in SparkKey.pem -check
```

If the command outputs the contents of the file, all is well.

11.6.2 Creating an EC2 standalone cluster

Now let's look at the main `spark-ec2` script for managing the EC2 cluster. It used to come bundled with Spark, but has since moved to a separate project. To use it, create an ec2 directory in your SPARK_HOME folder and then clone the AMPLab's spark-ec2 GitHub repository (https://github.com/amplab/spark-ec2) into it. The spark-ec2 script has the following syntax:

```
spark-ec2 options action cluster_name
```

Table 11.6 shows the possible actions you can specify.

Table 11.6 Possible actions for the `spark-ec2` script

Action	Description
launch	Launches EC2 instances, installs the required software packages, and starts the Spark master and slaves
login	Logs in to the instance running the Spark master
stop	Stops all the cluster instances
start	Starts all the cluster instances, and reconfigures the cluster
get-master	Returns the address of the instance where the Spark master is running
reboot-slaves	Reboots instances where workers are running
destroy	An unrecoverable action that terminates EC2 instances and destroys the cluster

Depending on the `action` argument, you can use the same script to launch the cluster; log in to it; stop, start, and destroy the cluster; and restart the slave machines. Every action requires the `cluster_name` argument, which is used to reference the machines that will be created; and security credentials, which are the AWS secret keys and the key pair you created before. Options depend on the action chosen and will be explained as we go.

SPECIFYING THE CREDENTIALS

AWS secret keys are specified as the system environment variables AWS_SECRET_ACCESS_KEY and AWS_ACCESS_KEY_ID:

```
export AWS_SECRET_ACCESS_KEY=<your_AWS_access_key>
export AWS_ACCESS_KEY_ID=<your_AWS_access_key_id>
```

The key pair is specified with the --key-pair option (-k for short) containing the key pair name and the --identity-file option (-i for short) pointing to the pem file with the private key created earlier.

You also have to specify the --region option (-r for short) for all actions if you chose a region other than the default us-east-1 as we did. Otherwise, the script won't be able to find your cluster's machines.

Up until this point, you have this (don't run this just yet)

```
spark-ec2 --key-pair=SparkKey --identity-file=SparkKey.pem \
--region=<your_region_if_dffrnt_than_us-east-1> launch spark-in-action
```

or the equivalent:

```
spark-ec2 -k SparkKey -i SparkKey.pem -r eu-west-1 launch spark-in-action
```

Running this command now would create a cluster called spark-in-action. But we'd like to change a few things before doing that.

CHANGING THE INSTANCE TYPES

Amazon offers many types of instances you can use for your VMs. These differ in number of CPUs, amount of memory available, and, of course, price.

The default instance type when creating EC2 instances with the spark-ec2 script is m1.large, which has two cores and 7.5 GB of RAM. The same instance type will be used for the master and slave machines, which usually isn't desirable because the master is less hungry for resources. So we decided to use m1.small for the master. We also opted for m1.medium for slaves. The option for changing a slave's instance type is --instance-type (-t for short), and the option for changing the master is --master-instance-type (-m for short).

CHANGING THE HADOOP VERSION

You'll probably be using Hadoop on your EC2 instances. The default Hadoop version the spark-ec2 script will install is 1.0.4, which may not be something you want. You can change that with the --hadoop-major-version parameter and set it to 2, which will install Spark prebuilt for Cloudera CDH 4.2.0, containing Hadoop 2.0.0 MR1.

CUSTOMIZING SECURITY GROUPS

By default, access to EC2 instances through internet ports isn't allowed. That prevents you from submitting applications to your Spark cluster running on EC2 instances directly from a client machine outside the EC2 cluster. EC2 security groups let you change inbound and outbound rules so that machines can communicate with the

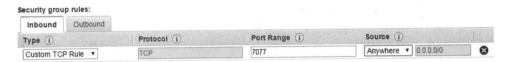

Figure 11.9   Adding a custom security rule to allow access to the master instance from anywhere on the internet

outside world. The `spark-ec2` script sets up security groups to allow communication between the machines in your cluster, but access to port 7077 (the Spark standalone master default port) from the internet still isn't allowed. That's why you should create a security group (accessible from Services > EC2 > Security Groups > Create Security Group) with a rule as shown in figure 11.9 (we named it *Allow7077*).

Although opening a port to everybody like this isn't recommended, it's acceptable for short time periods in test environments. For production environments, we recommend that you restrict access to a single address.

You can assign a security group to all of your instances with the option `--additional-security-group`. Because you need the security group you just created only for the master (you don't need to access workers through port 7077), you won't use this option now and will add this security group manually to the master instance after your cluster is running.

LAUNCHING THE CLUSTER

The last thing you need to change is the number of slave machines. By default, only one will be created, and in this case you'd like more. The option for changing that is `--slaves` (`-s` for short).

This is the complete command:

```
./spark-ec2 --key-pair=SparkKey --identity-file=SparkKey.pem \
--slaves=3 --region=eu-west-1 --instance-type=m1.medium \
--master-instance-type=m1.small --hadoop-major-version=2 \
launch spark-in-action
```

After you start the script, it will create security groups, launch the appropriate instances, and install these packages: Scala, Spark, Hadoop, and Tachyon. The script downloads appropriate packages from online repositories and distributes them to workers using the `rsync` (remotely copy) program.

You can instruct the script to use an existing master instance and only create the slaves with the option `--use-existing-master`. To launch the cluster on an Amazon Virtual Private Cloud (VPC), you use the options `--vpc-id` and `--subnet-id`; everything else remains the same.

After the script is done, you'll see the new instances running in your EC2 console (figure 11.10). The cluster is now ready to be used.

Figure 11.10 Spark cluster machines running on EC2

11.6.3 *Using the EC2 cluster*

Now that you have your cluster, you can log in to see what your command created.

LOGGING IN

You can log in to your cluster in a couple of ways. First, the `spark-ec2` script provides an action for this:

```
spark-ec2 -k SparkKey -i SparkKey.pem -r eu-west-1 login spark-in-action
```

This will print out something similar to the following:

```
Searching for existing cluster spark-in-action...
Found 1 master(s), 3 slaves
Logging into master ec2-52-16-244-147.eu-west-1.compute.amazonaws.com

Last login: ...

      __|  __|_  )
      _|  (     /   Amazon Linux AMI
     ___|\___|___|

https://aws.amazon.com/amazon-linux-ami/2013.03-release-notes/
There are 74 security update(s) out of 262 total update(s) available
Run "sudo yum update" to apply all updates.
Amazon Linux version 2014.09 is available.
root@ip-172-31-3-54 ~]$
```

And you're in! Another option is to add `ssh` directly to the public address of one of your instances, still using your private key (secret key environment variables aren't necessary in this case). You can find the addresses of your instances on the EC2 console. In this example, to log in to the master instance, you'd type

```
$ ssh -i SparkKey.pem root@52.16.171.131
```

If you don't feel like logging in to your EC2 console to find the address, you can use the `spark-ec2` script to obtain the master's hostname:

```
$ spark-ec2 -k SparkKey -i SparkKey.pem -r eu-west-1 login spark-in-action
Searching for existing cluster spark-in-action...
Found 1 master(s), 3 slaves
ec2-52-16-244-147.eu-west-1.compute.amazonaws.com
```

Then you can use that address for the `ssh` command.

CLUSTER CONFIGURATION

Upon logging in, you'll see that software packages were installed in the user's home directory. The default user is root (you can change that with the `--user` option), so the home directory is /root.

If you examine `spark-env.sh` in the spark/conf subdirectory, you'll see that the `spark-ec2` script added a few Spark configuration options. The ones we're most interested in are `SPARK_WORKER_INSTANCES` and `SPARK_WORKER_CORES`.

The number of instances per worker can be customized with the command-line option `--worker-instances`. Of course, you can manually alter the configuration in the `spark-env.sh` file, too. In that case, you should distribute the file to the workers.

`SPARK_WORKER_CORES` can't be customized using the `spark-ec2` script because the number of worker cores depends on the instance type selected. In the example, you used `m1.medium`, which has only one CPU, so the configured value was 1. For the default instance type (`m1.large` in the example), which has two CPUs, the configured default value is 2.

You'll also notice two Hadoop installations: `ephemeral-hdfs` and `persistent-hdfs`. Ephemeral HDFS is configured to use temporary storage available only while the machine is running. If the machine restarts, the ephemeral (temporary) data is lost.

Persistent HDFS is configured to use Elastic Block Store (EBS) storage, which means it won't be lost if the machine restarts. It also means keeping that data is going to cost you. You can add more EBS volumes to each instance with the `--ebs-vol-num`, `--ebs-vol-type`, and `--ebs-vol-size` options.

The spark-ec2 subdirectory contains the contents of the https://github.com/mesos/spark-ec2 GitHub repository. These are the actual scripts for setting up Spark EC2 clusters. One useful script there is `copy-dir`, enabling you to `rsync` a directory from one of the instances to the same path on all slave machines in a Spark configuration.

CONNECTING TO THE MASTER

If everything went smoothly, you should be able to start a Spark shell and connect to the master. For this, you should use the hostname returned by the `get-master` command and not its IP address.

If you assigned the Allow7077 security group to the master instance, you should be able to connect to the cluster from your client machine, too. Further configuration and application submission work as usual.

STOPPING, STARTING, AND REBOOTING

Stop and start actions obviously stop and start the entire cluster. After stopping, the machines will be in a stopped state, and data in temporary storage will be lost. After starting the cluster again, the necessary scripts will be called to rebuild the temporary data and repeat the cluster configuration. This will also cause any changes you may have made to your Spark configuration to be overwritten, although that data is kept in persistent storage. If you restart the machines using the EC2 console, your changes to your Spark configuration will be preserved.

spark-ec2 also lets you reboot slave machines. reboot-slaves is used similarly to other actions:

```
$ ./spark-ec2 -k SparkKey -i SparkKey.pem -r eu-west-1 \
reboot-slaves spark-in-action
Are you sure you want to reboot the cluster spark-in-action slaves?
Reboot cluster slaves spark-in-action (y/N): y
Searching for existing cluster spark-in-action...
Found 1 master(s), 3 slaves
Rebooting slaves...
Rebooting i-b87d0d5e
Rebooting i-8a7d0d6c
Rebooting i-8b7d0d6d
```

After a reboot, you'll have to run the start-slaves.sh script from the master machine, because slaves aren't started automatically.

11.6.4 Destroying the cluster

A destroy action (to use the AWS terminology) will terminate all cluster instances. Instances that are only stopped and not terminated may incur additional costs, although you may not be using them. For example, Spark instances use EBS permanent storage, and Amazon charges for EBS usage even though instances are stopped.

So it may be prudent to destroy the cluster if you won't be using it for a long time. It's straightforward to do:

```
spark-ec2 -k SparkKey -i SparkKey.pem destroy spark-in-action
Are you sure you want to destroy the cluster spark-in-action?
The following instances will be terminated:
Searching for existing cluster spark-in-action...
ALL DATA ON ALL NODES WILL BE LOST!!
Destroy cluster spark-in-action (y/N):
Terminating master...
Terminating slaves...
```

After this step, your only option is to launch another cluster (or pack up and go home).

11.7 Summary

- A standalone cluster comes bundled with Spark, has a simple architecture, and is easy to install and configure.
- It consists of master and worker processes.
- Spark applications on a Spark standalone cluster can run in cluster mode (the driver is running in the cluster) or client-deploy mode (the driver is running in the client JVM).
- You can start the standalone cluster with shell scripts or manually.

- The master process can be automatically restarted if it goes down, using filesystem master recovery or ZooKeeper recovery.
- The standalone cluster web UI gives useful information about running applications, master, and workers.
- You can specify extra classpath entries and files using the `SPARK_CLASSPATH` environment variable, using command-line options, using the `--jars` argument, and programmatically.
- The Spark History Server enables you to view the Spark web UI of applications that finished, but only if they were running while event logging was enabled.
- You can start a Spark standalone cluster on Amazon EC2 using the scripts in the Spark distribution.

Running on YARN and Mesos

This chapter covers

- YARN architecture
- YARN resource scheduling
- Configuring and running Spark on YARN
- Mesos architecture
- Mesos resource scheduling
- Configuring and running Spark on Mesos
- Running Spark from Docker

We examined a Spark standalone cluster in the previous chapter. Now it's time to tackle YARN and Mesos, two other cluster managers supported by Spark. They're both widely used (with YARN still more widespread) and offer similar functionalities, but each has its own specific strengths and weaknesses. Mesos is the only cluster manager supporting fine-grained resource scheduling mode; you can also use Mesos to run Spark tasks in Docker images. In fact, the Spark project was originally started to demonstrate the usefulness of Mesos,[1] which illustrates Mesos's importance. YARN lets you access Kerberos-secured HDFS (Hadoop distributed filesystem restricted to users authenticated using the Kerberos authentication protocol) from your Spark applications.

In this chapter, we'll describe the architectures, installation and configuration options, and resource scheduling mechanisms for Mesos and YARN. We'll also highlight the differences between them and how to avoid common pitfalls. In short, this chapter will help you decide which platform better suits your needs. We'll start with YARN.

12.1 Running Spark on YARN

YARN (which, as you may recall, stands for yet another resource negotiator) is the new generation of Hadoop's MapReduce execution engine (for more information about MapReduce, see appendix B). Unlike the previous MapReduce engine, which could only run MapReduce jobs, YARN can run other types of programs (such as Spark). Most Hadoop installations already have YARN configured alongside HDFS, so YARN is the most natural execution engine for many potential and existing Spark users.

Spark was designed to be agnostic to the underlying cluster manager, and running Spark applications on YARN doesn't differ much from running them on other cluster managers, but there are a few differences you should be aware of. We'll go through those differences here.

We'll begin our exploration of running Spark on YARN by first looking at the YARN architecture. Then we'll describe how to submit Spark applications to YARN, then explain the differences between running Spark applications on YARN compared to a Spark standalone cluster.

12.1.1 YARN architecture

The basic YARN architecture is similar to Spark's standalone cluster architecture. Its main components are a *resource manager* (it could be likened to Spark's master process) for each cluster and a *node manager* (similar to Spark's worker processes) for each node in the cluster. Unlike running on Spark's standalone cluster, applications on YARN run in *containers* (JVM processes to which CPU and memory resources are granted). An *application master* for each application is a special component. Running in its own container, it's responsible for requesting application resources from the resource manager. When Spark is running on YARN, the Spark driver process acts as the YARN application master. Node managers track resources used by containers and report to the resource manager.

Figure 12.1 shows a YARN cluster with two nodes and a Spark application running in the cluster. You'll notice that this figure is similar to figure 11.1, but the process of starting an application is somewhat different.

A *client* first submits an application to the resource manager (step 1), which directs one of the node managers to allocate a container for the application master (step 2). The node manager launches a container (step 3) for the application master (Spark's

---

[1] See "Mesos: A Platform for Fine-Grained Resource Sharing in the Data Center," by Benjamin Hindman et al., http://mesos.berkeley.edu/mesos_tech_report.pdf.

driver), which then asks the resource manager for more containers to be used as Spark executors (step 4). When the resources are granted, the application master asks the node managers to launch executors in the new containers (step 5), and the node managers obey (step 6). From that point on, driver and executors communicate independently of YARN components, in the same way as when they're running in other types of clusters. Clients can query the application's status at any time.

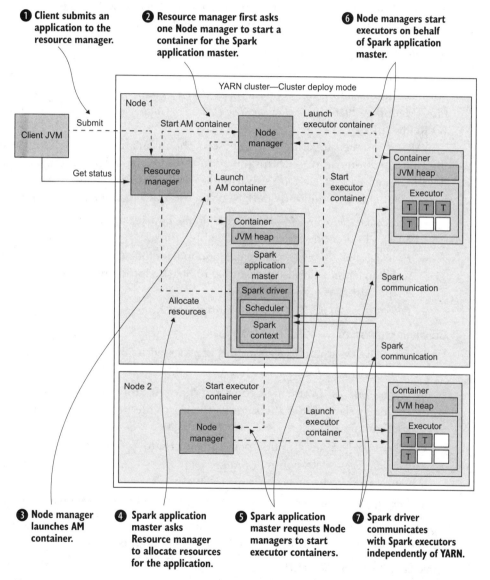

Figure 12.1 YARN architecture in an example cluster of two nodes. The client submits an application, whereby the resource manager starts the container for the application master (Spark driver). The application master requests more containers for Spark executors. Once the containers start, the Spark driver communicates directly with its executors.

Figure 12.1 shows only one application running in the cluster. But multiple applications can run in a single YARN cluster, be they Spark applications or applications of another type. In that case, each application has its own application master. The number of containers depends on the application type. At minimum, an application could consist of only an application master. Because Spark needs a driver *and* executors, it will always have a container for the application master (Spark driver) and one or more containers for its executors. Unlike Spark's workers, YARN's node managers can launch more than one container (executor) per application.

12.1.2 *Installing, configuring, and starting YARN*

This section contains an overview of YARN and Hadoop installation and configuration. For more information, we recommend *Hadoop in Practice, Second Edition*, by Alex Holmes (Manning, 2015) and *Hadoop: The Definitive Guide, Fourth Edition*, by Tom White (O'Reilly, 2015).

YARN is installed together with Hadoop. The installation is straightforward: from the Hadoop download page (https://hadoop.apache.org/releases.html), you need to download and extract Hadoop's distribution archive on every machine that is to be part of your cluster. Similar to Spark, you can use YARN in three possible modes:

- *Standalone (local) mode*—Runs as a single Java process. This is comparable to Spark's local mode, described in chapter 10.
- *Pseudo-distributed mode*—Runs all Hadoop daemons (several Java processes) on a single machine. This is comparable to Spark's local cluster mode, described in chapter 10.
- *Fully distributed mode*—Runs on multiple machines.

CONFIGURATION FILES

Hadoop's XML-based configuration files are located in the etc/hadoop directory of the main installation location. The main configuration files are as follows:

- *slaves*—List of hostnames (one per line) of the machines in the cluster. Hadoop's slaves file is the same as the slaves file in Spark's standalone cluster configuration.
- *hdfs-site.xml*—Configuration pertaining to Hadoop's filesystem.
- *yarn-site.xml*—YARN configuration.
- *yarn-env.sh*—YARN environment variables.
- *core-site.xml*—Various security, high-availability, and filesystem parameters.

Copy the configuration files to all the machines in the cluster. We'll mention specific configuration options pertinent to Spark in the coming sections.

STARTING AND STOPPING YARN

Table 12.1 lists the scripts for starting and stopping YARN and HDFS daemons. They're available in the sbin directory of the main Hadoop installation location.

Table 12.1 Scripts for starting and stopping YARN and HDFS daemons

Script file	What it does
`start-hdfs.sh` / `stop-hdfs.sh`	Starts/stops HDFS daemons on all machines listed in the slaves file
`start-yarn.sh` / `stop-yarn.sh`	Starts/stops YARN daemons on all machines listed in the slaves file
`start-all.sh` / `stop-all.sh`	Starts/stops both HDFS and YARN daemons on all machines listed in the slaves file

12.1.3 Resource scheduling in YARN

YARN's `ResourceManager`, mentioned previously, has a pluggable interface to allow different plug-ins to implement its resource-scheduling functions. There are three main scheduler plug-ins: the *FIFO scheduler*, the *capacity scheduler*, and the *fair scheduler*. You specify the desired scheduler by setting the property `yarn.resourcemanager.scheduler.class` in the yarn-site.xml file to the scheduler's class name. The default is the capacity scheduler (the value `org.apache.hadoop.yarn.server.resourcemanager.scheduler.capacity.CapacityScheduler`).

These schedulers treat Spark like any other application running in YARN. They allocate CPU and memory to Spark according to their logic. Once they do, Spark schedules resources for its own jobs internally, as discussed in chapter 10.

FIFO SCHEDULER

The FIFO scheduler is the simplest of the scheduler plug-ins. It lets applications take all the resources they need. If two applications require the same resources, the first application that requests them will be first served (FIFO).

CAPACITY SCHEDULER

The capacity scheduler (the default scheduler in YARN) was designed to allow for sharing of a single YARN cluster by different organizations, and it guarantees that each organization will always have a certain amount of resources available (*guaranteed capacity*). The main unit of resources scheduled by YARN is a *queue*. Each queue's capacity determines the percentage of cluster resources that can be used by applications submitted to it. A hierarchy of queues can be set up to reflect a hierarchy of capacity requirements by organizations, so that sub-queues (sub-organizations) can share the resources of a single queue and thus not affect others. In a single queue, the resources are scheduled in FIFO fashion.

If enabled, capacity scheduling can be elastic, meaning it allows organizations to use any excess capacity not used by others. Preemption isn't supported, which means the excess capacity temporarily allocated to some organizations isn't automatically freed when demanded by organizations originally entitled to use it. If that happens, the "rightful owners" have to wait until the "guests" have finished using their resources.

FAIR SCHEDULER

The fair scheduler tries to assign resources in such a way that all applications get (on average) an equal share. By default, it bases its decisions on memory only, but you can configure it to schedule with both memory and CPU.

Like the capacity scheduler, it also organizes applications into queues. The fair scheduler also supports application priorities (some applications should get more resources than others) and minimum capacity requirements. It offers more flexibility than the capacity scheduler. It enables preemption, meaning when an application demands resources, the fair scheduler can take some resources from other running applications. It can schedule resources according to FIFO scheduling, fair scheduling, and dominant resource fairness scheduling. Dominant resource fairness scheduling takes into account CPU and memory (whereas in normal operation, only memory affects scheduling decisions).

12.1.4 *Submitting Spark applications to YARN*

As with running applications in a Spark standalone cluster, depending on where the driver process is running, Spark has two modes of running applications on YARN: the driver can run in YARN or it can run on the client machine. If you want it to run in a cluster, the Spark master connection URL should be as follows:

```
--master yarn-cluster
```

If you want it to run on the client machine, use:

```
--master yarn-client
```

> **NOTE** The spark-shell can't be started in yarn-cluster mode because an interactive connection with the driver is required.

Figure 12.1 shows an example of running Spark on YARN in cluster-deploy mode. Figure 12.2 shows Spark running on YARN in client-deploy mode. As you can see, the order of calls is similar to cluster-deploy mode. What is different is that resource allocation and internal Spark communications are now split between Spark's application master and the driver. Spark's application master handles resource allocation and communication with the resource manager, and the driver communicates directly with Spark's executors. Communication between the driver and the application master is now necessary, too.

Submitting an application to YARN in client mode is similar to the way it's done for a standalone cluster. You'll see the output of your application in the client window. You can kill the application by stopping the client process.

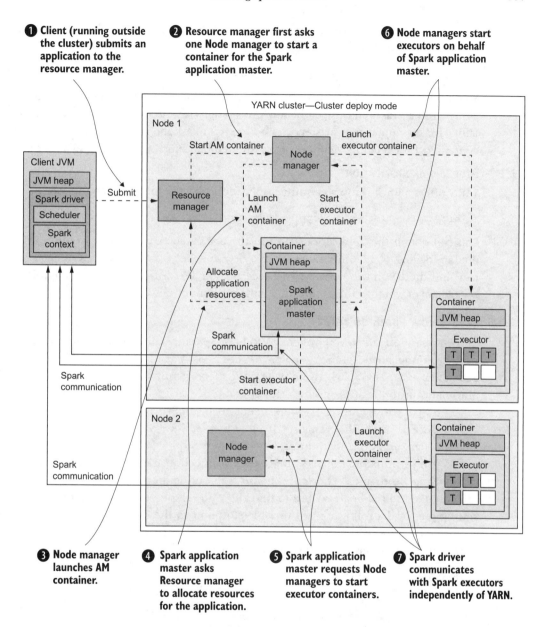

① Client (running outside the cluster) submits an application to the resource manager.

② Resource manager first asks one Node manager to start a container for the Spark application master.

⑥ Node managers start executors on behalf of Spark application master.

③ Node manager launches AM container.

④ Spark application master asks Resource manager to allocate resources for the application.

⑤ Spark application master requests Node managers to start executor containers.

⑦ Spark driver communicates with Spark executors independently of YARN.

Figure 12.2 Running spark in YARN client-deploy mode in a cluster with two nodes. The client submits an application, and the resource manager starts the container for the application master (Spark driver). The application master requests further containers for Spark executors. The Spark driver runs in the client JVM and directly communicates with the executors once the containers start.

When you submit an application to YARN in cluster mode, your client process will stay alive and wait for the application to finish. Killing the client process won't stop the application. If you've turned on information (INFO) message logging, your client process will display periodic messages like this one:

```
INFO Client: Application report for <application_id> (state: RUNNING)
```

You'll notice that application startup is somewhat slower on YARN than it is on a standalone cluster. This is because of the way YARN assigns resources: it first has to create a container for the application master, which then has to ask the resource manager to create containers for executors. This overhead isn't felt that much when running larger jobs.

STOPPING AN APPLICATION

YARN offers a way to stop a running application with the following command:

```
$ yarn application -kill <application_id>
```

You can obtain the application ID from the spark-submit command's output if you enable logging of INFO messages for the org.apache.spark package. Otherwise, you can find the ID on the YARN web UI (see section 12.1.5). You can kill an application regardless of whether the application runs in client or cluster mode.

12.1.5 *Configuring Spark on YARN*

To run Spark on YARN, you only need to have Spark installed on the client node (the node running spark-submit or spark-shell, or if your application instantiates a SparkContext). The Spark assembly JAR and all configuration options are transferred automatically to the appropriate YARN containers.

The Spark distribution package needs to be built with YARN support. You can download a prebuilt version from the Spark official website (https://spark.apache.org/downloads.html) or build your own.

As you've probably noticed, the master connection URL for connecting to YARN contains no hostnames. Therefore, before submitting an application to a YARN cluster, you need to tell Spark where to find the YARN resource manager. This is done by setting one of the following two variables to point to the directory that contains the YARN configuration: YARN_CONF_DIR or HADOOP_CONF_DIR. At minimum, the specified directory needs to have at least one file, yarn-site.xml, with this configuration:

```xml
<?xml version="1.0"?>
<configuration>
    <property>
        <name>yarn.resourcemanager.address</name>
        <value>{RM_hostname}:{RM_port}</value>
    </property>
</configuration>
```

RM_hostname and RM_port are the hostname and port of your resource manager (the default port is 8050). For other configuration options that you can specify in yarn-site.xml, please see the official Hadoop documentation (http://mng.bz/zB92).

If you need to access HDFS, the directory specified by YARN_CONF_DIR or HADOOP _CONF_DIR should also contain the core-site.xml file with the parameter fs.default

.name set to a value similar to this: `hdfs://yourhostname:9000`. This client-side configuration will be distributed to all Spark executors in the YARN cluster.

SPECIFYING A YARN QUEUE

As we discussed in section 12.1.3, when using capacity or fair schedulers, YARN applications' resources are allocated by specifying a queue. You set the queue name Spark will use with the `--queue` command-line parameter, the `spark.yarn.queue` configuration parameter, or the `SPARK_YARN_QUEUE` environment variable. If you don't specify a queue name, Spark will use the default name (`default`).

SHARING THE SPARK ASSEMBLY JAR

When submitting Spark applications to a YARN cluster, JAR files containing Spark classes (all the JARs from Spark installation's jars folder) need to be transferred to the containers on remote nodes. This upload can take some time because these files can take up more than 150 MB. You can shorten this time by uploading the JARs to a specific folder on all executor machines manually and set `spark.yarn.jars` configuration parameter to point to that folder. Or you can make it point to a central folder on HDFS.

There is a third option. You can put the JAR files in an archive and set the `spark.yarn.archive` parameter to point to the archive (in a folder on each node or in an HDFS folder).

This way, Spark will be able to access the JARs from each container when needed, instead of uploading the JARs from the client each time it runs.

MODIFYING THE CLASSPATH AND SHARING FILES

Most of the things we said in the previous chapter about specifying extra classpath entries and files for a standalone cluster also apply to YARN. You can use a `SPARK_CLASSPATH` variable, the `--jars` command-line parameter, or `spark.driver.extra-ClassPath` (and others in `spark.*.extra[Class|Library]Path`). For more details, see the official documentation at http://mng.bz/75KO.

There are a few differences, though. An additional command-line parameter, `--archives`, lets you specify an archive name that will be transferred to worker machines and extracted into the working directory of each executor. Additionally, for each file or archive specified with `--archives` and `--files`, you can add a reference filename so you can access it from your program running on executors. For example, you can submit your application with these parameters:

```
--files /path/to/myfile.txt#fileName.txt
```

Then, you can access the file myfile.txt from your program by using the name fileName.txt. This is specific to running on YARN.

12.1.6 *Configuring resources for Spark jobs*

YARN schedules CPU and memory resources. A few specifics that you should be aware of are described in this section. For example, the default number of executor cores should be changed in most circumstances (as described shortly). Also, to take advantage of Spark's memory management, it's important to configure it properly, especially on YARN. Several important, YARN-specific parameters are mentioned here as well.

SPECIFYING CPU RESOURCES FOR AN APPLICATION

The default setup when running on YARN is to have two executors and one core per executor. This usually isn't enough. To change this, use the following command-line options when submitting an application to YARN:

- `--num-executors`—Changes the number of executors
- `--executor-cores`—Changes the number of cores per executor

SPARK MEMORY MANAGEMENT WHEN RUNNING ON YARN

Just as on a standalone cluster, driver memory can be set with the `--driver-memory` command-line parameter, a `spark.driver.memory` configuration parameter, or the `SPARK_DRIVER_MEMORY` environment variable. For executors, the situation is a bit different. Similar to a standalone cluster, `spark.executor.memory` determines the executors' heap size (same as the `SPARK_EXECUTOR_MEMORY` environment variable or the `--executor-memory` command-line parameter). An additional parameter, `spark.executor.memoryOverhead`, determines additional memory beyond the Java heap that will be available to YARN containers running Spark executors. This memory is necessary for the JVM process itself. If your executor uses more memory than `spark.executor.memory` + `spark.executor.memoryOverhead`, YARN will shut down the container, and your jobs will repeatedly fail.

> **TIP** Failing to set `spark.executor.memoryOverhead` to a sufficiently high value can lead to problems that are hard to diagnose. Make sure to specify at least 1024 MB.

The memory layout of Spark's executors when running on YARN is shown in figure 12.3. It shows memory overhead along with the sections of the Java heap we described in section 10.2.4: storage memory (whose size is determined by `spark.storage.memoryFraction`), shuffle memory (size determined by `spark.shuffle.memoryFraction`), and the rest of the heap used for Java objects.

When your application is running in YARN cluster mode, `spark.yarn.driver.memoryOverhead` determines the memory overhead of the driver's container. `spark.yarn.am.memoryOverhead` determines the memory overhead of the application master in

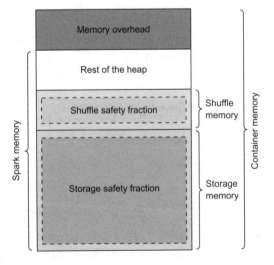

Figure 12.3 Components of Spark's executors' memory on YARN

client mode. Furthermore, a few YARN parameters (specified in yarn-site.xml) influence memory allocation:

- `yarn.scheduler.maximum-allocation-mb`—Determines the upper memory limit of YARN containers. The resource manager won't allow allocation of larger amounts of memory. The default value is 8192 MB.
- `yarn.scheduler.minimum-allocation-mb`—Determines the minimum amount of memory the resource manager can allocate. The resource manager allocates memory only in multiples of this parameter. The default value is 1024 MB.
- `yarn.nodemanager.resource.memory-mb`—Determines the maximum amount of memory YARN can use on a node overall. The default value is 8192 MB.

`yarn.nodemanager.resource.memory-mb` should be set to the amount of memory available on a node, minus the memory needed for the OS. `yarn.scheduler.maximum-allocation-mb` should be set to the same value. Because YARN will round up all allocation requests to multiples of `yarn.scheduler.minimum-allocation-mb`, that parameter should be set to a value small enough to not waste memory unnecessarily (for example, 256 MB).

CONFIGURING EXECUTOR RESOURCES PROGRAMMATICALLY

Executor resources can also be specified when creating Spark context objects programmatically with the `spark.executor.cores`, `spark.executor.instances`, and `spark.executor.memory` parameters. But if your application is running in YARN cluster mode, the driver is running in its own container, started in parallel with executor containers, so these parameters will have no effect. In that case, it's best to set these parameters in the spark-defaults.conf file or on the command line.

12.1.7 *YARN UI*

Similar to a Spark standalone cluster, YARN also provides a web interface for monitoring the cluster state. By default, it starts on port 8088 on the machine where the resource manager is running. You can see the state and various metrics of your nodes, the current capacity usage of the cluster, local and remote log files, and the status of finished and currently running applications. Figure 12.4 shows a sample YARN UI starting page with a list of applications.

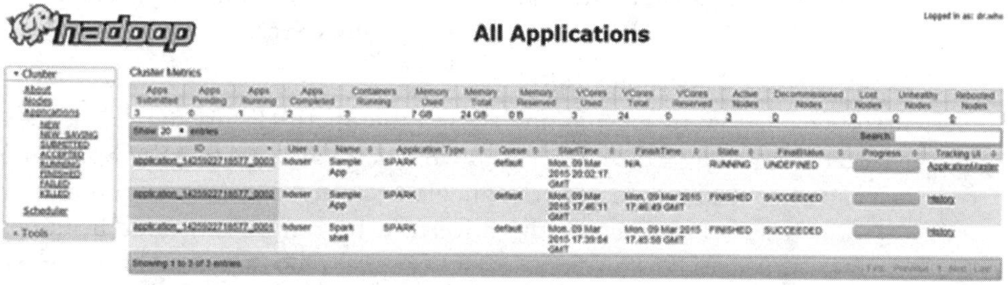

Figure 12.4 YARN UI: the All Applications page shows a list of running and finished applications

Figure 12.5   YARN UI: The Application Overview page

From this page, you can click an application's ID, which takes you to the Application Overview page (figure 12.5). There you can examine the application's name, status, and running time, and access its log files. The node at which the application master is running is also displayed.

ACCESSING THE SPARK WEB UI FROM THE YARN UI

The so-called *tracking UI* (or *tracking URL*) is available from the YARN UI Applications page and from the Application Overview page. The tracking URL takes you to the Spark web UI if the application is still running. We described the Spark web UI in chapter 10.

> **TIP**   If you get the error "Connection refused" in your browser when trying to access the Spark web UI through the Tracking UI link, you should set the YARN configuration parameter `yarn.resourcemanager.hostname` (in yarn-site.xml) to the exact value of your YARN hostname.

When the application finishes, you'll be taken to the YARN Application Overview page (figure 12.4). If you have the Spark History Server running, the tracking URL for the finished application will point to the Spark History Server.

SPARK HISTORY SERVER AND YARN

If you enabled event logging and started the Spark History Server (as described in chapter 10), you'll be able to access the Spark web UI of a finished Spark application, just like when running on a Spark standalone cluster. But if you're running your application in YARN cluster mode, the driver can be run on any node in the cluster. In order for the Spark History Server to see the event log files, don't use a local directory as an event log directory; put it on HDFS.

12.1.8 Finding logs on YARN

By default, YARN stores your application's logs locally on the machines where the containers are running. The directory for storing log files is determined by the parameter `yarn.nodemanager.log-dirs` (set in yarn-site.xml), which defaults to <Hadoop installation directory>/logs/userlogs. To view the log files, you need to look in this directory on each container's machine. The directory contains a subdirectory for each application.

You can also find the log files through the YARN web UI. The application master's logs are available from the Application Overview page. To view logs from other containers, you need to find the appropriate node by clicking Nodes and then clicking the node name in the list of nodes. Then go to its list of containers, where you can access logs for each of them.

USING LOG AGGREGATION

Another option on YARN is to enable the *log aggregation* feature by setting the `yarn.log-aggregation-enable` parameter in yarn-site.xml to `true`. After an application finishes, its log files will be transferred to a directory on HDFS as specified by the parameter `yarn.nodemanager.remote-app-log-dir`, which defaults to /tmp/logs. Under this directory, a hierarchy of subdirectories is created, first by the current user's username and then by the application ID. The final application aggregate log directory contains one file per node on which it executed.

You can view these aggregate log files by using the `yarn logs` command (only after the application has finished executing) and specifying the application ID:

```
$ yarn logs -applicationId <application_id>
```

As we already said, you can obtain the application ID from the `spark-submit` command's output if logging of `INFO` messages for the `org.apache.spark` package is enabled. Otherwise, you can find it on the YARN web UI (see section 12.1.5).

You can view a single container's logs by specifying the container's ID. To do so, you also need to specify the hostname and port of the node on which the container is executing. You can find this information on the Nodes page of the YARN web UI:

```
$ yarn logs -applicationId <application_id> -containerId <container_id> \
-nodeAddress <node hostname>:<node port>
```

You can then use shell utilities to further filter and grep the logs.

CONFIGURING THE LOGGING LEVEL

If you want to use an application-specific log4j configuration, you need to upload your log4j.properties file using the `--files` option while submitting the application. Alternatively, you can specify the location of the log4j.properties file (which should already be present on the node machines) using the `-Dlog4j.configuration` parameter in the `spark.executor.extraJavaOptions` option. For example, from the command line, you can do it like this:

```
$ spark-submit --master yarn-client --conf spark.executor.extraJavaOptions=
-Dlog4j.configuration=file:/usr/local/conf/log4j.properties" ...
```

12.1.9 *Security considerations*

Hadoop provides the means for authorizing access to resources (HDFS files, for example) to certain users, but it has no means of user authentication. Hadoop instead relies on Kerberos, a widely used and robust security framework. Hadoop allows user access or not, depending on Kerberos-provided identity and access control lists in the Hadoop configuration. If Kerberos is enabled in a Hadoop cluster (in other words, the cluster is *Kerberized*), only Kerberos-authenticated users can access it. YARN knows how to handle Kerberos authentication information and pass it on to HDFS. The Spark standalone and Mesos cluster managers don't have this functionality. You'll need to use YARN to run Spark if you need to access Kerberized HDFS.

To submit jobs to a Kerberized YARN cluster, you need a Kerberos *service principal name* (in the form username/host@KERBEROS_REALM_NAME; the *host* part is optional) and a *keytab* file. The service principal name serves as your Kerberos user name. Your keytab file contains pairs of user names and encryption keys used for encrypting Kerberos authentication messages. Your service principal name and keytab file are typically provided by your Kerberos administrator.

Before submitting a job to a Kerberized YARN cluster, you need to authenticate with a Kerberos server using the kinit command (on Linux systems):

```
$ kinit -kt <your_keytab_file> <your_service_principal>
```

Then submit your job as usual.

12.1.10 *Dynamic resource allocation*

As you may recall from the previous chapters, Spark applications obtain executors from the cluster manager and use them until they finish executing. The same executors are used for several jobs of the same application, and executors' resources remain allocated even though they may be idle between jobs. This enables tasks to reuse data from a previous job's tasks that ran on the same executors. For example, spark-shell may be idle for a long time while the user is away from their computer, but the executors it allocated remain, holding the cluster's resources.

Dynamic allocation is Spark's remedy for this situation, enabling applications to release executors temporarily so that other applications can use the allocated resources. This option has been available since Spark 1.2, but only for the YARN cluster manager. Since Spark 1.5, it's also available on Mesos and standalone clusters.

USING DYNAMIC ALLOCATION

You enable dynamic allocation by setting the spark.dynamicAllocation.enabled parameter to true. You should also enable Spark's shuffle service, which is used to serve executors' shuffle files even after the executors are no longer available. If an executor's shuffle files are requested and the executor isn't available while the service isn't enabled, shuffle files will need to be recalculated, which wastes resources. Therefore, you should always enable the shuffle service when enabling dynamic allocation.

To enable the shuffle service on YARN, you need to add spark-<version>-shuffle.jar (available from the lib directory of the Spark distribution) to the classpath of all node managers in the cluster. To do this, put the file in the share/hadoop/yarn/lib folder of your Hadoop installation and then add or edit the following properties in the yarn-site.xml file:

- Set the property `yarn.nodemanager.aux-services` to the value "mapreduce _shuffle,spark_shuffle" (basically, add `spark_shuffle` to the string).
- set the property `yarn.nodemanager.aux-services.spark_shuffle.class` to `org.apache.spark.network.yarn.YarnShuffleService`.

This will start the service in each node manager in your cluster. To tell Spark that it should use the service, you need to set the `spark.shuffle.service.enabled` Spark parameter to `true`.

When dynamic allocation is configured and running, Spark will measure the time during which there are pending tasks to be executed. If this period exceeds the interval specified by the parameter `spark.dynamicAllocation.schedulerBacklog-Timeout` (in seconds), Spark will request executors from the resource manager. It will continue to request them every `spark.dynamicAllocation.sustained-SchedulerBacklogTimeout` seconds if there are pending tasks. Every time Spark requests new executors, the number of executors requested increases exponentially so that it can respond to the demand quickly enough—but not too quickly, in case the application only needs a couple of them. The parameter `spark.dynamic-Allocation.executorIdleTimeout` specifies the number of seconds an executor needs to remain idle before it's removed.

You can control the number of executors with these parameters:

- `spark.dynamicAllocation.minExecutors`—Minimum number of executors for your application
- `spark.dynamicAllocation.maxExecutors`—Maximum number of executors for your application
- `spark.dynamicAllocation.initialExecutors`—Initial number of executors for your application

12.2 Running Spark on Mesos

Mesos is the last cluster manager supported by Spark that we'll talk about, but it's certainly not the least. We mentioned that the Spark project was originally started in order to demonstrate the usefulness of Mesos. Apple's Siri application runs on Mesos, as well as applications at eBay, Netflix, Twitter, Uber, and many other companies.

Mesos provides a distributed systems kernel and serves commodity cluster resources to applications, just like a Linux kernel manages a single computer's resources and serves them to applications running on a single machine. Mesos supports applications written in Java, C, C++, and Python. With version 0.20, Mesos can run Docker containers, which are packages containing all the libraries and configurations that an application needs in order to run. With Docker support, you can run Mesos on virtually any application that can run in a Docker container. Since Spark 1.4, Spark can run on Mesos in Docker containers, too.

A few points where Mesos can use some improvement are security and support to run stateful applications (ones that use persistent storage, such as databases). With the current version (1.0.1), it isn't advisable to run stateful applications on Mesos. The community is working on supporting these use cases, too.[2] Also, Kerberos-based authentication isn't supported yet (https://issues.apache.org/jira/browse/MESOS-907). Applications, however, can provide authentication using Simple Authentication and Security Layer (SASL, a widely used authentication and data security framework), and intra-cluster communication is secured with Secure Sockets Layer (SSL). Dynamic allocation (explained in section 12.1.10), previously reserved for YARN only, is available on Mesos with Spark 1.5.

To begin our exploration of running Spark on Mesos, we'll first examine the Mesos architecture more closely. Then we'll see how running Spark on Mesos is different than running it on YARN and in Spark standalone clusters.

12.2.1 *Mesos architecture*

It's simpler to compare the Mesos architecture to a Spark standalone cluster than to YARN. Mesos's basic components—*masters*, *slaves*, and *applications* (or *frameworks*, in Mesos terms)—should be familiar to you from chapter 11. As is the case with a Spark standalone cluster, a Mesos master schedules slave resources among applications that want to use them. Slaves launch the application's executors, which execute tasks.

So far, so good. Mesos is more powerful than a Spark standalone cluster and differs from it in several important points. First, it can schedule other types of applications besides Spark (Java, Scala, C, C++, and Python applications). It's also capable of scheduling disk space, network ports, and even custom resources (not just CPU and memory). And instead of applications *demanding* resources from the cluster (from its master), a Mesos cluster *offers* resources to applications, which they can accept or refuse.

Frameworks running on Mesos (such as Spark applications) consist of two components: a *scheduler* and an *executor*. The scheduler accepts or rejects resources offered by the Mesos master and automatically starts Mesos executors on slaves. Mesos executors run tasks as requested by the frameworks' schedulers.

Figure 12.6 shows Spark running on a two-node Mesos cluster in client-deploy and coarse-grained modes. You'll learn what *coarse-grained* means in an instant.

---

[2] For more information, see https://issues.apache.org/jira/browse/MESOS-1554.

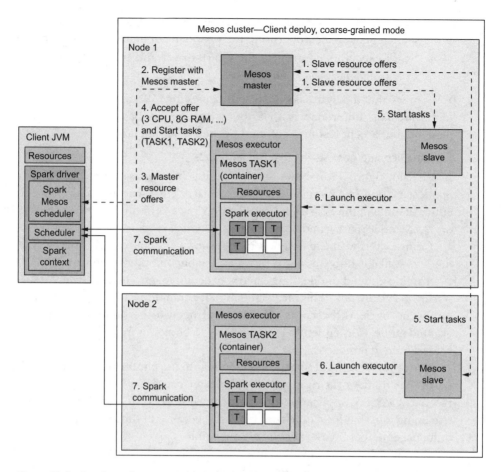

Figure 12.6 Spark running on a two-node Mesos cluster in client-deploy and coarse-grained modes

Let's explain the communication steps shown on the figure:

1 Mesos slaves offer their resources to the master.

2 Spark's Mesos-specific scheduler, running in a driver (the Spark `submit` command, for example) registers with the Mesos master.

3 The Mesos master in turn offers the available resources to the Spark Mesos scheduler (this happens continually: by default, every second while the framework is alive).

4 Spark's Mesos scheduler accepts some of the resources and sends a list of resources, along with a list of tasks it wants to run using the resources, to the Mesos master.

5 The master asks the slaves to start the tasks with the requested resources.

6 Slaves launch executors (in this case, Mesos's Command Executors), which launch Spark executors (using the provided command) in task containers.

7 Spark executors connect to the Spark driver and freely communicate with it, executing Spark tasks as usual.

You can see that the figure is similar to the ones for YARN and a Spark standalone cluster. The main difference is that the scheduling is backward: applications don't demand, but accept resources offered by the cluster manager.

FINE-GRAINED AND COARSE-GRAINED SPARK MODES

As we said, figure 12.6 shows Spark running in coarse-grained mode. This means Spark starts one Spark executor per Mesos slave. These executors stay alive during the entire lifetime of the Spark application and run tasks in much the same way as they do on YARN and a Spark standalone cluster.

Contrast this with fine-grained mode, shown on figure 12.7. Spark's fine-grained mode is available only on Mesos (it isn't available on other cluster types).

In fine-grained mode, one Spark executor—and, hence, one Mesos task—is started per Spark task. This means much more communication, data serialization, and setting up of Spark executor processes will need to be done, compared to coarse-grained mode. Consequently, jobs are likely to be slower in fine-grained mode than in coarse-grained mode.

The rationale behind fine-grained mode is to use cluster resources more flexibly so that other frameworks running on the cluster can get a chance to use some of the resources a Spark application may not currently need. It's used mainly for batch or streaming jobs that have long-running tasks, because in those cases, the slowdown due to management of Spark executors is negligible.

One additional detail visible in figure 12.7 is the Spark Mesos executor. This is a custom Mesos executor used only in Spark fine-grained mode.

Fine-grained mode is the default option, so if you try Mesos and see that it's much slower than YARN or a Spark standalone cluster, first switch to coarse-grained mode by setting the `spark.mesos.coarse` parameter to `true` (configuring Spark was described in chapter 10) and try your job again. Chances are, it will be much faster.

MESOS CONTAINERS

Tasks in Mesos are executed in *containers*, shown in figures 12.6 and 12.7, whose purpose is to isolate resources between processes (tasks) on the same slave so that tasks don't interfere with each other. The two basic types of containers in Mesos are *Linux cgroups containers* (default containers) and *Docker containers*.

- *cgroups (control groups)*—A feature of the Linux kernel that limits and isolates processes' resource usage. A control group is a collection of processes to which a set of resource limitations (CPU, memory, network, disk) is applied.
- Docker containers—Similar to VMs. In addition to limiting resources, as cgroups containers do, Docker containers provide the required system libraries. This is the crucial difference.

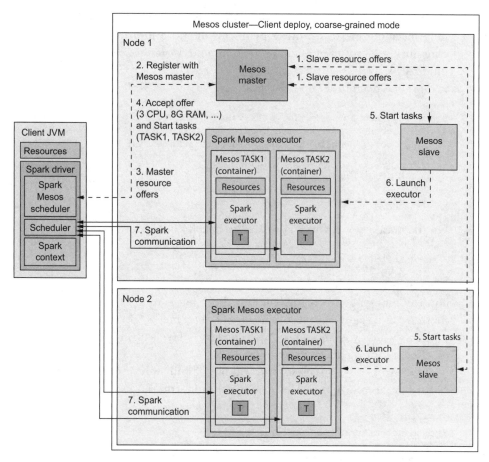

Figure 12.7 Spark running on a two-node Mesos cluster in client-deploy and fine-grained modes. Each Spark executor runs only one task.

We'll say more about using Docker in Mesos in section 12.2.6.

MASTER HIGH-AVAILABILITY

Similar to Spark standalone clusters, you can set up Mesos to use several master processes. Master processes use ZooKeeper to elect a leader among themselves. If the leader goes down, the standby masters will elect a new leader, again using ZooKeeper.

12.2.2 *Installing and configuring Mesos*

The officially recommended way to install Mesos is to build it from source code.[3] But if you're lucky enough to be running a Linux version supported by Mesosphere, a quicker and simpler way is to install Mesos from the Mesosphere package repository.[4]

---

[3] For more information, see the "Getting Started" guide at http://mesos.apache.org/gettingstarted.
[4] For more information, see https://mesosphere.com/downloads.

Here we show the steps for installing Mesos from Mesosphere on Ubuntu. If you need help installing Mesos on other platforms or more information about installing and configuring Mesos in general, we recommend *Mesos in Action* by Roger Ignazio (Manning, 2016).

You first need to set up the repository

```
$ sudo apt-key adv --keyserver keyserver.ubuntu.com --recv E56151BF
$ echo "deb http://repos.mesosphere.io/ubuntu trusty main" | \
    sudo tee /etc/apt/sources.list.d/mesosphere.list
```

and then install the package:

```
$ sudo apt-get install mesos
```

On the master node, you'll also need to install Zookeeper:

```
$ sudo apt-get install zookeeper
```

BASIC CONFIGURATION

You're (almost) good to go. The only thing left is to tell the slaves where to find the master. Master and slaves look in the file /etc/mesos/zk to find ZooKeeper's master address (which you should set up and start before starting Mesos). Slaves always ask ZooKeeper for the master's address.

Once you edit /etc/mesos/zk, you have a fully working Mesos cluster. If you want to further customize your Mesos configuration, you can use these locations:

```
/etc/mesos
/etc/mesos-master
/etc/mesos-slave
/etc/default/mesos
/etc/default/mesos-master
/etc/default/mesos-slave
```

The list of all configuration options is available at the official documentation page (http://mesos.apache.org/documentation/latest/configuration). You can also obtain it by running the `mesos-master --help` and `mesos-slave --help` commands. Environment variables are specified in the /etc/default/mesos* files just listed. Command-line parameters can also be specified on the command line and in the /etc/mesos/* directories. Place each parameter in a separate file, where the name of the file matches the parameter name and the contents of the file contain the parameter value.

STARTING MESOS

You run Mesos by starting the corresponding service. To start the master, you should use

```
$ sudo service mesos-master start
```

Use this for slaves:

```
$ sudo service mesos-slave start
```

These commands automatically pick up the configurations from the configuration files previously described. You can verify that the services are running by accessing the Mesos web UI at port 5050 (the default port).

12.2.3 *Mesos web UI*

When you start a Mesos master, it automatically starts a web UI interface. Figure 12.8 shows the main page.

Figure 12.8 **The main Mesos web UI page shows active and completed tasks and basic information about the cluster.**

On the main page, you'll find a list of active and completed tasks, information about the master and slaves, and an overview of the cluster's CPU and memory (figure 12.9). The list of active and terminated frameworks is available on the Frameworks page (figure 12.10).

You can click one of the frameworks to examine a list of its active and terminated tasks. The Slaves page (figure 12.11) shows a list of registered slaves and their resources. This is where

Resources

	CPUs	Mem
Total	6	14.5 GB
Used	6	4.1 GB
Offered	0	0 B
Idle	0	10.4 GB

Figure 12.9 **Overview of the state of the cluster's CPU and memory resources on the main Mesos web UI page**

Active Frameworks

ID ▼	Host	User	Name	Active Tasks	CPUs	Mem	Max Share	Registered	Re-Registered
5050-17096-0003			Sample App	0	3	4.1 GB	50%	2 minutes ago	-

Terminated Frameworks

ID ▼	Host	User	Name	Registered	Unregistered
5050-17096-0002			Sample App	5 minutes ago	4 minutes ago
5050-17096-0001			Sample App	an hour ago	an hour ago
5050-17096-0000			Sample App	an hour ago	an hour ago

Figure 12.10 **The Mesos Frameworks page shows active and terminated frameworks, with an overview of their resources.**

you can check whether all of your slaves have registered with the master and are available. You can click one of the slaves to see a list of previous or currently running frameworks. If you click one of the frameworks, you'll also see a list of its running and completed executors on that slave.

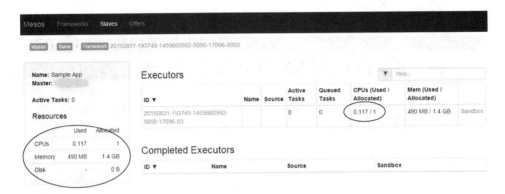

Figure 12.11   A list of a framework's executors on a slave. The executor's environment is available from the Sandbox link.

From this screen, you can access an executor's environment by clicking the Sandbox link. Figure 12.12 shows the resulting page.

The Sandbox page lets you see your executor's environment: application files and its log files. When you click one of the log files, a separate window opens with a live view of your application's logs, which is automatically updated as new lines become available. This is useful for debugging your application.

Mesos	Frameworks	**Slaves**	Offers				

Master	/	Slave	/	Browse

mode	nlink	uid	gid	size	mtime		
-rwxr-xr-x	1	hduser	hadoop	72 KB	Aug 31 20:56	sample-app.jar	Download
-rw-r--r--	1	root	root	153 KB	Aug 31 20:59	stderr	Download
-rw-r--r--	1	root	root	0 B	Aug 31 20:56	stdout	Download

Figure 12.12   An executor's Sandbox page shows the executor's working folder. You can also download application files and system out and system error log files.

12.2.4 *Mesos resource scheduling*

The fine-grained and coarse-grained scheduling described in section 12.2.1 are Spark's scheduling policies when running on Mesos. Mesos itself knows nothing about them.

Resource scheduling decisions in Mesos are made on two levels: by the *resource-allocation module* running in the Mesos master, and by the *framework's scheduler*, which we mentioned previously. A resource-allocation module decides which resources to offer to which frameworks and in which order. As we mentioned, Mesos can schedule memory, CPU, disk, network ports, and even custom resources. It seeks to satisfy the needs of all frameworks while fairly distributing resources among them.

Different types of workloads and different frameworks require different allocation policies, because some are long-running and some are short-running, some mostly use memory, some CPU, and so forth. That's why a resource-allocation module allows for use of plug-ins that can change resource-allocation decisions.

By default, Mesos uses the Dominant Resource Fairness (DRF) algorithm, which is appropriate for the majority of use cases. It tracks each framework's resources and determines the *dominant resource* for each framework, which is the resource type the framework uses the most. Then it calculates the framework's *dominant share*, which is the share of all cluster resources of the dominant resource type used by the framework. If a framework is using 1 CPU and 6 GB of RAM in a cluster of 20 CPUs and 36 GB of RAM, then it's using 1/20 of all CPUs and 1/6 of all RAM; thus its dominant resource is RAM, and its dominant share is 1/6.

DRF allocates the newest resource to the framework with the lowest dominant share. The framework can accept or reject the offer. If it currently has no work to do, or if the offer doesn't contain enough resources for its needs, the framework can reject the offer. This can be useful if the framework needs a specific locality level for its tasks. It can wait until a resource offer with an acceptable locality level becomes available. If a framework is holding on to some resources for too long, Mesos can revoke the tasks taking up the resources.

ROLES, WEIGHTS, AND RESOURCE ALLOCATIONS

Roles and weights let you prioritize frameworks so that some get more resource offers than others. *Roles* are names attached to typical groups of users or frameworks, and *weights* are numbers attached to roles that specify priorities the roles will have when resource-allocation decisions are made.

You can initialize a master with a list of acceptable roles with the `--roles` option (for example, `--roles=dev,test,stage,prod`) or with a list of weights per role (for example, `--weights='dev=30,test=50,stage=80,prod=100'`). As we explained in the previous section, you can place these values in the /etc/mesos-master/roles and /etc/mesos-master/weights files, respectively. In this example, the `prod` role will get twice as many resource offers as the `test` role.

Furthermore, resource allocations can be used on slaves to reserve some resources for a particular role. When starting a slave, you can specify the `--resources` parameter with the contents formatted as follows: `'resource_name1(role_name1):value1;` `'resource_name2(role_name2):value2'`. For example, `--resources='cpu(prod):3;` `mem(prod):2048'` will reserve 3 CPUs and 2 GB of RAM exclusively for frameworks in the `prod` role.

Frameworks can specify a role when registering with a master. To tell Spark which role to use when registering Mesos, you can use the `spark.mesos.role` parameter (which is available with Spark version 1.5).

MESOS ATTRIBUTES AND SPARK CONSTRAINTS

Mesos also lets you specify custom attributes per slave with the `--attributes` parameter. You can use attributes to specify the type and version of the slave's operating system or the rack the slave is running on. Mesos supports attributes of the following types: float, integer, range, set, and text. For more information, see the official documentation (http://mesos.apache.org/documentation/attributes-resources/). Once specified, the attributes are sent with each resource offer.

Beginning with Spark 1.5, you can specify attribute constraints using the `spark.mesos.constraints` parameter. This instructs Spark to accept only those offers whose attributes match the specified constraints. You specify the constraints as key-value pairs, separated by semicolons (`;`). Keys and values themselves are separated by colons (`:`); and if the value is composed of several values, they're separated by commas (`,`) (for example, `os:ubuntu,redhat;zone:EU1,EU2`).

12.2.5 *Submitting Spark applications to Mesos*

The master URL for submitting Spark applications to Mesos starts with mesos:// and needs to specify the master's hostname and port:

```
$ spark-submit --master mesos://<master_hostname>:<master_port>
```

The default Mesos master port is 5050. If you have several masters running, synchronized through Zookeeper, you can instruct Spark to ask Zookeeper for the currently elected leader by specifying a master URL in this format:

```
mesos://zk://<zookeeper_hostname>:<zookeeper_port>
```

The ZooKeeper port defaults to 2181.

MAKING SPARK AVAILABLE TO SLAVES

Mesos's slaves need to know where to find the Spark classes to start your tasks. If you have Spark installed on the slave machines in the same location as on the driver, then there's nothing special you need to do to make Spark available on the slave machines. Mesos's slaves will automatically pick up Spark from the same location.

If Spark is installed on the slave machines, but in a different location, then you can specify this location with the Spark parameter `spark.mesos.executor.home`. If you don't have Spark installed on the slave machines, then you need to upload Spark's binary package to a location accessible by slaves. This can be an NFS shared filesystem or a location on HDFS or Amazon S3. You can get Spark's binary package either by downloading it from Spark's official download page or by building Spark yourself and packaging the distribution with the `make-distribution.sh` command. Then you need to set this location as the value of the parameter `spark.executor.uri` *and* as the value of the environment variable `SPARK_EXECUTOR_URI`.

RUNNING IN CLUSTER MODE

Mesos's cluster mode is available with Spark 1.4. A new component was added to Spark for this purpose: MesosClusterDispatcher. It's a separate Mesos framework used only for submitting Spark drivers to Mesos.

You start `MesosClusterDispatcher` with the script `start-mesos-dispatcher.sh` from Spark's sbin directory and then pass the master URL to it. Start the cluster dispatcher with ZooKeeper's version of the master's URL. Otherwise, you may have problems submitting jobs (for example, `submit` could hang). The complete `start` command looks like this:

```
$ start-mesos-dispatcher.sh --master mesos://zk://<bind_address>:2181/mesos
```

The dispatcher process will start listening at port 7077. You can then submit applications to the dispatcher process instead of the Mesos master. You also need to specify cluster-deploy mode when submitting applications:

```
$ spark-submit --deploy-mode cluster --master \
    mesos://<dispatcher_hostname>:7077 ...
```

If everything goes OK, the driver's Mesos task will be visible in the Mesos UI, and you'll be able to see which slave it's running. You can use that information to access the driver's Spark web UI.

OTHER CONFIGURATION OPTIONS

A few more parameters are available for configuring how Spark runs on Mesos, in addition to the `spark.mesos.coarse`, `spark.mesos.role`, and `spark.mesos.constraints` parameters that we mentioned before. They're shown in table 12.2.

Table 12.2 Additional configuration parameters for running Spark on Mesos

Parameter	Default	Description
`spark.cores.max`	All available cores	Limits the number of tasks your cluster can run in parallel. It's available on other cluster managers, too.
`spark.mesos .mesosExecutor.cores`	1	Tells Spark how many cores to reserve per Mesos executor, in addition to the resources it takes for its tasks. The value can be a decimal number.

Table 12.2 Additional configuration parameters for running Spark on Mesos *(continued)*

Parameter	Default	Description
`spark.mesos.extra.cores`	0	Specifies the extra number of cores to reserve per task in coarse-grained mode.
`spark.mesos.executor .memoryOverhead`	10% of `spark.executor .memory`	Specifies the amount of extra memory to reserve per executor. This is similar to the memory overhead parameter on YARN.

12.2.6 *Running Spark with Docker*

As we said earlier, Mesos uses Linux cgroups as the default "containerizer" for the tasks it's running, but it can also use Docker. Docker lets you package an application along with all of its library and configuration requirements. The name *Docker* comes from an analogy to freight containers, which all adhere to the same specifications and sizes so they can be handled and transported the same way regardless of their contents. The same principle runs true for Docker containers: they can run in different environments (different OSes with different versions of Java, Python, or other libraries), but they behave the same way on all of them because they bring their own libraries with them. So, you only need to set up your machines to run Docker containers. Docker containers bring everything needed for whichever application they contain.

You can use Docker, Mesos, and Spark in several interesting ways and combinations. You can run Mesos in Docker containers, or you can run Spark in Docker containers. You can have Mesos run Spark and other applications in Docker containers, or you can do both—run Mesos in Docker containers and have it run other Docker containers. EBay, for example, uses Mesos to run Jenkins servers for continuous delivery in the company's development department (http://mng.bz/MLtO).

The benefit of running Docker containers on Mesos is that Docker and Mesos provide two layers of abstraction between your application and the infrastructure it's running on, so you can write your application for a specific environment (contained in Docker) and distribute it to hundreds and thousands of different machines. We'll first show you how to install and configure Docker and then how to use it to run Spark jobs on Mesos.

INSTALLING DOCKER

Installing Docker on Ubuntu is simple because the installation script is available online at https://get.docker.com/.[5] You only need to pass it to your shell:

```
$ curl -sSL https://get.docker.com/ | sh
```

You can verify your installation with this command:

```
$ sudo docker run hello-world
```

---

[5] For other environments, see the official installation documentation: https://docs.docker.com/installation.

To enable other users to run the docker command without having to use sudo every time, create a user group named docker and add your user to the group:

```
$ sudo addgroup docker
$ sudo usermod -aG docker <your_username>
```

After logging out and logging back in, you should be able to run docker without using the sudo command.

USING DOCKER

Docker uses *images* to run containers. Images are comparable to templates, and containers are comparable to concrete instances of the images. You can *build* new images from *Dockerfiles*, which describe the image contents, and you can *pull* images from Docker Hub, an online repository of public Docker images. If you visit Docker Hub (https://hub.docker.com) and search for *mesos* or *spark*, you'll see that dozens of images are available for you to use. In this section, you'll build a Docker image based on the mesosphere/mesos image available from Docker Hub.

When you have *built* or *pulled* an image to your local machine, it's available locally, and you can *run* it. If you try to run an image that doesn't exist locally, Docker pulls it automatically from the Docker Hub. To list all the images available locally, you can use the docker images command. To see the running containers, use the docker ps command. For the complete command reference, use the docker --help command.

You can also run a command in a container in interactive mode by using the -i and -t flags, and by specifying the command as an additional argument. For example, this command starts a bash shell in a container of an image called spark-image:

```
$ docker run -it spark-image bash
```

BUILDING A SPARK DOCKER IMAGE

This is the contents of a Dockerfile for building a Docker image that can be used to run Spark on Mesos:

```
FROM mesosphere/mesos:0.20.1
RUN apt-get update && \
    apt-get install -y python libnss3 openjdk-7-jre-headless curl
RUN mkdir /opt/spark && \
    curl http://www-us.apache.org/dist/spark/
spark-2.0.0/spark-2.0.0-bin-hadoop2.7.tgz | tar -xzC /opt
ENV SPARK_HOME /opt/spark-2.0.0-bin-hadoop2.7
ENV MESOS_NATIVE_JAVA_LIBRARY /usr/local/lib/libmesos.so
```

Copy those lines into a file called Dockerfile in a folder of your choosing. Then, position yourself in the folder and build the image using this command:

```
$ docker build -t spark-mesos .
```

This command instructs Docker to build an image called *spark-mesos* using the Docker file in the current directory. You can verify that your image is available with the `docker images` command. You need to do this *on all the slave machines* in your Mesos cluster.

PREPARING MESOS TO USE DOCKER

Before using Docker in Mesos, the Docker containerizer needs to be enabled. You need to execute the following two commands on each of the slave machines in your Mesos cluster:

```
$ echo 'docker,mesos' > /etc/mesos-slave/containerizers
$ echo '5mins' > /etc/mesos-slave/executor_registration_timeout
```

Then restart your slaves:

```
$ sudo service mesos-slave restart
```

Mesos should now be ready to run Spark executors in Docker images.

RUNNING SPARK TASKS IN DOCKER IMAGES

Before running Spark tasks in your newly built Docker image, you need to set a couple of configuration parameters. First, you need to tell Spark the name of the image by specifying it in the `spark.mesos.executor.docker.image` parameter (in your spark-defaults.conf file). The image you built has Spark installed in the folder /opt/ spark-2.0.0-bin-hadoop2.7, which is probably different than your Spark installation location. So, you'll need to set the parameter `spark.mesos.executor.home` to the image's Spark installation location. And you'll need to tell Spark executors where to find Mesos's system library. You can do this with the parameter `spark.executorEnv` `.MESOS_NATIVE_JAVA_LIBRARY`.

Your spark-defaults.conf file should now contain these lines:

```
spark.mesos.executor.docker.image          spark-mesos
spark.mesos.executor.home                  /opt/spark-2.0.0-bin-hadoop2.7
spark.executorEnv.MESOS_NATIVE_JAVA_LIBRARY  /usr/local/lib/libmesos.so
```

We'll use the `SparkPi` example to demonstrate submitting an application to Docker, but you can use your own (for example, the one built in chapter 3). Position yourself in your Spark home directory, and issue the following command (the name of the JAR file could be different, depending on your Spark version):

```
$ spark-submit --master mesos://zk://<your_hostname>:2181/mesos \
    --class org.apache.spark.examples.SparkPi \
    examples/jars/spark-examples_2.11-2.0.0.jar
```

If everything goes well, you should see the message *Pi is roughly 3.13972* in your console output. To verify that Mesos really used a Docker container to run Spark tasks, you can use the Mesos UI to find your framework. Click the Sandbox link next to one of framework's completed tasks, and then open its standard output log file. It should contain the following line:

```
Registered docker executor on <slave's_hostname>
```

FURTHER DOCKER CONFIGURATION

If you need to access the slave's filesystem from within your Docker image, Docker lets you mount the host's folders to the folders in your image with the -v flag. You can instruct Spark to do this for you when launching Docker executors by specifying the parameter spark.mesos.executor.docker.volumes containing a comma-separated list of volume (folder) mappings in the following format:

```
[host_path:]container_path[:ro|:rw]
```

The host path is optional if it's the same as the container path.

Docker also lets you connect certain network ports on your image to the ones on the slave's host. You can specify these port mappings with the parameter spark.mesos.executor.docker.portmaps in this format:

```
host_port:container_port[:tcp|:udp]
```

This way, you'll be able to access the container through ports on the host.

12.3 *Summary*

- YARN is the new generation of Hadoop's MapReduce execution engine and can run MapReduce, Spark, and other types of programs.
- YARN consists of a resource manager and several node managers.
- Applications on YARN run in containers and provide their application masters.
- YARN supports three different schedulers: FIFO, capacity, and fair.
- Spark on YARN runs in yarn-cluster and yarn-client modes.
- YARN kills containers that use more memory than allowed, so tuning spark.executor.memoryOverhead is important.
- YARN provides log aggregation for easy log inspection.
- YARN was the first cluster manager to support dynamic allocation.
- YARN is the only cluster manager on which Spark can access HDFS secured with Kerberos.
- Mesos can also run different types of applications (you can even run YARN on Mesos), but unlike YARN, it's capable of scheduling disk, network, and even custom resources.
- Mesos consists of masters, slaves, frameworks, and executors.
- Spark on Mesos can run in fine-grained or coarse-grained mode.
- Mesos provides resource isolation for its tasks through containers, implemented with Linux cgroups or Docker.

- Mesos's resource scheduling operates on two levels: by a framework's scheduler and by Mesos's resource-allocation module.
- Mesos allows framework prioritization through roles, weights, and resource allocations.
- You can use Spark's contraints to accept resource requests from only some of the slaves in the cluster.
- Spark on Mesos supports both client and cluster modes. Cluster mode is implemented with Spark's Mesos dispatcher.
- You can run Spark's executors on Mesos from Docker images.

Part 4

Bringing it together

In chapter 13, you'll bring it all together and explore a Spark streaming application for analyzing log files and displaying the results on a real-time dashboard. The application implemented in chapter 13 can be used as a basis for your own future applications.

Chapter 14 introduces H2O, a scalable, fast machine-learning framework with implementations of many machine-learning algorithms, most notably deep learning, which Spark lacks; and Sparkling Water, H2O's package that enables you to start and use an H2O cluster from Spark. Through Sparkling Water, you can use Spark's Core, SQL, Streaming, and GraphX components to ingest, prepare, and analyze data, and transfer it to H2O to be used in H2O's deep-learning algorithms. You can then transfer the results back to Spark and use them in subsequent computations.

13
Case study:
real-time dashboard

In this chapter, we'll show you how to use Spark in a real-life application. For the example application in this chapter, we'll show you how to build a real-time dashboard (a control panel with monitoring instruments) for viewing statistics calculated from a web server's access log files. We'll first explain the main idea behind the application. Then we'll show you how to run it using shell scripts and a Docker image (which we prepared for you at https://github.com/spark-in-action/uc1-docker) and how to run the components manually, if you choose to do so. At the end of the chapter, we'll explain the application code.

You can use this example application as a starting point for your own dashboard. You can extend the example to track additional metrics, or you can use it to show a dashboard for something entirely different than web-access logs. You can replace some of the components with your own, and more. The first step is to see it in action and understand how it works. Let's get to it.

13.1   Understanding the use case

In this section, you'll first learn what this case study is all about. Then we'll explain the components of the application that we built to realize the use case. You'll also get the answers to the "what" and "why" questions you may have (the "how" question will be answered in sections 13.2 and 13.3).

13.1.1   The overall picture

Real-time dashboards are common. People generally want to have insight into the state of their applications and systems, and they want to be able to react quickly to any challenges that may arise. Dashboards can display sensor data, resource-utilization data, click-stream data (log traces that users leave while browsing a website), and so on.

The use case in this chapter analyzes click-stream data coming from access log files and displays the results in a web application called *Web Stats Dashboard*. You want to receive access log files; calculate the number of active user sessions in each second and the number of requests, errors, and ads clicked per second; and display all that information in real-time graphs. The result is shown in figure 13.1.

As you can see, the web page (the only page in the web application) has two graphs: the upper graph shows the number of active user sessions, and the lower graph shows the number of requests, errors, and ads clicked per second. For debugging purposes, you log the last 100 messages received (shown in the text area on the right). Using the button in the upper-left corner, you can start or stop consuming messages; and using the row of buttons at the top of the page, you can change the time range displayed.

The access log data is in this format:

```
<date> <time> <IPaddress> <sessionId> <URL> <method> <respCode> <duration>
```

For example:

```
2016-04-12 21:38:39.138 192.168.0.123 514304dd-dbf4-4ad9-9cff-557dcff47d7b
⮑ / GET 200 500
2016-04-12 21:38:39.138 192.168.0.252 d7a074e5-77c2-4045-9447-245f7b80269d
⮑ sia.org/ads/10/123/clickfw GET 200 500
2016-04-12 21:38:39.138 192.168.0.51 df870e59-b67c-45d4-b02b-458aa492052f /
⮑ GET 200 500
```

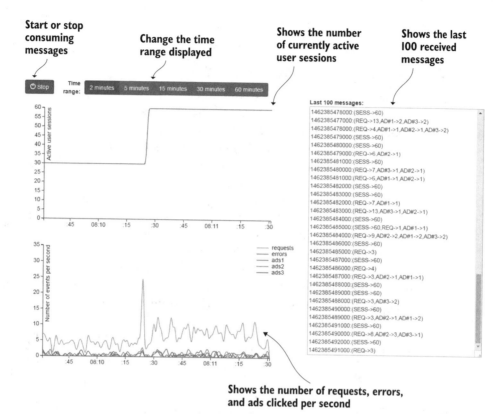

Figure 13.1 Web Stats Dashboard displays two graphs: one showing the number of active user sessions and the other showing the number of requests, errors, and ads clicked per second. You can change the displayed time range using the buttons at the top, and start or stop consuming messages using the button in the upper-left corner. The last 100 messages are shown on the right for debugging purposes.

Actual fields are described in table 13.1.

Table 13.1 Data stored in access logs for each user request in the example application

Field	Description
date and time	Date and time formatted as `yyyy-MM-dd hh:mm:ss.SSS` (for example, "2016-02-01 13:10:50.738")
IPaddress	Client's IP address
sessionId	Contents of the client's session cookie
URL	Visited URL
method	HTTP method used (`GET`, `POST`, and so on)
respCode	Server's HTTP response code
duration	Time it took the server to respond to the request

This is, more or less, the data that's usually stored in web server access log files. But you won't use all of these fields to calculate statistics.

13.1.2 *Understanding the application's components*

Figure 13.2 shows the components of this application. Because you don't have a real, running website that would generate access logs, you use *Log Simulator*, a Java application that simulates access logs generated by users visiting URLs on the website. Log Simulator sends the formatted click data directly to a Kafka topic. (As mentioned in chapter 6, Kafka is a distributed queuing system used in many organizations today for streaming data.)

If you were dealing with click-stream data from a real website (or several sites), you'd need a method of collecting the log files and sending them to Kafka. Apache Flume (mentioned in chapter 1) would be a good choice for that. It can execute the `tail -F` command, for example, and direct its output to Kafka.

The next component, a Spark Streaming application called Web Log Analyzer, is the main component of the system. It reads log data from Kafka, calculates several statistics, and writes the statistics back to Kafka, but to a different topic.

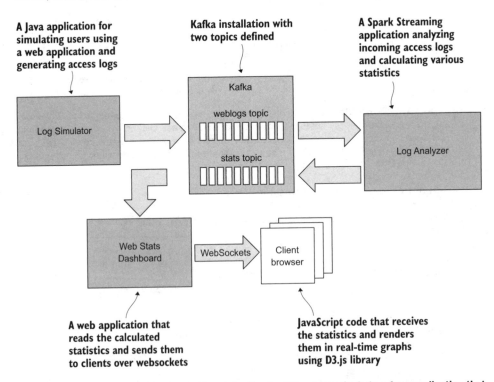

Figure 13.2 Components of the example application for this chapter include a Java application that simulates user traffic, a Spark Streaming application that analyzes incoming access logs and calculates various statistics, and a web application (including the JavaScript code running in the client browser) to display the calculated statistics in real-time graphs. All three communicate through Kafka.

The Log Analyzer component calculates statistics and sends the results to the second Kafka topic in this format:

```
<timestamp>:(key->value,...)
```

The timestamp is a long number containing the number of milliseconds since Jan. 1, 1970, (the standard representation of time in Java and several other languages). Table 13.2 shows the possible keys and their meanings. It's assumed that every banner click takes the user to a URL of the format /ads/<ad_category>/<ad_id>/clickfw, logs the click event, and redirects the user to the corresponding partner site. Keys are encoded as integers in order to save some network bandwidth, which is a good practice.

Table 13.2 Statistics, descriptions, and matching keys calculated by Log Analyzer to format messages sent to Kafka

Statistic	Key	Description
Active sessions	SESS	Number of active sessions. Each request has an associated session ID. The number of active sessions is the number of unique session IDs whose last request occurred less than some fixed number of seconds ago. This fixed number of seconds is the session timeout parameter, which should be equal to the application server's session timeout.
Requests	REQ	Number of requests per second, calculated based on timestamps parsed from log file entries.
Errors	ERR	Number of error response codes (400 and higher) per second.
Ads 1	AD#1	Number of clicks per second on banners of category 1.
Ads 2	AD#2	Number of clicks per second on banners of category 2.
Ads 3	AD#3	Number of clicks per second on banners of category 3.

You can easily extend this application and track other statistics as well. You'll see how to do that in section 13.3.

Finally, Web Stats Dashboard reads the calculated statistical data from Kafka again and sends it to client browsers over WebSockets to display on real-time graphs using the D3.js JavaScript library. Additionally, the JavaScript code running in the browser aggregates and sorts the statistics per timestamp (in case the data comes in out of order).

13.2 Running the application

Now that you understand what the application does, you're ready to start the components and see them in action. You have two main options:

- You can use the scripts and the Docker image (for the application server) that we prepared for you, and run all the components on a single machine, as described in section 13.2.1. The spark-in-action VM already has Spark, Kafka, and Docker installed. Using the scripts in the spark-in-action VM is the easier option for getting everything up and running quickly.

- You can start the application components manually if you have your own Kafka, Spark, and application server installations, as described in section 13.2.2.

Of course, you could use a combination of the two approaches and run some of the components using our scripts and/or the Docker image, and some of the components on your own. But we recommend that you use the VM, because that way you can be sure everything will work as planned and that you won't have any version clashes and incompatibilities.

13.2.1 Starting the application in the spark-in-action VM

We prepared a Docker image and a set of bash scripts to run the application components in the spark-in-action VM. The scripts make it easy for you to set up the environment and run the application, but they run all of the components on a single machine (your VM) with minimal capacity. To use more resources, you can manually run the application components on different machines and/or using your own Spark cluster (see section 13.2.2).

To get the images for running the application components, first clone the ucl-docker project into your home directory from our GitHub repository using `git`:

```
$ git clone https://github.com/spark-in-action/ucl-docker
```

Then make all the scripts in the folder executable:

```
$ cd ucl-docker
$ chmod +x *.sh
```

The ucl-docker folder contains the following scripts for starting the application:

- `start-kafka.sh`—Starts ZooKeeper and Kafka in the background
- `start-dashboard.sh`—Downloads the Web Stats Dashboard web application, builds the sia-dashboard Docker image containing the IBM WebSphere Liberty Profile application server, and deploys and starts the web application
- `start-spark.sh`—Downloads the Log Analyzer JAR file and submits it to a local Spark cluster
- `start-simulator.sh`—Downloads and runs the Log Simulator Java process, which generates web-traffic log entries and sends them to Kafka

All the scripts (except `start-simulator.sh`) should be run in the spark-in-action VM, because they use its IP address (192.168.10.2) and Spark and Kafka install locations.

To start the application components, run the scripts in this order:

```
$ ./start-kafka.sh
$ ./start-dashboard.sh
$ ./start-spark.sh
```

Or use the `run-all.sh` script, which will call all of these scripts consecutively:

```
$ ./run-all.sh
```

The scripts start ZooKeeper, Kafka, the web application, and Spark. It will take some time to download all the archives and build the sia-dashboard Docker image. This image is based on the websphere-liberty:webProfile7 image from the Docker Hub (https://hub.docker.com/_/websphere-liberty), which contains an IBM WebSphere Liberty Profile application server. The `sia-dashboard` image automatically downloads, installs, and runs the Web Stats Dashboard web application.

The last script starts Spark in the foreground, which means you'll see the results directly in the console. You can stop the Spark streaming job by pressing Ctrl-C.

To see if the web application has started, open your browser and go to the following URL: http://192.168.10.2/WebStatsDashboard. If you don't get any response, or if you see a "Context Root Not Found" message, wait a minute or two and then try again. You should finally see a screen similar to the one in figure 13.3. If the page looks broken, the problem could be in your ad-blocking software. Please disable it if you're using one. If you don't see any messages in the box on the right, see the next section for troubleshooting.

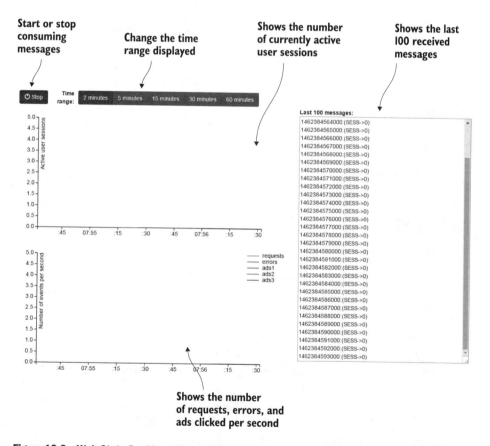

Figure 13.3 Web Stats Dashboard immediately after starting the application components, before starting Log Simulator

The messages contain only zeros for now, and the lines in the graphs are flat. In order to see some activity, you'll need to start Log Simulator. You can use the `start-simulator.sh` script for that; but because you left Spark in the foreground, open another shell and position yourself in the uc1-docker folder. If you run the script with the `-help` argument, it shows all the possible options you can specify; they're listed in table 13.3.

Table 13.3   Arguments for the `start-simulator.sh` script

Argument	Description
`-brokerList=HOST1:PORT1,...`	Comma-separated list of Kafka broker `host:port` pairs (default is 192.168.10.2:9092).
`-topic=NAME`	Optional. Name of the Kafka topic for sending log messages (default is `webstats`).
`-usersToRun=NUM`	Optional. Number of users to simulate (default is 10).
`-runSeconds=NUM`	Optional. Number of seconds to run and simulate user traffic (default is 120).
`-thinkMin=NUM`	Optional. Minimum think time between simulated actions, in seconds (default is 5).
`-thinkMax=NUM`	Optional. Maximum think time between simulated actions, in seconds (default is 10).
`-silent`	Optional. Suppresses all messages.
`-help`	Shows help, and exits.

If you call the `start-simulator.sh` script with no arguments, it runs 10 simulated users for 2 minutes (120 seconds) and sends those messages to the Kafka topic weblogs. You can send it to the background by adding an ampersand (&) at the end of the command line:

```
$ ./start-simulator.sh &
```

You can start several processes like this to generate even more traffic. After starting Log Simulator, you should see some activity in the graphs, similar to what is shown in figure 13.4.

STOPPING THE APPLICATION

If you wish to stop the application, it's best to stop the components in the opposite order of that they were started. To stop Log Simulator, you *kill* the appropriate process or press Ctrl-C if it's running in the foreground. It's the same for the Spark job.

To stop the Web Dashboard application, you can use the `stop-dashboard.sh` script. It will kill the appropriate Docker container. If you wish to remove the Docker images from your system (or from the VM), you need to list the Docker images:

```
$ docker images
```

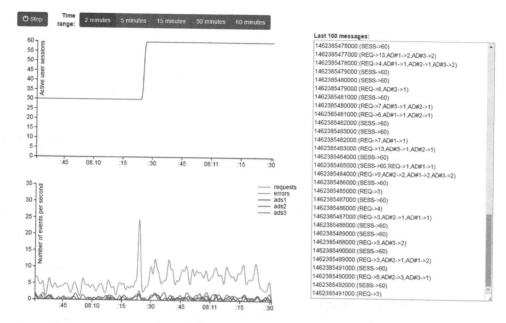

Figure 13.4   Activity on Web Stats Dashboard's graphs after starting two instances of Log Simulator. The upper graph shows that the number of users increased from 30 to 60 at one point. The lower graph shows that the requests and errors generated and ads clicked by the simulated users also increased.

Find the image ID of the Docker image you wish to remove, and use the ID in the docker rmi command:

```
$ docker rmi --force <image_id>
```

Finally, to stop Kafka and ZooKeeper, run the stop-kafka.sh script.

TROUBLESHOOTING THE APPLICATION

If you don't see any messages or activity on the web page after starting the components, you can check a couple of things. First, see whether the Spark Streaming Log Analyzer is working as expected. You can execute the consume-messages.sh script, which starts a Kafka console consumer, reads messages from the stats topic (to which Log Analyzer should be writing), and writes them to standard output.

If consume-messages.sh doesn't output any messages, examine the output from the Spark streaming job. You should be able to diagnose the problem using the job's output. If Log Analyzer is producing messages but you still don't see them on the web page, you can examine the web application's log using the show-dashboard-log.sh script, and try to correct the problem.

Note that the time scale on the X-axis of the graphs depends on the date and time of the machine where your browser is running, which may be different from the date and time of the machine where the application is running. Log Simulator generates log events using its machine's local time. If there's a large difference between the two times, the data may not be displayed in the graph, because it may fall outside of the X-axis' time range. So, the time offset on the two machines is another thing to check (if you're using two machines).

Finally, there's a known issue with the Kafka version installed in the spark-in-action VM. If you stop Spark and Kafka and then start them again, you may see the message "Kafka scheduler has not been started" (the issue is reported here: https://issues.apache.org/jira/browse/KAFKA-1724). The solution is to stop and start Spark and Kafka one more time, after which the application should work. If you're still experiencing problems, you can report them to us using the book's forum at https://forums.manning.com/forums/spark-in-action.

13.2.2 *Starting the application manually*

If you want to use your existing ZooKeeper and Kafka installations, your existing Spark cluster to run Log Analyzer, or your existing application server to run Web Stats Dashboard, you can manually install, configure, and run the required components as described in this section.

OBTAINING THE ARCHIVES

First, you need to obtain the component archives. You can build them yourself, or you can download them from our GitHub repository.

The archive locations are as follows:

- http://mng.bz/8uuF
- http://mng.bz/QJvi
- http://mng.bz/Ak6K
- The projects with the source files are in our repository's ch13 folder.

CREATING THE KAFKA TOPICS

You'll need to create two Kafka topics: one for log events and one for statistics. We named them `weblogs` and `stats`, but you can use different names. In our scripts, we used a replication factor of 1, and one partition for each topic. To use different values, use this command (you need to start ZooKeeper and Kafka before running the command):

```
$ kafka-topics.sh --create --topic <topic_name> --replication-factor
➥ <repl_factor> --partitions <num_partitions> --zookeeper <zk_ip>:2181
```

STARTING LOG ANALYZER

After you create the topics, you can start the Log Analyzer job. You submit the job to Spark as usual, specifying the `StreamingLogAnalyzer` class and at least two additional arguments (`brokerList` and `checkpointDir`):

- `brokerList` depends on your Kafka installation and should contain a comma-separated list of the Kafka broker IP addresses and ports.
- `checkpointDir` is a URL pointing to a directory (local or HDFS) for storing Spark checkpoint data (for details, see section 4.4.3).

The command looks like this:

```
$ spark-submit --master <your_master_url> \
  --class org.sia.loganalyzer.StreamingLogAnalyzer \
  streaming-log-analyzer.jar -brokerList=<kafka_ip>:<kafka_port> \
  -checkpointDir=hdfs://<hdfs_host>:<hdfs_port>/<checkpoint_dir>
```

Additionally, you can specify several optional parameters:

- `inputTopic`—Name of the input topic with log events
- `outputTopic`—Name of the output topic for writing statistics
- `sessionTimeout`—How many seconds should pass since the last request before a session is considered timed out
- `numberPartitions`—Number of RDD partitions to use during statistical calculations

STARTING WEB STATS DASHBOARD

Web Stats Dashboard is a Java web application, so you can use any Java application server supporting WebSockets to run it. We chose IBM WebSphere Liberty Profile. Whichever server you choose, you need to set two Java system variables:

- `zookeeper.address`—ZooKeeper's host name and port, which are used for connecting to Kafka
- `kafka.topic`—Topic name for reading statistical messages

The URL to the application depends on the chosen application server and your installation method. If you change the default URL (/WebStatsDashboard), make sure to change it in the webstats.js file, too. As soon as you visit the page, if everything was set up correctly, the application will start consuming messages from Kafka and displaying them in the graphs. Your application server's System Out log file should contain the following entries:

```
LogStatsReceiver getting consumer
LogStatsReceiver getting KafkaStream
LogStatsReceiver iterating
```

The result on the screen should be the same as when using the VM. If not, you'll need to examine log files from the Spark job and the web application server. As we explained in the previous section, it's important that all machines running your components have synchronized clocks. Otherwise, data may display with an offset.

STARTING LOG SIMULATOR

Once all the components are running, you can start Log Simulator, as explained previously. When you're starting everything manually, provide the address of the Kafka broker (probably `localhost:9092`):

```
$ ./start-simulator.sh --brokerList=<kafka_host>:<kafka_port>
```

For the full list of arguments, see table 13.3.

13.3   Understanding the source code

If you're curious about how the application works, this is the moment when you learn the answer. The ch13 folder in this book's GitHub repository (https://github.com/spark-in-action/first-edition/tree/master/ch13) contains the three required projects:

- KafkaLogsSimulator
- StreamingLogAnalyzer
- WebStatsDashboard

We examine these projects in this section.

13.3.1   *The KafkaLogsSimulator project*

KafkaLogsSimulator is a pure Java application consisting of only two classes: Log-Simulator and IPPartitioner. This is all straightforward and not Spark-specific, so we won't spend much time on it.

LogSimulator is an executable Java class (it has a main method) and extends the Thread class, which means it can be run as a thread. The main method takes the arguments described in table 13.3. It then spawns the required number of LogSimulator threads and waits for all of them to finish.

Each thread has its own IP address and a session ID (generated in the main method), which remain constant throughout the life of the thread. Each thread creates access-log entries containing the current time, IP address, session ID, URL, HTTP method, response code, and response duration in milliseconds. The response code that Log Simulator generates is 404 (not found) in 2% of cases and 200 (OK) otherwise. The session URL (in the format /ads/<ad_category>/<ad_id>/clickfw) represents a click to an ad in 3% of cases and a forward slash (/) otherwise. Log Simulator uses only three categories (1, 2, and 3), each of which has an equal probability of appearing.

The constructed message is then sent to Kafka as a KeyedMessage (line 191):

```
KeyedMessage<String, String> data = new KeyedMessage<String, String>
    (TOPIC_NAME, ipAddress, message);
producer.send(data);
```

The IP address is used as the partitioning key. IPPartitioner, used for constructing the producer, partitions messages based on the lowest octet of the IP address key (the number after the last dot in the address).

13.3.2   *The StreamingLogAnalyzer project*

StreamingLogAnalyzer is a Scala project containing only one file with two classes: StreamingLogAnalyzer and KafkaProducerWrapper. Figure 13.5 shows their relationship. As explained in chapter 6, StreamingLogAnalyzer uses KafkaProducerWrapper to open a single connection per partition to Kafka. In this way, multiple tasks on a single partition can reuse the same connection.

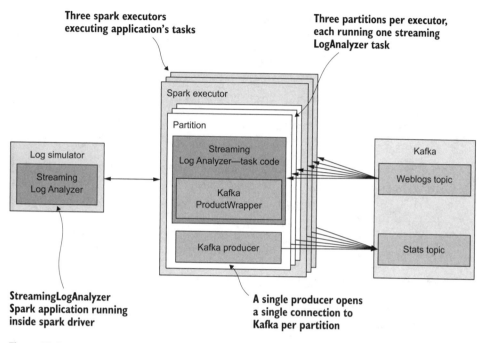

Figure 13.5 An instance of `StreamingLogAnalyzer` running in a Spark cluster with three executors, each running three Spark Streaming Log Analyzer tasks within the matching partitions. Using a single Kafka producer and a single connection, each task reads data from the `weblogs` Kafka topic, calculates the statistics, and writes them to the `stats` topic.

These classes are the core of the example application. We'll analyze the source code thoroughly in this section; it's available in the single file at http://mng.bz/NSOr.

INITIALIZING THE SPARK CONTEXT

`StreamingLogAnalyzer` takes several arguments, which we described in section 13.2.2. As we said, the two required arguments are `brokerList` and `checkpointDir`. After argument validation, the Spark streaming context is initialized:

```
println("Starting Kafka direct stream to broker list: "+brokerList.get)
val conf = new SparkConf().setAppName("Streaming Log Analyzer")
val ssc = new StreamingContext(conf, Seconds(1))
```

This is the standard way of streaming context initialization. The batch duration of 1 second is important, as you'll see later.

The `updateStateByKey` functionality, which you use to keep track of active sessions, requires checkpointing, so you set the checkpoint folder:

```
ssc.checkpoint(checkpointDir.get)
```

INITIALIZING THE KAFKA INPUT STREAM

Next, the Kafka stream is initialized using the `KafkaUtils` helper class. You need to pass to `KafkaUtils` a list of Kafka brokers as the `metadata.broker.list` parameter:

```
val kafkaReceiverParams = Map[String, String](
  "metadata.broker.list" -> brokerList.get)
val kafkaStream = KafkaUtils.
  createDirectStream[String, String, StringDecoder, StringDecoder](
    ssc, kafkaReceiverParams, Set(logsTopic.get))
```

The `createDirectStream` method is parameterized with key and value types (both strings) and their decoders (both `StringDecoders`).

The `LogLine` case class is used to store parsed access log lines, and `df SimpleDate-Format` is used for parsing the date and time:

```
case class LogLine(time: Long, ipAddr: String, sessId: String, url: String,
        method: String, respCode: Int, respTime: Int)
val df = new SimpleDateFormat("yyyy-MM-dd hh:mm:ss.SSS")
```

PARSING ACCESS-LOG LINES

The first step in analyzing access logs is to read the access-log lines coming in as Kafka messages and parse them into `LogLine` objects:

```
val logsStream = kafkaStream.flatMap { t => {
  val fields = t._2.split(" ")
  try {
    List(LogLine(df.parse(fields(0) + " " + fields(1)).getTime(),
      fields(2), fields(3), fields(4), fields(5), fields(6).toInt,
      fields(7).toInt))
  }
  catch {
    case e: Exception => {
      System.err.println("Wrong line format: "+t);
      List()
    }
  }
} }}
```

If a line doesn't conform to the expected format, a message is printed to the standard error output and the line is discarded.

COUNTING ACTIVE SESSIONS

To count all active sessions, you need to find when the last request happened for each session ID. So, you first map `LogLine` objects to tuples with the session ID as the key and the time as the value. Then, using `reduceByKey`, you find the maximum time per session (in case several requests with the same session ID are returned during this batch):

```
val maxTimeBySession = logsStream.map(r => (r.sessId, r.time)).reduceByKey(
  (max1, max2) => { Math.max(max1, max2) })
```

The RDDs in the `maxTimeBySession` DStream now contain one tuple per session ID. You can use the `updateStateByKey` function to maintain state during the lifetime of your streaming application (for details, see chapter 6). Here, you use it to keep track of all session IDs whose requests happened at most `SESSION_TIMEOUT_MILLIS` milliseconds ago. You'll "forget" all session IDs with no requests during that timeframe.

`updateStateByKey` gives you the set of new values from the current batch (the `maxTimeNewValues` variable, which always has a size of 1 in this case because of the previous `reduceByKey`) and the maintained state for that key (the `maxTimeOldState` variable). For each key, you can use `updateStateByKey` to delete the key by returning `None` or to change the key's state value by returning the new value:

```
val stateBySession = maxTimeBySession.updateStateByKey(
  (maxTimeNewValues: Seq[Long], maxTimeOldState: Option[Long]) => {
    if (maxTimeNewValues.size == 0) {
      if (System.currentTimeMillis() - maxTimeOldState.get >
          SESSION_TIMEOUT_MILLIS)
        None
      else
        maxTimeOldState
    }
    else if(maxTimeOldState.isEmpty)
      Some(maxTimeNewValues(0))
    else
      Some(Math.max(maxTimeNewValues(0), maxTimeOldState.get))
  })
```

For each key (session ID), only the last (maximum) request time is retained. If there are no new requests for a session ID (`maxTimeNewValues` is empty), you need to check whether the session has expired by comparing the last request time with the current time. If it has expired, you delete it from the state by returning `None`; you leave the old maximum request time otherwise.

If the session ID doesn't have any state yet (this is the first request for that session ID), you return the new request's time. And if the session ID has both a new request and an old state, you return the larger of the two.

Finally, you count all the elements in the `stateBySession` DStream to get the current count of active sessions:

```
val sessionCount = stateBySession.count()
```

COUNTING REQUESTS PER SECOND

Before counting requests, errors, and ad clicks per second, you need to map `LogLine` objects in the `logsStream` DStream to key-value tuples, where the key is the second (the request's time with milliseconds removed):

```
val logLinesPerSecond = logsStream.map(l => ((l.time / 1000) * 1000, 1))
```

Now that you have second LogLine tuples in the logLinesPerSecond DStream, you need to count them by key to get the number of requests per second. Because DStream doesn't have a countByKey method, you use combineByKey for that:

```
val reqsPerSecond = logLinesPerSecond.combineByKey(
  l => 1L,
  (c: Long, ll: LogLine) => c + 1,
  (c1: Long, c2: Long) => c1 + c2,
  new HashPartitioner(numberPartitions),
  true)
```

COUNTING ERRORS PER SECOND

Counting errors per second is done the same way as counting requests, except that requests first need to be filtered to include only errors. To do that, you check whether the response code starts with 4 or 5:

```
val errorsPerSecond = logLinesPerSecond.filter(l => {
    val respCode = l._2.respCode / 100
    respCode == 4 || respCode == 5
}).
  combineByKey ...
```

The combineByKey part is identical to what you did to count requests.

COUNTING AD CLICKS PER SECOND

To count ad clicks, not only do you need to filter requests based on their URLs, but you also need to find the ad category that the user clicked to display it on the dashboard. You assume that the web application whose logs you are analyzing accepts ad clicks at URLs of this format: /ads/<ad_category>/<ad_id>/clickfw. The web application then redirects the user to the appropriate partner website.

As we said, you need to parse the ad category. You use the following regular expression to accomplish that:

```
val adUrlPattern = new Regex(".*/ads/(\\d+)/\\d+/clickfw", "adtype")
```

Because you need to find the ad category too, you can't use filter as you did previously. You flatMap logLinesPerSecond to key-value tuples, where the keys are tuples of the timestamp (second) and ad category. If the request URL doesn't match the regular expression adUrlPattern, the flatMap function removes that element from the results:

```
val adsPerSecondAndType = logLinesPerSecond.flatMap(l => {
    adUrlPattern.findFirstMatchIn(l._2.url) match {
      case Some(urlmatch) => List(((l._1, urlmatch.group("adtype")), l._2))
      case None => List()
    }
}).combineByKey ...
```

COMBINING ALL STATISTICS

Now you have four DStreams with different statistics: sessionCount, reqsPerSecond, errorsPerSecond, and adsPerSecondAndType. But you need to display them all in a single dashboard. You could send them to Kafka separately, thus sending four messages for a single timestamp (second), or you could combine all the statistics and send only one message per second. How can you combine the statistics?

Well, you can put the different statistics under different keys in a single Map per timestamp. That's exactly what you're going to do. You first need to define the keys:

```
val SESSION_COUNT = "SESS"
val REQ_PER_SEC = "REQ"
val ERR_PER_SEC = "ERR"
val ADS_PER_SEC = "AD"
```

Then you map each statistic count value to a Map with the statistic under the appropriate key. The corresponding DStream also has to be keyed by timestamp. Because reqsPerSecond and errorsPerSecond are already keyed by timestamp, you just map the values:

```
val requests = reqsPerSecond.map(sc => (sc._1, Map(REQ_PER_SEC -> sc._2)))
val errors = errorsPerSecond.map(sc => (sc._1, Map(ERR_PER_SEC -> sc._2)))
```

The sessionCount DStream, however, isn't keyed by timestamp. It contains only one count per batch (per DStream's RDD), so you also create the key with the current timestamp with milliseconds removed:

```
val finalSessionCount = sessionCount.map(c =>
  ((System.currentTimeMillis / 1000) * 1000, Map(SESSION_COUNT -> c)))
```

By the way: this is why the Spark batch duration of 1 second is important. You want to generate a single statistic per second. The granularity of other statistics doesn't depend on the batch duration, because their timestamps are taken from log files and always aggregated per second. For the session count, you generate the key yourself. If the batch duration were set to 2 seconds, for example, you'd generate a session-count statistic for every other second. Then the final graph, showing active sessions, would oscillate unrealistically (it would have a gap every other second). One possible solution is to fill in the missing values when displaying the graph or change the way the graph is displayed. Another solution is to fix the batch size to 1 second. We opted for the latter.

As for the adsPerSecondAndType DStream, it's keyed by timestamp and ad category. So, you map its keys to keep only the timestamp part and use the ad category for the key in the value Map:

```
val ads = adsPerSecondAndType.map(stc =>
  (stc._1._1, Map(s"$ADS_PER_SEC#${stc._1._2}" -> stc._2)))
```

Thus, all the ad keys in the `Map` will begin with 4# and end with the ad category.

Finally, you need to combine all the `Map` objects into a single `Map` per timestamp. You `union` them into a single `DStream` and reduce all value `Maps` per key into a single `Map` object:

```
val finalStats = finalSessionCount.union(requests).
  union(errors).
  union(ads).
  reduceByKey((m1, m2) => m1 ++ m2)
```

SENDING THE RESULTS TO KAFKA

You're finally ready to send the statistics to Kafka. Here you have a challenge. Kafka `Producer` objects aren't serializable, because they need to open a connection to Kafka and maintain it. Therefore, you can't instantiate producers on the driver side and transfer them to the workers. You need to instantiate producers in the tasks running in Spark workers. You use the `KafkaProducerWrapper` class for that purpose. `KafkaProducerWrapper`'s *companion object* (companion objects hold the equivalent to static methods and fields in Java, as discussed in section 4.1.1) is used to instantiate a single, lazily instantiated instance of `KafkaProducerWrapper`, which itself instantiates one instance of a Kafka `Producer`. `KafkaProducerWrapper` is parameterized by a list of Kafka brokers:

```
case class KafkaProducerWrapper(brokerList: String) {
  val producerProps = {
    val prop = new Properties
    prop.put("metadata.broker.list", brokerList)
    prop
  }
  val p = new Producer[Array[Byte], Array[Byte]](
    new ProducerConfig(producerProps))
  def send(topic: String, key: String, value: String) {
    p.send(new KeyedMessage(topic,
      key.toCharArray.map(_.toByte), value.toCharArray.map(_.toByte)))
  }
}
object KafkaProducerWrapper {
  var brokerList = ""
  lazy val instance = new KafkaProducerWrapper(brokerList)
}
```

Using the `KafkaProducerWrapper` class and the RDD's `foreachPartition` function, you can instantiate a single Kafka `Producer` per JVM (multiple partitions can share the same executor's JVM; they would all use the same static instance) and use it to send messages to Kafka:

```
finalStats.foreachRDD(rdd => {
  rdd.foreachPartition(partition => {
    KafkaProducerWrapper.brokerList = brokerList.get
    val producer = KafkaProducerWrapper.instance
```

```
      partition.foreach {
        case (s, map) =>
          producer.send(
            statsTopic.get,
            s.toString,
            s.toString + ":(" + map.foldLeft(new Array[String](0)) {
              case (x, y) => { x :+ y._1 + "->" + y._2 } }.
                mkString(",")+")")
      }//foreach
    })//foreachPartition
  })//foreachRDD
```

Using Scala `Map`'s `foldLeft` function, the message is formatted as `timestamp:(key1->value1,key2->value2,...)`. The timestamp is used as the Kafka topic's partitioning key.

The only thing left to do now is to start the Spark Streaming application and wait for its termination:

```
println("Starting the streaming context... Kill me with ^C")
ssc.start()
ssc.awaitTermination()
```

13.3.3 *The WebStatsDashboard project*

The `WebStatsDashboard` project is a web application that reads messages from Kafka and sends them to the clients' browsers over WebSockets. Using the D3.js library, the JavaScript code running in the client's browsers displays the statistics in real-time graphs.

The `WebStatsDashboard` project consists of four main files:

- LogStatsObserver.java—Interface denoting classes that receive messages from `LogStatsReceiver` when they arrive
- LogStatsReceiver.java—Singleton that reads messages from Kafka and dispatches them to all `LogStatsObservers`
- WebStatsEndpoint.java—WebSockets endpoint for managing WebSockets connections and for forwarding messages to clients
- webstats.js—JavaScript code for receiving statistics from the WebSockets endpoint and displaying that data using the D3.js library

The `LogStatsReceiver` thread continuously receives messages from a Kafka topic and dispatches them to the registered `LogStatsObservers`. It functions as a singleton object and starts receiving only when at least one `LogStatsObserver` is registered. It stops receiving when the last `LogStatsObserver` deregisters.

The `WebStatsEndpoint` is a WebSockets endpoint used to connect clients, but it's also a `LogStatsObserver`. It forwards messages received from the `LogStatsReceiver` to its clients.

webstats.js is a JavaScript application based on the Multi-Series Line Chart D3.js example (http://bl.ocks.org/mbostock/3884955). It connects to the `WebStatsEndpoint` and starts displaying the messages. This book isn't about JavaScript, so we won't explain the code in the webstats.js file.

13.3.4 *Building the projects*

If you want to build the projects on your own, you'll need to have Maven and Java installed. For each project, we've included a Maven pom.xml file in the root of the project folder. Just issue a `maven install` command from the root folder, and find the resulting kafka-logs-simulator.jar, streaming-log-analyzer.jar, or WebStatsDashboard.war file in the target subfolder.

13.4 *Summary*

- The use case in this chapter is about analyzing click-stream data coming from access log files.
- The application consists of a a Log Simulator application that simulates user activity on a website, Log Analyzer (a Spark Streaming application) to analyze log data and produce statistics, Kafka topics to exchange messages between components, and a Web Stats Dashboard application to consume the statistics. Web Stats Dashboard also sends statistics over WebSockets to client browsers to be displayed in real-time graphs using the D3.js library.
- The statistics tracked are active user sessions, requests per second, errors per second, and clicks on ads per second and per ad category.
- We prepared several scripts and a Docker image to run the application components: ZooKeeper, Kafka, Spark, and a WebSphere Liberty Profile application server to run the Web Dashboard web application.
- Using a set of available scripts, you can easily start, stop, and troubleshoot the application.
- You can also manually start individual components on your own infrastructure.
- The source code is organized into three projects: `KafkaLogsSimulator`, `StreamingLogAnalyzer`, and `WebStatsDashboard`.

Deep learning on Spark with H2O

Deep learning is a hot topic in the machine-learning world today. We could say that there's a deep-learning revolution going on. *Deep learning* is a general term denoting a family of machine-learning methods characterized by the use of multiple processing layers of nonlinear transformations. These layers are almost universally implemented as neural networks.

Although the core principles aren't new, a lack of computing power and efficient algorithms prevented those principles from being further developed in the previous decades. This has changed in recent years, with many advances in deep-learning algorithms and their successful applications. One of the many recent breakthroughs is the DeepID system for learning high-level features,[1] which is capable of recognizing tens of thousands of faces with a close-to-human accuracy of 97.45% (unlike its accuracy, its capacity is obviously superhuman).

Likewise, several software frameworks for doing deep learning have sprung up in recent years. In this chapter, we'll give you an overview of the H2O framework, which seamlessly integrates with Spark and coexists with it nicely. You'll create an H2O cluster and use the housing prices dataset from chapter 7 and the adult dataset from chapter 8 to perform regression and classification using deep learning (H2O neural networks). You'll train deep-learning models through H2O's UI, and we'll show you how to do the same thing using the H2O API from Spark. The datasets will be kept small so that you can use them even without a large Spark cluster, but you can use the same techniques to build deep-learning models using larger datasets.

14.1 *What is deep learning?*

Deep learning can help you model complex nonlinear relationships in the data and build powerful regression and classification models. Deep learning is an area of machine learning based on usage of artificial neural networks for learning high-level features of the underlying data. *Artificial neural networks* (ANNs) are modeled according to biological neural networks and consist of artificial neurons (*nodes*) organized in layers. Each neuron's output depends on outputs from several neurons in the previous layer, on a set of learned weights, and on an activation function, which combines inputs and weights to produce a single output value. A single neuron functions similarly to the logistic regression model described in chapter 8 and learns the values of its input weights through the process of training the ANN. The complete ANN, consisting of many tens, hundreds, or thousands of neurons, is capable of modeling complex, nonlinear functions.

Each ANN has an input layer, used to feed the feature values of input examples into the network; an output layer, to output the results; and one or more hidden layers (layers that aren't input or output layers). A *deep neural network* (DNN) is an ANN with two or more hidden layers. An illustration of a DNN with three layers is shown in figure 14.1. The output from each neuron is 0 or 1, and each neuron calculates its output using the activation function (usually the logistic function we introduced in chapter 8). The input to the activation function is the sum of its inputs multiplied by their weight parameters. For example, the output of neuron h^k equals the following (assuming the logistic function is used)

$$h_k = \frac{1}{1 + e^{-\sum_{j=1}^{3} i_j w_{jk}}}$$

where i_j is output from neuron i_j and w_{jk} is the j-th input weight of neuron h^k.

---

[1] Yi Sun et al., "Deep Learning Face Representation from Predicting 10,000 Classes," http://mng.bz/W01w.

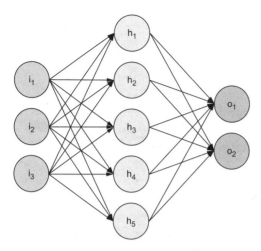

Figure 14.1 An artificial neural network consisting of three layers: an input layer, a hidden layer, and an output layer. Each neuron's output depends on the outputs from neurons in the previous layer and on a set of weights, learned through the process of training the ANN.

Weights of individual nodes are learned through processes of forward and backward propagation. For each example, forward propagation uses already-learned weights to calculate the output values and the error between calculated and real output values. Backward propagation then goes from the last layer toward the first (for each example) and changes the weights based on a measure of how much each neuron participated in the overall error. The process then repeats with another wave of forward and backward propagations until convergence.

Each layer in an ANN learns features on different levels of abstraction. In ANNs built for recognizing faces, the first layer may learn to recognize low-level features, such as edges and their directions. The second layer may learn to recognize basic shapes based on edge features from the previous layer. The third layer may recognize eyes, noses, and so on. This description is just an illustration; interpreting in this way what specific layers learn is very difficult, and ANNs function mostly like black boxes.

Mathematical foundations for ANNs were laid down in the 1940s, and the first ANN machines appeared in the 1950s. Although neglected for some time during '80s and '90s, they're seeing wide adoption again today because of advances in computational capacity and the efficiency of learning algorithms and distributed computing. Neural networks and deep-learning methods are outperforming traditional machine-learning algorithms today in a wide range of application areas, such as image analysis and pattern recognition, speech analysis, decision making, robotics, autonomous driving, and so on.

14.2 Using H2O with Spark

In this section, you'll see how H2O can help you do deep learning on Spark. We'll first give you a short introduction to H2O and Sparkling Water, H2O's Spark package that enables integration between H2O and Spark. Then you'll start an H2O cluster from Spark, using the Sparkling Water API. After that, you'll get acquainted with the H2O Flow UI, its graphical interface.

14.2.1 *What is H2O?*

H2O is a fast, open source, machine-learning platform. It's backed by the H2O.ai company (http://www.h2o.ai, previously called 0xdata), which was cofounded in 2011 by SriSatish Ambati and Cliff Click, the lead developer of the JVM (Cliff wrote JIT, Java's just-in-time compiler). Arno Candel serves as the chief architect.

H2O is an excellent machine-learning platform with basic data-transformation capabilities (fast parse, columnar transformations and joins), but it isn't a general computing engine like Spark. Using them together, you can get the best of both worlds. With Spark, you can read and join data from various sources, parse the data, transform it, transfer it to H2O, and then build and use the H2O machine-learning models. In this way, H2O and Spark can nicely complement each other.

H2O algorithms overlap somewhat with Spark's machine-learning algorithms. Although H2O has a few algorithms that Spark still doesn't have (deep learning and generalized low-rank modeling), Spark has several algorithms not available in H2O, such as alternating least squares (ALS), latent Dirichlet allocation, SVMs, tf-idf, Word2vec, and others.

H2O supports these machine-learning algorithms:

- *Deep learning*—Algorithm used in this chapter.
- *Generalized linear modeling*—Generalization of ordinary linear regression (explained in chapter 7) to also cover other types of regressions (such as elastic net regularized logistic regression). Can be used for both classification and regression.
- *Generalized low-rank modeling*—New machine-learning approach for reconstructing missing values and identifying important features in heterogeneous data (http://mng.bz/w4OJ).
- *Distributed random forest*—Regression and classification algorithm, covered in chapter 8.
- *Naïve Bayes*—Probability-based multiclass classification algorithm, also available in Spark.
- *Principal component analysis*—Algorithm for dimensionality reduction, also available in Spark.
- *K-means*—Clustering algorithm, explained in chapter 8.
- *Gradient-boosting machines*—Form of ensemble method, using decision trees as the base learner, similarly to random forests. Can be used for both classification and regression.

14.2.2 *Starting Sparkling Water on Spark*

Sparkling Water is the integration layer between Spark and H2O and is implemented as a Spark package. You can use it to start an H2O cluster in a Spark cluster and exchange data between the two. This is shown in figure 14.2.

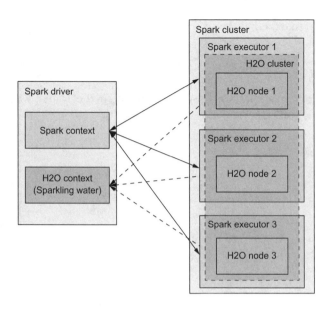

Figure 14.2 Sparkling Water architecture. H2O nodes are running in Spark executors, forming an H2O cluster.

When starting an H2O cluster in Spark, you first use a Spark context to start or connect to a Spark cluster as usual. You then use the Sparkling Water API to instantiate an instance of H2OContext, which starts H2O nodes in Spark executors. These nodes form an H2O cluster and are used to store compressed data and machine-learning models.

Similar to Spark, you have several options for starting Sparkling Water:

- Start the Sparkling Water shell, and start a new Spark cluster or connect to an existing one
- Start the Spark shell by specifying the Sparkling Water package (recommended method).
- Embed Sparkling Water in your application, and submit it to a Spark cluster.

STARTING SPARKLING WATER WITH THE SPARKLING WATER SHELL

To start the Sparkling Water shell, you first need to build or download Sparkling Water for your version of Spark (www.h2o.ai/download). In the spark-in-action VM, Sparkling Water is already downloaded and unzipped in your home directory (/home/spark/sparkling-water-1.6.3). You also need to set the SPARK_HOME environment variable to point to the root directory of your Spark installation. The Spark version you will use has to correspond to the version of Sparkling Water you will use. At the time of writing, Sparkling Water for Spark 2.0 was still not available, so set this variable to the Spark 1.6.1 folder, which is also available in the spark-in-action VM:

```
$ export SPARK_HOME=/opt/spark-1.6.1-bin-hadoop2.6
```

You can also set the MASTER environment variable to the Spark master you wish to use. If you don't set it, the default is local[*]. For a local, single-JVM cluster, you can use this value:

```
$ export MASTER=local
```

For a local cluster with three executors, one core, and 1024 MB per executor, you can use the following:

```
$ export MASTER=local-cluster[3,1,1024]
```

After you set the environment variables, position yourself in the folder where you extracted Sparkling Water, and start the Sparkling Water shell:

```
$ bin/sparkling-shell
-----
  Spark master (MASTER)       : local[3,1,1024]
  Spark home    (SPARK_HOME) : /usr/local/spark
  H2O build version           : 3.8.1.3 (turan)
  Spark build version         : 1.6.1
----
Welcome to

      ____              __
     / __/__  ___ _____/ /__
    _\ \/ _ \/ _ `/ __/  '_/
   /___/ .__/\_,_/_/ /_/\_\   version 1.6.1
      /_/

Using Scala version 2.10.5 (Java HotSpot(TM) 64-Bit Server VM, Java 1.8.0_72)
Type in expressions to have them evaluated.
Type :help for more information.
Spark context available as sc.
SQL context available as sqlContext.

scala>
```

If your Spark master is a local cluster, the Sparkling Water shell will start it automatically. If you're connecting to YARN, Mesos, or a Spark standalone cluster, you'll need to specify the number of executors you wish to use. For a Spark standalone cluster, you need to specify the `spark.executor.cores`, `spark.cores.max`, and `spark.executor.instances` parameters. For YARN, only `spark.executor.instances` is needed.

To connect to a Spark standalone cluster and use six executors, issue the following command:

```
$ bin/sparkling-shell --master spark://<master_address> \
--conf "spark.cores.max=6" --conf "spark.executor.cores=1" \
--conf "spark.executor.instances=6"
```

STARTING SPARKLING WATER WITH THE SPARK SHELL

You can download Sparkling Water automatically to your local Maven repository with the `--packages` option (you'll also need to download the `sparkling-water-examples` package, which you'll need in this chapter):

```
$ spark-shell --packages \
ai.h2o:sparkling-water-core_2.10:1.6.3,\
ai.h2o:sparkling-water-examples_2.10:1.6.3 <other options>
```

You can also load Sparkling Water into a Spark shell by specifying the Sparkling Water assembly JAR with the `--jars` option. If you're running in the spark-in-action VM as the `spark` user, `spark-shell` should already be in your path and Sparkling Water should be available from the sparkling-water-1.6.3 directory in your home directory:

```
$ spark-shell --jars /home/spark/sparkling-water-1.6.3/assembly/build/libs/
  sparkling-water-assembly-1.6.3-all.jar <other options>
```

STARTING SPARKLING WATER FROM YOUR APPLICATION

Finally, to use Sparkling Water from your application, embed it in your fat JAR (using dependencies with your packaging manager) or add it with the `jars` or `packages` option while submitting the application as usual.

14.2.3 Starting the H2O cluster

No matter which method you use to start Sparkling Water, once you have your shell open, you can start the H2O cluster by creating and starting an instance of `H2OContext`:

```
scala> import org.apache.spark.h2o._
scala> val h2oContext = new H2OContext(sc).start()
```

The default number of H2O nodes that will be started is the value of the `spark.ext.h2o.cluster.size` Spark configuration parameter. If it's not specified, the `spark.executor.instances` parameter will be used.

> **NOTE** If running in a local, single-JVM cluster, Sparkling Water always starts a single H2O node.

If all goes well, you should see output similar to the following. In this example, the Sparkling Shell was started using six executors on a Spark Standalone cluster:

```
Sparkling Water Context:
 * H2O name: sparkling-water-<user>_876327168
 * number of executors: 6
 * list of used executors:
  (executorId, host, port)
  ------------------------
  (4,<IP4>,<PORT4>)
  (0,<IP0>,<PORT0>)
  (5,<IP5>,<PORT5>)
  (2,<IP2>,<PORT2>)
  (1,<IP1>,<PORT1>)
  (3,<IP3>,<PORT3>)
  ------------------------

  Open H2O Flow in browser: http://<IP>:<PORT> (CMD + click in Mac OSX)
```

The H2O cluster has started, and you're good to go.

14.2.4 *Accessing the Flow UI*

H2O features a web-based console called Flow UI, which enables you to quickly load the data, train models using the supported algorithms, use the trained models, and inspect the results. It also has a helpful assistant to guide you through possible actions. You can use the assistant's forms to manipulate data in the Flow UI, or you can directly enter Flow commands.

If you visit the URL that was printed after the H2OContext was started, you'll land on the H2O Flow UI page shown in figure 14.3. The functioning of the Flow UI may look familiar if you've used Jupyter notebooks (http://jupyter.org) or Zeppelin (https://zeppelin.incubator.apache.org).

The Flow UI manages notebooks called *flows*, which are web pages you can save and execute. Each flow has a name and a set of *cells* for executing commands and displaying the results. Similar to Jupyter notebooks and Zeppelin, cells can also contain markdown code, which can be used as portable documentation.

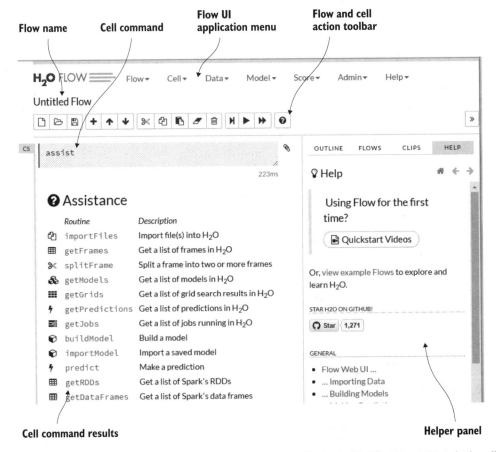

Figure 14.3 The starting page of the H2O Flow UI, showing a flow called Untitled Flow with a single cell that displays the results of the `assist` command. You can manipulate cells through the action toolbar.

At the top of the Flow UI screen is the main Flow UI menu. You can use it to manipulate flows (create, load, save, run all cells in a flow, and so on), cells (run, cut, delete, move, and so on), data (import and split), and models (create, export, import, and so on). Through the Admin submenu, you can view running jobs, view cluster status and CPU usage, inspect logs, and access other advanced options (such as network test). And through the Help submenu, you can get information about using H2O.

If you press the H key, the Flow UI presents a helpful pop-up showing keyboard shortcuts. Using the Flow UI is intuitive, and you should find your way around it easily. We'll get you on the right track in the next section, where you'll train several deep-learning models.

14.3 Performing regression with H2O's deep learning

In chapter 7, you used the UCI Boston housing dataset to predict the mean values of owner-occupied homes in suburbs of Boston. You'll use it again here to build a deep-learning model with H2O. By using the same dataset as in chapter 7, we'll be able to concentrate on the features in H2O and Sparkling Water without explaining the details of the dataset and regression, and you can compare the techniques and ease of use of Spark ML against H2O.

After loading data into H2O, we'll show you how to build and evaluate a deep-learning model using the H2O Flow UI. Then we'll teach you how to do the same thing using the Sparkling Water API so that you can use H2O machine-learning algorithms from your Spark applications.

14.3.1 Loading data into an H2O frame

The first step is to load data into Sparkling Water and make it available to the H2O cluster as an H2O *frame*. H2O frames are similar to Spark `DataFrames`; implicit and explicit conversions from Spark `DataFrames` and RDDs to H2O frames, and vice versa, are available from the `H2OContext` class. To use the conversions, you need to import them from your `H2OContext` object:

```
import h2oContext._
```

The housing dataset is available from our online repository (http://mng.bz/o8e0). You can either import this file directly into an `H2OFrame` from this URL (we'll show you how to do that later) or download it and parse it into a Spark `DataFrame` and then into an `H2OFrame`. In this section, you'll do the latter. In the subsequent example, you'll load it directly into H2O.

You can use the following code to import the file into a Spark `DataFrame`. Just replace the path to housing.data and the number of partitions with your own (you can use three partitions for this small dataset):

```
val housingLines = sc.textFile("first-edition/ch07/housing.data", 3)
val housingVals = housingLines.map(x => x.split(",").
    map(_.trim().toDouble))
import org.apache.spark.sql.types.{StructType,StructField,DoubleType}
```

```
val housingSchema = StructType(Array(
    StructField("crim",DoubleType,true),
    StructField("zn",DoubleType,true),
    StructField("indus",DoubleType,true),
    StructField("chas",DoubleType,true),
    StructField("nox",DoubleType,true),
    StructField("rm",DoubleType,true),
    StructField("age",DoubleType,true),
    StructField("dis",DoubleType,true),
    StructField("rad",DoubleType,true),
    StructField("tax",DoubleType,true),
    StructField("ptratio",DoubleType,true),
    StructField("b",DoubleType,true),
    StructField("lstat",DoubleType,true),
    StructField("medv",DoubleType,true)
))
import org.apache.spark.sql.Row
val housingDF = sqlContext.applySchema(housingVals.map(Row.fromSeq(_)),
    housingSchema)
```

This code should be familiar to you by now. If not, please consult chapters 4 and 5. The column names and their meanings are explained in the housing.names file (http://mng.bz/k6kE).

To convert the `housingDF` DataFrame to an H2O frame, use the `asH2OFrame` method of `H2OContext`:

```
val housingH2o = h2oContext.asH2OFrame(housingDF, "housing")
```

The second argument is optional and specifies the name of the frame. You should now be able to find the new frame in the Flow UI. Select Data > List All Frames from the main Flow UI menu (or click the same option in the Assist cell). This will execute the `getFrames` Flow command in a new cell, as shown in figure 14.4.

By clicking the frame name, you get another cell executing the command `get-FrameSummary "housing"`, as shown in figure 14.5. The frame-summary cell shows basic column statistics, such as the number of zeros; the number of missing values;

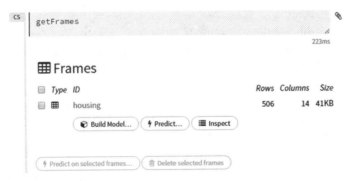

Figure 14.4 Cell created after selecting the List All Frames menu action, showing all frames in the current flow. The housing frame was created using the Sparkling Water API.

minimum, mean, and maximum values and so on. The frame-summary cell also contains several action buttons: you can use them to preview frame data, download the data, split the frame, build a model from a frame, or use the frame's data for predictions on an already-built model.

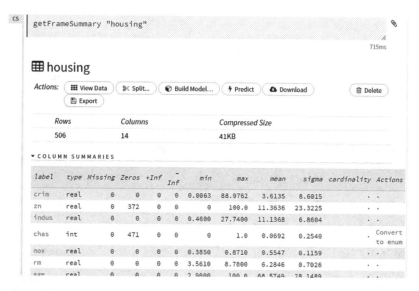

```
cs    getFrameSummary "housing"
```

Figure 14.5   Frame summary displayed after clicking the frame name. It shows basic column statistics and action buttons.

If you click any of the columns, you'll get further information about the data it contains in the column summary cell. Among other things, it contains a graphical representation of the data distribution. The distribution graph for the Lstat column is shown in figure 14.6.

Before building a model, you need to split the data into training and test sets. Go back to the housing frame summary cell by deleting the current cell (select the cell and press D twice) or by scrolling upward, and click the Split button. (You can also find all your cells in the Outline view on the right side of the screen.) Another cell appears (see figure 14.7), where you need to define ratios for frame splits. Accept the default ratios of 0.75 and 0.25, but rename the split frames (change

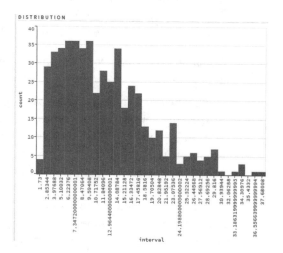

Figure 14.6   Distribution graph for the Lstat column's summary cell

Figure 14.7   Defining the frame's split ratios and the future frames' names

their key names) to something recognizable (housing750 and housing250) and then click the Create button. The resulting frames will be displayed (see figure 14.8).

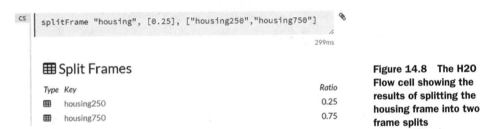

Figure 14.8   The H2O Flow cell showing the results of splitting the housing frame into two frame splits

The results in the rest of the chapter are highly dependent on the exact frames used for training and testing. If you'd like to get results similar to ours, you can download the splits we used from our online repository (housing750.csv and housing250.csv from http://mng.bz/IS40). See section 14.4.1 on how to load files into H2O directly, or load them by parsing them into SQL DataFrames, as you did in this section.

14.3.2   *Building and evaluating a deep-learning model using the Flow UI*

You'll now use the two new frames to build and evaluate a deep-learning model. Supervised machine-learning models (to which deep-learning models belong), as you learned in chapters 7 and 8, consist of a set of algorithm-specific parameters estimated according to the training data used to train the models and to a set of hyper-parameters used during the training process. A deep-learning model learns a large number of parameters, which determine the functioning of particular neurons in its layers, as described in section 4.1.

Hyper-parameters are specified outside of the learning process. Deep-learning hyper-parameters include, for example, the number of hidden layers in the neural network. We'll call hyper-parameters *parameters* from now on.

Once trained, models are evaluated on validation datasets; and once their accuracy is satisfactory, they're used to make predictions and classify samples in a production environment. Deep-learning models can be used both for regression and classification. H2O automatically determines this according to the target variable.

Click the Housing750 frame, and then click the Build Model button; a Build a Model assistant will be displayed, asking you to choose the algorithm to be used. We're interested in deep learning in this chapter, so select Deep Learning. You should then see an assistant (a wizard) similar to the one shown in figure 14.9.

```
CS   assist buildModel, null, training_frame: "housing750"
```

🎁 Build a Model

Select an algorithm: Deep Learning ▼

PARAMETERS

model_id	housingDL-flow2	Destination id for this model; auto-generated if nc
training_frame	housing750 ▼	Training frame
validation_frame	housing250 ▼	Validation frame
nfolds	0	Number of folds for N-fold cross-validation
response_column	medv ▼	Response column
ignored_columns	Search...	
	Showing page 1 of 1.	
	☐ crim REAL	

Figure 14.9   An assistant for building a deep-learning model. The housing750 frame will be used for training, and housing250 will be used for validation. The target variable is in the Medv response column.

Select Housing750 as the training dataset and Medv as the response column (target variable). These are the only two mandatory parameters. But because you want to use a validation dataset, select Housing250 as the validation frame.

You can also specify a large number of other parameters. We'll explain some of them as we go along. Leave the parameters at their defaults, and click the Build Model button. A new cell will be created, executing the `buildModel` Flow command with all the parameters you previously selected. You can watch the progress as the job is executing (see figure 14.10).

≣ Job

Run Time	00:00:09.821
Type	Model
Key	deeplearning-95948c64-4d00-4e74-b95b-9d47781af154
Description	DeepLearning
Status	RUNNING
Progress	10% ▬▬
	Iterations: 1. Epochs: 3,98387. Speed: 305 samples/sec.
Actions	🔍 View ⊘ Cancel Job

Figure 14.10   H2O Flow cell showing the progress of building a deep-learning model

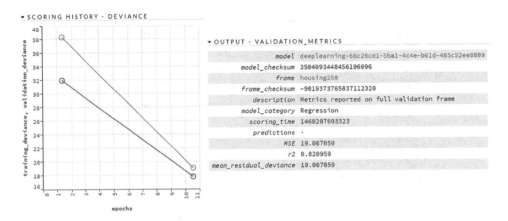

Figure 14.11   Two metrics of the built deep-learning model shown side by side: the scoring history showing mean deviance (equal to MSE) as a function of the number of epochs, and the final validation metrics.

Once the model is built, click the View button. This will display the built model and the various metrics. The metrics will depend on the exact data splits and may differ from our results (you can see our results in figure 14.11).

> **NOTE** By the way, H2O deep-learning model results are almost never repro-ducible because of the way the algorithm functions. You can make them reproducible by setting the Reproducible parameter to true and setting a seed, but this is slow and should be done only on small datasets.

The graph on the left in figure 14.11 shows deviance, which is equal to the mean squared error (MSE). You can see in the graph that deviance is still falling and that you probably stopped too early. If you continue to increase the number of epochs, you'll probably get better results (but we'll skip that and continue to a more complex model in the next section). The output on the right shows a couple of metrics, most notably the final deviance and MSE of 19.07 (equal to the RMSE of 4.37). This isn't great, but it's better than the first result you got in chapter 7 when you were using linear regres-sion on this dataset, which was 22.806 (RMSE of 4.78).

BUILDING A MORE COMPLEX MODEL

In chapter 7, you added second-order polynomials to capture nonlinear relationships in the data but used a linear regression model. With higher-order polynomials, you increased the complexity of the model. To increase complexity in a deep-learning model, you can add additional hidden layers, and that is what you'll do now.

You should train several models to get a feeling for the dataset and for the algo-rithm parameters. We don't have the means here to walk you through all the parame-ters and options, so we invite you to do that yourself. We'll just show you a set of parameters that will give you the best results on the housing dataset.

Go back to the Build a Model assistant (you can use the Outline view on the right side of the screen to navigate more easily), and set the model name to something human-readable, such as `housingDL`. Then enter `200, 200, 200` in the Hidden field. As you'll recall from chapters 7 and 8, more complex models need more iterations to converge, so enter `200` in the Epochs field. Finally, add L1 regularization by setting L1 to 1e-5. That will help the model suppress the features that don't contribute to its performance. Click the Build Model button, and wait for the job to finish (it may take longer than the first time). The results we got are shown in figure 14.12.

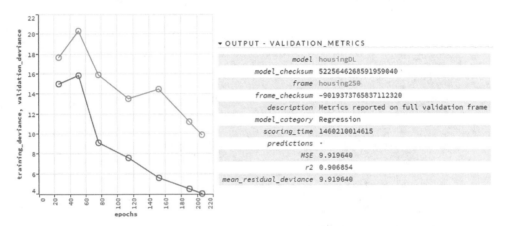

Figure 14.12   Results of building a deep-learning model with three hidden layers, 200 epochs, and L1 regularization

As you can see in the scoring history graph, the validation deviation (equal to the MSE) is now 9.92, which gives an RMSE of 3.15. R2 is 0.907. That is better than the best result you had in chapter 7 (RMSE of 3.4655119390 and R2 of 0.8567), and the Flow UI made it much easier to do.

SAVING THE MODEL

You can now save the model by clicking Export. This will open another cell where you need to enter a directory path (on the server where your Spark driver is running). Then, click Export (see figure 14.13). You can import a saved model using the main menu (Model > Import Model).

```
CS   exportModel "housingDL"
```

🎁 Export Model

Model: | housingDL ▼ |

Path: /models/housingDL

Overwrite: ☐

Actions: (💾 Export)

Figure 14.13   Exporting a model to the /models/ housingDL folder on the server where the Spark driver is running

14.3.3   *Building and evaluating a deep-learning model using the Sparkling Water API*

In this section, you'll learn how to do all the steps from the previous sections directly from Spark, using the Sparkling Water API, which may come in handy if you plan to use H2O with Spark. First, you need to load and split the data and use it to build an H2O deep-learning model. After that, you'll evaluate the model's performance; and finally, you'll learn how to load and save H2O models.

SPLITTING THE DATA

If you wish to use the same split frames as in the previous section (we recommend doing so, because that way you can get comparable results), you can load them in your Spark shell (the one from which you started the H2O cluster) using the following command:

```
scala> val housing750 = new H2OFrame("housing750")
scala> val housing250 = new H2OFrame("housing250")
```

Otherwise, you can create splits using the Sparkling Water API:

```
import org.apache.spark.examples.h2o.DemoUtils
val housingSplit = DemoUtils.split(housingH2o, Array("housing750sw",
  "housing250sw"), Array(0.75))
val housing750 = housingSplit(0)
val housing250 = housingSplit(1)
```

`DemoUtils` is a helper class available from the Sparkling Water examples package. You can examine its source (http://mng.bz/pT30) to see how it splits frames.

BUILDING THE MODEL

The first step in building the model is to create a `DeepLearningParameters` object, which will hold the algorithm's parameters:

```
import _root_.hex.deeplearning.DeepLearningModel.DeepLearningParameters
val dlParams = new DeepLearningParameters()
```

To get results similar to those from the model built from the Flow UI, you'll use the exact same parameters you used there. First you need to set the train frame and the validation frame. Every object in H2O (frames, models, and jobs) has a key with which it's referenced in H2O's distributed key-value store:

```
dlParams._train = housing750._key
dlParams._valid = housing250._key
```

Next, set the other parameters you used through the Flow UI. Parameters that aren't explicitly set will take the same defaults as those in the Flow UI:

```
dlParams._response_column = "medv"
dlParams._epochs = 200
dlParams._l1 = 1e-5
dlParams._hidden = Array(200, 200, 200)
```

As a last step, construct a DeepLearning object by passing it the parameters object you just built, and call the trainModel method. trainModel will return a water.Job object, which is used for tracking long-running user actions. Its get method will block until the job's completion and return the result:

```
import _root_.hex.deeplearning.DeepLearning
val dlBuildJob = new DeepLearning(dlParams).trainModel
val housingModel = dlBuildJob.get
```

That last command will trigger the model training job and output the results once it's finished:

```
housingModel: hex.deeplearning.DeepLearningModel =
Model Metrics Type: Regression
 Description: Metrics reported on full training frame
 model id: DeepLearning_model_1460198303597_1
 frame id: housing750-2
 MSE: 5.7617407
 R^2: 0.92605346
 mean residual deviance: 5.7617407
Model Metrics Type: Regression
 Description: Metrics reported on full validation frame
 model id: DeepLearning_model_1460198303597_1
 frame id: housing250-2
 MSE: 10.819859
 R^2: 0.89840055
 mean residual deviance: 10.819859
Status of Neuron Layers (predicting medv, regression, gaussian
➡ distribution, Quadratic loss, 83.401 weights/biases, 989,5 KB, 82.616
➡ training samples, mini-batch size 1):
Layer Units      Type Dropout       L1      L2 Mean Rate Rate RMS
➡ Momentum Mean Weight Weight RMS Mean Bias Bias RMS
    1 ...
```

The resulting model is automatically stored in the H2O cluster (its distributed key-value store) under its key.

EVALUATING THE MODEL

The model-training step also automatically puts into the H2O's key-value store a ModelMetricsRegression object (because housingModel is a regression model), containing results of the model's evaluation against the validation dataset. You can retrieve the metrics object with the following code:

```
scala> val housingMetrics = _root_.hex.ModelMetricsRegression.getFromDKV(
    housingModel, housing250)
housingMetrics: hex.ModelMetricsRegression =
```

```
Model Metrics Type: Regression
 Description: Metrics reported on full validation frame
 model id: DeepLearning_model_1460198303597_1
 frame id: housing250-2
 MSE: 10.819859
 R^2: 0.89840055
 mean residual deviance: 10.819859
```

The model is also available from the Flow UI. You can find it by clicking Models and then List All Models. When you click the model name (DeepLearning_model_146…), you can see that the scoring history graph and the validation metrics (see figure 14.14) are similar to those from the housingDL model (figure 14.12).

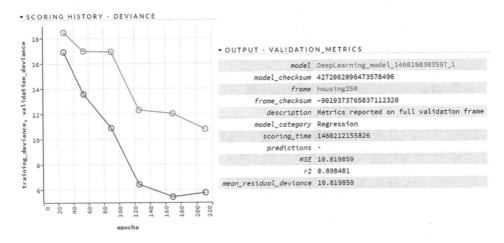

Figure 14.14   Scoring history and validation metrics of the model built from Sparkling Water with the same parameters as the model built through the Flow UI

TRANSFERRING H2O RESULTS BACK TO SPARK

You can now use the model to create predictions based on new data samples. For example, you can get a new H2OFrame, with the individual predictions the model makes on samples from the validation dataset, by calling the model's score method:

```
scala> val housingValPreds = housingModel.score(housing250)
housingValPreds: water.fvec.Frame =
Frame _972a703785fcceb561ec3310fa0f4b43 (114 rows and 1 cols):
                   predict
     min    6.744033282852284
    mean   24.105874992201343
  stddev    9.2411335636329
     max   51.844403675884294
 missing               0.0
       0    33.76862113111221
       1    20.826654125442147
       2    21.0116710955151
```

```
3  21.966950826024252
4   18.81179674838294
...
```

To convert these results back to a Spark `DataFrame`, call the `H2OContext`'s `asDataFrame` method:

```
scala> val housingPredictions = h2oContext.asDataFrame(
  housingValPreds)(sqlContext)
scala> housingPredictions.show()
+------------------+
|           predict|
+------------------+
|  33.76862113111221|
|20.826654125442147|
|   21.0116710955151|
|21.966950826024252|
|  18.81179674838294|
|  18.02565778065803|
|17.795387663167254|
|18.419968615600666|
|  22.92203005950029|
|21.225224043197787|
|   20.0887430162838|
|  21.45854177762687|
|  23.76300250484211|
|  23.48128403269915|
|   21.354705723607|
|  29.75633627046893|
|24.705942488206933|
|  22.37385360846257|
|30.439123158814077|
|  32.83702131412606|
+------------------+
only showing top 20 rows
```

The resulting `DataFrame` contains a single Predict column, which contains the predictions for individual rows in the input frame.

LOADING AND SAVING MODELS USING THE SPARKLING WATER API

You can save a model to a file and load a saved model using the `ModelSerialization-Support` class. To save a model, pass the model and a URI pointing to a file (it can also be an HDFS or S3 URI) to its `exportH2OModel` method:

```
import water.app.ModelSerializationSupport
import _root_.hex.deeplearning.DeepLearningModel

ModelSerializationSupport.exportH2OModel(housingModel,
  new java.net.URI("file:///path/to/model/file"))
```

You can load a saved model with the `loadH2OModel` method the same way:

```
val modelImported:DeepLearningModel = ModelSerializationSupport.loadH2OModel(
  new java.net.URI("file:///path/to/model/file"))
```

14.4   *Performing classification with H2O's deep learning*

Deep learning can be used for classification as well as for regression. In this section, you'll again use a dataset you used before: the adult dataset from chapter 8. To refresh your memory, the adult dataset was extracted from the 1994 United States census data. It contains 13 attributes with data about a person's sex, age, education, marital status, race, native country, and so on, and the target variable (income). The goal is to predict whether a person earns more or less than $50,000 per year. You can find the dataset in our online repository (http://mng.bz/bnCf). You can find descriptions of the columns in the file adult.names (http://mng.bz/KF4i).

14.4.1   *Loading and splitting the data*

As we said previously, in this section you'll load the data from a file directly to an H2OFrame. It's straightforward—you need only to provide a path to the file to load:

```
val censusH2O = new H2OFrame(new java.net.URI("first-edition/ch08/adult.raw"))
```

The frame is now also available through H2O Flow UI under the name adult_raw.hex. H2O automatically detects which columns contain numbers and which contain categorical values (the enum type in H2O terms). Categorical values are those that can take on only a limited number of possible values, such as education and marital_status. The resulting frame is shown in figure 14.15.

⊞ adult_raw.hex

Actions: (▦ View Data) (✂ Split...) (◐ Build Model...) (⚡ Predict) (⬇ Download) (🖺 Export)

Rows	Columns	Compressed Size
48842	14	1MB

▾ COLUMN SUMMARIES

label	type	Missing	Zeros	+Inf	-Inf	min	max	mean	sigma	cardinality	Actions
C1	int	0	0	0	0	17.0	90.0	38.6436	13.7105	·	Convert to enum
C2	enum	0	2799	0	0	·	8.0	·	·	9	Convert to numeric
C3	int	0	0	0	0	12285.0	1490400.0	189664.1346	105604.0254	·	Convert to enum
C4	enum	0	1389	0	0	0	15.0	·	·	16	Convert to numeric
C5	enum	0	6633	0	0	0	6.0	·	·	7	Convert to numeric
C6	enum	0	2809	0	0	0	14.0	·	·	15	Convert to numeric
C7	enum	0	19716	0	0	0	5.0	·	·	6	Convert to numeric
C8	enum	0	470	0	0	0	4.0	·	·	5	Convert to numeric
C9	enum	0	16192	0	0	0	1.0	0.6685	0.4708	2	Convert to numeric
C10	int	0	44807	0	0	0	99999.0	1079.0676	7452.0191	·	Convert to enum
C11	int	0	46560	0	0	0	4356.0	87.5023	403.0046	·	Convert to enum
C12	int	0	0	0	0	1.0	99.0	40.4224	12.3914	·	Convert to enum
C13	enum	0	857	0	0	0	41.0	·	·	42	Convert to numeric
C14	enum	0	37155	0	0	0	1.0	0.2393	0.4266	2	Convert to numeric

(⬅ Previous 20 Columns) (➡ Next 20 Columns)

Figure 14.15   Census frame summary showing that H2O sees categorical columns as strings and not as enums

But there's a problem with the names of the columns. The adult.raw file doesn't include the column names. So, you can change the column names using the H2O API. This is how you do that:

```
censusH2o.setNames(Array("age1", "workclass", "fnlwgt", "education",
  "marital_status", "occupation", "relationship", "race", "sex",
  "capital_gain", "capital_loss", "hours_per_week", "native_country",
  "income"))
```

That line sets the new names for the columns. You can check it with the following command:

```
scala> censusH2o.name(0)
res0: String = age
```

But if you execute the Flow command `getFrameSummary "adult_raw.hex"` from the Flow UI, you'll see that the names haven't changed. You need to update them in H2O's distributed key-value store in order for them to become visible in the Flow UI. You can accomplish that with the following line:

```
censusH2o.update()
```

SPLITTING THE DATASET

Unlike the housing dataset, you'll split the census dataset directly using the Sparkling Water API to learn how it's done. The most straightforward way is to use the `DemoUtils` class from the Sparkling Water examples (this is why you needed to include the examples package when you started Sparkling Water in section 14.2.2):

```
import org.apache.spark.examples.h2o.DemoUtils
val censusSplit = DemoUtils.split(censusH2o,
    Array("census750", "census250"), Array(0.75))
val census750 = censusSplit(0)
val census250 = censusSplit(1)
```

The new frames are now also accessible through the Flow UI. If you'd like to use the same splits we used, you can find them in our online repository (files census750.csv and census250.csv at http://mng.bz/IS40). You can load them using the line from the beginning of this section.

14.4.2 Building the model through the Flow UI

Building a classification deep-learning model is no different than building a regression model. But you must be wondering what to do with the categorical data—after all, in chapter 8 you had to use the `StringIndexer` and `OneHotEncoder` classes to one-hot encode those features. The good news is that H2O does all that automatically; you don't have to worry about it. Just open the Build Model assistant, select the Deep Learning algorithm, and enter the parameters from table 14.1. They're almost identical to the ones you used to build the regression model previously.

Table 14.1   Parameters to build a deep-learning model for classification of census data

Parameter	Value
Model ID	`censusDL-Flow`
Training frame	`census750`
Validation frame	`census250`
Response column	`income`
Hidden	`200, 200, 200`
Epochs	`50`
L1	`1e-5`

The training will take longer than for the housing data because the adult dataset is larger. Click the Build Model button, and then click View once the job finishes.

EVALUATING THE MODEL'S PERFORMANCE

Because the target variable (response column) is categorical, H2O automatically builds a classification model and chooses the appropriate evaluation metrics: f1, r2, and ROC curve (to refresh your memory on these terms, consult section 8.2.4). It also shows log-loss (defined in section 8.2.1), not just MSE.

The resulting validation metrics are shown in figure 14.16, and the ROC curve is shown in figure 14.17. As you can see, the corresponding area under the curve (AUC) is 0.9118, which is slightly better than the best result from chapter 8.

The table on the right in figure 14.17 is associated with the value selected under the criterion drop-down menu (or the threshold, if a criterion isn't selected). You have to select one of those fields in order to see the table. The table shows the threshold and all other metrics that would apply if the selected criterion were to be enforced. The selected criterion in figure 14.17 is the maximum f1 measure. This tells you that if you wanted the maximum f1 measure possible, the threshold would need to be 0.2905 (anything above that value is considered to belong to the target category, meaning the income is greater than $50,000), the TPR would be 0.8007, the FPR would be 0.1550, and so on.

You can also examine the scoring history graphs (figure 14.18) that show log-loss and MSE as functions of the number of epochs. You can use them to see if the validation error is

```
           model  censusDL-Flow
  model_checksum  2074392514228507136
           frame  census250
  frame_checksum  -662556047399127936
     description  Metrics reported on full validation frame
  model_category  Binomial
    scoring_time  1460223045883
     predictions  ·
             MSE  0.097116
              r2  0.461146
         logloss  0.306352
             AUC  0.911823
            Gini  0.823647
```

Figure 14.16   Validation metrics of the built deep-learning model

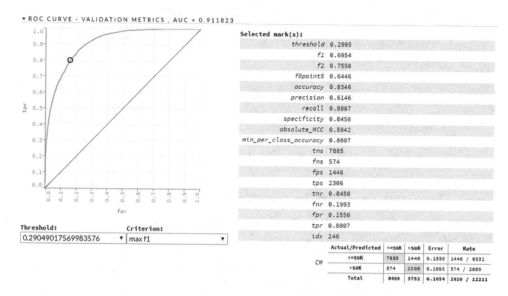

Figure 14.17 **The ROC curve of the built deep-learning model with an area under the curve of 0.911823. The values in the tables on the right correspond to the maximum possible value of the f1 measure that can be obtained with this model and this dataset.**

rising or falling and to determine whether you're using too few or too many epochs. In this case, we could say that a smaller number of epochs may lead to slightly better results, because the validation error has started to rise. Your results may be different, depending on the frame splits.

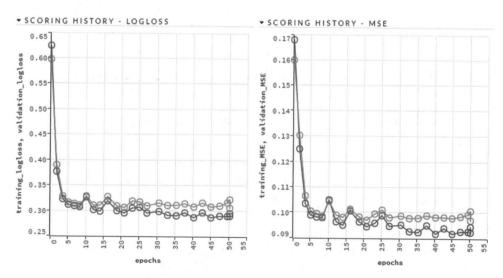

Figure 14.18 **Scoring history for the built deep-learning model, showing log-loss and MSE as functions of the number of epochs**

14.4.3 *Building the model with the Sparkling Water API*

Using the Sparkling Water API to build a classification deep-learning model is the same as building a regression model:

```
val censusdlParams = new DeepLearningParameters()
censusdlParams._train = census750._key
censusdlParams._valid = census250._key
censusdlParams._response_column = "income"
censusdlParams._epochs = 50
censusdlParams._l1 = 1e-5
censusdlParams._hidden = Array(200, 200, 200)
```

The following line starts the training job:

```
import _root_.hex.deeplearning.DeepLearning
val censusModel = new DeepLearning(censusdlParams).trainModel.get
Model Metrics Type: Binomial
 Description: Metrics reported on temporary training frame with 9890 samples
 model id: DeepLearning_model_1460198303597_64
 frame id: census750.temporary.sample.27,30%
 MSE: 0.09550598
 R^2: 0.48424917
 AUC: 0.9206606
 logloss: 0.2964316
 CM: Confusion Matrix (vertical: actual; across: predicted):
          <=50K  >50K   Error            Rate
 <=50K   6619    844    0,1131  =    844 / 7.463
  >50K    595   1832    0,2452  =    595 / 2.427
 Totals  7214   2676    0,1455  = 1.439 / 9.890
 Gains/Lift Table (Avg response rate: 24,54 %):
   Group  Cumulative Data Fraction  Lower Threshold      Lift   Cumulative
 ➥ Lift   Response Rate  Cumulative Response Rate  Capture Rate   Cumulative
 ➥ Capture Rate        Gain  Cumulative Gain
    ...
```

The only difference is the class used for validation. In this case, it's `ModelMetricsBinomial`:

```
val censusPredictions = censusModel.score(census250)
val censusMetrics = _root_.hex.ModelMetricsBinomial.getFromDKV(censusModel,
➥ census250)
```

Looking at the AUC metric values, this model gives very similar results to the censusDL-Flow model and, again, better results than the best results from chapter 8, on the same dataset.

14.4.4 *Stopping the H2O cluster*

When you're finished using the H2O cluster, you can shut it down by calling the H2OContext's `stop` method:

```
h2oContext.stop(false)
```

The argument (`true` or `false`; `false` is the default) tells Sparkling Water whether to first stop the Spark context. The Spark context stops in either case, because the `stop` method performs the system exit, which causes the JVM to stop.

14.5 *Summary*

- Deep learning is an area of machine learning based on using artificial neural networks to learn high-level features of the underlying data.
- Artificial neural networks are modeled according to biological neural networks and consist of artificial neurons organized in layers. A deep neural network is an ANN with two or more hidden layers.
- H2O is a fast, open-source, machine-learning platform, featuring a deep-learning algorithm, among others.
- Sparkling Water is a Spark package that you can use to run an H2O cluster on top of Spark. With Sparkling Water, you can use H2O API directly from Spark.
- H2O's web-based console is called the Flow UI. It enables you to quickly load data, train models using the supported algorithms, use the trained models, and inspect the results.
- Spark `DataFrames` can be converted to H2O frames, and vice versa. Once converted to H2O frames, they're immediately available in the Flow UI. This way, you can load, transform, and clean data in Spark, transfer it to H2O to build machine-learning models, and transfer the results back to Spark.
- The Flow UI can be used to examine data distributions, split frames, train models, and load and save data and machine-learning models. The same actions can be accomplished using the Sparkling Water API.
- H2O automatically chooses the appropriate metrics and deep-learning model (classification or regression) based on the type of the target variable, and provides a wealth of information about your model's performance.

appendix A
Installing Apache Spark

Although we provide a VM image where Spark is already installed, we also wanted to give you step-by-step instructions on how to install Apache Spark as it would be done in the real world. This appendix contains instructions for the following:

- Installing Java (JDK)
- Downloading, installing, and configuring Apache Spark

If you aren't using Ubuntu, we suggest that you install the VirtualBox hardware-virtualization software and create a Ubuntu VM (www.wikihow.com/Install-Ubuntu-on-VirtualBox).

Prerequisites: installing the JDK

Let's get started. From now on, we'll assume that you're logged in to your Ubuntu OS.

If you aren't sure whether you already have the JDK installed and set up correctly, open your terminal (Ctrl-Alt-T) and issue the following command (you can paste the command in the Ubuntu terminal with Ctrl-Shift-V and, if needed, copy from the terminal with Ctrl-Shift-C):

```
$ which javac
```

> **NOTE** Skip the dollar sign ($) when you enter commands—that's just the standard way of designating that commands should be entered into the terminal.

The `which` command basically tells you which executable file on your filesystem would be triggered if you were to execute the `javac` command (javac is the Java compiler, which comes only with the JDK).

If the command returns a path, such as /usr/bin/javac, make sure your `JAVA_HOME` environment variable is correctly set (echo `$JAVA_HOME` should return the root JDK installation folder: for example, /usr/lib/jvm/java-8-openjdk-amd64), and continue from "Downloading, installing, and configuring Spark." If the JDK is installed but `JAVA_HOME` isn't set, continue from "Setting the `JAVA_HOME` environment variable."

If the `which` command returns an empty line, you'll need to install the JDK. Still in your terminal, execute the following set of commands (requires internet access):

```
$ sudo apt-get update
$ sudo apt-get -y install openjdk-8-jdk
```

Updates the apt package repository

Downloads and installs the latest available build of the JDK

`sudo` is a way to run commands with elevated privileges (as the root user). `apt` is Ubuntu's *package manager*: a way to install programs using online package repositories (or deb prepackaged installations from the local filesystem).

SETTING THE JAVA_HOME ENVIRONMENT VARIABLE

There's one more thing to do, once the installation completes: permanently set the `JAVA_HOME` environment variable to refer to the open-jdk installation folder (*permanently* meaning not only for the duration of the current session, but after a reboot too). Here's how:

```
$ echo "export JAVA_HOME=/usr/lib/jvm/java-8-openjdk-amd64" | sudo tee
/etc/profile.d/sia.sh
export JAVA_HOME=/usr/lib/jvm/java-8-openjdk-amd64
```

The `echo` command sends its input to the standard output. The standard output is normally the terminal window, but here you use a *pipe* command (|), which temporarily redirects standard output to a command that comes after it (`tee`, in this case). (We provide more details about the pipe command in chapter 3.) The `tee` command sends its input to both a file, which it received as a parameter, and the standard output (the terminal, because there's no pipe after `tee`). You again need the `sudo` command because writing to any file in /etc requires elevated privileges.

To summarize, you echo the `JAVA_HOME` assignment string (`export` is used to set environment variables), which the pipe redirects to the `tee` command, which in turn writes that string to both the provided file and to the terminal window.

Every file located in /etc/profile.d that has the .sh extension is executed on Ubuntu startup, so you'll have `JAVA_HOME` set even after you restart Ubuntu. But all the previous command did was to create a new file, sia.sh, and add the export of the `JAVA_HOME` assignment line to the file; it didn't set `JAVA_HOME`. Let's see whether that's the case with `echo`, and then fix it with the `source` command (which executes the contents of a file):

```
$ echo $JAVA_HOME
-----empty-line-----
$ source /etc/profile.d/sia.sh
$ echo $JAVA_HOME
/usr/lib/jvm/java-8-openjdk-amd64
```

Placing $ in front of an environment variable retrieves the variable's value.

Now, with the prerequisites out of your way, you'll finally start dealing with fun stuff: downloading and setting up the latest version of Spark.

Downloading, installing, and configuring Spark

Use Mozilla Firefox, which comes with Ubuntu out of the box, to open the Apache Spark project page (http://spark.apache.org/downloads.html). Make the following selections:

1　Choose a Spark Release: select the latest Spark release.
2　Choose a Package Type: select the latest prebuilt version of Hadoop (or your version of Hadoop, if you have one at your disposal).
3　Choose a Download Type: select Apache Mirror.
4　Click the link that comes after Download Spark in step 3.

When a page with a list of mirrors appears, click the suggested, topmost Apache Mirror site. In the dialog that opens, make sure Save File is selected (this may differ depending on your browser), and click OK. The file will be saved in the Downloads folder in your home folder.

Once the download completes, in your terminal, navigate to the $HOME/Downloads folder (if that's where you downloaded Spark), and unpack the Spark bundle:

```
$ cd $HOME/Downloads
$ tar -xvf spark*
$ rm spark*tgz
```

Deletes the downloaded Spark tgz archive.

Instead of using *, you can type "`tar -xvf spark`" and then press Tab to autocomplete the filename.

When you log in to Ubuntu, the HOME environment variable is populated with a path to your home directory.[1] For example, because we used the username mbo, HOME points to /home/mbo:

```
$ echo $HOME
/home/mbo
```

Prints out the provided input, as you saw when setting JAVA_HOME.

From now on, we'll refer to this directory as your *home directory* (or just *home*), and you'll use the HOME environment variable to navigate to it (as shown in the next set of commands).

Because the purpose of this Spark installation is not to put Spark in production, but rather to learn, and because it will be used only by you, let's follow a Linux convention (http://mng.bz/0ezc) and place the Spark binaries[2] in the bin directory in your home. You have full access rights (read/write/execute, or *rwx*) to your home directory, so you won't have to fiddle with sudo every time you need to make a change (for example, to a configuration file).

---

[1]　More on the home directory: https://help.ubuntu.com/community/HomeFolder.
[2]　A fancy name for a compiled program (for example, you can download Spark's *source code* or Spark *binaries*).

Because new versions of Spark are flying out every couple of months, you need a way to manage them so you can have multiple versions installed and easily choose which one to use. You'll create a sparks directory, where you'll put the current and all future versions of Spark.

Create the bin directory with the sparks directory in it, and then move your unpacked Spark binaries from Downloads to this new sparks directory, as follows:

Creates the bin/sparks directory → | **Navigates to your home directory** | **Moves the uncompressed spark directory from Downloads to bin/sparks.**

```
$ cd $HOME
$ mkdir -p bin/sparks
$ mv Downloads/spark-* bin/sparks
```

Our home/bin directory looked like this after moving the Spark binaries to bin/sparks. Yours should look the same, but without earlier versions of Spark:

```
bin
├── spark
└── sparks
    ├── spark-1.2.0-bin-hadoop2.4
    ├── spark-1.2.1-bin-hadoop2.4
    ├── spark-1.2.2-bin-hadoop2.4
    ├── spark-1.3.0-bin-hadoop2.4
    ├── spark-1.3.1-bin-hadoop2.6
    ├── spark-1.4.0-bin-hadoop2.6
    ├── spark-1.4.1-bin-hadoop2.6
    ...
    └── spark-1.6.1-bin-hadoop2.6
spark-2.0.0-bin-hadoop2.7
```

Great! You're nearly there. There's one thing left to do, if you're going to follow good Linux practices for managing multiple versions of a program: you need to create a symbolic link directory named Spark in your $HOME/bin directory, which will point to a Spark installation directory you want to use. Let's do that now:

Creates a symbolic link | **Navigates to the bin directory in your home directory**

```
$ cd $HOME/bin
$ ln -s sparks/spark-2.0.0-bin-hadoop2.7 spark
```

Now, still in the ~/bin folder, execute the tree -L 2 command. You'll see that the spark folder is actually a symbolic link that points to another folder in the sparks directory.

The idea is to always refer to the spark root (see the sidebar) the same way, using the spark symbolic link. When you want to use some other version of Spark, you can change the symbolic link to point to a different version.

SPARK-SHELL

Now you should be able to start the spark-shell command-line interface using these commands in your terminal:

Navigates to the spark root directory

```
$ cd $HOME/bin/spark
$ ./bin/spark-shell
```
Starts the spark-shell

> ## Symbolic links
>
> A symbolic link (or *symlink*) is a reference to a file or a folder (the latter, in this case). It behaves as though you have access to the same folder from two different places in your filesystem. The symlink isn't a copy; it's a reference to the target folder, with the ability to navigate within it, as if it were the target folder. Every change you make in the symlink is applied directly to the target folder and reflected in the symlink.
>
> By using the symlink this way, regardless of the current version of Spark, you're always using $HOME/bin/spark. You switch versions by deleting the symlink (`rm` command) and creating one that points to the root installation folder of a Spark version you want to work with. If you wanted to switch to version 1.6.1, you would do this:
>
> ```
> $ rm spark
> $ ln -s spark-1.6.1-bin-hadoop2.6 spark
> ```
>
> From now on, we'll call $HOME/bin/spark directory the *spark root*.

Boom! You have a running spark-shell on your machine. The default logging settings are much too verbose, so let's tone that down a bit.

You'll make spark-shell print only errors, but you'll maintain the complete log in the logs/info.log file (relative to the spark root) for troubleshooting. Exit the shell by typing `:quit` or just `:q` (or pressing Ctrl-D), and create a log4j.properties file in the conf subfolder, like this:

```
$ gedit conf/log4j.properties
```

gedit is Ubuntu's built-in text editor. You are, of course, free to use any other text editor. Now, copy the following listing into the newly created log4j.properties file in gedit.

Listing A.1 log4j.properties file

```
# set global logging severity to INFO (and upwards: WARN, ERROR, FATAL)
log4j.rootCategory=INFO, console, file

# console config (restrict only to ERROR and FATAL)
log4j.appender.console=org.apache.log4j.ConsoleAppender
log4j.appender.console.target=System.err
log4j.appender.console.threshold=ERROR
log4j.appender.console.layout=org.apache.log4j.PatternLayout
log4j.appender.console.layout.ConversionPattern=%d{yy/MM/dd HH:mm:ss} %p
➥ %c{1}: %m%n

# file config
log4j.appender.file=org.apache.log4j.RollingFileAppender
log4j.appender.file.File=logs/info.log
log4j.appender.file.MaxFileSize=5MB
log4j.appender.file.MaxBackupIndex=10
log4j.appender.file.layout=org.apache.log4j.PatternLayout
```

```
log4j.appender.file.layout.ConversionPattern=%d{yy/MM/dd HH:mm:ss} %p
➥ %c{1}: %m%n

# Settings to quiet third party logs that are too verbose
log4j.logger.org.eclipse.jetty=WARN
log4j.logger.org.eclipse.jetty.util.component.AbstractLifeCycle=ERROR
log4j.logger.org.apache.spark.repl.SparkIMain$exprTyper=INFO
log4j.logger.org.apache.spark.repl.SparkILoop$SparkILoopInterpreter=INFO
```

Save the file, and close gedit.

> **log4j**
>
> Although it has been superseded by the logback library and is almost two decades old, log4j is still one of the most widely used Java logging libraries, due to the simplicity of its design.

Make sure your current directory is still spark root, and then use the same command as before (instead of writing it again, you can press the up-arrow key two times) to start spark-shell:

```
$ ./bin/spark-shell
```

Cleaner, right? So, what is this spark-shell about?

There are two ways you can interact with Spark. One way is to write a program in Scala, Java, or Python that uses Spark's library (that is, its API; more on programs in chapter 3). The other is to use the Scala shell or the Python shell.

The *shell* is primarily used for exploratory data analysis, usually one-off jobs, because a program written in the shell is discarded after you exit the shell. The other common shell-use scenario is testing and developing Spark applications. It's much easier to test a hypothesis in a shell (for example, probing a dataset) than it is to write an application, submit it to be executed, write the results to an output file, and then analyze that output.

spark-shell is also known as Spark REPL, which, as you recall, stands for read-eval-print-loop. It reads your input, evaluates it, prints the result, and then does it all over again (after a command returns a result, it doesn't exit the scala> prompt but rather stays ready for your next command—thus *loop*).

As you can see in the REPL's initial printout, as you start it, it provides you with the Spark context in the form of the sc variable and the SparkSession as spark. Spark-Session is the entry point for interacting with Spark. You use it for things like connecting to Spark from an application, configuring a session, managing job execution, loading or saving a file, and so on. If you type spark. and press the Tab key, you'll see a printout of all the functions SparkSession provides.

appendix B
Understanding MapReduce

In December 2004, Google published a paper, "MapReduce: Simplified Data Processing on Large Clusters," by Jeffrey Dean and Sanjay Ghemawat, summarizing the authors' solution to Google's urgent need to simplify cluster computing. Dean and Ghemawat settled on a paradigm in which parts of a job are *mapped* (dispatched) to all nodes in a cluster. Each node produces a slice of the intermediary result set. All those slices are then *reduced* (aggregated) back to the final result.

The MapReduce paper (http://mng.bz/8s06) solves these three main problems:

- *Parallelization*—How to parallelize the computation
- *Distribution*—How to distribute the data
- *Fault-tolerance*—How to handle component failure

The core of MapReduce deals with programmatic resolution of those three problems, which effectively hides most of the complexities of dealing with large-scale distributed systems and allows MapReduce to expose a minimal API that consists only of two functions: (wait for it …) `map` and `reduce`.

One of the key insights from MapReduce is that you shouldn't be forced to move data in order to process it. Instead, a program is sent to where the data resides. That is a key differentiator, compared to traditional data warehouse systems and relational databases. There's simply too much data to be moved around.

We'll explain how MapReduce works with a simple example—we'll use the good-old simplified word count (big data's "Hello World").

Suppose you'd like to find the most common words on a website. Let's say there are two pages on this website, each with a single paragraph:

- "Is it easy to program with MapReduce?"
- "It is as easy as Map and Reduce are."

First, the map function takes each paragraph, tokenizes it into words, normalizes the case and punctuation, and emits 1 for each word:

map → ("is", 1)	map → ("it", 1)
map → ("it", 1)	map → ("is", 1)
map → ("easy", 1)	map → ("as", 1)
map → ("to", 1)	map → ("easy", 1)
map → ("program", 1)	map → ("as", 1)
map → ("with", 1)	map → ("map", 1)
map → ("mapreduce", 1)	map → ("and", 1)
	map → ("reduce", 1)
	map → ("are", 1)

So, for each input paragraph, map takes a key and a value and returns a list of keys/values.

In this intermediate phase, the MapReduce library takes care that the same word always goes to the same reducer, so counts can be summed up and computation finalized without any subsequent steps. That is called the *shuffle phase*, and for the overwhelming majority of applications, it takes the longest time to complete.

The reduce function receives map's output, adds up the words, and emits the result:

reduce → ("is", 2)	reduce → ("it", 2)
reduce → ("easy", 2)	reduce → ("to", 1)
reduce → ("program", 1)	reduce → ("with", 1)
reduce → ("mapreduce", 1)	reduce → ("as", 2)
reduce → ("map", 1)	reduce → ("and", 1)
reduce → ("reduce", 1)	reduce → ("are", 1)

We can generalize that map takes a key/value pair, applies some arbitrary transformation, and returns a list of so-called *intermediate* key/value pairs. MapReduce then, behind the scenes, groups those pairs by key, and they become input for the reduce function. reduce combines those values in some useful way and writes the result to a final output file. When all reducers have finished their task, control is returned to the user program.

This is just one version of the word-count example. You could do it differently: for example, you could make `map` do the counting within each paragraph (`"as"`, `2`), or you could use natural language processing analysis and stem each word to its root. You could split words on CamelCase (*MapReduce → map reduce*). Also, you could use a *stop-word filter,* which uses a list of the most common words in each language to remove those words from the final count because they don't add value or relevance (that would then be TermVector, not WordCount). But those additions would only complicate and obscure the example. We skipped them because they're not important when explaining how MapReduce works.

Having seen MapReduce in action, your first instinct may be that MapReduce is overly complicated for the simple task of counting the frequency of words in two sentences. And you're right, of course—there are simpler and more intuitive ways to write a trivial method for the task at hand. But keep in mind that MapReduce was designed to tackle terabytes and even petabytes of sentences, from billions of websites, server logs, click streams, and so on.

MapReduce fault-tolerance

Thisis an excerpt from Dean's and Ghemawat's MapReduce paper (slightly paraphrased):

> *The master pings every worker periodically. If no response is received from a worker in a certain amount of time, the master marks the worker as failed. Any map tasks, in-progress or completed by the failed worker are reset back to their initial idle state, and therefore become eligible for scheduling on other workers.*

A primer on linear algebra

This appendix presents the basic linear algebra operations. They're important for understanding much of the math behind most machine-learning algorithms. In case you skipped your linear algebra classes, this is your chance to come to grips with it.

Matrices and vectors

A *matrix* is a set of elements arranged in rows and columns (we'll only use matrices whose elements are numbers). This is a matrix with two rows and three columns, so it's called a 2×3 matrix:

$$x = \begin{bmatrix} 1 & 2 & 3 \\ 4 & 5 & 6 \end{bmatrix}$$

Usually, the number of rows in a matrix is denoted by the letter m and the number of columns by the letter n. m and n are the matrix's dimensions, and we say its *size* is $m \times n$. We'll denote matrices with bold, uppercase letters (X in the previous example) and its elements with plain, lowercase letters with subscript indices. For example:

$$x = \begin{bmatrix} x_{11} & x_{12} & x_{13} \\ x_{21} & x_{22} & x_{23} \end{bmatrix}$$

A *column vector* is a matrix of size $n \times 1$, and a *row vector* is a matrix of size $1 \times n$. We'll refer to column vectors with lowercase, italic, bold letters (for example, u)

and row vectors just like column vectors, but with an added superscript letter T (for example, u^T):

$$u = \begin{bmatrix} 1 \\ 2 \\ 3 \end{bmatrix} \qquad u^T = \begin{bmatrix} 1 & 2 & 3 \end{bmatrix}$$

The letter T here means *transposed*. Transposition is an operation in which the rows of a matrix become its columns, and vice versa. For our example matrix **X**, its transposed matrix would be as follows:

$$X^T = \begin{bmatrix} x_{11} & x_{21} \\ x_{12} & x_{22} \\ x_{13} & x_{23} \end{bmatrix}$$

So, if the size of the original matrix is $m \times n$, the size of the transposed matrix will be $n \times m$. Note that $(\mathbf{X}^T)^T = \mathbf{X}$.

Matrix addition

Two matrices (or vectors, which are matrix special cases) can be added if they have the same size. The addition is performed element-wise:

$$\begin{bmatrix} a_{11} & a_{12} \\ a_{21} & a_{22} \end{bmatrix} + \begin{bmatrix} b_{11} & b_{12} \\ b_{21} & b_{22} \end{bmatrix} = \begin{bmatrix} a_{11} + b_{12} & a_{12} + b_{12} \\ a_{21} + b_{22} & a_{21} + b_{22} \end{bmatrix}$$

Matrix addition is associative, which means $\mathbf{A} + (\mathbf{B} + \mathbf{C}) = (\mathbf{A} + \mathbf{B}) + \mathbf{C}$. It's also a commutative operation, which means $\mathbf{A} + \mathbf{B} = \mathbf{B} + \mathbf{A}$.

Scalar multiplication

A scalar, in contrast to vectors and matrices, is a regular number. Multiplication of matrices by scalars is also performed element-wise, by multiplying each element with the scalar value:

$$\lambda \begin{bmatrix} a_{11} & a_{12} \\ a_{21} & a_{22} \end{bmatrix} = \begin{bmatrix} \lambda a_{11} & \lambda a_{12} \\ \lambda a_{21} & \lambda a_{22} \end{bmatrix}$$

Matrix multiplication

Two matrices can be multiplied only if the number of columns in the left matrix is equal to the number of rows in the right matrix. If two matrices being multiplied have sizes $m \times n$ and $n \times k$, the resulting matrix will be of size $m \times k$.

In the case of vectors, when multiplying a row vector ($1 \times n$) and a column vector ($n \times 1$), the result will be a scalar value. This is also called a *dot product* or a *scalar product*:

$$a^T b = \begin{bmatrix} a_{11} & a_{12} & a_{13} \end{bmatrix} \begin{bmatrix} b_{11} \\ b_{21} \\ b_{31} \end{bmatrix} = a_{11}b_{11} + a_{12}b_{21} + a_{13}b_{31}$$

Conversely, when multiplying a column vector of size $m \times 1$ and a row vector of size $1 \times n$, the result will be a matrix of size $m \times n$.

Generally, when multiplying matrices **A** and **B**, you can use this formula to calculate each element of the resulting matrix **C**:

$$c_{ij} = \sum_{r=1}^{n} a_{ir}b_{rj} \quad , 0 < i \leq m, 0 < j \leq k$$

For example:

$$\begin{bmatrix} a_{11} & a_{12} & a_{13} \\ a_{21} & a_{22} & a_{23} \end{bmatrix} \begin{bmatrix} b_{11} & b_{12} \\ b_{21} & b_{22} \\ b_{31} & b_{32} \end{bmatrix} = \begin{bmatrix} a_{11}b_{11} + a_{12}b_{21} + a_{13}b_{31} & a_{11}b_{12} + a_{12}b_{22} + a_{13}b_{32} \\ a_{21}b_{11} + a_{22}b_{21} + a_{23}b_{31} & a_{21}b_{12} + a_{22}b_{22} + a_{23}b_{32} \end{bmatrix}$$

In other words, the value of the element in the row i and column j of the resulting matrix will be equal to the dot product of the i-th row of the first matrix and the j-th column of the second matrix.

Identity matrix

A *square matrix* is a matrix with the same number of rows and columns (its size is $m \times m$). An *identity matrix* is a square matrix with all elements on its main diagonal equal to 1 and all other elements equal to 0. For example, this is an identity matrix of size 2:

$$I_2 = \begin{bmatrix} 1 & 0 \\ 0 & 1 \end{bmatrix}$$

Any matrix **A** of size $m \times n$, multiplied by an identity matrix, stays the same: $\mathbf{A}I^n = I^m\mathbf{A} = \mathbf{A}$.

Matrix inverse

The final definition for this appendix is the *matrix inverse*. Any matrix **A** multiplied by its inverse (denoted by $\mathbf{A}^{-1}$) gives an identity matrix. Only square matrices can have an inverse. But some square matrices don't have an inverse. If a square matrix has an inverse, it's called an *invertible* or *non-singular* matrix.

index

MORE TITLES FROM MANNING

Spark GraphX in Action
by Michael S. Malak and Robin East

ISBN: 9781617292521
280 pages
$49.99
June 2016

Big Data
Principles and best practices of scalable realtime data systems

by Nathan Marz and James Warren

ISBN: 9781617290343
328 pages
$49.99
April 2015

Streaming Data
Understanding the real-time pipeline
by Andrew G. Psaltis

ISBN: 9781617292286
300 pages
$49.99
December 2016

For ordering information go to www.manning.com